Winner, American Battlefield T

Finalist, *Los Angeles Times* Bool

Praise for *Longstreet*

"[Longstreet's] story is a reminder that the arc of history is sometimes bent by those who had the courage to change their convictions. . . . And for that, Ms. Varon contends, he commands our attention as one of the most enduringly relevant voices in American history."

—Peter Cozzens, *The Wall Street Journal*

"For readers interested in the tragedy of America's Civil War, the horrors of Reconstruction and their implications for our own divided time, *Longstreet* is an essential book."

—Mary Ann Gwinn, *Minneapolis Star-Tribune*

"James Longstreet's evolution from an ardent secessionist and prominent Confederate general to a postwar Republican and supporter of Black civil rights who repudiated Lost Cause mythologies has long puzzled contemporaries and historians. Elizabeth Varon brilliantly solves this puzzle and links it to the persistent efforts to scapegoat Longstreet for Confederate defeat at Gettysburg."

—James M. McPherson, author of
Battle Cry of Freedom: The Civil War Era

"Tells Longstreet's story with authority and insight. . . . Readers interested in the Civil War and the horrors of Reconstruction should not miss this book."

—*Kirkus Reviews*

"[Varon's] study of the Confederate general—one of Robert E. Lee's closest confidants, yet an outcast in the post–Civil War South for his embrace of Black emancipation and civil rights—is insightful, well-executed, and sorely needed."

—Richard Kreitner, *Slate*

"A fresh and balanced appraisal of Longstreet's life and postwar career. Readers interested in American history, the Civil War, and biographies will enjoy this well-written treatment."

—*Library Journal* (starred review)

"At a time when it seems an open question whether human beings have the capacity to learn and to change in politics, the great historian Elizabeth Varon has given us a compelling portrait of a man who did just that: James Longstreet. A Confederate general who became an advocate for justice in the painful aftermath of the Civil War, Longstreet has much to teach us in our own hour of polarization."

—Jon Meacham, author of *And There Was Light:*
Abraham Lincoln and the American Struggle

"A fresh take on Confederate general James Longstreet. . . . A must-read for Civil War buffs that contains valuable insight on today's political polarization."

—*Publishers Weekly*

"Elizabeth R. Varon's engaging biography of James Longstreet delivers a long overdue reassessment of the Confederate general turned Republican politician and businessman. . . . Combining rigorous research with engaging prose, Varon pairs the full life of this fascinating and controversial figure with brilliant insights into a complicated period of U.S. history."

—Joan Waugh, professor emerita,
UCLA Department of History

"Elizabeth Varon's much anticipated and insightful new biography of James Longstreet deepens our understanding not only of the controversial general himself, but also of the profound and painful complexities of the Reconstruction Era and beyond."

—Elizabeth D. Leonard, author of
Benjamin Franklin Butler: A Noisy, Fearless Life

ALSO BY ELIZABETH R. VARON

Armies of Deliverance: A New History of the Civil War

Appomattox: Victory, Defeat, and Freedom at the End of the Civil War

Disunion! The Coming of the American Civil War, 1789–1859

Southern Lady, Yankee Spy: The True Story of Elizabeth Van Lew, a Union Agent in the Heart of the Confederacy

LONGSTREET

The CONFEDERATE GENERAL WHO DEFIED the SOUTH

Elizabeth R. Varon

SIMON & SCHUSTER PAPERBACKS
New York   London   Toronto   Sydney   New Delhi

An Imprint of Simon & Schuster, LLC
1230 Avenue of the Americas
New York, NY 10020

Copyright © 2023 by Elizabeth R. Varon

All rights reserved, including the right to reproduce this book or portions thereof in any form whatsoever. For information, address Simon & Schuster Paperbacks Subsidiary Rights Department, 1230 Avenue of the Americas, New York, NY 10020.

First Simon & Schuster trade paperback edition November 2024

SIMON & SCHUSTER PAPERBACKS and colophon are registered trademarks of Simon & Schuster, LLC

Simon & Schuster: Celebrating 100 Years of Publishing in 2024

For information about special discounts for bulk purchases, please contact Simon & Schuster Special Sales at 1-866-506-1949 or business@simonandschuster.com.

The Simon & Schuster Speakers Bureau can bring authors to your live event. For more information or to book an event, contact the Simon & Schuster Speakers Bureau at 1-866-248-3049 or visit our website at www.simonspeakers.com.

Interior design by Wendy Blum

Manufactured in the United States of America

1   3   5   7   9   10   8   6   4   2

Library of Congress Cataloging-in-Publication Data is available.

ISBN 978-1-9821-4827-0
ISBN 978-1-9821-4828-7 (pbk)
ISBN 978-1-9821-4829-4 (ebook)

To David and Bension

CONTENTS

LONGSTREET

Prologue

CONFEDERATE JUDAS

I

It was a quintessentially American scene. Although the event was slated to begin at four o'clock in the afternoon, the city square began to fill up hours earlier, as thousands of spectators gathered in eager anticipation of a venerable civic ritual: a militia parade and flag presentation ceremony. Such occasions, in which volunteer citizen soldiers displayed their martial prowess and their patriotic devotion to the state, generally followed time-honored scripts. And this parade was, in key respects, no different from countless others that had come before. The arrival of the militia was heralded by the martial airs of a regimental band. Having made their way to the square, the troops drew up in line of battle and opened ranks, to be inspected by their officers and demonstrate their skill in marching in close order. The regiment then wheeled into column by companies and passed a reviewing stand, where dignitaries and distinguished guests—military and civil—looked on with approval. "One might be easily excused for mistaking them for regulars, so admirable was their marching," crowed the local newspaper, comparing the militiamen favorably to professional soldiers.[1]

The militia formed a line of battle again, and its commissioned officers marched forward to receive a stand of colors—featuring a brightly colored flag bearing the coat of arms of the state—from the general who commanded the militia force. The general made a short speech in which he expressed his faith that if the troops were ever called into battle, they would do the state proud. The regiment's colonel, accepting the stand of colors on behalf of his fellow officers, then gave a speech of his own, expressing his sincere thanks for "the honor you have done us and the confidence you have reposed in us."[2]

Such events had a timeless quality, as celebrations of the vital role non-professional soldiers have played, in times of peace and war, as auxiliaries to the standing, full-time, professional US military.

But this particular ceremony also marked a unique moment in American history—a moment of fleeting possibility. The year was 1870, the zenith of Reconstruction in the post–Civil War South. The place was New Orleans, a key proving ground for testing whether Reconstruction would succeed. The soldiers, the 2nd Regiment of the Louisiana State Militia, were African American. They pledged themselves to defend not only the flag of Louisiana but also the flag of the Union.

And positioned conspicuously in the reviewing stand, radiating his approval, was a man who had waged four years of bloody war against that very Union: the famed Confederate general James Longstreet.

II

Longstreet did not make a speech at this October review, but his presence spoke volumes. Like the militia's commander, a former Union colonel named Hugh J. Campbell, Longstreet was there as a representative of Louisiana's governor, Henry Warmoth, and of Warmoth's governing coalition. Warmoth had appointed Longstreet adjutant general (chief of staff) of the state force, in recognition of his military experience as a career soldier and, more important, of the bold and unlikely political position that Longstreet took on Reconstruction: namely, to support the US Congress's ambitious, revolutionary program for remaking the American South. The centerpiece of its plan was the enfranchisement of Black Southern men as voters and their inclusion in the body politic as citizens. In aligning himself with this program, Longstreet joined ranks with the Republican Party—the party of the North, of Lincoln, of emancipation, of Union victory, of everything Confederates had loathed and feared. The Republicans rewarded him with a major federal patronage position as customs surveyor in New Orleans (bestowed in 1869 by President Ulysses S. Grant) and with various leadership positions within the Louisiana party apparatus.[3]

Longstreet threw himself into his role as an agent of Reconstruction, in his capacity as a civil servant and warrior. As Hugh J. Campbell noted in his remarks during the October 1870 flag presentation ceremony, Longstreet showed "every favor in his power" to the Black regiments in the Louisiana State Militia, seeing to it that they were properly armed, equipped, and trained; promoting the careers of the LSM's Black officers; and according them, from his position as one of the most "illustrious soldiers of America" (so Campbell put it), their rightful legitimacy and respect. Indeed, during the ceremony, Longstreet singled out one of the companies of the 2nd Regiment, led by United States Colored Troops veteran Captain R. R. Ray, for its drilling, praising it "in the most complimentary manner," according to newspaper coverage of the event. Such a show of support was meant to nerve the men to do battle, as the regiment's colonel, James B. Lewis, intoned in his comments, with their ultimate enemy, that "great monster, the most formidable of all": the "caste prejudice" that had so long subordinated Southern Blacks.[4]

How did Longstreet, a man who had gone to war in 1861 to destroy the Union and perpetuate slavery, find his way onto that reviewing stand, among his former enemies? This biography will answer that question, and in so doing reintroduce Americans to one of the Civil War era's best-known—but least understood—figures.

The basic outlines of Longstreet's story have long been familiar to scholars and the interested general public. During the Civil War, he commanded the Army of Northern Virginia's fabled First Corps, and won laurels in Confederate victories at Second Manassas, Fredericksburg, and Chickamauga, among other battles, earning a reputation as Robert E. Lee's hardy and dependable "war-horse." Longstreet's postwar embrace of Radical Reconstruction infuriated his fellow white ex-Confederates, who promptly cast him out of the pantheon of Confederate heroes—and then proceeded, in a decades-long campaign, to blame Longstreet retroactively for their defeat in the Battle of Gettysburg, as well as for the loss of the war itself. Longstreet's efforts to defend himself were muddled and contradictory, and he remained a social pariah, remembered in the South as Lee's "tarnished lieutenant."[5]

The vast majority of popular writing and academic scholarship on Longstreet has revolved around the question of whether, militarily speaking, he deserved this fate: his performance as a commander in the Civil War, especially at Gettysburg, has been litigated over and over in painstaking detail, with various verdicts (mostly negative) offered on his generalship. But Longstreet's remarkable postwar political conversion—the very event that sparked the endless debates over his military leadership—has never been the subject of an extended, thorough account. Longstreet's 1867 decision to support Reconstruction launched him on a lifelong career as a Republican political operative and national celebrity whose iconoclastic positions on race relations, sectional reunion, military history, foreign affairs, and even marriage kept him consistently in the public eye. A prolific writer and speaker and interviewee who produced a vast oeuvre of political commentary, Longstreet ruminated at length on the issues of loyalty and treason, victory and defeat, progress and reaction—and his distinct voice can help us better understand both the transformative changes and the entrenched inequities of the postwar era. Longstreet was not, by the standards of Radical Republicans and abolitionists such as Thaddeus Stevens and Frederick Douglass, a true racial egalitarian. But even his circumscribed challenge to the racial caste system—his insistence that Blacks could exercise, through the Republican Party, a measure of political influence and leadership in the Southern polity—was a clear and present threat to Lost Cause orthodoxies. Defenders of the Lost Cause, such as Confederate general Jubal Early, insisted on the righteousness of slavery, secession, the Confederacy, and white supremacy. Longstreet rejected the conservative South's demand for ideological purity, and that was enough to cast him forever as an apostate in the eyes of those who rejected change. Longstreet was "le Judas Confederé," as the reactionary francophone New Orleans paper *Le Carillon* charged, to go along with the labels of "Benedict Arnold," "Lucifer," and other such favorites of the unreconstructed press.[6]

III

Longstreet's political journey from ardent Confederate to ardent Republican was an exceedingly unlikely one. As this biography will show, his remarkable life played out in three distinct acts, each with its own dramatic arc. The first act saw Longstreet, bred for battle and steeped in proslavery ideology, seize the mantle of rebel when the South seceded and fight tenaciously for Southern independence until the bitter end. Longstreet was a true believer in the Confederacy's racial politics. As a military commander, he tried to preempt and to punish the many forms of Black resistance to the Confederacy, such as the flight of slaves and their offering their services as spies, scouts, and soldiers to the Union army. And he worked to forestall and undermine emancipation, through acts such as seizing free Blacks during the Gettysburg campaign and sending them South as slaves.

While his belief in the Confederate cause did not waver during the four long years of war, Longstreet's confidence in it did. His growing bitterness about the human costs of the conflict and the failings in Confederate leadership primed him to contemplate the prospect of defeat and to formulate a critique of the fatal flaws that beset Southern society—especially the flaw of hubris. It was not the battle at Gettysburg that defined Longstreet's Civil War but rather the surrender at Appomattox. There, on April 9, 1865, Longstreet's West Point classmate and dear old friend, U. S. Grant, extended the hand of clemency to the surrendering Confederates, to effect their submission to a new order. Longstreet took that offer to heart.

In his second act, during the turbulent era of Reconstruction, Longstreet affirmed the finality and necessity of both Union victory and of emancipation. Motivated by a complex blend of personal and political factors—including his respect for Grant and his exposure to the unique racial politics of New Orleans—Longstreet announced his support for Reconstruction to the public in the spring of 1867. "There can be no discredit to a conquered people for accepting the conditions offered by their conquerors. Nor is there any occasion for a feeling of humiliation. We have made an honest, and I hope I may say, a creditable fight, but we have lost. Let us come forward, then, and accept the ends involved in the struggle." This simple sentiment drew the wrath of ex-Confederates, who reviled Longstreet as a race traitor—even as Northern and Southern Unionists, Longstreet's wartime foes, rallied to his defense.[7]

Stung by Confederate condemnation of his stance, Longstreet doubled down and became deeply immersed in Republican Party politics. He chose, in Louisiana's bitter gubernatorial election cycle of 1872, to back the faction led by Union veterans William P. Kellogg (a white Northerner) and Pinckney Benton Stewart Pinchback (a Black Southerner). As conservative whites wielded propaganda, fraud, intimidation, and violence to suppress Black votes and undermine the Republican coalition, Longstreet defended Black voting as a key to rebuilding the South. In what became known as the battle of Canal Street, on September 14, 1874, Longstreet, leading the interracial New Orleans Metropolitan Police and the state militia, fought to defend the Republican state government against a violent takeover by the White League, the Democratic Party's white supremacist paramilitary arm, full of Confederate veterans. It took federal troops, sent by President Grant, to pacify the city.[8]

The traumatic events of 1874 drew the curtain on Longstreet's second act, in which he had battled alongside Radical Republican allies against racial segregation and oppression. Making a strategic retreat from the turmoil in Louisiana, Longstreet resettled his family in Gainesville, Georgia. During his third act, lasting thirty years until his passing in 1904, he remained active in government, holding patronage posts as an internal revenue collector, postmaster, ambassador to the Ottoman Empire, US marshal for Georgia, and US railroad commissioner. He continued to support Black voting and officeholding, working closely, sometimes at cross-purposes, with Georgia's leading Black activists and politicians. But Longstreet also tried in these years to claw back some of his lost popularity among white Southerners, especially Confederate veterans. He emphasized the need for white Southerners to firmly control the Republican coalition, and he fashioned himself as a herald of sectional reconciliation who was equally proud of his Confederate record and his Republican affiliation.

Limbering up his pen, Longstreet did literary battle with a clique of Confederate veterans, led by Jubal Early and William Nelson Pendleton, who worked relentlessly to scapegoat him for the South's defeat and to immortalize Robert E. Lee as a faultless saint. Longstreet labored doggedly, and with considerable skill, to set the record straight on his military performance during the war. As he put it in 1876, "I should have been willing to have any one, who wished to use it, appropriate any or all of my part in the war if it had been done without arraigning me before the world as the person, and the only one, responsible for the loss of the cause. Under the severest provocations I have remained silent, until the importunities have forced me to speak."[9] Speak Longstreet did, in torrents of prose, including published interviews, letters, speeches, essays, articles, and a 690-page memoir, *From Manassas to Appomattox: Memoirs of the Civil War in America* (1896), all of which were eagerly consumed by a rapt public.

Longstreet's tireless campaign at self-reinvention—one that received a jolt of energy when he married a maverick young journalist, Helen Dortch, in 1897—paid off. His popularity and visibility surged in the last years of his life, as he managed to build reservoirs of goodwill among divergent groups in American society, each of which saw in him, as he did in them, some political value. Those groups included Southern Blacks competing for

Republican patronage in the nadir years of Jim Crow; Northern Republicans eager to devise a winning "Southern strategy" for capturing votes; "New South" boosters, like the editors of the influential *Atlanta Constitution*, who hoped to fuse economic modernization and social conservatism; and Civil War veterans, blue and gray alike, swept up in the burgeoning cult of sectional reunion. But Longstreet's skill at cultivating these alliances only further pointed up his iconoclasm. His stubborn efforts to reconcile his Confederate and Republican identities meant that he never secured the full trust of either conservatives or progressives. His impassioned critiques of Southern intolerance boomeranged back on him, as whites in the region simply would not tolerate his challenges to the cult of Lee worship or the "Solid South" political dominance of Democrats.

Debates over the current landscape of Civil War memorialization invariably invoke the fate of Longstreet, who, unlike Lee and his ilk, never became a "marble man," immortalized among the Confederate statues erected in town squares across the South. Longstreet could not be used as a symbol of white supremacy and the Lost Cause because, in the eyes of Confederates, he had repudiated both.[10] But Longstreet's legacy is so complex that he does not fit easily the mold of either hero or villain. His long life is a revealing window into nearly a century of Southern history. He embodied antebellum Southern society's commitment to slavery and white supremacy; the wartime elusiveness, for Confederates, of command harmony and social cohesion; the suppression of dissent in the postwar South (with Longstreet taking up the mantle of an embattled dissenter); and American culture's unfolding contests over the Civil War's legacies. In the face of ex-Confederates' intransigence, his greatest provocation was his very willingness to change. He is one of nineteenth-century America's most significant public figures precisely because he confounds our labels and forces us to confront the haunting complexity of Southern history—and the elusiveness of reconciliation among Southerners over the meaning of the Civil War.

PART I

Disunion

Chapter 1

THE MAKING OF A REBEL

I

On June 17, 1862, at a crucial juncture in the Civil War's famed Peninsula campaign, Major General James Longstreet rallied his troops to the defense of Richmond, Virginia, against the invading Yankees with the following words:

> Soldiers—You have marched out to fight the battles of your country, and by these battles you must be rescued from the shame of slavery. Your foes have declared their purpose of bringing you to beggary; and avarice, their natural characteristic, incites them to redoubled efforts for the conquest of the South, in order that they may seize her sunny fields and happy homes.... [T]hey care not for the blood of babes nor carnage of innocent women which servile insurrection thus stirred up may bring upon their heads.... [D]eath would be better than the fate that defeat would entail upon us all.[1]

Such rhetoric was an archetypal expression of proslavery ideology: Longstreet staked the claim that Northern society was irredeemably radical, intent on fomenting race war ("servile insurrection") in the South to fasten the shame of political enslavement on the region's whites.

3

Longstreet's upbringing had primed him to make such a speech. He was shaped by the plantation South and by the political mentorship of his uncle Augustus Baldwin Longstreet. Augustus, an influential proslavery ideologue, saw the antebellum era's slavery debates as a form of warfare. And he groomed his nephew James to carry the South's banner into battle.

II

James Longstreet was born in Edgefield County, South Carolina, on January 8, 1821. His ancestors had roots in the Netherlands and had settled in Dutch New York and in New Jersey in the seventeenth century; descendants of these settlers made their way to Augusta, Georgia, in the eighteenth century. Longstreet's grandfather William made a name for himself in Georgia as a second-tier inventor, experimenting with steam engines for riverboats and improvements to the cotton gin. William and his family moved at the dawn of the nineteenth century to rural Edgefield, where they acquired a small plantation. Over the course of the antebellum era, the county would acquire a reputation as a seedbed of proslavery and states' rights sentiment, "famous for its state and national troublemakers," such as the US senator-turned-secessionist James Henry Hammond, and for its high yields of cotton, as the historian Orville Vernon Burton has noted.[2]

William Longstreet's son James eventually became a cotton planter, settling near Gainesville in northeastern Georgia and marrying Mary Ann Dent of Augusta in 1814. Ann gave birth to a son, James Jr., the couple's fifth child, while visiting her mother-in-law in South Carolina. Young James Longstreet's boyhood was spent mostly in the Gainesville region, a sparsely populated district that was still undergoing the transition from forested frontier to settled farmland. His father owned and bought and sold dozens of slaves to work family properties near Gainesville and also near Augusta and back in Edgefield. An advertisement James Sr. placed in an Augusta newspaper in 1816 seeking a reward for the return of two "negro boys" who had fled the Edgefield district is a glimpse into the Longstreet family's slaveholding, as is the December 1822 record of James's purchase, for the price of $401, of a "negro girl" named Nance.[3]

At age nine, James Jr. was sent to live with his uncle Augustus Baldwin Longstreet in Augusta in order to attend the Richmond County Academy there and to acquire some education and polish; James would divide his time between school and his uncle's nearby plantation, Westover. For eight years, from 1830 to 1838, he was under the care and increasingly under the sway of Augustus; James's father's death in an 1833 cholera epidemic, and his mother's decision to resettle in northern Alabama, further augmented Augustus's role as James's mentor and a father figure. In these years, Augustus was well on his way to fashioning a reputation as one of the South's most strident defenders of slavery. In his overlapping careers as a lawyer and jurist, Methodist minister, politician, newspaper editor, fiction writer, and college president of four different institutions, Augustus used all of the platforms at his disposal to elaborate the states' rights, proslavery creed. Like his friend and Yale University classmate John C. Calhoun, the fiery US senator who defended the sovereignty of Southern states against any abolitionist incursions, Augustus was instrumental in transmuting Southern disunion prophecies and threats into a disunion program. A lifelong adherent of the Democratic Party, he vociferously promoted the doctrine of nullification: South Carolina's protest against tariffs (import taxes) that were, so nullifiers charged, harmful to the plantation economy.[4]

Even as Augustus Longstreet defended slavery as a "positive good," he struggled to establish Westover as a profitable plantation. In a passage that reveals the mentality of Southern slaveholders, Augustus attributed his failings as a planter to the criminality of his slaves, casting himself as their victim. He failed to recognize that what he saw as their faithlessness was, in fact, resistance to his domination. "My crops barely paid the expenses of making them," he recalled in 1870 of his Westover days, as "my negroes became thieves, they stole my hogs, my corn, my bacon (by false keys), and every thing they could sell. Security debts I had to pay by thousands; in short, you can hardly name a trouble to which I was not subjected." Frustrated with plantation management, Augustus eventually put Westover on the market and sold nearly fifty of its enslaved persons (with his wife's permission, as she had brought this property to the marriage) so that he could focus on his law practice. In 1832, as part of divesting himself of his large plantation workforce, Augustus transferred to his young nephew James Longstreet, then only eleven years of age, ownership of eight slaves: the "carpenter Dennis, Guss for Augustus, Daniel and Zanya, Charity and her children, Joe and Ned and Little May daughter of Nelly." As he embarked on his career as a college president in the 1840s, Augustus would continue to own a domestic workforce of roughly a dozen enslaved persons, which classified him as a "middling" slaveowner rather than an elite "planter." But he considered himself a mouthpiece for the interests of elite planters and sought public acclaim as such.[5]

III

Young James had grown to be an impressive physical specimen if not a particularly promising student, and Augustus saw him as the vehicle for his own ambition. To that end, he finagled his nephew an appointment to the United States Military Academy at West Point, on the Hudson River in New York. Their Georgia district's vacancy had already been filled by another nominee, so Augustus reached out to an Alabama relative, Congressman Reuben Chapman, who could appoint Longstreet out of the district to which James's widowed mother had relocated. West Point, one of the nation's most prestigious and rigorous institutions of higher education, sought to train an elite officer corps of professional soldiers and to steep them in a distinct, emerging military subculture that "united men from different regions and social classes" by socializing them to "avoid strident political partisanship and instead be a neutral instrument of government policy." This emphasis on political neutrality ran counter to James Longstreet's family culture of intense partisanship; in the future, the tension between these two creeds would at times become quite acute.[6]

James Longstreet's biographers have portrayed him as a jovial, fun-loving, boisterous young man. An indifferent student at West Point, Longstreet relished the physical challenges of soldiering, but showed little intellectual motivation for scholastics. His poor grades and low class rank lend credence to this portrait, as does Longstreet's own recollection that he was more interested in "horsemanship, sword exercise, and the outside game of foot-ball than in the academic courses." But Longstreet's future Civil War tactical and strategic decision-making, and his voluminous post-war writings on what he called, following the military lingo of the day, the "art" and the "science" of war, reveal that at least some of the West Point academic curriculum took. Longstreet was clearly influenced by French military theorist Antoine Henri Jomini, whose writings on the Napoleonic art of war were conveyed to West Point cadets in the antebellum period through professors such as Dennis Mahan. Jomini's emphasis on throwing force upon decisive points; on the value of the strategic offensive but potential pitfalls of the tactical offensive; and most of all his emphasis on "moral courage"—those key qualities of character that were the most essential attributes of a great leader—would all echo in Longstreet's writings on the Civil War, as would Jomini's view that one of the key tests of a leader's character was whether he could resist having "too great a contempt for the enemy."[7]

West Point's demanding curriculum and discipline generally suppressed its graduation rate, but as the historian Jeffry D. Wert explains, Longstreet's West Point class of '42 defied the odds and "proved to be one of the better ones of the decade," graduating a roster of future Civil War generals, including the Confederates Daniel Harvey Hill and Lafayette McLaws and Unionists William S. Rosecrans and John Pope. The most important connection Longstreet made at West Point was his friendship with fellow cadet Ulysses S. Grant of Ohio from the class of '43. Although Pete and Sam, as they were known to their classmates, came from very different backgrounds, the prankish Georgian and the quiet Midwesterner quickly became best friends. Reflecting on his West Point years in his memoir, Longstreet described Grant reverently as "the man who was to eclipse all."[8]

After their respective graduations, Longstreet and Grant were both posted to Jefferson Barracks, Missouri, where the steady routine of military drills and exercises and garrison duty was pleasantly punctuated by each man's courtship of his future wife: Grant wooed Julia Dent, a distant cousin of Longstreet's mother, while Longstreet courted Maria Louisa Garland, the daughter of his regimental commander, Lieutenant Colonel John Garland.[9]

But first duty intervened. As Longstreet recalled, "In May, 1844, all of our pleasures were broken by orders sending both regiments to Louisiana, near Fort Jessup, where with other troops we were organized as 'The Army of Observation,' under General Zachary Taylor." This was the staging ground for the Mexican War, as Taylor was monitoring the border with Mexico in the wake of fierce congressional debates that had culminated in the annexation of Texas. Observation soon turned to occupation, as Taylor's troops were ordered by President James K. Polk to Corpus Christi in the contested boundary zone between Mexico and the United States, even as diplomatic relations between the two republics were breaking down.[10]

While Longstreet, a second lieutenant in the US Army's 8th Infantry, patrolled this volatile borderland, his uncle Augustus was busy sowing the seeds of sectionalism. Scorning the notion that ministers and educators should avoid partisan politics, Augustus Longstreet used the pulpit and lecture hall, as well as the printed page, to preach the proslavery creed. He was instrumental in the sectional schism that divided the Methodist Church into Northern and Southern branches, and integral to the biblical defense of slavery, telling Northern abolitionists in an 1845 pamphlet, "What you believe to be sinful, we believe to be perfectly innocent." Augustus fancied himself a molder of the South's young men and an anti-abolition prophet, who warned the white South early and often of the growing sway of antislavery sentiment in the North. He portrayed abolitionists as a "tribe of self-infuriated madmen, rushing through the country with the Bible in one hand and a torch in the other—preaching peace, and scattering the flames of civil war." Augustus Longstreet resented what he considered the abolitionists' condescension and hypocrisy, and he accused them of devising a ruthless "system of warfare against Slavery," as he put it in 1847. Southerners must, Augustus insisted, be ruthless and systematic in slavery's defense.[11]

At this juncture in the road to civil war, James Longstreet's military duties and his uncle's political agenda aligned: the slaveholding South embraced both Texas annexation and the Mexican War as vehicles for slavery's westward expansion and for augmenting slaveholder power, through the addition of new slave states, within the Union. Prowar propaganda tapped into two strains of American nationalism. One was an idealistic tradition in which America was a model republic that could redeem the people of the world from tyranny; seen in this light, the Mexican War was a war of liberation that would bring the blessings of a republican government to a struggling, factionalized country. The second strain was an ascendant racial nationalism that asserted the superiority of Anglo-Saxon civilization and cast Mexicans as an unassimilable, inferior race that must yield to Anglo expansion and dominance. Racial nationalism resonated with Southern Democrats such as James Longstreet. While U. S. Grant would deem the Mexican War, in retrospect, a wicked one, provoked needlessly by Polk's aggressive deployment of troops in the disputed territory between the Nueces and Rio Grande Rivers, Longstreet accepted the Polk administration's arguments that Mexico had instigated the war. As Longstreet would put it in 1885, reminiscing on the war's origins, "[T]he Mexicans were committing outrages which called for repression at the hands of the United States."[12]

IV

In the eyes of his family, his commanders, and the prowar press, Longstreet acquitted himself with honor in the Mexican War. During Zachary

Taylor's initial campaign to control Mexico's northern provinces, Longstreet performed well in the string of US victories, stretching from the fall of 1846 to the first months of 1847, at Palo Alto, Resaca de la Palma, and Monterrey. Longstreet's combat leadership in storming Monterrey's imposing fortifications led to his promotion to first lieutenant and adjutant of the 8th Infantry Regiment. As Mexican authorities remained unwilling to negotiate even after having lost control of their northern and western provinces, President Polk and Major General Winfield Scott decided to invade central Mexico with a combined naval and army force that would first encircle the port city of Veracruz and then march inland toward Mexico City.[13]

Longstreet and the 8th Infantry were reassigned to Scott's Army of Invasion and participated in the assault on Veracruz; the city fell after a merciless artillery bombardment that laid waste to homes, churches, and schools as well as its defenses and defenders. Scott's army then moved into the interior, advancing on the National Road through the Valley of Mexico, a volcanic plateau ringed by mountains and blocked by the fortified positions of General Antonio López de Santa Anna. Scott's tactics of outflanking Santa Anna's fixed defenses worked, and, by mid-August, the American army had reached Mexico City's southern outskirts. Surrounded by a flood-prone lake system and marshes and canals, the city was ringed by causeways, like spokes from a wheel, which constituted its only approaches. Scott was determined to strike the retreating Mexican army before it could bolster the defenses of the city.[14]

On August 20, 1847, Scott's army clashed with Santa Anna's rear guard at Churubusco in one of the most desperate battles of the war. On the orders of division commander Colonel David Worth, Longstreet and his 8th Infantry attacked the *tête de pont* (earthworks protecting a bridge) at Churubusco, advancing into withering enemy fire. The dogged Mexican defenders faltered as they ran out of ammunition, but the battle nonetheless inflicted heavy casualties on the American attackers and bought Santa Anna time, permitting the bulk of his forces to fall back toward Mexico

City. Scott chose to regroup rather than to press on and assault the city, agreeing to a brief armistice with Santa Anna during which the Mexican army established a new defensive line. Longstreet earned a promotion to brevet captain for his bravery at Churubusco and also earned favorable coverage from the press back home. Improvements in transportation and communication, such as the advent of railroads and telegraphs and steam printing presses and the penny press, stoked the public's appetite for news from the front. In November the *Charleston Mercury* of South Carolina published a letter from a South Carolina officer on the "exploit of our friend Longstreet, who highly distinguished himself" at Churubusco. "In a hail-storm of musket balls," Longstreet had "rushed forward, calling upon all brave men to follow their standard."[15]

The paper also revealed that Longstreet was badly wounded in a subsequent US attack on another imposing position: the fortified stone mansion of Chapultepec, home to Mexico's national military academy. That assault took place on September 13, as Scott resumed his campaign after the abortive armistice. In keeping with his preference for flanking maneuvers, the general decided to attack the city from the drier land to the west rather than the more direct route from the south. After winning a meaningless victory on September 8, overrunning an entrenched Mexican position at Molino del Rey—a flour mill that the Americans mistakenly believed had been converted into a foundry—Scott's army set its sights on the two causeways that entered the city from the southwest and were guarded by Mexican forces arrayed on the steep, rocky hill of Chapultepec. Scott created a diversion by having a small force feint against the southern causeways, and then softened up the Mexican defenses at Chapultepec with a blistering artillery bombardment. In the ensuing assault, the American attackers fought their way into the fortress, overcoming a desperate last-ditch defense by Mexican troops, who included young military cadets.[16]

Longstreet played a conspicuous role in the storming party, carrying the US flag toward the fortress heights, and suffered a grievous wound to the thigh. As Longstreet fell, Lieutenant George E. Pickett took the colors from him and carried them to the castle summit, in a dramatic set piece that entered the annals of the war's heroic moments. The victorious Americans surged down the causeways toward the capital of Mexico City, forcing Mexico to surrender on September 14. Winfield Scott took up residence in the country's National Palace. On February 2, 1848, Mexico signed the Treaty of Guadalupe Hidalgo, agreeing to cede more than half of its territory, including lands that would become the states of Arizona, California, New Mexico, Texas, Colorado, Nevada, and Utah.[17]

In its coverage of Longstreet's heroics during the Mexico City campaign, the *Charleston Mercury* reassured readers that the recently brevetted major was "recovering rapidly" from his wounding at Churubusco. But, in fact, the musket ball wound to his thigh was severe enough to require a prolonged convalescence, first at an American hospital and then with an elite Mexican family, the Escandones, who were friendly to US troops. Longstreet eventually made his way back to his mother's home in Huntsville, Alabama, to recuperate for another two months before proceeding on to Augusta, Georgia, in February 1848. Upon his arrival there, he received a warm welcome as a native son, the local papers noting that Longstreet had "behaved with a gallantry worthy of all praise" in the war.[18]

Longstreet could glean many lessons in combat leadership and tactical decision-making from the Mexican War. As the historian Alexander Mendoza has noted, Longstreet had "witnessed how troops, if properly motivated, could overcome great odds and overtake a strongly fortified position," especially through flanking movements. Longstreet also derived lessons about the political nature of military command: on high-ranking officers' perennial jockeying for credit and doling out blame, and the need to guard and promote one's own reputation zealously.

These lessons were driven home when Longstreet was embroiled, in the spring of 1848, in a bitter feud between General Gideon Pillow and his superior, the war hero Winfield Scott. Scott court-martialed Pillow for publicly magnifying his own heroism and trying to take unwarranted credit for Scott's successful tactics in the Mexico City campaign. But politics were at the heart of the feud: Pillow, a close ally of Democratic president James K. Polk, had political aspirations of his own, and stoked Polk's fear that Scott, a member of the Whig Party, might be a rival for the presidency. Polk fired Scott as commander of the US Army and canceled the court martial; instead, he set up a court of inquiry stacked with Pillow supporters. Most soldiers took Scott's side. As the Whigs were more willing to spend federal dollars on funding the military, they were generally favored by the career army officers. Although the party was more interested in economic modernization than territorial expansion, and had been ambivalent about "Mr. Polk's War," it saw the merit in riding the tide of military victory and in choosing a soldier as its standard-bearer. The Whigs would run the Mexican War's second greatest hero, Zachary Taylor, for president in 1848, and then run Winfield Scott in 1852.[19]

Longstreet, during the Pillow-Scott imbroglio, stood strongly with Scott. When Scott arrived in Frederick, Maryland, in June 1848 for the military court of inquiry, Longstreet was in the small party of associates accompanying him. Longstreet's testimony deflated one of Pillow's overblown claims. Among the many acts Pillow took credit for was shooting a captured Mexican officer off his horse when the officer attempted to escape the custody of US troops in the aftermath of Churubusco. Longstreet testified that many soldiers in various regiments saw the attempted escape and that "at least fifty muskets were fired at the officer before he fell"; Longstreet could not recall even seeing Pillow at the scene. However, faced with a parade of conflicting witnesses, the court of inquiry eventually dropped the case. Pillow claimed vindication, and the hearings, which were covered in the national press, served his end of casting a shadow over Scott's reputation.[20]

Over the course of his life, Longstreet had surprisingly little to say publicly about either the military or political lessons of the Mexican War. In postwar speeches and interviews, he often took the opportunity to praise the conduct of U. S. Grant. For example, Longstreet recalled in 1890 that at the Battle of Molino del Rey, he "had occasion to notice [Grant's] superb coolness and courage under fire. So noticeable was his bearing that his gallantry was alluded to in official reports." In Longstreet's lengthy memoir, only ten pages would be devoted to the Mexican War, and they featured intimate anecdotes: of officers setting up a makeshift theater for performing plays to pass the time; of mosquitoes "as thick as the blades of grass on the prairies" swarming the troops on the march; of Longstreet's being "unnerved" at the sight of a dead young Mexican woman, "her expression life-like."

Longstreet also remembered that his spirits were lifted by the image of Maria Louisa Garland, whose daguerreotype he carried in his breast pocket. When Longstreet returned home, he promptly married "Louise," as he called her, at her family home in Lynchburg, Virginia. A few months after their own wedding, on March 8, 1848, the young couple attended the August 1848 nuptials of Grant and Julia Dent in Missouri.[21]

Louise Longstreet was no stranger to the vicissitudes of military life: she was born in 1827 at the army post of Fort Snelling, in the Minnesota Territory, to career soldier John Garland of Virginia and Harriet Smith, descended from a part-Chippewa fur-trading family. As historian and Longstreet biographer William Garrett Piston has noted, James Longstreet married well not only by finding a devoted, resilient wife but also in riding the coattails of John Garland, who rose to the rank of colonel during the Mexican War and would help James in his own rise through the ranks. After a brief stint in Carlisle Barracks, Pennsylvania, where the first of their ten children (named John Garland, after Louise's father), was born, the Longstreets were transferred, in the spring of 1849, to San Antonio, Texas, headquarters of the Department of Texas (one of the army's geographic districts). John Garland Sr. arrived there in January 1850 to assume command of the 8th Infantry. Fortuitously, that same month, James was reassigned from detached duty at the western outpost of Fort Lincoln back to San Antonio to serve as commissary chief for Military Department No. 8, thus reuniting him with his wife and son. For nearly eleven of the next twelve years, Piston writes, Longstreet "served with or near his father-in-law under circumstances which suggest Longstreet benefitted from his favoritism."[22]

V

When Longstreet was deployed to Texas in 1849, he entered a complex, shifting geopolitical terrain. Texas grew explosively in the mid-1840s, as settlers from the Deep South surged into the region, bringing the cotton economy and infringing on the borders of Comancheria—the vast trading empire, built through commerce, diplomacy, and raids, that the Comanche Indians had established in the Southwest and on the Southern Plains. One of the pretexts for the Mexican War had been Mexico's inability to pacify and control this frontier. "The U.S. takeover of the Southwest was significantly assisted by the fact that Comanches and Apaches had already destabilized Mexico's Far North," the historian Pekka Hämäläinen observes, adding that Anglo settlers imagined they *"earned* Texas because they alone possessed the masculine and martial vigor to wrestle the land away from the Comanches and savagery." But wrestling the land away took years and years of effort: when Longstreet arrived in Texas in 1849, half the state remained under Comanche control. The US Army's mission in the region was to establish national authority; to protect the gold rushers, merchants, ranchers, and other Anglos who entered the Southwest; to provide supplies and escorts to those proceeding farther west on trade routes such as the San Antonio–El Paso Road; and to enforce the provisions of the Treaty of Guadalupe Hidalgo. In Article 11, the one element of the treaty favorable to Mexico, "[T]he United States agreed to police the border to prevent Indian raids from crossing the Rio Grande into Mexico," Hämäläinen explains. The US Army established a double ring of forts at the peripheries of Anglo settlements, arcing from the Trinity and Washita Rivers in North Texas to the Rio Grande in the south, to guard against Indian raids and to press outward into Comancheria. The first ring was established in the late 1840s, in wake of the Mexican War, and the second ring, roughly a hundred dred miles to the west, was established a few years later.[23]

Longstreet's first assignment, in the summer of 1849, was as the commander at Fort Lincoln, a small garrison of approximately a hundred men located a two days' ride west of San Antonio. Named in honor of a fallen Mexican War officer, the fort was part of the initial outer ring of federal posts in Texas. Longstreet left very little record of his experiences in these years, but a communication he submitted in the fall of 1849, which made its way into the report of the US Congress's Joint Committee on Indian Affairs in 1850, hinted at the escalation of clashes between Anglos and Native Americans in this borderland. Longstreet's description of how a "private in his command was killed on the night of the 21st November last, at Fort Lincoln, on the Rio Seco, Bexar County, by a party of Indians—tribe unknown" was folded into the committee's case that so-called Indian outrages necessitated a firmer national commitment to frontier defense.[24]

Longstreet's reassignment in January 1850 to San Antonio afforded him some physical safety, but posed its own challenges: "He was responsible for feeding every person and animal the Army employed in southeastern Texas," as William Garrett Piston has succinctly put it. The site of the famous Alamo, San Antonio was, as a fellow soldier named Lewis Harvie Blair described it, "a mere village of adobe huts and American buildings of very cheap grade; with two plazas—one military, and the other civil, with a Mexican cathedral on the latter." Although slavery was less of a presence in San Antonio than in Galveston and Houston, the institution grew exponentially in Texas in the 1850s, in urban as well as rural areas, and, by 1860, there were several hundred enslaved persons in San Antonio. The US Federal Census for 1850 shows that James Longstreet owned two enslaved persons while he lived in San Antonio: a woman age thirty-five and a thirteen-year-old girl.[25]

As the biggest city in Texas, San Antonio was an important staging ground for travelers heading west to California in the gold rush years. Longstreet, as commissary chief, ran afoul of a particularly notorious such emigrant in the fall of 1850: one Parker H. French, a practiced con man. French arrived in the city posing as the head of an emigrant company undertaking the journey from New York to California. Flashing a letter of credit from the New York merchant firm of Howland & Aspinwall, French persuaded Lieutenant Longstreet and two other officers to furnish supplies to the emigrants, consisting of quartermaster, ordnance, and subsistence stores worth roughly $2,000. War Department regulations permitted army officers to undertake such transactions, provided that the proper paperwork was done and excess supplies were available. But unfortunately for Longstreet, the method of payment French had offered turned out to be a forgery. When the fraud came to light, a search party was sent to track down the swindler, but he had already escaped into Mexico. In 1855–56, Longstreet and his fellow aggrieved officers successfully petitioned the War Department to be remunerated for the funds they had been defrauded of.[26]

Although Longstreet had otherwise done a commendable job as commissary, this incident likely contributed to his desire to get away from desk work and return to field duties; he got his wish when he was assigned in March 1851 to Fort Martin Scott in Fredericksburg, Texas, to resume scouting duty with the 8th Infantry. Another in the first ring of frontier garrisons, Fort Martin Scott was crude at best. "The face of nature here is lovely, noble hills, fine fields and beautiful streams, but botched and deformed by the works of man," wrote the post doctor, US Army assistant surgeon Ebenezer Swift. The fort consisted of "a few log houses for officers and soldiers quarters . . . inclosed with a stick and brush fence that don't keep the hogs out," he continued. However "botched" the fort was, the town served as a key supply station for wagon trains bound for California.[27]

Longstreet was promoted to captain in December 1852. A glimpse of his activities in this period is afforded by a surviving unfinished painting by the German-born Texas artist Friedrich Richard Petri, who had immigrated to the United States in 1851 and settled in Pedernales, Texas, near Fredericksburg. In early 1853 Petri painted a scene set at Fort Martin Scott in which a military man is shown returning captured horses, mules, and supplies to a delegation of Lipan Apaches, who had allied with Texans and the US Army against the Comanches and Mexicans. Those resources had been issued to the Lipans by government agents and then violently seized by US troops on the false rumor that they were stolen goods. Petri's biographer William W. Newcomb has argued that the soldier in the painting is Longstreet. The resemblance is strong—and records show that Longstreet, who had been reassigned to nearby Fort Chadbourne, located on the new outer ring of Texas's cordon of garrisons, was the officer put in charge of the captured horses and supplies.[28]

Longstreet's next western posting, in 1854, was as commander of Company I, 8th Infantry, at the recently established Fort Bliss in El Paso, on the western edge of Texas. In early 1855 he led a major 240-man mounted infantry expedition in the Trans-Pecos region's Guadalupe Mountains against Mescalero Apaches, who had conducted raids on the San Antonio–El Paso Road. This was forbidding terrain. Three years later, a correspondent traveling through the Guadalupe Pass came across a chilling sight: two graves, one of which belonged to Longstreet's Mexican scout in the 1855 expedition, Jose Maria Palancio, who had been "sent forward to look for water, and when in the narrowest portion of the pass, [was] shot full of arrows" by Apaches. While the Apaches dodged their pursuers, and the mission resulted in no combat, it was "an important element of the military pressure that led the Mescaleros to seek peace the following May," as the historian David A. Clary has noted. It also represented Longstreet's most extensive command experience before the Civil War.[29]

Longstreet would remain at Fort Bliss until the spring of 1858, when he took a leave of absence to head east and arrange for his ten-year-old son, Garland, to be placed in a school in Yonkers, New York. The family had been wracked with grief at the loss of two infant children: William Dent Longstreet, born in San Antonio in 1853, had died of illness during the family's sojourn east to Washington, DC, where Longstreet was ordered on assignment as a courier, in the summer of 1854, and Harriet Margaret Longstreet died at Fort Bliss in 1856 at only six months of age. Longstreet was preoccupied with the welfare of his remaining sons: Garland, Augustus (named after his uncle), and his own namesake, James, who was born in 1857 in Santa Fe. Longstreet confided to his uncle Augustus in 1859 that if he could find a suitable education for the boys, it would "reconcile [him] to living anywhere on the continent."[30]

Newly promoted to the rank of major and assigned to the Pay Department, Longstreet briefly took up a new post at Fort Leavenworth, in the Kansas Territory. Then he relocated his family yet again to Albuquerque, New Mexico Territory, in another instance of his being transferred to the same post as his father-in-law, John Garland. While there in February 1860, James penned a revealing letter to South Carolina congressman William Porcher Miles in Washington, DC. "Some one or two friends and myself have been working very hard for several years past to put Chihuahua into the US," Longstreet revealed, adding, "She is now ready to come in and has applied to the Pres. for support or protection." Highlighting the political implications of this maneuver to annex the sizable Mexican state, bordering Texas and New Mexico, Longstreet expressly noted that "if it can be granted, she can very readily be brought in as a slave state."[31]

The historian Robert E. May has read this exchange as evidence of the seductive power of filibustering—the raising of private armies to invade foreign countries in peacetime—for young men, even career military officers, in the late antebellum United States. Filibustering exploits such as William Walker's brief and ill-fated seizure of Nicaragua in 1856 "attracted front-page headlines," May explains, by tapping a pervasive spirit of expansionism and martial manhood. Although the US Army was officially tasked with anti-filibustering duties, such as intercepting illicit expeditions before they could wreak much mischief, many soldiers nonetheless "held latent pro-filibuster sentiments." According to May, Longstreet's letter to Representative Miles, disclosing his designs on Chihuahua, was evidence of how a "sectionalist imperative reinforced filibustering inclinations": soldiers such as Longstreet "shared civilian ideologies of Anglo-American racial superiority and Manifest Destiny."[32]

While May's points are well taken, an equally important context for the letter is President James Buchanan's foreign policy. Longstreet specified that he intended to "raise a Regiment of Volunteers" that would march on

Chihuahua *after* Buchanan had officially authorized them to do so. Longstreet was taking signals from the embattled Democratic chief executive, who, in the face of escalating sectional conflict between the North and South, hoped to divert the public's attention with some sanctioned imperial ventures. Establishing a temporary American protectorate over the northwestern Mexican states of Chihuahua and Sonora, would, so Buchanan claimed, help Mexicans in their battles against "predatory" Indians. But Congress, preoccupied with the slavery debates and the upcoming 1860 presidential election, rebuffed the president's request that it raise expeditionary forces for an invasion of Mexico, seeing such machinations as an unwarranted intervention in the affairs of a sovereign nation.[33]

Instead, the Southwest was swept up in the unfolding secession drama. In the late 1850s Deep South secessionists led the movement for Southern independence, reviling the new antislavery Republican Party that had taken root in the North as radicals hell-bent on forcing abolition on the South. Abraham Lincoln and other Republicans disavowed any intent to federally mandate emancipation; the party sought only to ban slavery's spread to the west, in the hope that such a restriction might motivate Southerners to dismantle the institution voluntarily and gradually. But the reassurances left proslavery Southerners cold. The Republican critique of slavery as undemocratic and unproductive was an intolerable affront to Southern honor, secessionists claimed. Militant "fire-eaters"—whose leadership ranks included Congressmen Miles and J. L. M. Curry of Alabama, both friends of Longstreet's—appealed to white solidarity and ginned up racial fears, warning that Lincoln's election would bring race war, race competition, and race mixing. Lincoln fended off three other parties' candidates to win the 1860 presidential contest on the strength of Northern votes. In the four months between the election and the new commander in chief's inauguration on March 4, 1861, seven Deep South states, including Texas, seceded from the Union to form the Confederate States of America in Montgomery, Alabama. Four Upper South states would join the Confederacy that spring.[34]

Secessionists, especially those in Texas, eyed the New Mexico Territory as a possible addition to the roster of Southern states. In March 1861, disunionists in Mesilla, in the southern half of the New Mexico territory, seceded from the Union to form the Arizona Territory and expressed the hope that they would be absorbed into the new Southern Confederacy. US Army officers on duty in the Department of New Mexico in the turbulent months after Lincoln's election did not stand in the way of secessionist demonstrations and mobilization. Instead, many of them, including Longstreet, resigned their commissions and headed east to join their state forces or the Confederate military.[35]

VI

Resigning from the US Army and taking up leadership roles in the rebel military was not a foreordained course for Southern soldiers like Longstreet, but rather a choice. A small but symbolically significant number of Southern men chose the Union—most notably the Virginians Winfield Scott, general-in-chief of the US Army at the Civil War's outset, and General George Thomas, who would face off against Longstreet at Chickamauga, Georgia, in 1864. (Roughly 30 percent of Virginia-born officers in the US Army remained loyal.) Many more Southern military men qualified as "reluctant Confederates," agonizing about forsaking the Union army for the Confederate one. Generally, they were committed to defending slavery and believed that the South had the right to secede, but they worried about the Union's advantages in manpower and resources, and struggled to break their sentimental attachment to the Union. As the case of Virginia-born Robert E. Lee illustrates, events such as South Carolina's April 1861 firing on Fort Sumter and Lincoln's subsequent call for troops to suppress the rebellion moved such "conditional Unionists" off the fence and into the Confederate column. Lee resigned his US commission and joined the Virginia state forces, which he headed for

21

six weeks before becoming a Confederate officer. Lincoln, men like Lee believed, had chosen the path of coercion rather than compromise.[36]

Longstreet would suggest in postwar interviews and in his memoir that he had been among those who struggled with the decision of whether to join the Southern cause, and that he had in part yielded to family pressure from secessionist relatives. As he put it in 1879,

> I was paymaster in the United States Army when the trouble between the states began. I had the rank of major and was stationed in New Mexico. I viewed from my distant point of observation the agitation of the Southern leaders with impatience. I was devoted to the Union and failed to see any cause for breaking it up when secession was accomplished. I held on. I was determined to remain where I was if secession was peacefully accomplished, of which, however, I had little hope. My relatives in Georgia wrote me urgently to come on at once, saying that "all the good officers were being taken up." I replied that if there was going to be any war, it would last for several years, and that in time every soldier would find his level, and so that it mattered little whether he commenced at the top or the bottom. At length Sumter was fired upon, and then I knew that war was inevitable and felt that my place was with my people. I resigned my commission and came home.[37]

Longstreet's claim that his family pressured him to head east and join the Confederate army finds some corroboration in an April 17, 1861, letter he wrote to a fellow paymaster about arranging passage from Albuquerque: "My letters by the last mail call me home, and I cannot, at present, see that I can do otherwise than go." But as Longstreet biographer Jeffry Wert's sleuthing has revealed, the image of Longstreet as a reluctant secessionist is controverted by documents showing that he "acted with surprising haste" in embracing Southern independence. Deep South secessionists regarded the election of Lincoln as a virtual declaration of war. They did not adopt a wait-and-see attitude about Lincoln's intentions—and neither did Longstreet. As soon as Alabama seceded in January 1861, making it the fourth state to do so, Longstreet wasted no time in lobbying its governor, Andrew B. Moore, for a Confederate military appointment. (Alabama had sponsored Longstreet's West Point nomination.) In a February 1861 letter on Longstreet's behalf, J. L. M. Curry explained to Moore that Longstreet, though still a paymaster in the US Army, had "asserted his determination to go wherever his state went, to bide her fortunes, and to serve her in any capacity, where his services were needed." Curry urged Moore to appoint Longstreet "to an office of at least equal rank with that held by him under the government of the United States." Wert speculates that ambition drove Longstreet's choice of Alabama over Georgia as his designated home base, as he was the state's senior West Point alumnus and thus poised to assume a leadership role in its armed forces.[38]

Wert's interpretation rings true, for Longstreet had made no secret of his ambitions—or his frustrations. Back in 1850, stationed in San Antonio, Brevet Major Longstreet wrote US Secretary of War George W. Crawford requesting promotion on the grounds he had performed "as much service as any officer of my grade could have rendered" to the US Army in the Mexican War and in frontier duty. Longstreet was dissatisfied with his brevetting, a temporary symbolic promotion that recognized merit but did not necessarily bring additional pay or authority. He lamented to Crawford, "[B]revets have been given in such promiscuous profusion" that they conferred "neither fame nor reward." A Confederate appointment promised a chance for that deferred recognition and for future acclaim. "Major Longstreet expects to get a good position in the Southern Army," Captain Edmunds Holloway of the 8th Infantry wrote from New Mexico on February 10, 1861, to his wife, Eliza, in Illinois. Holloway, a proslavery Missourian and close friend of Longstreet's who had served alongside him in the Mexican War and on frontier duty in the Southwest, thus provides additional confirmation of Longstreet's yearning for promotion.[39]

At the same time he was pursuing a state-level appointment in the secessionist cause, Longstreet was also reaching out to Confederate authorities in Richmond, the new capital of the South. He had his older brother, William Dent Longstreet, of Mississippi, send a letter directly to Confederate president Jefferson Davis on February 22, 1861, tendering James's "services to any new government or Southern organization to serve in any capacity that is within the scope of his profession." The letter noted that right after Lincoln's election, James had requested a US Army escort for himself and his family from Albuquerque through "Indian country" to Texas so that he could proceed to points east—but that the request had been denied. William editorialized that should Lincoln provoke war, the Confederacy should "not be on the defensive entirely, but carry [the war] into Africa"—namely, invade the antislavery North. "What I am and what I have belongs to this Southern Movement," Longstreet's brother proclaimed, speaking for the entire family. William Dent Longstreet would serve as a second lieutenant in the Mississippi 11th Infantry Regiment.[40]

As further evidence of James's keen enthusiasm for secession, Wert reveals that Longstreet was appointed a lieutenant colonel in the Confederate infantry in March 1861 and accepted that appointment on May 1, well before he had tendered his official resignation from the US Army ranks (May 9) and before the War Department accepted the resignation (June 1). "As a U.S. Army officer, he accepted a commission in an enemy army," Wert writes, and thereby "crossed the delicate line between honor and dishonor." Further complicating Longstreet's claim that he went "home" to defend "his people": from Texas, he went straight to Richmond to join the army there rather than going to Alabama. "He did not go to answer Alabama's 'call,'" Wert notes, "but to answer the Confederacy's."[41]

Siding with the South had immediate implications for Longstreet's role as a slaveowner. When Longstreet was young, he had been deeded (by either his father or uncle) an enslaved man named Daniel. But because Longstreet's army career often took him to places that were "not in favor of slavery"—such as the Kansas and New Mexico Territories—he could not, as he would later put it, "have Daniel with me." When Longstreet returned to the slaveholding South to enter the Confederate service, he soon "called for Daniel" to act as his body servant in the army, despite the fact that "by this time, [Daniel] was old and had the rheumatism." Tasked with cooking, foraging, tending horses, and other chores of camp life, body servants answered to their individual masters, not to the Confederate authorities, and thus were considered valuable assets by the slaveholding officer class. Like thousands of other enslaved men and women forced to work as laborers for the Confederate army, Daniel was released from bondage only with Union victory at the war's end.[42]

VII

In choosing the Confederacy, James Longstreet aligned himself with the proslavery secessionist ideology that his uncle Augustus had done so much to promote. Over the course of the 1850s, Augustus had escalated his own personal war against abolitionism and the "radical" North, calling on Southerners to reject "polluted" Northern books and schools and journals and to develop their own proslavery literary culture in order to "elevate and purify the education of the South." Emphasizing the theme of Southern victimization, Augustus, in his capacity as college president, told the graduating class of South Carolina College in the spring of 1859, "You are embarking upon a strange world, my young friends. . . . You may expect, therefore, at times to be depressed by your rivals, condemned for your patriotism, and tormented for your benefactions." In the wake of white abolitionist John Brown's failed attempt at inciting a slave revolt that fall in Harpers Ferry, Virginia, Augustus postured as a prophet, telling his students that he had predicted the "present crisis": "I foretold its course and results as though I had been inspired."[43]

Augustus did everything he could to be provocative. In the summer of 1860 he engaged in an attention-grabbing stunt that shocked Northerners and thrilled Southern secessionists: while in London as a US delegate at a prestigious scholarly gathering called the International Statistical Congress, he withdrew in a huff to protest the presence there of a Black delegate, the American abolitionist and physician Martin Delany. Augustus fumed that Delany's inclusion was an insult to the South. In a torrent of anti-abolition vitriol, Augustus Longstreet urged Southerners to "declare war against [their] oppressors" and vindicate their honor, lest history write them down as "the most arrogant cowards that ever disgraced the earth," as he put it in his December 1860 polemical essay "An Appeal to the South."

"I do not believe that there exists on the face of the earth two nations who more cordially detest each other than the slaveholding and nonslaveholding states of this Republic," he intoned. "It was bad enough before Lincoln's election; it is ten times worse, if possible, now." For secessionists like Augustus, the ascendancy of Lincoln's Republican Party represented both a political and social revolution: the eclipse of slaveholders' power to control the US government, and the specter of social leveling, of "high, low, white, black, male, female—all on a level, all tongue-clattering, all furious," as he warned. Augustus vastly exaggerated the egalitarianism of Northern Republicans, most of whom, like Lincoln himself, were political moderates. Casting all Northerners as radical abolitionists was a core secession strategy for engineering solidarity among Southern whites.[44]

A letter from Longstreet to his uncle in March 1861 testifies to their personal and political bonds. Written in Albuquerque as Longstreet was arranging his passage east, it recounted how he had, back in February, already offered his services to the Confederate cause. He hoped to delay his family's difficult and long journey home until winter was over, but he was prepared to leave them behind and hurry back east if Lincoln "attempted or threatened" the "coercion" of the seceded states back into the Union. Longstreet confided that Louise was "quite distressed" at the prospect of being left behind. "But I shall not flinch from any sacrifice that I feel I may be called upon to make," he vowed, signing the letter "most affectionately, yours."[45]

In the eyes of the secessionist public and press in the Deep South,

Augustus Longstreet's reputation as a spokesman for the South was linked to James's reputation as a soldier. As James traveled from the southwest to the seat of war in the spring of 1861, the newspapers reported his progress. According to Mississippi's *Oxford Intelligencer*, "Major James Longstreet, nephew of our distinguished friend, Judge Longstreet, and late of the United States Army, passed up on Monday last en route for Richmond.... He is reported to be a splendid officer," the paper observed, citing James's Mexican War record. "We welcome him to the service of his native South."[46]

Chapter 2

ENEMIES WITHOUT AND WITHIN

I

Longstreet achieved renown as a Confederate national hero during the first two years of the war, despite enduring personal tragedy and military setbacks. He was sustained by his fervent ideological commitment to the Confederate cause and by his faith in his own ability to mold his men and lead them in combat. But even as it brought battlefield victories that stoked Longstreet's confidence, the early war also forced him to confront what the historian Stephanie McCurry has called "the problem of the slaves' political allegiance." Confederate ideology defined the enslaved as existing outside of politics, with no duties or obligations as citizens, only the duty to obey the authority of their masters. During the secession crisis, Southern nationalists depicted the enslaved as submissive and loyal—and dangerous only if they fell under the spell of abolitionists and became instruments of Northern conquest. When the enslaved ratcheted up their resistance in the South during the war, "work[ing] toward the destruction of slavery tactically and in stages," whites like Longstreet faced a reckoning: the realization that there was a Unionist enemy within.[1]

Initially, at least, hopes ran high among soldiers on both sides that the war might be resolved swiftly in a grand military showdown. In June 1861 Longstreet was appointed to command of the Fourth Brigade (made up of the three regiments of the Virginia Volunteer Infantry) and ordered to join the forces of the hero of Fort Sumter, Brigadier General P. G. T. Beauregard, at Manassas Junction in Northern Virginia. Longstreet's primary role was to help anchor Beauregard's far-right flank, in the Confederate defensive position guarding the rail junction at Manassas. With this Confederate force massed a mere day's march southwest of Washington, DC, the pressure was on Union forces to dislodge the foe from the threshold of the capital. So, a Federal army under Union brigadier general Irvin McDowell set out for Manassas in mid-July, hoping to land a devasting blow on the insurgents.[2]

Beauregard, anticipating such a move, deployed Longstreet's brigade to guard the Bull Run crossing point at Blackburn's Ford. As the historian Edward G. Longacre has explained, Beauregard intended that "when the Federals struck, Longstreet was to move his entire command to the north side of Blackburn's Ford and lash the Union left flank and rear." McDowell's troops reached the village of Fairfax Court House by noon on July 17, and, the next day, a Federal vanguard probed at the Confederates at Blackburn's Ford, only to be turned back by Longstreet's men in a sharp skirmish. From a favorable defensive position of earthworks on the south side of the Bull Run, Longstreet's force pummeled the attacking Federals with a series of musket volleys and artillery blasts. Then they executed a blistering counterattack that sent the Federals reeling back and in need of a new plan for approaching Manassas.

As he described it in his after-action report, Longstreet's preparation had paid off: "My line of defense being quite extended, I threw out a line of skirmishers to the water's edge, covering my entire front, holding strong reserves in readiness to defend with the bayonet any point that might be violently attacked." Despite sixty-three casualties, the new recruits' performance gave momentum to Longstreet and his army, and won him plaudits in the Southern press. In the eyes of Confederates eager to prove their mettle, the affair on the 18th was a full-blown battle, in which "Longstreet displayed a courage and military skill that astonished every one," according to one Richmond paper. Longstreet would briefly second-guess himself about Blackburn's Ford, writing to his uncle Augustus in mid-August that he wished he had further attacked and pursued the retreating Federals—but the magnitude of the subsequent victory at Manassas largely kept such doubts at bay.[3]

Longstreet missed the main show at Manassas on the 21st. The setback at Blackburn's Ford helped convince McDowell that the best plan of action was to send part of his force against the center of the Confederate defensive position, while the other part executed a flank attack on the Confederate left. But this plan was foiled by Federal mistakes and Confederate counterstrokes—delays in McDowell's advance afforded the enemy time to reinforce its own front and to counterattack, sending the Union army taking flight across the Bull Run toward Washington. The Confederates scored a tactical as well as strategic victory in this first major battle of the war, inflicting nearly 3,000 casualties on the Federals, while suffering nearly 2,000 of their own.[4]

Having waited in vain at Blackburn's Ford for orders to advance, Longstreet seemed fleetingly to get the chance to contribute to the unfolding victory at Manassas when Beauregard directed him to intercept McDowell's retreating troops and cut off their avenues for withdrawal. But to Longstreet's profound frustration, Beauregard ultimately aborted that pursuit as being too risky. For Longstreet, the battle at Manassas illustrated both a key tactical principle—the effectiveness of a counterattack from a strong defensive position—and a key "moral" dictum, namely, "Never despise your enemy." By this, Longstreet meant that military commanders should take care not to underestimate the fighting capacity of their foes. He attributed the Federals' defeat to McDowell's "overconfidence" in his own troops and underrating the Confederate soldiery. In the weeks after Bull Run, Confederates reveled in their victory, seeing the Yankee "invasion" of the Virginia countryside as the fulfillment of secessionist prophecy that the enemy would wage war without mercy. When a British correspondent visited the rebel encampments a few days after the battle, Longstreet pointed out to him a nearby small Episcopal church on which Union soldiers had scrawled graffiti slogans such as "Death to traitors—thus saith the Lord!" Here was proof of Northern condescension and barbarity—and an intimation that the war could not be restricted to the battlefield.[5]

II

Longstreet was assigned by Beauregard to hold down Centreville, north of Manassas. Over the next six months, he trained his troops and attended to the many often mundane duties of a brigade commander. Longstreet was preoccupied with obtaining and transporting supplies, from rations to maps to ambulances. "We can only get four or five days' rations at a time," he complained to Colonel Thomas Jordan, adjutant general for Beauregard's army, in late August, adding, "This keeps me constantly on the watch and is exceedingly annoying." Longstreet's other duties included sifting through various intelligence reports from scouts, spies, civilians, and Yankee prisoners and deserters, to try to distinguish fact from rumor; resolving scuffles between his troops; meting out discipline to malcontents and troublemakers, such as when he sent a mutinous company of Marylanders to the rear in September 1861; and maintaining troop morale through inspirational speeches, promotions, furloughs, and other incentives. As was to be expected, there was a competence gap between the experienced career soldiers among his troops and the large numbers of inexperienced volunteers. For example, in September 1861 Longstreet issued a general order commending Colonel James Ewell Brown "J. E. B." Stuart and his cavalry for their performance in a minor engagement at Lewinsville, Virginia, proclaiming that "this handsome affair should remind our forces that numbers are of little avail compared with the importance of coolness, firmness, and careful attention to orders." But behind the scenes, in letters to Jordan, Longstreet complained of his green recruits' occasional fecklessness on the battlefield: in one incident, a sentry, "by his own carelessness," got shot in the leg by friendly fire after changing stations without informing the other pickets.[6]

Longstreet was generous in his praise and promotion of any man who rose to the occasion and acquitted himself well. Over the course of the war, he cultivated the confidence and loyalty of a core group of staff officers, such as his chief of staff, Gilbert Moxley Sorrel, and assistant staff John Walter Fairfax, Osmun Latrobe, and Thomas J. Goree. Longstreet reveled in the chance to praise these men's combat mettle in the romanticized language typical of the early war. Of Sorrel's conduct at Manassas, Longstreet wrote, "He came into battle as gaily as a beau, and seemed to receive orders which threw him into more exposed positions with peculiar delight." These men in turn all left extensive wartime writings that provide windows into Longstreet's own performance and morale. For example, Goree's letters to his family in Texas in this period reveal that Longstreet and the men in his inner circle were frustrated by their inaction and by the lingering sense that the Confederates had missed the opportunity at Bull Run to pursue the enemy all the way into Washington, DC, and perhaps take the capital and end the war in one decisive blow. The moment had slipped away: from the Confederates' advanced picket positions at Mason's and Munson's Hills, they had full view of Alexandria, Georgetown, and Washington and could see the Federals fortifying their defenses.

Goree also provides the most intimate portrait of Longstreet at this juncture of the war. "At home with his staff, he is some days very sociable and agreeable," Goree related in a December 1861 letter home, adding, "then again, for a few days he will confine himself mostly to his room, or tent, without having much to say to anyone, and is grim as you please.... We all know now how to take him and do not now talk much to him without we find out he is in a talkative mood."[7]

On October 7, 1861, Longstreet was rewarded for his exploits at Blackburn's Ford and his effective stewardship over his brigade with a promotion to major general and his own division to lead. The key development in this period of the war was Longstreet's growing connection to General Joseph Johnston, who assumed command of this sector once Beauregard was reassigned in early 1862 to the western theater. Johnston, a decorated and experienced Mexican War veteran and career soldier, was already at odds with Confederate president Jefferson Davis, resenting how Davis had placed Robert E. Lee and other generals ahead of him in the command chain. Longstreet made no secret of his admiration for Johnston and began to gain a reputation as a member of the general's clique, in the escalating feud between Johnston and Davis. In the early spring of 1862 Longstreet joined with Johnston's forces in relocating from Northern Virginia to the eastern Peninsula, bounded by the James and York Rivers, to form a defensive barrier protecting the Confederate capital of Richmond from the Union's new offensive. But first Longstreet would be jolted by a string of staggering personal tragedies.[8]

III

Writing under the pen name "Via" from winter quarters at Centreville in December 1861 to the *Richmond Daily Dispatch*, an infantryman in the 1st Virginia Regiment wistfully captured the perennial dilemma of soldiers, caught between duties to home and to country. "It is hard to forget home," he lamented. "In most instances, when a man gives himself to his country, he not only withdraws the cheering influence of his presence from those who have a natural claim upon him, but he also abandons the means by which they have obtained shelter and support. Can any man do this without a painful struggle? Are these not sacrifices worthy of hesitation?"[9]

Such questions took on an agonizing immediacy for Longstreet when, in the space of just six days in January 1862, he and Louise suffered the losses of three of their four children to a scarlet fever epidemic that was ravaging Richmond. The bacterial illness preyed especially on the young.

Longstreet had visited his family, which was boarding with friends in Richmond while he was in Centreville, early in the month. He then returned to his post, only to be beckoned back to his wife's side by the news that the children had fallen dangerously ill. One-year-old Mary died on January 25, 1862, followed by four-year-old James the very next day, and eleven-year-old Augustus on February 1. Only thirteen-year-old John Garland (known in the family as Garland) survived. The Longstreets had already lost two infants, a boy and a girl, before the war. This series of blows was nearly unbearable. "Just think of it—three children within one week," Tom Goree wrote home to his own family on February 9. "The General is very low spirited."[10]

As his biographer Jeffry Wert notes, Longstreet did not pause for a long period of mourning but instead returned to Centreville on February 5. "Perhaps he could find solace only in work and with old comrades," Wert speculates. Certainly Richmond remained in the grip of panic over the epidemic. "Ladies with young families are fleeing from town to escape the scarlet fever," the Richmond correspondent for the *Charleston Mercury* reported in early February, taking note of Longstreet's losses. The grief-stricken general returned to his command "a changed man," Moxley Sorrel recalled. "He had become very serious and reserved and a consistent member of the Episcopal Church."[11]

Longstreet threw himself into the task of securing the reenlistment of men whose initial twelve-month enlistment terms would expire that spring. Inuring his men against the "allurements of home" that might "entice the citizen solider from the field," Longstreet, in an address he promulgated to his army on February 8, painted a dystopian picture of what would befall the South if his veteran soldiers failed to reenlist. The "unchecked Yankee horde" would "overrun and destroy Virginia, the Carolinas, and the entire South," and "leave for our mothers, wives, and children a country polluted, desolated, and enslaved," he thundered. In time, Longstreet would channel some of his sadness over his family's tragedy into anger at the war itself and at the Confederate leadership. But for now, his personal grief fired his indignation at the Yankee foe.[12]

IV

In March 1862 that foe launched a massive offensive targeting Richmond. The man in charge of the Federal forces, Major General George Brinton McClellan, would face off in the ensuing Peninsula campaign against the general tasked with defending the rebel capital, Joseph Johnston. After McClellan's troops were transported down the Chesapeake Bay to the York River Peninsula, Confederates kept the Federals stalled in siege operations at Yorktown before executing a well-planned retreat that caught the cautious McClellan off guard. Longstreet, in charge of the rear guard of Johnston's army, played a key role in the withdrawal, clashing with the Federals' advance units in the inconclusive Battle of Williamsburg, Virginia, Longstreet's first as a division commander. McClellan declared the fight a great Union victory, but Longstreet's division had been effective in protecting Johnston's retreat; in his official report on the action, Johnston praised Longstreet's "clear head and brave heart." McClellan had squandered almost a month at Yorktown—during which time the arrival of Confederate reinforcements shrank the Union manpower advantage from nearly 6 to 1 to 2 to 1.[13]

Meanwhile, the Confederate leadership debated its own tactical options. Jefferson Davis grew impatient with General Johnston, who failed to offer stern enough resistance to the Yankees as they made their way up the Peninsula toward Richmond. By May 31, the Federals were on the city's outskirts. Johnston, hoping to take advantage of the fact that McClellan's army was divided—with some of it positioned north of the Chickahominy River and some to the south—ordered Longstreet, commanding the Confederate right wing, to lunge at McClellan's left. The two armies clashed on May 31 near a plantation called Seven Pines. A poorly executed Confederate attack on that day was followed on June 1 by a successful Federal counterattack. Johnston himself numbered among the 6,000 Confederate casualties—he was grievously wounded while conducting reconnaissance on May 31, and would be, to Longstreet's chagrin, out of action for six months.[14]

Longstreet, historians agree, mismanaged his own assignments. He literally lost his way to the front on the first day, wasted precious time squabbling with Major General Benjamin Huger over how to proceed, and then needlessly divided his own force, attenuating its attacking power. He "also acted indecisively during the second day of fighting by giving imprecise orders to his subordinates," as Alexander Mendoza explains. Adding insult to injury, Longstreet then tried to pin the blame for these poor results on Huger. He lamented to Johnston, who was convalescing in Richmond, that the "slow movement of Gen. Huger's command . . . threw perhaps the hardest part of the battle on my own poor Division"; although Longstreet's men had performed bravely, Huger's failure to hit the enemy's left flank had squandered their efforts. In modern-day assessments, Jeffry Wert has called this grousing "unjustifiable, even reprehensible," while Mendoza observes that such scapegoating was pervasive in both armies. Both points are sound, but it should be noted that commanders who took fellow officers to task were often motivated by a desire to protect not only their own personal reputations but also that of their collective rank and file. Even as he scapegoated Huger, Longstreet reported of his army's performance that a "better body of men never marched upon a battlefield." His division was "greatly cut up," Longstreet wrote to Johnston, "but as true and ready as ever." In a sign of their strengthening bond, Johnston took Longstreet's side in this feud, describing Longstreet's conduct in the battle as "worthy of the highest praise."[15]

Jefferson Davis named his trusted military adviser Robert E. Lee as Johnston's replacement on June 1; Lee christened his new command the Army of Northern Virginia. Davis granted him broader authority than

Johnston had held, placing under Lee's purview armies in the Shenandoah Valley and North Carolina. Lee sought to retake the initiative by maneuvering McClellan out into the open and turning the Federal right flank to threaten McClellan's supply and communications line; Lee counted on the support of Major General Thomas Jonathan "Stonewall" Jackson, who was summoned east after winning a series of battles in the Shenandoah Valley.

During this tense prelude to the epic Seven Days battles, Longstreet found himself in the spotlight among Confederates not for what he did but for what he said. On June 17, 1862, Longstreet appealed to his troops with a stem-winding speech, portraying Yankees as merciless despoilers who "attempted to make the negro your equal by declaring his freedom." Intent on the "dishonor and violation" of Southern homes and firesides, the Yankees "care not for the blood of babes, nor carnage of innocent women," and would knowingly foment insurrection by the enslaved, Longstreet fumed. The speech not only echoed the rhetoric of fire-eaters such as Augustus Baldwin Longstreet, but also had a personal edge, reflecting Longstreet's desolation at his family's recent trials. His references to the "blood of babes" and to the desecration of once "happy homes" tapped his grief at the death of his children—while he could not blame the Yankees for the scarlet fever per se, he did blame them for bringing the scourge of war into Southern communities.[16]

Moreover, the speech reflected Confederate alarm at the rising tide of slave flight and resistance. With his reference to Black freedom, Longstreet condemned Federal commanders such as Generals Benjamin F. Butler and John Frémont, who were laying the groundwork for the Union's emancipation policy. In the spring of 1861 Butler inaugurated the practice of "confiscating" fugitive slaves who ran to Union lines as "contraband of war" so that they could be put to work aiding the Northern war effort as laborers, on the grounds of military necessity; Butler hoped thereby to undercut the Confederate army, which extracted the coerced manual labor of the enslaved to clear roads, build fortifications, and work as teamsters and camp servants for their rebel masters. Butler's improvised policy was formalized in the US

Congress's Confiscation Act of 1861. Frémont went Butler one better, with an August 1861 proclamation of emancipation in the slaveholding loyal border state of Missouri. Although the US Congress tried initially to limit the scope of confiscation to slaves who were military assets, and although Abraham Lincoln voided Frémont's proclamation, the tide of resistance kept rising wherever the Union army made inroads in the South. In the spring and summer of 1862, slaves flocked to Union lines during the Yorktown siege, the move up the Peninsula, and the fighting around Richmond, offering their services to the Union war effort.[17]

Longstreet's speech conjured images of slave resistance and race war because he knew this kind of rhetoric would resonate with his troops. Thirty-six percent of the men in the Army of Northern Virginia owned slaves or lived with slaveholding families—a greater percentage than the 25 percent of families that owned slaves in the general Southern population. The broad swath of Confederates, nonslaveholders included, were deeply invested in the institution of slavery as a system of social control, racial hierarchy, and economic profit. The experience of war, the historian Aaron Sheehan-Dean has noted, made Confederate soldiers "more committed to preserving slavery" and more inclined to see the enslaved as "active and conspiring enemies."[18]

Along with venting his grief and anger, Longstreet sought in this speech to steel his troops for combat. Eager to reassure the "fresh and inexperienced troops" in his command, Longstreet told them that although the "fiery noise of battle" was "terrifying," it was "not so destructive as it seems." "Few soldiers, after all, are slain," Longstreet declared, in a message that strained credulity, as Richmond's hospitals and private residences overflowed with casualties from Seven Pines. Longstreet meant in this speech to sustain a fundamental premise of nineteenth-century definitions of masculinity and of soldiering: that courage was the essence of manhood, and that it would ultimately win out on the battlefield and guarantee success and survival. "Preserve a quiet demeanor and self-possessed temper," he continued. "Keep cool, obey orders, and aim low." If men could do as he commanded, he promised "the bright sunlight of peace" would soon "be a sufficient reward for the sacrifices we are now called upon to make."[19]

Longstreet's "flaming address," as the press called it, circulated widely in the South. It was initially published on June 23 by the *Richmond Daily Dispatch,* which editorialized that it "had the ring of true metal, and will be read with interest by soldiers and civilians." It was then picked up by papers in Charleston, Macon, and elsewhere, solidifying Longstreet's reputation as a fearsome warrior. Northern papers, too, took note of the address, but saw it in a different light. A correspondent to the *New York Times* observed that Longstreet "shows the desperation of his cause by the falsehoods by which he seeks to sustain it."[20]

V

In the next phase of the Union's grand offensive, it was Lee's turn to try to dislodge McClellan from Richmond's front. The two armies battered each other in a series of clashes that came to be known as the Seven Days battles (June 25 to July 1), with Confederate blows compelling McClellan to scrap his plan of besieging Richmond and to instead essay a strategic withdrawal, southeast across the Chickahominy, to Harrison's Landing on the James River. There he could establish a new base of operations and restore his access to Federal gunboats. Confederates launched a determined pursuit, and the June 27 Battle of Gaines' Mill gave Longstreet the chance to weigh in. When Union brigadier general Fitz John Porter established a defensive line near the military bridges crossing the Chickahominy, Lee hit him. After some uncoordinated assaults during the day, in which Porter held off the attackers, Lee launched the largest Confederate tactical offensive of the war: a concentrated onslaught of more than 32,000 men at Porter's line at dusk, with Longstreet's men driving Porter on the Union left, from the west. As night fell, this final wave broke the Northerners' position and forced Porter to fall back toward the Chickahominy. According to Longstreet's memoir, Lee had relied on him to turn the tide of the battle. "All other efforts had failed, and unless I could do something, the day was lost," Longstreet recalled. The largest of the Seven Days battles, Gaines' Mill was another costly victory for which the Confederates paid dearly, as their roughly 8,700 casualties exceeded the Union's 6,800.[21]

For the next four days, Lee's harassing columns ensured that McClellan's retreat toward the James would be a fighting one. Confederates struck the Union rear guard at Savage's Station on June 29 and Glendale/White Oak Swamp on the 30th. Longstreet anchored the Glendale assault on the center of the Union line, and his troops pressed the Federals back in brutal hand-to-hand combat. But those efforts were in vain, as Huger and General John B. Magruder did not provide the necessary support and reinforcements in flank attacks on the Union left and right, and Jackson failed to strike a blow from the north. Lee's attacks unnerved McClellan but fell short of ensnaring the Union army and cutting off its retreat, in part because Lee's army was plagued by what Longstreet called "a succession of mishaps," especially on Jackson's part.[22]

The last of the Seven Days battles, at Malvern Hill on July 1, found the Confederates assaulting an imposing Federal defensive line in a last determined attempt to disable McClellan's army before it reached the James. Despite waves of attacks, the Union forces remained intact and slipped away from the Confederate grasp, remaining on the Peninsula until Lincoln summoned McClellan back to the North in mid-August. Although he had won tactical victories (measured in casualties inflicted) in all but one of the Seven Days battles and extracted his army from a trap, McClellan was deemed the loser in his showdown with Lee. All told, this week of carnage, unprecedented in American history, cost the Confederacy approximately 20,600 casualties to the Union's 15,800.[23]

It was quite clear to Confederates at the time that although they had saved Richmond, victory was "not as decisive as could be wished," as Longstreet's trusted aide Tom Goree put it in a letter home on July 21, 1862. Lee's plan for the campaign, Goree maintained, had been well conceived, but his subordinates' execution of it imperfect; indeed, afterward, Lee transferred some senior major generals in the Army of Northern Virginia who had performed poorly. Goree nonetheless saw the Seven Days as a breakthrough for Longstreet. "He was the staff in my right hand," Lee said of Longstreet after the battle. Lee had sought Longstreet's advice in conceptualizing the offensive and was impressed by his battlefield conduct at Gaines' Mill and Glendale. As Goree declared with pride, "Genl. Longstreet has undoubtedly acquired as much or more reputation than any other officer in this army. He is now next in command in Virginia to Genl. Lee." Lee rewarded Longstreet's relatively strong performance in the Seven Days by dividing his army into Longstreet's Command and Jackson's Command, with Longstreet designated Lee's senior subordinate, ahead of Jackson—a position he would hold for the duration of the war.[24]

In the aftermath of the Seven Days, a dustup over Longstreet's effectiveness at the Battle of Glendale (Frayser's Farm) revealed his willingness to do public battle with his detractors. The controversy was sparked by an article in the *Richmond Examiner* that gave General Ambrose Powell Hill undue credit for heroism at the battle while denigrating Longstreet's role and the contributions of his brigades. Longstreet penned an indignant reply and asked Major Sorrel to place it in a rival Richmond newspaper, under Sorrel's name. The letter sought to set the record straight, taking the *Examiner* to task for inflating Hill's role and the losses sustained by Hill's division. "Exaggerated statements of casualties," Longstreet objected, "are calculated to be of great injury to the army, both at home and abroad." Hill in turn felt disrespected by Longstreet's account and decided that he would no longer comply with Longstreet's orders. In response, Longstreet ordered Sorrel to arrest Hill and take him into custody, prompting Hill to challenge Longstreet to a duel. Lee finally stepped in to resolve the matter by transferring Hill and his division to Stonewall Jackson's command. But relations between Longstreet and Hill remained sour, hinting at internecine strife to come.[25]

VI

Longstreet would soon have the chance to prove himself worthy of Lee's trust, as the Army of Northern Virginia resumed offensive operations in mid-July. A new Northern force, under Major General John Pope, entered the lists and threatened to link up with McClellan's army and target Richmond anew. Determined to prevent such a combination, Lee positioned a small force to defend the Confederate capital and then headed northward to drive back Pope. On August 24 Lee launched a daring assault in which he divided his army: he and Longstreet would hold down the Rappahannock front while Jackson undertook a flank march around Pope's right to cut off Federal communications and supply lines.[26]

Lee's plan, the historian John J. Hennessy has explained, held "dire risks": it would "leave the two wings of his army separated by more than fifty miles, with a Yankee army nearly twice the size of either of them in between," and with reinforcements from McClellan's army en route to the scene. But the risk paid off. Jackson seized the Federal supply depot at Manassas and lured Pope, who had to respond to this threat to his flank, into a trap: on August 29 Pope attacked Jackson's strong defensive line, which ran across the original Manassas battlefield, to no avail.[27]

Meanwhile, Longstreet was rushing to the front with reinforcements. The prospect of battle "seemed to give new life and strength to our jaded men," he wrote in his official report. He and Lee arrived at the Manassas battlefield on the morning of the 29th. After a careful reconnaissance of the Yankee positions, Longstreet repeatedly persuaded Lee to delay their offensive and prepare the way for a decisive strike the next day. Three times on the 29th, Lee called for Longstreet to launch assaults, and each time, Longstreet cautioned that they hold off and instead aim to land a counterpunch when the Federals renewed their offensive the following day. Lee's willingness to trust his senior subordinate paid off. Fitz John Porter's attack on August 30 was met with a shattering blow by Longstreet against the Union general's left flank; an artillery barrage scattered the attackers, and the infantry then swept down upon them "like an avalanche." The Federals once again retreated back to Washington, DC, over the very same ground they had covered in the first Bull Run debacle. Like his experience at Blackburn's Ford, the battle "solidified Longstreet's belief in defensive tactics, specifically, allowing the enemy to attack a fortified position, then counterattacking the weakened foe," Alexander Mendoza has noted.[28]

The men in Longstreet's inner circle would look back on the August 30 fighting as a signature triumph for the general. "Longstreet was seen at his best during the battle," Moxley Sorrel remembered. "His consummate ability in managing troops was well displayed that day, and his large bodies of men were moved with great skill." Modern scholars have echoed this assessment. Longstreet's was "one of the finest counterattacks of the war," Jeffry Wert has observed, adding that it would have taken a more decisive toll on the Federals had Stonewall Jackson's men done more to support Longstreet. In his own reminiscences, Longstreet would cast Lee's willingness to heed his counsel as illustrating "the character of the relations that existed between us."[29]

The Second Battle of Bull Run was both a tactical and strategic triumph for the Confederacy, with Federal casualties numbering roughly 16,000 and the South's, 9,000. Longstreet attributed the Union's failure not only to Pope's tactical mistakes but also his hubris: Pope had unwisely boasted that he was the man to subdue the rebels, and his "great contempt for his enemy" had led the Union general to underestimate Lee's men. Confederate morale surged, and the stage was set for Lee's movement in Maryland. On the Federal side, a disgusted Lincoln turned Pope's men over to McClellan, despite rumors that McClellan had purposely undermined Pope's campaign by withholding his own troops from it.[30]

A parallel drama was unfolding, as slave resistance continued to roil the Confederate army and Southern society, and to shape the Union's emerging emancipation policy. The summer's fighting in Virginia accelerated the pace of slave flight to Union lines. In Washington, DC, Radical Republicans in the US Congress sought to leverage the changes that were under way: as the Peninsula campaign unfolded, they pushed for the broader military use of African Americans. While the Confiscation Act of 1861 had applied only to slaves employed by the Confederate army or navy and had left the legal status of forfeited slaves unclear, the second Confiscation Act, passed in July 1862, authorized the seizure of slaves from all disloyal masters and declared such persons "captives of war" and "forever free." Republican politicians built the case that emancipation was a military necessity, as the Northern press featured countless illustrative stories of how "contrabands" were aiding the Union war effort.[31]

One such story implicated Longstreet himself. On July 25, 1862, a Washington, DC–based correspondent to the newspaper *Boston Traveller* reported that he'd had an extensive conversation in DC with a "fugitive from rebeldom" who had been a servant to Longstreet. The "intelligent contraband," as the correspondent called the fugitive, was a free Black man from Northern Virginia whom the Confederate army had "impressed" (forced) into menial service as a camp servant early in the war; his principal responsibility was making "cocktails" for Longstreet—of which the general, the article claimed, partook liberally. The fugitive had stealthily gathered military intelligence on the troop strength, disposition, and morale of Confederate forces, and seized the opportunity of the "noise and confusion" of the battles around Richmond to escape to Federal lines and then make his way to DC. His report to Union authorities there was valuable in its details, but sobering in its overall tone. The "contraband" reported that the rebels had an "undoubted faith in the righteousness of their cause." They "will fight to the bitter end with a zeal and desperation we little imagine," he prophesized.[32]

VII

Lee sought to capitalize on the advantage he had seized from the overmatched Pope by launching a large-scale raid of the North. The decision to cross the Potomac River into Maryland—and thus to assume the strategic offensive—reflected both long-standing assumptions and new contingencies. The idea that slaveholding Maryland was a natural part of the South and that Marylanders longed for "liberation" from Yankee rule was one such assumption. The hope that decisive Confederate battlefield victories would undermine Lincoln's popularity in the North and perhaps unseat him was a second. Confederate hopes for British recognition of and support for the Confederacy, too, factored into Lee's plans. Moreover, the abundant crops and brimming larders of rural Maryland and Pennsylvania beckoned the poorly fed Confederates. Lee intended to keep up the initiative and to strike while the Federals were still demoralized.[33]

Meanwhile, Lincoln chose after the Second Bull Run setback to reinstate McClellan as commander of the Army of the Potomac. At first, McClellan seemed to justify this vote of confidence, moving his army of 85,000 men out from the Washington defenses and northwest into Maryland in pursuit of Lee. Confederate forces converged on the town of Frederick on September 7, with military bands playing the secessionist anthem "Maryland, My Maryland" to announce the deliverance of this Southern territory from the Yankees. But Marylanders failed to hew to Lee's script and generally scorned the Confederate army. Lee had miscalculated: if he had entered the southeastern plantation districts of Maryland, he might have encountered a far warmer reception than he did in the Unionist northwest.[34]

To Longstreet's exasperation, more miscalculations ensued. On September 9, while in Frederick, Lee issued Special Order No. 191. This plan for a northern raid directed Stonewall Jackson to capture the federal garrison at Harpers Ferry, Virginia, while Lee and Longstreet would proceed west through the South Mountain gaps to the vicinity of Boonsboro, Maryland, where they would await Jackson. Once the armies were reunited, they could forge on into Pennsylvania and dare McClellan to attack them on terrain chosen by Lee. Longstreet objected to this plan, maintaining that the Confederate army was "in no condition to divide in the enemy's country" where the Yankees could "get information, in six or eight hours, of any movement we might make." He preferred that the South concentrate its forces and recruit more men and supplies. But Lee, in what Longstreet would later call a "fatal error," chose not to heed these objections.[35]

Lee was counting on McClellan to be hesitant in his pursuit, as had been his habit. But on September 13, as McClellan's men camped on ground near Frederick that Confederates had just passed through, a Yankee corporal found a copy of Lee's Special Order No. 191 lying in the grass. It was wrapped around three cigars and tucked into an envelope. This intelligence windfall might have permitted McClellan to catch the rebels in their own trap. But Lee moved decisively to neutralize the Federal advantage, ordering Longstreet and Major General D. H. Hill to focus on blocking the passes at South Mountain to buy time and prevent the Federals from relieving Harpers Ferry. Moreover, McClellan diminished some of his advantage by waiting until the morning of September 14 to send his columns forward. Nonetheless, the Federals prevailed in the fight for South Mountain that day, forcing Longstreet and Hill to fall back to the town of Sharpsburg, near the Antietam Creek. At day's end, Confederate prospects seemed so poor that Lee considered calling off the campaign and returning to Virginia. Longstreet, for his part, felt that the "moral effect" of the Confederates' move into Maryland—their bid to legitimate their cause and dispirit the Yankees—had been attenuated by their struggles at South Mountain.[36]

But daybreak on the 15th breathed new life into Lee's proposed raid, as he learned that Jackson had secured the surrender of the garrison at Harpers Ferry and could thus join forces with him and Longstreet. The terrain on the west side of the Antietam Creek—a commanding plateau overlooking the creek valley—seemed to Lee to afford the Confederates a strong defensive position. So, he decided to make a stand, aware that until Jackson could reinforce him, his 19,000 men would confront a Federal force of more than 80,000. McClellan, meanwhile, plagued by his old indecisiveness, tarried in moving his troops through the South Mountain passes, and this delay enabled Jackson to arrive at the Antietam front, meaning Lee was outnumbered only two to one rather than four to one.[37]

VIII

McClellan's battle plan for the fateful day of September 17, 1862, called for serial attacks on the Confederate defensive position. Major General Joseph Hooker's First Corps would strike first, at Jackson's command, on Lee's left, northernmost flank. Then Major General Ambrose Burnside would attack the Confederate's southernmost right flank, forcing Lee to weaken his center to bolster the flanks. When these movements had pinned back the Confederates, the Union center would finish off Lee. For the Federals, the day began well: Hooker's columns pushed Jackson's brigades through the West Woods in furious fighting. But a timely counterattack by Major General John B. Hood's troops stalled the North, compelling McClellan to send more men into the fray. The frenzied armies churned up a thirty-acre cornfield at the edge of the West Woods in some of the war's most horrific combat.[38]

The Army of the Potomac's Second Corps now weighed in, with one division joining the action on the Confederate left, at the Dunker Church, and two more attacking the Confederate center, along a sunken, rutted farm road that would go down in history as the "Bloody Lane." The Confederates' defensive position there was encircled by waves of Union attacks. But rather than sending in his reserve units to follow up on the momentum on the left and center of Lee's line, McClellan held back these reinforcements, thus permitting the battle to shift to the south. Longstreet's men, especially his old West Point friend and future confidant D. H. Hill, thwarted the Union assault; Longstreet, by all accounts, managed his lines expertly.[39]

In its third act, the battle moved to the Confederate right, where Longstreet's command, this time with A. P. Hill in the starring role, would make another dramatic defensive stand and counterattack. Burnside was trying to take the stone bridge crossing the Antietam Creek, but the bluffs on its west bank gave the outnumbered Confederates a strong vantage point for blunting repeated Union frontal assaults. "Brigadier-General [Robert] Toombs held the bridge and defended it most gallantly, driving back repeated attacks, and only yielded it after the forces brought against him became overwhelming," Longstreet recounted. After hours of ferocious fighting, just as Burnside's men seemed to have sealed a victory, Hill's reinforcements arrived from Harpers Ferry and struck back, enabling the Confederates to recover their lost ground. "Before it was entirely dark, the 100,000 men that had been threatening our destruction for twelve hours had melted away into a few stragglers," Longstreet wrote—with some literary flair and hyperbole—in his official report. The battle ended in a tactical draw, with the two armies having each suffered roughly 12,000 casualties and scarcely shifted the positions they had assumed at the battle's outset. Rather than withdrawing his troops across the Potomac and back into Virginia on the night of the 17th, Lee chose to stand his ground and dared McClellan to renew the contest. The Union general chose not to risk a new attack, and the Confederates executed an orderly retreat, on their own terms, after dusk on the 18th.[40]

Capturing both the horror and exhilaration of combat, Confederate staff officer Osmun Latrobe described Antietam in his September 17 diary entry as a "*terrible* battle, slaughter heavy on both sides" and also as "a long, exciting, amazing day." In Latrobe's view, Longstreet had comported himself "like a man god" as the fighting raged; Latrobe recounted a "special deed of bravery" in which Longstreet dismounted his horse and manned an artillery battery against Burnside "with such tremendous effect that the Federal advance was checked." The battle affirmed Longstreet's reputation, in Lee's eyes, as a consummate combat leader. Lee dubbed Longstreet his trusted "old *warhorse*," and the Confederacy formalized Lee's informal designation of two commands into two official corps under Longstreet and Jackson, with each man promoted to lieutenant general.[41]

Antietam further strengthened Longstreet's belief in the tactical defensive; "he preferred the counterstrike to the attack," as Jeffry Wert puts it. Historians have carefully analyzed an October 6 letter Longstreet sent to Joseph Johnston from Winchester, Virginia (where the Army of Northern Virginia was rehabilitating after the battle), for insights into his relationships with both Johnston and Lee. Had Longstreet's allegiance to Johnston—whose defensive mindset he shared—superseded his allegiance to the more aggressive Lee? In the letter, Longstreet flattered Johnston, telling him that he was still the army's favorite. Attuned to rumors that Johnston would soon assume command of Confederate forces in the West, Longstreet also offered to go west in his place, ostensibly to protect Johnston, still recuperating from his Seven Pines wound, from hardships. Wert has argued persuasively that Longstreet held both Johnston and Lee in high regard at this stage and was not signaling any discontent with the latter. But one can also see in this letter Longstreet's taste for and growing skill at ingratiation and back-channel politicking. He insinuates that he would have confided more deeply in Johnston if he could. "T'would do my heart a great deal of good to have one good talk with you," Longstreet related, adding, "Cant always write what we would like to say." Longstreet professed his regard for the fire-eating secessionist and Confederate senator Louis T. Wigfall of Texas, a strong promoter of Johnston's and an outspoken critic of Jefferson Davis's conduct of the war; Longstreet told Johnston he relished the chance to advance the career of Wigfall's son, Francis, who had joined the Confederate army.[42]

Perhaps the most revealing aspect of Longstreet's October 6 letter was its assessment of Confederate morale. In his postwar memoir, with the benefit of hindsight, Longstreet would take the Confederacy, not the Union, to task for hubris at Antietam. The "Army of Northern Virginia should have held in profound respect its formidable adversary"; instead, "the hallucination that McClellan was not capable of serious work seemed to pervade our army," he reflected. But in the moment, in the fall of 1862, Longstreet shared in the defiant confidence and optimism of Lee and his men. "We are now beginning to feel like gamecocks again," Longstreet reassured Johnston, "and some begin [to] wish for the chance to convince the Yankees that Sharpsburg is but a trifle to what they can do." That chance would soon come at Fredericksburg, Virginia.[43]

IX

In early November Lincoln replaced McClellan with Major General Ambrose E. Burnside. As Moxley Sorrel of Longstreet's staff saw it, even though Burnside had "conspicuously failed at Sharpsburg," the president turned to him because at least Burnside "could and would fight, even if he did not know how, and after 'Little Mac,' this was what Mr. Lincoln was trying for." Sorrel's assessment was astute. After turning back Lee at Antietam, McClellan had squandered much of the fall, allowing Lee to position himself favorably between the Federal army and Richmond. Burnside hoped to avoid McClellan's flaws and his fate, and sought to move the Army of the Potomac, 120,000 men strong, with alacrity across the Rappahannock River to seize Fredericksburg and thus clear the way for a new push southward to Richmond. The Federal army reached the outskirts of Fredericksburg by November 17, but the pontoon bridges they needed to cross the river did not arrive until a week later, and this logistical delay gave Lee time to concentrate forces to defend the city, fortifying the high ground at Marye's Heights. Longstreet established extensive field fortifications, taking full advantage of the terrain features: "He ordered the construction of trenches for his infantry, pits for his cannon, and placed abatis in front of the works as well as in the flat fields that lay between the town's edge and his positions," the military historian Harold M. Knudsen explains. (Abatis were field fortifications of felled trees.) Longstreet's meticulous preparation would succeed in minimizing his own casualties.[44]

As Federal artillery massed on Stafford Heights, across the river from the Confederate defenses, and Longstreet's men dug in, perfecting their earthworks, most of Fredericksburg's civilians evacuated their homes and took to the road as refugees in anticipation of a shattering clash. The Union army's odds of success worsened each day, as Lee bolstered his forces; nevertheless, Burnside was determined to act boldly and sent a division across pontoon bridges and right through Fredericksburg in order to drive Longstreet's men off the high ground. On December 11, 150 Federal artillery guns on Stafford Heights blazed away at Fredericksburg for two hours, reducing many blocks to rubble. Civilians sought safety in basements and cellars or fled in a panic as advance Union assault parties began entering Fredericksburg and ransacking the city.[45]

On December 12, in the bitter cold, as many as 80,000 soldiers in blue crossed into Fredericksburg over the pontoon bridges. Confederates in their defensive lines behind the city "watched the pageantry before them," as Jeffry Wert has put it. Longstreet's divisions anchored three hills: Taylor's, Marye's, and Telegraph. "Burnside's men wanted it," Sorrel wrote of the central Confederate strongpoint of Marye's Hill, and "there he threw his men in blind and impotent fury." Burnside hoped that an initial attack on the Confederate right flank, toward Hamilton's Crossing, might force Lee to transfer troops from his own left and open the way for Union troops to capture Marye's Heights. But Burnside's orders lacked clarity and were poorly communicated, and thus the attack on the rebel right flank proceeded piecemeal, with a single division rather than in force. The Confederates launched a successful counterattack, plugging the gap in their lines.[46]

This failure on the right should have prompted Burnside to call off the attack on the enemy left, but he chose instead to send two divisions to assail Longstreet's impregnable position at Marye's Heights. The Union mounted fifteen hopeless assaults across daunting terrain: its troops had to move through a valley, across a canal ditch, and then across upward-sloping open ground toward the Confederate line, where men and artillery were entrenched in a sunken road behind a half-mile-long stone wall. Burnside could send in only one or two brigades at a time, as the canal ditch served as a funnel. Longstreet conveyed the futility of the Federal attack in his after-action report:

Our artillery, being in position, opened fire as soon as the masses became dense enough to warrant it. This fire was very destructive and demoralizing in its effects, and frequently made gaps in the enemy's ranks that could be seen at the distance of a mile. The enemy continued his advance and made his attack at the Marye Hill in handsome style. He did not meet the fire of our infantry with any heart, however, and was therefore readily repulsed. Another effort was speedily made, but with little more success. The attack was again renewed, and again repulsed.

As the Federals ran the rebel gauntlet, the area in front of the stone wall soon became a slaughter pen. The Northern army sustained nearly 13,000 casualties—more than twice as many as the Confederates—with most of them on Marye's Heights.[47]

The news of the Fredericksburg defeat shook Union confidence and stoked criticism of the Army of the Potomac's leaders. Confederate morale rose not only because of the lopsided military victory but also the ideological vindication Southerners derived from the Yankee bombardment of Fredericksburg—it was interpreted as further proof of Yankee perfidy, and the carnage of Marye's Heights as fitting retribution. Osmun Latrobe wrote in his diary on December 12 that the shelling of the city was "a monument to the barbarity of the abolitionists." "I rode over the battlefield and enjoyed the sight of hundreds of dead Yankees," he added. "Saw much of the work I had done in the way of several limbs, decapitated bodies, and mutilated remains of all kinds. Doing my soul good. Would that the whole Northern army were as such."

Longstreet, in his congratulatory order to his troops, invoked the suffering of civilians whose homes had been "sacked by the foe" and the "humiliating retreat to which the invader has been forced." "Every such disaster to his arms brings us nearer to the happy and peaceful enjoyments of our homes and our families," he noted. An exhilarated Robert E. Lee, watching his men repulse the Yankee attack on December 13, uttered, "It is well this is so terrible! We should grow too fond of it!"[48]

But even as they crowed over their military momentum, Confederates were losing the battle to preserve slavery and were about to receive Lincoln's coup de grâce. Throughout most of 1862, the mass exodus of the enslaved from farms and plantations to Union lines had accelerated. Meanwhile, the president of the United States caught up to the US Congress at last, embracing its confiscation policy and finally announcing his preliminary Emancipation Proclamation on September 22, 1862. The executive order freeing all slaves in the rebel South was to go into effect on the first day of the new year. All of these developments reverberated loudly and ominously in Longstreet's army. Enslaved laborers continued to flee and to provide intelligence and labor for the Union army. In November 1862, for example, the *Philadelphia Inquirer* reported that two "contrabands"—one of whom was a "private servant of Ge. Longstreet"—had escaped north and shed light on the recent disposition of Longstreet's force as it retreated from Maryland into Virginia.

This scene played out again and again over the course of the war, with Black refugees divulging the movements and condition of Longstreet's army. For example, an enslaved couple, the Walkers, who escaped across the Rappahannock to Union lines during the Fredericksburg campaign, set up an unusual intelligence-gathering operation. Dabney Walker worked as a scout and cook at General Joe Hooker's encampment, while Walker's intrepid wife, Lucy Ann, volunteered to go back across the river and seek work as a laundress in the Confederate camp so that she could gather intelligence and convey it using a color-coded system of hanging clothes from a clothesline: Longstreet was represented by a gray shirt; A. P. Hill, by a white one; and Stonewall Jackson by a red one. In addition, a shirt's position on the line indicated where each general was deployed.[49]

Longstreet fully understood the import of Lincoln's new policies. The preliminary Emancipation Proclamation "was one of the decisive political events of the war," he would observe in his memoir, "and at once put the great struggle outwardly and openly on the basis where it had before only rested by tacit and covert understanding." The Union war was now expressly a war against slavery, not only against slaveholders. Confederates sought to roll back this tide of escapes by enslaving or re-enslaving African Americans in areas of the South in which the Confederates drove back the Yankees. For example, after the Federals surrendered Harpers Ferry in mid-September 1862, Stonewall Jackson's army seized hundreds of Blacks in the town and its outskirts, sending them into slavery; the Confederate press cast this as the reclaiming of property that "the Yankees had stolen." Lincoln's January 1, 1863, final Emancipation Proclamation inaugurated the Union's mass enlistment of Black men in the Federal army; Confederate soldiers viewed this policy with derision and were determined to roll it back, too. "We are all anxious to meet their regiments of negroes," wrote Alexander McNeill, a South Carolina infantryman in Longstreet's corps in February 1863. "We hope to be able to capture many of them and send them South to instruct them in the more useful occupation of growing cotton."

Longstreet shared this mentality and would counter the Union's policy of liberation with a Confederate policy of re-enslavement, aimed not only at the occupied South, but eventually, during the Gettysburg campaign, at the North. Longstreet was present in the Confederate Congress in late February 1863, as a guest of House speaker J. L. M. Curry, when that body passed a preliminary version of what would become the May 1, 1863, Retaliatory Act. The final act ruled that Black Union soldiers, when captured in the South, would be considered rebellious slaves and "delivered to the authorities" of the states to face punishment for "servile insurrection."[50]

X

As the Emancipation Proclamation went into effect, Longstreet accepted a new assignment from Lee: independent command of some 43,000 troops in the Department of Virginia and North Carolina, spanning southeast Virginia and northeast North Carolina. His overlapping missions were to safeguard Richmond on its southern and eastern perimeters and to scour the countryside for food and forage and other supplies that Lee's army desperately lacked. And if conditions favored offensive moves, he was to wrest coastal towns such as Suffolk in Virginia and New Bern in North Carolina out of the hands of Yankee occupiers. In a tenure that culminated with a siege of Suffolk from April 11, 1863, to May 3, 1863, Longstreet would succeed in the first two goals but fall short in the third. Although militarily less consequential than his previous campaigning, the Suffolk campaign provides a revealing window into Longstreet's psyche, morale, and command calculations through his extensive correspondence with Lee and with the commanders of his own subdepartments.[51]

The keynote in Longstreet's communications in the spring of 1863 is apprehensiveness. He was under some pressure from James Seddon, the Confederacy's secretary of war, and from Lee to initiate a move against Suffolk. But he worried that, given the occupied city's strong defenses, such a move could not succeed without an infusion of more cavalry units and without help from the Confederate navy to keep Yankee gunboats out of the Nansemond River. Longstreet was also anxious about confiding his plans to Seddon or Lee or to his own subdepartment commanders, lest they were leaked unwittingly or gleaned by Yankee spies. "I do not consider it prudent under any circumstances to explain fully my plans," Longstreet wrote to his subordinate commander Arnold Elzey in Richmond on March 12, 1863, from department headquarters in Petersburg, Virginia, "for the reason that if no one knows them but myself, the enemy will surely not hear of them. If they are made known to any one but myself, that person might in his sleep speak of them, and they might reach the enemy." Surely the fact that Longstreet had already seen "personal servants" run away and convey intelligence to the Yankees contributed to his unease.[52]

Longstreet fretted, too, about his obligations to Lee—namely, to keep some units in reserve, ready to be sent quickly to Lee in Fredericksburg should the Federals resume the offensive there. Longstreet felt he needed to keep and deploy his available force to fulfill his mission of protecting Richmond and of gathering supplies for Lee's army. "I know that it is the habit with individuals in all armies to represent their own positions as the most important ones, and it may be that this feeling is operating with me; but I am not prompted by any desire to do, or to attempt to do, great things," he confided to Lee on March 19. "I only wish to do what I regard as my duty." It was "a matter of prime necessity," as Longstreet saw it, to "keep the enemy out of North Carolina in order that we may draw out all the supplies there." Rather than concentrating to crush the Federals on the Rappahannock, Longstreet hoped the Confederates could win some minor victories by defeating Union detachments. This was the best way, he reckoned, "to avail ourselves of the opportunity to produce a favorable political impression at the North."[53]

But what sort of minor victories were possible? The question surrounding Suffolk was whether Longstreet could find a way to draw the Federals out of their defenses there, perhaps by threatening their communication lines, or whether, instead, the Federals would remain entrenched within their formidable fortifications, leaving the Confederates little choice but to pin them there and focus on foraging in the surrounding countryside. Lee held out some hope that Longstreet might succeed in the former task, but Longstreet opted for the latter: besieging Suffolk rather than attempting what would surely be a costly assault. As a result, "skirmishing and artillery exchanges marked the fighting at Suffolk," Jeffry Wert has explained, while the "campaign's primary objective—the collection of foodstuffs and supplies—rolled on unimpeded."[54]

As revealed by a published letter from an artillerist (identified as "C.J.M.") in Longstreet's siege force, the Black population—enslaved, free, and refugee—was caught up in the fighting around Suffolk. Although "the negroes have nearly all ran away to the Yankees," C.J.M. lamented, the campaign was enabling the Confederates to strike back: "Several negroes have fallen into our hands and have been sent with the captured Yankees to

Richmond, where they will either be returned to their owners or sold into bondage." The Suffolk siege dramatizes the profound stakes of Civil War battles—even the lesser-known ones—for Southern Blacks in the path of the two armies. Union-occupied Suffolk was the site of a sizable contraband camp, Uniontown, to which Black refugees in the region had fled; the Federal army drew on their labor power to help build its fortifications.[55]

Longstreet, meanwhile, relied on the coerced labor of a "negro work force," as he called it, raised through impressment—seizing public property for use by the army—to clear roads, construct bridges, and build works. At Suffolk, and, indeed, throughout the war, Longstreet was anxious about securing enough Black laborers. When Confederate forces crossed the Blackwater River to advance on Suffolk, he thus left the bulk of his Black labor force on the other side of the river, to prevent its escape. Those who did manage to flee told the Union commander there, General John J. Peck, that they "prayed very long that 'Massa Longstreet might be whipped by you folks.'" If the siege succeeded and Suffolk reverted to rebel control, Peck would note later, conjuring the campaign's significance, many thousand "contrabands" would have been re-enslaved by the Confederates.[56]

Longstreet's army acted aggressively both to preempt and to punish Black military assistance to the Union. A Suffolk correspondent for the *New York Herald* would report in May, after the siege was lifted, that local Blacks rejoiced that the enemy was gone, but also spoke of rebel depredations. A free Black man living four miles from Suffolk informed the correspondent that the "rebels had taken his three sons (free), fearing that they would give information to our forces." No mercy was shown by Longstreet's army to any Blacks suspected of or caught providing espionage to the Union. At the end of April, near Suffolk, he ordered the hanging of a "free negro, acting in the capacity of a spy for the enemy." The executed man, Eli Johnson, had been caught by a Confederate expeditionary force that Longstreet had ordered to roust out "negro runners": civilians who smuggled slaves through Confederate lines to the North. Johnson, deemed the "leader of the Runners," was made a conspicuous example of: he was hung "within 200 yards of Longstreet's headquarters . . . in the presence of at least 1,000 soldiers," as eyewitnesses testified later.[57]

Those Blacks who furnished intelligence reports to the Yankee army risked reprisals from Southern whites for years to come. John Bentford, whose spying led to the capture of rebel letters revealing Longstreet's plans at Suffolk, was found out by Confederates and fled to Union lines, enlisting in the 36th Regiment of the USCT; he testified in 1867 to receiving death threats, when he returned home to Suffolk after the war, for having provided information contributing to Longstreet's defeat back in 1863.[58]

Longstreet's Suffolk operations came to a close when Lee summoned him back to the Army of Northern Virginia at the end of April, as the Union general Joseph Hooker, the new chief of the Army of the Potomac, began to menace Lee on the Fredericksburg front. While Longstreet moved to consolidate his disparate troops and wagon trains for transport northwest toward Richmond, Lee fought and won the Battle of Chancellorsville. On May 1 and 2, 1863, in what is widely considered his tactical masterpiece, Lee audaciously divided his outnumbered army twice: first, leaving a single division to pin down the Federals at Fredericksburg, while Stonewall Jackson launched a surprise attack on the Union corps advancing through the Wilderness, and then, in a second risky gambit, sending Jackson on a long march around Hooker's exposed flank, while Lee and a force of only 15,000 occupied the Federals at the current Confederate position. On May 5 and 6, after days of fierce combat in the woods, Hooker's broken army withdrew back across the Rappahannock toward Washington.

Lee's victory took a sobering toll, though, as his approximately 13,000 casualties amounted to nearly a quarter of his men. Most unnerving for the Confederates was the death of Stonewall Jackson, who was struck in the left arm and right hand by friendly fire on the evening of May 2. Eight days later, the thirty-nine-year-old general succumbed to postoperative pneumonia after his left arm had to be amputated. The Confederate public took solace in the fact that heroes remained to fill the breach. Of Jackson's death, the *Richmond Dispatch* commented, "True it is that amongst the galaxy of Confederate stars one has disappeared, but others are left equal in magnitude and brilliancy," listing Longstreet first among those left to lead the way.[59]

Two of Longstreet's divisions participated in the Chancellorsville triumph, yielding him some reflected glory. Although Longstreet's personal absence from the battle made him vulnerable to postwar criticism that he had failed Lee at this crucial juncture, Lee himself did not cast blame; he wrote Longstreet on May 7 that his letter summoning Longstreet had expressed "the wish rather than the expectation" that his "war-horse" could return from Suffolk soon enough to join the fray. Indeed, despite the shortcomings of the Suffolk campaign, Longstreet's standing among Confederates was very high in the early summer of 1863, on the eve of the Gettysburg campaign. While a few commentators in the press chided Longstreet for failing to take Suffolk, the broad consensus was that his foraging operation there had been successful on a grand scale, drawing off loads of corn and bacon and other subsistence from the countryside to fill Confederate commissaries. Throughout that campaign, the press continued to portray Longstreet as "the synonym of victory" and the "best [corps] commander in the army." With leaders such as Longstreet and Lee, was it any wonder, a Confederate army correspondent wrote home in the spring of 1863, "that the army of Northern Virginia should have proved thus far invincible?" That very attitude would prove a fatal flaw as the Confederates moved north into Pennsylvania.[60]

Chapter 3

CROSSROADS AT GETTYSBURG

I

"Would General Lee have trusted General Longstreet after the battle of Gettysburg had he been in the least disloyal to his commands?" So asked Confederate veteran J. W. Matthews, in a tribute offered in 1904, when Longstreet passed away. Matthews added, wryly: "One more word about Gettysburg. I happened to be there (but at the time would have liked to have been elsewhere), and I decided then and am still of the opinion that the Yankees are to blame for our defeat."[1]

This clear-eyed perspective on Longstreet's performance at Gettysburg stood no chance of prevailing, given the epic scope and high stakes of the battle, and the egos involved. The Gettysburg campaign further exposed fault lines and flaws within the Confederate leadership and exacerbated its tendencies to infighting. But, crucially, in 1863 this recrimination had a different purpose than the postwar blame game in which Gettysburg would loom in hindsight as the "turning point" on the road to Appomattox, and Longstreet as the scapegoat. In the summer of 1863, Confederates, Longstreet included, sought to derive from their second invasion of the North the key lessons that could lead to their ultimate victory.

II

In early June, in the wake of its Chancellorsville triumph, the Army of Northern Virginia sought to take the fight to enemy territory. After the death of Stonewall Jackson, Lee reorganized his army: Longstreet retained command of the First Corps, General Richard S. Ewell inherited the Second from Jackson, and A. P. Hill was assigned the new Third Corps. Leaving Hill's corps to pin down Hooker at Fredericksburg, Lee moved the bulk of his force, under Longstreet and Ewell, northwest from the Wilderness to Culpeper. J. E. B. Stuart's cavalry was to screen the infantry's movement as it pressed on into the Shenandoah Valley, where it could veer north shielded by the Blue Ridge Mountains. With Ewell's corps in the lead position, the Confederates seized the Federal garrison at Winchester and set their sights on Maryland; Longstreet's and Hill's corps followed behind. As he had been during the Antietam campaign in the fall of 1862, Lee was eager to appropriate Northern resources for his undersupplied army, as well as to shake Northern confidence in the Lincoln administration and to relieve war-torn Virginia.[2]

Lee's faith in his troops, and his sense of invincibility, were at a peak. So, too, was his relationship of mutual trust and admiration with Longstreet. Arthur Fremantle, a British officer who had attached himself unofficially to Lee's forces and who chronicled the Gettysburg campaign in his diary, reported that during the Southern army's trip northward from Fredericksburg into Pennsylvania, Longstreet was "never far from General Lee, who relies very much upon his judgement." "The relations between him and Longstreet are very touching," Fremantle added. "It is impossible to please Longstreet more than by praising Lee."[3]

This assessment underscores that Longstreet had, at this critical juncture, yielded to Lee on matters of grand strategy. During the first few months of 1863, Longstreet advocated repeatedly to Lee, as well as to Secretary of War Seddon, Senator Wigfall, and others, for reinforcements to be sent from Lee's forces in the eastern theater to the western forces of Johnston and General Braxton Bragg, to relieve the pressure that U. S. Grant was exerting on the Confederate bastion in Vicksburg, Mississippi. After neutralizing the Federals there, the Confederates could then, Longstreet imagined, mount an offensive into Kentucky and perhaps onward into Ohio. However, a letter from Longstreet to Wigfall on May 13, 1863, reveals that Lee had brought him around to the idea that a northeastern offensive strategy was better calculated to shift momentum in the West than a defensive posture was. "[W]e can spare nothing from this army to re-enforce in the West." "If we could cross the Potomac with one hundred & fifty thousand men, I think we could demand Lincoln to declare his purpose," Longstreet added. "Every available man and means should be brought to bear" against the Yankees, to weaken their morale and their support for a protracted, decimating war. Longstreet, in other words, shared Lee's view that military triumphs could be a catalyst to a major shift in public opinion in the North. The specter of a rebel invasion could bring the Union to the negotiating table, where Northern leaders would learn that Confederate independence was the nonnegotiable price of peace.[4]

Lee reckoned that the aim of influencing Northern public opinion could be achieved only if his invading army refrained from indiscriminately plundering Northern property, in order to demonstrate the purported contrast between Southern "civility" and the hard war tactics carried out by Yankees in Southern territory. Lee thus directed his troops in General Orders No. 72 and 73 not to despoil civilian property during their Northern campaign; instead, they were to pay for "requisitioned" supplies with Confederate money or vouchers.

Such orders were largely disregarded, however. The Confederate army cut a swath of forcible confiscation during Lee's second invasion of the North, seizing people as well as property. Southern soldiers practiced "slave raiding," as the historian David G. Smith has called it: rounding up free and fugitive African Americans to send them to the South's slave markets for sale. In the path of an enslaving army, Blacks in Pennsylvania took flight as refugees, many heading for Harrisburg and Philadelphia. This policy, Smith explains, was officially sanctioned by the Confederate government and high command. It was an extension of the antebellum regime of hunting down and recapturing fugitive slaves who had made it to Northern soil (crossing from slaveholding Maryland into free Pennsylvania), and of the ubiquitous wartime practice of seizing and re-enslaving Blacks who had fled to Union lines but then fell back into Confederate hands in places where the Union army suffered military defeats. The slave raiding of the Gettysburg campaign represented, too, an escalating cycle of retaliation, with Confederates seeking to strike back against the Emancipation Proclamation and the new Federal policy of the mass enlistment of Black troops in the Union army.[5]

Cavalry units, the lead elements of the invasion force, inflicted the early damage at Gettysburg. Brigadier General Albert Gallatin Jenkins led slave raiding in the Pennsylvania towns of Chambersburg and Greencastle, just north of the Maryland border, while Captain John H. McNeill's cavalry raided Mercersburg; and General J. E. B. Stuart struck in Rockville, Maryland. The Northern press featured horrified reports from Pennsylvania civilians who had witnessed the invaders "carrying off negroes."

"The rebels took old people, and even very young children," one account noted. "Some were driven along the road like sheep." According to another journalist, "The stronger and more refractory ones were tied together, making somewhat of an extemporized coffle-gang." When some citizens of Greencastle rescued a group of thirty Blacks who were being "conveyed South under rebel guard," one of the Confederate commanding officers threatened to burn the town to the ground if the rescued captives were not remanded to his custody. Dozens of other Greencastle Blacks were forced south without rescue.[6]

Infantry in all three of Lee's corps were soon engaged in such raiding. "Quite a number of negroes were stolen by the army of General Lee, and evidently with the sanction of the officers," the *Franklin Repository* reported on the mercenary conduct of the legions of infantrymen that followed in the cavalry's wake. "All ages and conditions were taken and carried off to their rear, and as they were taken past rebel encampments, cheer after cheer would go up at the triumph of the negro stealers." Longstreet was centrally implicated in this policy. Indeed, his July 1, 1863, orders (conveyed through Moxley Sorrel) to Major General George E. Pickett, to proceed from Chambersburg to Gettysburg, directed Pickett that "the captured contrabands had better be brought along with you for further disposition." By "further disposition," Longstreet meant sale to slave traders, incarceration in Southern prisons, or seizure by Southern whites claiming ownership. Some such white civilians actually accompanied the Confederate army into Maryland and Pennsylvania, looking to recapture fugitives or to seize laborers to replace escaped ones. David G. Smith estimates that "over a thousand African Americans may have been seized" by Confederates during the Gettysburg campaign.[7]

The Confederate press, for its part, reported on the slave raiding as positive evidence that Lee's campaign was succeeding. Much of that coverage trafficked in the fiction that all Blacks in Maryland and Pennsylvania were slaves who had been enticed or coerced by the Yankees into leaving the South; it did not count as plunder, in Confederate eyes, to reclaim such "stolen property." For example, Peter W. Alexander, one of the most influential Confederate war correspondents (known by the byline "P.W.A."), wrote to a Georgia paper about the Greencastle rescue and subsequent Confederate threat of retaliation. "The kidnappers took the hint; the negroes were produced in the time specified, and were sent on to Virginia whence they had escaped." But some press coverage did acknowledge that Northern free Blacks who had never been slaves were among those rounded up by the rebel soldiers. An article in the *Richmond Enquirer*, for example, noted derisively that dozens of Pennsylvania-born Blacks were captured during the Gettysburg campaign and then jailed in Richmond's Castle Thunder Prison. Among them was a "haughty claret colored dame," who defiantly told her jailers: "My name is Mrs. Ellen Darks, from Pennsylvania; my maiden name was Miss Ellen Stratton." The *Enquirer* mocked her "affectation" and missed the pathos of her story: "I suppose I may term myself a widow now," she said, "as my husband was not captured and remains in Pennsylvania."[8]

III

On June 28 General George G. Meade replaced Hooker as the head of the Army of the Potomac. Meade, a native Pennsylvanian, had impressive qualifications, having led a division at Antietam and Fredericksburg and the Fifth Corps at Chancellorsville. Upon taking command, he displayed welcome decisiveness, ordering his men to advance from Frederick, Maryland, into Pennsylvania. He hoped to lure the Confederates back across the border toward Pipe Creek, Maryland, where he had identified a strong defensive position for the Federals to hold.[9]

That evening, the Confederates received an unexpected boon in the form of an intelligence report from Henry Harrison, an "enterprising scout" whom Longstreet had recruited during the Suffolk campaign and then tasked with "secret orders" to go to Washington and bring back "information of importance." The crafty Harrison, a onetime actor from Tennessee, returned with the news that Meade was advancing. "Harrison gave us the first complete account of the operations of the enemy since Hooker left our front," Moxley Sorrel wrote, "and described how they were even then marching in great numbers in the direction of Gettysburg, with intention apparently of concentrating there." Longstreet "was immediately on fire at such news" and sent Harrison to General Lee's nearby camp to update him.

"It was on this, the report of a single scout," Sorrel notes, "that the army moved." Lee modified his own plans accordingly, gathering together his far-flung elements. Ewell had taken part of his corps north to Carlisle, while sending the other men, under Major General Jubal Early, eastward to York, Pennsylvania; Harrisburg was their ultimate aim. On the afternoon of June 28, Early's division, seeking to cross the Susquehanna River at Wrightsville, was repulsed by local militiamen, including a company of free Blacks, at the Columbia Bridge. Acting on Harrison's intelligence, Lee recalled Ewell and ordered the Confederate forces to concentrate either in Cashtown or Gettysburg to the west; the goal was to reunite Ewell with the rest of Lee's command (Longstreet's and A. P. Hill's corps), which pressed through the South Mountain gap, from Chambersburg toward Cashtown.[10]

Lee had an army of roughly 70,000 at his disposal, to Meade's 93,000. But Harrison's crucial June 28 news notwithstanding, Lee would be, in the coming days, largely ignorant as to the exact disposition of the Federal forces, due to the misguided maneuvers of J. E. B. Stuart: the thirty-year-old general, another West Point graduate, had embarked on a June 25 ride around Hooker's army, baiting and badgering it, and sounding Northern alarms for the safety of Washington, DC. These tactics backfired, as Stuart's absence prevented Lee from receiving regular intelligence reports from his cavalry.[11]

The town of Gettysburg, a hub at which ten roads converged from every direction, drew both armies as a point of concentration. On June 30, as Lee and Longstreet were approaching South Mountain and heading toward Gettysburg from the west, Meade's vanguard, consisting of Buford's two cavalry brigades on reconnaissance, entered the town from the south and arrayed itself on McPherson Ridge, on the northwestern outskirts of Gettysburg. That afternoon a Confederate foraging party, looking to secure some shoes, made contact with the Federals and then withdrew after a brief skirmish. Buford, knowing that the main bulk of Lee's force was heading his way, and anticipating that the high ground just south of Gettysburg could confer a formidable advantage to whichever army held it, called for reinforcements. The next day, July 1, A. P. Hill's lead division under Major General Henry Heth approached Gettysburg from the west and was met by Buford's cavalry, which stubbornly kept the Confederates at bay until reinforcements arrived in the form of Major General John F. Reynolds's First Corps. Reynolds swept in just as Buford's troops were about to give way, but Reynolds was soon shot dead in the saddle. As Union major general Oliver Otis Howard of the Eleventh Corps tried to rally the Federals, Confederate reinforcements from Ewell's and Hill's corps entered the fray from the northeast and northwest, giving the Southern forces a 3-to-2 manpower advantage. The Confederates turned the Union right flank and then assaulted the left, and the Federal line collapsed, with retreating Union soldiers falling back through the town to the high ground on Cemetery Ridge to the south.[12]

Lee, who had arrived at the battlefield at around 2:00 p.m., ordered General Ewell to follow up on his success of that afternoon and to drive the Yankees off the heights, Cemetery Hill and Culp's Hill, south of town, if Ewell found it "practicable." However, Federal Second Corps major general Winfield Scott Hancock had established a new defensive line south of town, and Ewell, deeming it too strong, declined to attack. With the Confederates' momentum squandered, Lee and Longstreet engaged in a fateful conversation about how best to regain it. Longstreet had yielded to Lee's vision of a grand strategic offensive in Pennsylvania, in the hopes that Lee would commit to the tactical defensive in drawing up battle plans. Watching the Federals consolidate their own defenses in the late afternoon of July 1, Longstreet advocated a turning movement rather than a direct assault.

"My idea was to throw ourselves between the enemy and Washington, select a strong position, and force the enemy to attack us," he explained in a letter to his uncle Augustus Longstreet from Culpeper, Virginia, three weeks later. Lee should dislodge the army from the unfavorable low ground it occupied and invite a defensive battle, akin to Fredericksburg. To Longstreet's enduring disappointment, Lee rejected this advice, vowing, "If the enemy is there tomorrow, we must attack him." As Longstreet saw it, Lee's blood was up: "The sharp battle fought by Hill and Ewell on that day had given him a taste of victory." Longstreet was palpably worried, on the night of July 1, about resuming the offensive the next day. He "spoke of the enemy's position as being 'very formidable,'" Arthur Fremantle observed, and "he also said they would doubtless intrench themselves strongly during the night."[13]

Just how unnerved and angry Longstreet was at this moment has been a source of bitter controversies among his contemporaries during the post-war period and among historians ever since. Had Lee, in their mid-May conversations about the coming campaign, promised Longstreet, in a pact of sorts, that the Confederates would seek to fight on the defensive? Or had Lee merely entertained Longstreet's suggestion of defensive tactics, with no agreement, explicit or implicit, reached? While the postwar writings of Longstreet and of his supporters and detractors can, when culled selectively, seem to lend credence to either proposition, the totality of the written record suggests that the truth lay somewhere in between. Surely, modern historians agree, Lee made no blanket promise to avoid the tactical offensive—although, in his after-action report on the Gettysburg campaign, written in January 1864, Lee did attest that he had hoped to avoid "deliver[ing] a general battle . . . unless attacked." But this was far from a settled plan: Lee reserved the crucial right and authority to improvise and adapt his tactics to the fluid dynamics of the campaign, and he would not have entered into a binding agreement—one that tied his hands—with a subordinate. In an 1868 interview with William Allan, a former Confederate officer who became an influential educator and writer, Lee reprised his January 1864 report, indicating that, in Allan's words, he "did not intend to give general battle in Pa. if he could avoid it." Furthermore, Lee categorically denied making any compact with Longstreet not to fight such a battle, telling Allan that he "had never made any such promise, and had never thought of doing any such thing."[14]

At the same time, it is clear that Longstreet felt he and Lee had agreed in principle "that we should work so as to force the enemy to attack us, in such good position as we might find in his own country, so well adapted to that purposes,—which might assure us of a grand triumph." In Longstreet's memoir, he claims that Lee "assented" to this idea "as an important and material adjunct to his general plan." No promise was made, but neither was Longstreet's opinion a mere suggestion that Lee could swat away. Longstreet prided himself on his status as Lee's war-horse, his confidant, his right-hand man. When he proposed to Lee on July 1 that the Confederates "file around [Meade's] left and secure good ground between him and his capital," he did so thinking, based on their many earlier conversations, that this was "the opinion of my commander as much as my own." It was not only Lee's decision to attack that took Longstreet aback, but also his "impatience": Longstreet was stung to be brushed off by a man who so often sought his counsel.[15]

As for the tactical merits of Longstreet's proposal to turn the Union left, while it "made a lot of sense in the abstract," the historian Harry W. Pfanz has explained, it would have been difficult and risky for the Confederates to execute. The Southern forces, which lacked clear information on the disposition of the Union army, would have had to move swiftly and surreptitiously through enemy terrain, "virtually into the unknown." In doing so, they would also be risking their supply lines and leaving themselves vulnerable to counterattacks. And while Longstreet's notion of selecting a strong position between the Union army and Washington, DC, was also promising in theory, it, too, entailed "surrendering the initiative to the enemy, who could restrict or prevent foraging and whose strength would grow as Confederate strength declined," observes Pfanz. With these variables in mind, Lee opted instead to give battle.[16]

Longstreet's ex post facto claim that Lee had agreed to a defensive policy for the campaign, like many other phrases in Longstreet's postwar writings, brought scrutiny and scorn, as his detractors tried to read into his accounts of the Gettysburg campaign a haughty self-righteousness, a long-standing animus against Lee, and even a lack of commitment to the Confederate cause.[17] But the key to understanding Longstreet's outlook on the evening of July 1, 1863, is to avoid the temptations of hindsight. The loss in the ensuing battle, the Confederate defeat in the war, the deterioration of his relationship with Lee, the war of words over who was to blame—all these lay in the future. The crucial context for Longstreet's mindset and conduct at Gettysburg was his prized relationship with Lee; his belief that defensive tactics were the surest, although not the only, way for the South to win battlefield victories; and his profound hope for and commitment to Confederate victory.

IV

The questions about Longstreet's outlook on July 1 have hung like a cloud over his performance on July 2. Did his misgivings about Lee's plan translate into battlefield insubordination on day two of the epic clash? Longstreet's political enemies in the postwar period argued that he deliberately sabotaged Lee's battle plan, delaying his attack and thus dooming it to failure. Modern historians, on balance, have subscribed to a "toned-down" version of this critique, in which Longstreet did his duty but without his usual enthusiasm, efficiency, or fervor. The toned-down critique has some merit, rooted as it is in the testimony of reliable firsthand witnesses who bore no animus against Longstreet—most notably Sorrel, who wrote later that Longstreet "lacked the fire and point of his usual bearing on the battlefield." But even the moderate appraisal fails to account fully for Longstreet's own perspective on these events.[18]

"The stars were shining brightly on the morning of the 2d when I reported at General Lee's head-quarters and asked for orders," Longstreet would write later, setting the scene. "The enemy occupied the commanding heights of the city cemetery, from which point, in irregular grade, the ridge slopes southward two miles and a half to a bold outcropping height of three hundred feet called Little Round Top, and farther south half a mile ends in the greater elevation called [Big] Round Top." In other words, Meade's army was arrayed in what would come to be known as a "fish-hook" formation, occupying a series of tree-lined high ridges, with Cemetery Hill to its right and the Round Top hills to its left. This compact position, as compared with the Confederates' more extended one, gave the

Federals the advantage of "interior lines," or greater ease at moving assets. As Longstreet's First Corps artillery expert Edward Porter Alexander explained, "Our line was like a big fishhook outside the enemy's small one. Communication between our flanks was very long—roundabout & slow, while the enemy were practically all in one convenient-sized bunch." But the Confederates had their own potential advantage: Meade's army was not yet at full strength, as roughly 25 percent of his command was still en route to the front.[19]

Lee had not yet finalized his battle plans that morning, beyond his commitment to attacking the Federal lines. He and Longstreet consulted in the predawn darkness, with Longstreet again registering his discontent at the prospect of an offensive. Longstreet persisted in preferring that the Confederates leave behind this unfavorable terrain, slip south between the Yankees and Washington, DC, and force the Union army to engage on terrain that the Confederates chose. The commanding general shut him down again. After dispatching a detail of officers to conduct reconnaissance of the Federal left, and receiving their report that only a smattering of cavalry, and not masses of infantry, anchored the Union position, Lee settled, sometime before 9:00 a.m., on his tactical plan: "for Longstreet to make the principal attack against the Union left while Hill and Ewell supported him with secondary assaults against the enemy's center and right," as the historian Gary W. Gallagher has succinctly explained. Longstreet's attack itself was to unfold en echelon: at an oblique angle northward up Emmitsburg Road, rolling up the Federal flank.

Having spelled out his plan, Lee then rode off to consult with Richard Ewell at the other end of the Confederate battle line; Lee would spend two hours in that quadrant, assessing the situation on Cemetery and Culp's Hills. He returned to Seminary Ridge at around 11:00 and gave Longstreet the order to attack. Longstreet requested that they await the anticipated arrival of Brigadier General Evander M. Law's brigade, from General Hood's division, and Lee agreed—but Longstreet continued to fret about the fact that the third of his three divisions, Pickett's, was still in the army's rear guard, in Chambersburg. "I never like to go into battle with one boot off," Longstreet told Hood.[20]

After Law and his troops arrived around noon, Longstreet began to move his men into position. But his efforts were star-crossed: faulty information from their scouts set the army on a route that would have been visible to a Union signal station on Little Round Top. Discovering this, Longstreet's lead brigades under Major General Lafayette McLaws sought out an alternate path, countermarching in a circuitous journey to the designated starting point of their flank attack, facing Cemetery Ridge and the Round Tops across a peach orchard. Meanwhile, the Federals experienced their own missteps in the form of battlefield improvisation by Major General Daniel E. Sickles, commander of the Third Corps. Without authorization from Meade, the imprudent Sickles advanced his corps nearly a mile west of the Union line to what he imagined was some stronger high ground, leaving his men terribly vulnerable and isolated from the rest of the Northern army. McLaws, surprised to see the enemy massed before him, tarried, even as Lee and Longstreet formulated a new attack plan in which Hood's division would take the lead. Hood, after his own round of reconnaissance, asked Longstreet for permission to launch a flank attack east of the Round Tops rather than a direct assault on Cemetery Ridge, but Longstreet deemed this impractical and denied each of Hood's imploring, repeated requests for this late change to Lee's plans. Lee was "already fretting over the delay which had occurred" and Longstreet was "unwilling to add to it by offering further suggestions," as E. P. Alexander related the scene.

Rank-and-file soldiers were anxious about the delays, but tried to give their commanders the benefit of the doubt. As a South Carolina infantryman put it, the "great loss of time" it took to position the attack regiments was understandable, as Longstreet "doubtless believe[ed] that it would be better to have the great fighter Hood on his right." When the Confederates finally stormed Cemetery Ridge around 4:00 p.m., led by Hood's division, scenes of carnage ensued at the nest of boulders called the Devil's Den, and the adjacent peach orchard and wheat field, to the north. "My men charged with great spirit and dislodged the Federals from the peach orchard," Longstreet would recall in a vivid postwar account, "and soon reached the marshy ground that lay between Seminary and Cemetery Ridges, fighting their way over every foot of ground and against overwhelming odds.

"In front of them was a high and rugged ridge, on its crest the Army of the Potomac, numbering six to one, and securely resting behind strong positions," Longstreet continued. In the face of "withering fire," Longstreet's "brave fellows" attacked the heights in "splendid style," only to be driven back by the "heavy stroke of fresh troops"—namely, the Federal reinforcements that turned the Round Top hills anchoring the southernmost end of the Federal line, "as if by magic, into Gibraltar." Longstreet's men, by contrast, "received no support at all" in the form of reinforcements, nor was there any "evidence of cooperation" from his fellow corps commanders. Lieutenant General Ewell once again squandered the initiative, waiting until sundown to launch a series of uncoordinated attacks on the hills at the top of the fishhook. Again Federal counterattacks halted the Confederates' initial progress. John Bell Hood was grievously wounded in the arm and forced to leave the field.[21]

How much was Longstreet to blame for these reverses? As he had done before so often, he won praise from his soldiers for displaying personal bravery on the battlefield. For example, Longstreet rode to the front in the first phase of the day's fighting to rally General William T. Wofford's Georgia Brigade in "gallant and inspiring" fashion, as McLaws noted. But Longstreet's tactical decision-making came under some fire, most notably from McLaws, who complained in the immediate aftermath of the battle that Longstreet had adjusted poorly to the dynamic situation and had given "contradictory orders," such as the last-minute directive that Hood initiate the attack. McLaws would go on to describe Longstreet as "conceited" and "selfish." Some of Longstreet's modern critics, led by the historian Robert K. Krick, have echoed Longstreet's contemporaries in scathing arraignments of the general's behavior and attitude. For instance, according to Krick, Longstreet, with his "dismally tardy" movements on July 2, had "put on a display of pettiness of heroic proportions." Most historians take a more moderate line, following Wert's assessment that Longstreet's comportment on the 2nd lacked "the energetic and careful preparation that had been a hallmark of his generalship." Longstreet, he continues, "allowed his disagreement with Lee's decision to affect his conduct," noting his failure to prepare his army—particularly during the two crucial hours that Lee spent with General Ewell on the Confederates' left flank. Surely Longstreet could have used that time for reconnaissance or for coordinating with key subordinates such as artillerist E. P. Alexander.[22]

Alexander himself, arguably the most astute and least self-serving of the major Confederate memoirists, stands out among Longstreet's contemporaries for his efforts to offer a balanced assessment of the Gettysburg campaign. Alexander rued the delays on July 2. He noted that he and his artillerymen had found an expeditious route out of view of the Federal signal station, thus enabling the Confederates to get into position without a long countermarch, but no one heeded his advice. "There is no telling the value of the hours that were lost," he lamented. "If our corps had made its attack even two or three hours sooner than it did, our chances of success would have been immensely increased," for the Yankee reinforcements would not have proven so decisive. But Alexander also stressed that Lee had granted Longstreet's request to wait for Law's brigade and that Lee was "present on the field all the time & was apparently consenting to the situation from hour to hour." Alexander noted that the delay itself need not have had such negative effects, if only Hill and Ewell had used the extra hours to get "thoroughly prepared" to "press the enemy everywhere at once." Alexander credited the First Corps with some of the most heroic fighting of the Civil War, "or any other war," on July 2. "If the whole fighting force of our army could have been concentrated & brought to bear together upon that of the enemy," he maintained, "I cannot doubt that we would have broken it to pieces."[23]

More recently, Longstreet scholar Cory M. Pfarr echoed Alexander, emphasizing that the delays on the morning of the 2nd—such as waiting for Law's brigade or countermarching to avoid being seen by the enemy—were "necessary and approved," authorized by Lee. Longstreet himself, in his after-action report written a little over three weeks after the battle, on July 27, cast the morning's maneuvers as an effort to strengthen the Confederates' hand in what he regarded as a winnable scenario. His army waited for Law and then sought a "more concealed route" to the battlefront in order to maximize its chances of successfully attacking an enemy position that was, at the outset, "but little better" than its own.[24]

In his memoir's account of day two, Longstreet emphasized not his distrust of Lee's battle plan but instead his deference to Lee, especially with regard to Hood's request to turn the Federal flank on Big Round Top. Longstreet reminded Hood repeatedly "that the move to the right had been proposed the day before and rejected; that General Lee's orders were to guide my left by the Emmitsburg Road." In a sense, Hood was proposing a variant on Longstreet's own earlier proposal that the Confederates swing round the Union left—only Hood was now urging that the Confederates attack Big Round Top from the rear rather than draw the Yankees into attacking a Confederate position. This Hood plan, the historian Harry Pfanz has observed, had some of the same drawbacks as Longstreet's version: not only would it have been difficult for the Southern troops to get into position undetected, but also their knowledge of the enemy's disposition was tenuous. What's more, the risk of a counterattack on a vulnerable part of the Confederate line was high; and the rebel soldiers were already battle weary. Nonetheless, if Longstreet had been intent on rejecting Lee's plan and implementing his own, Hood's proposal would have furnished the perfect pretext for doing so. Instead, Longstreet stuck by Lee's orders. In a postwar letter to Longstreet, Hood called his July 2 request to turn the Round Top an "urgent protest"—the "first and only one" he would ever make during his entire military career. Hood confirmed that Longstreet dismissed this protest with the mantra "We must obey the orders of General Lee."[25]

Longstreet's principal complaint about the battle's second day was that Lee was not attentive enough to the First Corps and to Longstreet himself. Lee "had seen and carefully examined the left of his line" during his long visit with Richard Ewell, but left affairs on the right "to be adjusted to formidable and difficult grounds without his assistance," Longstreet recalled with regret. "If he had been with us, General Hood's messengers could have been referred to general headquarters," Longstreet elaborated, "but to delay and send messengers five miles in favor of a move that he had rejected would have been contumacious." This choice of words—*contumacious* means "stubbornly or willfully disobedient to authority"—is revealing. In Longstreet's own telling, he had expressly chosen obedience to Lee over disobedience on July 2.[26]

Longstreet's version occludes the fact that he, as the tactical chief on that part of the battlefield, had the authority to adapt Lee's earlier plan, in order to take into account new contingencies: namely, Hood's reconnaissance and proposed flank attack east of the Round Tops. Moreover, Longstreet was on shaky ground in suggesting that Lee should have positioned himself with Longstreet on the far right of the Confederate lines; it made more sense for Lee to be near the middle, where he could be in contact with his corps commanders Hill and Ewell (neither of whom had commanded a corps under Lee before) on both flanks. Longstreet's own positioning on his march to the front is also questionable. Arguably, he should have led his own column and directed its course, rather than relying on reconnaissance officer Captain Samuel R. Johnston to do so, in order to be more responsive to updates and requests such as Hood's.[27]

Longstreet clearly deserves some blame for the Confederate failure on the second day of the battle. But the enduring debates over his performance have turned on much more tendentious questions. Should he bear the primary or even sole responsibility for that failure? And did it reveal deep flaws in his generalship and character? The more Longstreet was pressed to refute the charges of having single-handedly lost the battle, the less willing he became to accept any blame whatsoever, lest in giving an inch, his critics would take a mile. Longstreet felt enduring pride in his men's performance on the second day of Gettysburg, writing that it was "the best three hours' fighting ever done by any troops on any battle-field." The Confederate attack that day ultimately fell short, in Longstreet's view, because of a convergence of multiple factors: the "great pertinacity" of the Yankee defense; its ability to fall back onto the high ground; the wounding in battle of key Confederate commanders, especially Hood; inadequate reconnaissance due to J. E. B. Stuart's absence; and the failures of Ewell and Hill to come to Longstreet's aid.[28]

V

While the battle plan for day two of Gettysburg—for an "inferior force" to "drive out the masses of troops upon the heights"—had been "problematical," according to Longstreet, the plan for the third day was, in his view, utterly hopeless. Factoring in the arrival at the front of General George Pickett's division of Virginia soldiers and of J. E. B. Stuart's wayward cavalry at sundown on July 2, Lee hoped for Longstreet and Ewell to launch concerted assaults on the Federal flanks. But Lee scrapped that plan. Instead, he chose to throw Pickett's men, along with divisions led by Brigadier General James Johnston Pettigrew and Major General Isaac Trimble, at the center of the Federal line on Cemetery Ridge, while Stuart harassed Meade from the rear after a massive artillery bombardment had weakened the Yankee defenses. Lee reckoned that the previous day's assaults had failed because they had unfolded serially rather than simultaneously; this time he would concentrate his forces for an all-out, coordinated attack.

Longstreet thought this was misguided, and, in another fraught meeting, on the morning of the 3rd, he told Lee so. The Confederates still had an excellent opportunity to move around the right of Meade's army and maneuver him into attacking a strong defensive position of the Confederates' choosing, Longstreet pleaded, based on reports from his scouts. Lee, "pointing with his fist at Cemetery Hill," countered, "The enemy is there, and I am going to strike him." Longstreet objected that "no fifteen thousand men ever arrayed for battle can take that position"—he felt that at least 30,000 men were required. "I should not have been so urgent had I not foreseen the hopelessness of the proposed assault," Longstreet would recall. "I felt that I must say a word against the sacrifice of my men." Lee, "impatient of listening," did not budge, and Longstreet turned away in silence.[29]

The ensuing offensive came to be known misleadingly as "Pickett's Charge," when, in fact, Pickett commanded fewer than half of the men engaged. As the historian Earl Hess has explained, it was "one of the most complex and difficult attacks to organize during the war, involving elements of two corps, dozens of artillery units, and the thorny problem of coordinating supporting troops." Confederate hopes rested on the success of their artillery in unleashing a massive bombardment that would cripple the Union's own artillery and perhaps thin out the infantry as well. Deeply distressed by the prospect of ordering his men to "make a hopeless charge," Longstreet entrusted tactical control of the July 3 bombardment to battalion commander Edward Porter Alexander, whom he regarded as the best artillerist in the army, rather than to chief of the First Corps Artillery Reserve, James B. Walton. This was an indication of Longstreet's willingness to sidestep protocol to achieve the best result, and the source of lingering resentment on Walton's part. Longstreet directed Alexander to position the First Corps' batteries for maximum effectiveness: to "cripple" the enemy and "tear him limbless." Crucially, Longstreet also asked Alexander to assess the overall effectiveness of the Confederate artillery barrage and to signal Pickett if and when the Federal defenses were sufficiently softened up as to warrant sending in the infantry. [30]

Longstreet told Alexander, "If the artillery fire does not have the effect to drive off the enemy or greatly demoralize him, so as to make our efforts pretty certain, I would prefer that you should not advise Pickett to make the charge." When Alexander noted that cannon smoke would obscure his sight lines and make it difficult to offer a precise assessment, Longstreet simply reiterated his instructions. Alexander, trying to fulfill his forlorn assignment, consulted with Pickett; finding him hopeful about the impending attack, Alexander decided that when the Confederate artillery fire was at its strongest, he would give the signal for the infantry assault to begin.[31]

At 1:00 p.m. the Confederate artillery unlimbered its barrage, setting the earth trembling; the din could be heard a hundred miles away. "The cannonading which opened along both lines was grand," Longstreet observed. The Federal batteries answered, setting up an epic artillery duel. After forty minutes or so, Alexander sensed a slackening of the Federals' artillery fire. Perhaps he had disabled some of their gunners. Then the Yankee guns fell strangely silent; it was a ruse designed to fool the Confederates into believing that the enemy had no firepower left. Alexander sent Pickett a note saying, "If you are coming at all, you must come at once, or I cannot give you proper support." Upon receiving the note, Pickett asked Longstreet, who was nearby, "General, shall I advance?" "My feelings had so overcome me that I would not speak, for fear of betraying my want of confidence to him," Longstreet later wrote of this portentous moment. "I bowed affirmation and turned to mount my horse." Longstreet then rode off to speak with Alexander directly, urging him to replenish his ammunition before Pickett moved forward. Upon learning that there was "no ammunition to replenish," Longstreet fatalistically accepted that there was "no help" to muster and that Pickett "must advance."

Alexander's own actions were motivated by his unflinching faith in Robert E. Lee. "The fact is that like all the rest of the army, I believed that it would come out right, because Gen. Lee had planned it," Alexander observed later. Longstreet's actions were still motivated by deference, now tinged with despair. Pickett's advance was Lee's will. "The order was imperative," Longstreet noted in his memoir. "The Confederate commander had his heart fixed upon the work."[32]

At about 3:00 p.m., the Confederate attack brigades, some 12,500 massed men, appeared from out of the woods along Seminary Ridge and began advancing—flags fluttering, as if on parade—along the half-mile gap that separated them from the Federal line, which was anchored by Winfield Scott Hancock's corps. Longstreet described the fate of these Confederates:

> As they started up the ridge, over one hundred cannon from the breastworks of the Federals hurled a rain of canister, grape, and shell down upon them; still they pressed on until half way up the slope, when the crest of the hill was lit with a solid sheet of flame as the masses of infantry rose and fired. When the smoke cleared away, Pickett's division was gone. Nearly two-thirds of his men lay dead on the field, and the survivors were sullenly retreating down the hill. Mortal man could not have stood that fire. In a half hour, the contested field was cleared, and the Battle of Gettysburg was over.

The entrenched Yankee infantry, protected by embankments, stone walls, and boulders, poured forth lead, shattering Confederate bodies. For a few tantalizing moments it seemed that that Yankee line might give way, as several hundred Confederates led by General Lewis Addison Armistead breached the low stone wall at what would come to be remembered as the "High Water Mark" of the Confederacy—only to have Yankee reinforcements stream in and overwhelm them. For the Union troops, Pickett's Charge played out as a parable of retribution, the soldiers shouting, "Fredericksburg! Fredericksburg!" as they obliterated the onrushing rebel ranks.[33]

VI

The Confederates suffered a staggering 24,000 casualties in the Battle of Gettysburg, to an equally shocking 23,000 for the Federals. Fifty-four percent of the men who made Pickett's Charge were killed or wounded. The command structure of the Army of Northern Virginia was ravaged, with a third of Lee's fifty-two generals numbering among the casualties. "The sights and smells" of the battlefield were "simply indescribable," as Confederate artillery lieutenant Robert Stiles put it: "corpses swollen to twice their original size, some of them actually burst asunder with the pressure of foul gases and vapors . . . the shocking distension and protrusion of the eyeballs of dead men and dead horses . . . showing us what we essentially were and might at any moment become."

The Confederates stood their ground on July 4, expecting that "Meade would be inspired to try & win a real victory" on Independence Day, Stiles wrote many years later. But Meade—to Abraham Lincoln's profound disappointment—decided not to renew the fight. Lee skillfully withdrew his army, retreating back to Virginia by mid-July, with the Federals offering only a tentative pursuit. Meanwhile, in an even greater blow to Confederate prospects, the Union army seized Vicksburg, the Confederate "Gibraltar" on the Mississippi River, after a long, grueling siege. Upon receiving the ill tidings from the western theater, wrote a Confederate war correspondent in Virginia, "All at once, we are plunged into a whirlpool from which I fear we shall never be able to extricate ourselves." The news of Vicksburg's surrender "started us like a clap of thunder on a cloudless day."[34]

In a recurring pattern, many Confederates tried to spin the Gettysburg campaign as a qualified success rather than a crushing defeat, taking solace in their army's successes on the battle's first day, the stores and prisoners they captured, and the casualties they inflicted. But Lee soberly accepted full responsibility for the failed campaign, saying "all this has been my fault" on July 3 and even offering to resign his position—an offer Jefferson Davis rejected. In time, Lee would retroactively shift blame onto not only cavalry chief J. E. B. Stuart but also his three corps commanders, who "could not be gotten to act in concert," as he told William Allan in 1868. Alluding to the "imperfect, halting way" in which these commanders conducted battle, Lee singled out Ewell, but not Longstreet. Lee clearly did not consider Longstreet his biggest disappointment at Gettysburg.[35]

Taking the onus off Lee, modern historians have analyzed the many factors at play, emphasizing that Lee had grounds for his confidence in his army's ability to beat the odds, as well as good reason to assume that Meade, like his Union predecessors, would underperform. Although other culprits behind the Confederate failure, such as Stuart and Ewell, have borne some blame, no one has come under greater scrutiny than Longstreet. Did his misgivings about Lee's offensive tactics became a self-fulfilling prophecy? Did Longstreet make "deliberate attempts to limit the chances of success" of Lee's battle plans at Gettysburg, as Earl Hess suggests in his book *Pickett's Charge: The Last Attack at Gettysburg?* The prolific military historian has argued that Longstreet not only displayed "lapses of judgment" on the third day of the battle, but also intentionally undermined the Confederate operation in a misguided attempt to "limit the loss of valuable manpower." Hess takes Longstreet to task for failing to coordinate Pickett's First Corps unit with those of Pettigrew and Trimble (in Hill's Third Corps), and failing to support the flanks of the attacking columns with reserves, to take "some pressure off the centrally positioned troops." Hess also critiques Longstreet for saddling Alexander with too much responsibility for Pickett's Charge. Longstreet hoped thereby "to create a situation where the attack would be called off by someone else; thus the lives of the infantry would be saved, and he would avoid the primary blame." Echoing Harry Pfanz, Hess deems Longstreet's preferred plan of turning Meade's left flank as impractical, noting that Meade had anticipated and prepared for such a move and identified a strong fallback position at Pipe Creek if forced to abandon his Gettysburg line.[36]

Other historians have dismissed the charge that Longstreet was willfully disobedient. Allen C. Guelzo, in his meticulous analysis of the Gettysburg campaign, has emphasized that "if Longstreet was somehow in violation of Lee's wishes, Lee certainly showed no evidence of it at the time." "Men up and down the line" on July 3 saw Lee and Longstreet conferring "without any sign of impatience or bad feeling." In Guelzo's view, "Longstreet might have been reluctant to initiate an attack on

July 3rd, but that is far from being the same thing as deliberately refusing to implement it."[37]

The most insistent of Longstreet's modern defenders, Cory M. Pfarr, answers Hess's critiques by noting that it was justifiable for Longstreet to be focused on his own First Corps troops and that General A. P. Hill should have played a more active role in positioning and advocating for the Third Corps. Pfarr, too, notes that Longstreet worked very closely with Lee in preparing for the July 3 assault and that all such preparations and orders were approved by Lee. Pfarr sees no attempt to shirk responsibility in Longstreet's exchanges with Alexander—instead, Longstreet was "simply leaning on Alexander's expertise and trained eye," as commanders often did with subordinate officers. When Alexander told Longstreet, in their last pre-charge exchange, that the Confederate artillery was running low on ammunition, Longstreet could have used this as a pretext for calling off the attack. But he did no such thing, instead yielding to Lee's wishes. Citing in-the-moment accounts, Pfarr asserts, too, that Longstreet again displayed conspicuous courage during the fighting, exposing himself to enemy skirmish fire while encouraging the troops and inspecting their lines. Certainly such images of Longstreet in the heat of combat belie the image of him as sullen and sulking: the British observer Arthur Fremantle, bearing witness to Longstreet's fervent efforts to rally his troops on July 3, contended, "Difficulties seem to make no other impression upon him than to make him a little more savage."[38]

Longstreet biographer William Garrett Piston stakes out a middle ground in these debates. He spotlights some of Longstreet's missteps—such as his failure to report to and meet with Lee in person on the evening of July 2, or to position Pickett's division that evening "where it would be ready at dawn" to attack Cemetery Ridge. But Piston rejects the idea that Longstreet had a "diabolical" plan to thwart Lee and observes instead that the two men were "at cross-purposes," blinkered by "tragic oversights, the fog of war, and Lee's command style, which routinely delegated important decisions to subordinates." Longstreet's mistakes "hardly caused the defeat at Gettysburg," Piston concludes sensibly.[39]

VII

What of Longstreet's own assessments of the third day of fighting and of the battle's overall results? In time, as he came under fire in the postwar period, Longstreet would elaborate a searing critique of Lee's leadership at Gettysburg: Lee had rejected Longstreet's sage advice about turning the Federal left because Lee's judgment was impaired. Lee had been thrown off balance and lost his "matchless equipoise," due both to the "deplorable absence" of his cavalry chief, J. E. B. Stuart, and to Lee's own overexcitement at the prospect of another underdog victory. Notably, Longstreet's postwar accounts give some credence to the idea that his doubts impaired his performance during the battle. He makes it clear that these reservations pertained to means, not ends: to Lee's preferred tactics, not the broader Southern cause. Lee should have "put an officer in charge who had more confidence in his plans," Longstreet would suggest in hindsight.[40]

But in the immediate aftermath of the battle, Longstreet sang a different tune, stressing, in his July 24, 1863, letter to Augustus Longstreet, the theme of deference rather than that of doubt. Explaining to his uncle how he had proposed a turning movement only to have that suggestion rejected, Longstreet wrote,

> I consider it a part of my duty to express my views to the commanding general. If he approves and adopts them, it is well; if he does not, it is my duty to adopt his views, and to execute his orders as faithfully as if they were my own. I cannot help but think that great results would have been obtained had my views been thought better of; yet I am much inclined to accept the present condition as for the best. I hope and trust that it is so. . . . As General Lee is our commander, he should have the support and influence we can give him. If the blame, if there is any, can be shifted from him to me, I shall help him and our cause by taking it.

This letter is revealing of Confederate priorities in the late summer of 1863: namely, to soften the sting of defeat by emphasizing that the Army of Northern Virginia had survived to fight another day, and "the cause" was still viable.[41]

In this spirit, Longstreet attempted, in his official after-action report of July 27, 1863, to inscribe into the historical record a version of the Gettysburg campaign he could live with—one that registered his reservations about Lee's chosen tactics but also played up the themes of heroism and resilience rather than that of failure. The report did not disclose Longstreet's proposal to throw the Confederate army between the Union forces and Washington, but it did matter-of-factly share his view that the July 3 assault was ill-conceived. "The distance to be passed over under the fire of the enemy's batteries, and in plain view, seemed too great to insure great results," Longstreet wrote, adding, "The order for this attack . . . would have been revoked had I felt I had the privilege." Longstreet found some fault with Pettigrew and Trimble, whose "wavering columns" did not prove as stalwart as Pickett's. But he ended the report on a redemptive note, praising the rank and file for their "great determination and courage" during the campaign, and lauding the "great gallantry and skill" not only of Pickett but also of Trimble, Pettigrew, Hood, Alexander, and other key officers.[42]

Invariably, Confederates on the home front did devolve into fingerpointing in the weeks and months after the battle. But, crucially, the Southern press flagged a litany of factors in accounting for the overall result. War correspondent Peter W. Alexander ("P.W.A.") offered a firsthand account of Gettysburg in a series of dispatches and digests he sent to his home newspaper, the *Savannah Republican*, in July 1863; these were widely reprinted in newspapers across the South. P.W.A. soberly enumerated the many disadvantages and miscalculations that had plagued the Confederates: the fact that the Southern forces had been too dispersed as the battle opened and not concentrated quickly enough; that Yankees had seized the favorable high ground; that Confederates had failed to "undertake a proper reconnaissance" of Yankee positions; that the assaults on July 2 and 3 had not been properly coordinated, to make simultaneous use of all three of Lee's corps; that the Confederates had lacked crucial supplies, including ammunition; that Meade, whom Lee underestimated, "displayed much skill and judgement" and dictated not only the place but also the time of the battle; and that certain Confederate units, Pettigrew's especially, had acquitted themselves poorly.[43]

In the late summer of 1863, Confederates scrutinized the results of the battle in order to identify problems they could fix—to bring about their ultimate victory in the war, not to presage their ultimate defeat. In the Southern press and public discourse, Longstreet was cast as a stalwart hero, not as a problem. P.W.A. discerned no cross-purposes in the Confederate high command. He attributed Lee's decision-making to the conviction that "his troops were able to carry any position however formidable," and he portrayed Longstreet as being in lockstep with Lee; the choice to attack Cemetery Hill on July 2 was, he reported, "the decision of Generals Lee and Longstreet." Revealingly, P.W.A. folded his account of the battle into an argument that the South could still win the war: it would prevail, he advised, only if it refrained from any further invasions of the North, and, instead, "[fought] the battle of freedom upon our own soil and in front of our own hearthstones." "In such a struggle as this, righteous God will give us the victory, and with it peace and independence," he wrote, capturing the mood of Confederate defiance in defeat.[44]

This account was echoed by other Confederate correspondents, who bemoaned the lack of reconnaissance and coordination but found no particular fault with Longstreet and no reason to despair of their ultimate vindication and victory. A pair of accounts in the July 24 issue of the *Richmond Enquirer*, by correspondents using the pen names "A" and "T," reassured the public that the Army of Northern Virginia had survived its ordeal in Pennsylvania with its faith in Lee fully intact and its "zeal unabated" and "devotion unchilled," ready to "repel any new invasion of the Confederacy." In these accounts, Longstreet's troops came in for special praise, with Pickett garnering adulation for his intrepid advance and Pettigrew taking blame for the assault's ultimate failure; such coverage showed the favoritism of the Richmond press for Pickett's Virginia unit over Pettigrew's North Carolinians. A *Richmond Dispatch* correspondent, writing under the pen name "X" in the spring of 1864, did allude to Longstreet's preference, on day three of the battle, that the Confederate advance target the Federal left flank rather than the center of the Union line; "X" reported that Lee "overruled" Longstreet. But "X" went on to say, reflecting back on July 2 and 3, that "on no part of our whole line was there more bravery displayed than by Longstreet, when in person he superintended the operation of his corps in both days' engagements. His noble and well-known form was always foremost in the rudest shock of battle, encouraging by his presence and stimulating by his example to the highest deeds of bravery and daring."[45]

As these early narratives of the battle were taking shape, the Confederates were encamped in Virginia's Piedmont region, the rolling hills and valleys east of the Blue Ridge, for a prolonged period of recuperation after the Pennsylvania campaign. Despite his efforts to make his own peace with the Gettysburg outcome, Longstreet brooded and began to fantasize again about being transferred to the western theater of war, to be Joe Johnston's right-hand man. In a letter to Robert E. Lee on September 2, 1863, he wrote: "I know little of the conditions of our affairs in the west, but am inclined to the opinion that our best opportunity for great results is in Tennessee." Some in the Richmond press joined Longstreet in speculating that he could make a decisive difference in Tennessee and Kentucky. "There is no officer in the army, except General Lee, who enjoys the confidence of the country and the army to a greater degree than General Longstreet," the *Richmond Enquirer* asserted, asking, "Can he not be spared and put in command of the Army of the West?" Little did Longstreet know that Tennessee campaigns would deal a greater blow to his reputation and morale—in the short term—than the failed Pennsylvania invasion had.[46]

Chapter 4

TOWARD APPOMATTOX

I

"I doubt if General Bragg has confidence in his troops or himself either," Longstreet wrote to Lee on September 5, 1863. "He is not likely to do a great deal for us." By the end of his own stint in the western theater of war, it was Longstreet who was losing confidence—in his government, not in his cause—as Confederate victory at Chickamauga was followed by disappointment and disarray in East Tennessee. Longstreet's commitment to Southern independence and a slaveholders' republic remained resilient. But he also began, in the winter of 1863–64, to grapple with the prospect of defeat. Increasingly, there was a gap between his public bravado and his inner despair. He brooded over the Confederacy's logistical failings, which left his soldiers desperate for supplies, and its lack of command harmony, which left it ill-equipped to match the North's formidable leadership of President Abraham Lincoln and of General U. S. Grant.[1]

Those failings would prove decisive when Lee finally faced off against Grant in the war's long-awaited showdown in Virginia. Severely wounded in the Wilderness in May 1864 in the showdown's first phase, Longstreet rallied and pushed on, clinging to the hope that the Confederacy could somehow still turn battlefield victories into political leverage and thereby control its own destiny. Those hopes evaporated in April 1865 at Appomattox.

II

Longstreet's September 1863 letter deriding Braxton Bragg—sent from his headquarters in Orange County, in central Virginia, to Lee at Richmond—was one of a series of appeals he made to his higher-ups that summer after the Gettysburg campaign, advocating that the Confederacy concentrate forces in the West and that he and his corps be reassigned there. He was preoccupied with what the Union high command was thinking and planning, observing to Lee that "the enemy intends to confine his great operations to the west, and . . . it is time that we were shaping our movements to meet him. . . . I think that it would be better for us to remain on the defensive here, and to re-enforce the west, and take the offensive there." Understanding that his request could be seen as a bid for promotion and to unseat Bragg, Longstreet reassured Lee, "I feel that I am influenced by no personal motive in this suggestion, and will most cheerfully give up, when we have a fair prospect of holding our western country."[2]

Confederate prospects in the western theater looked poor at this juncture, as Bragg had been outperformed by his Union rival William S. Rosecrans. Bragg had bungled his attempt to "liberate" Kentucky in 1862; had repeatedly clashed with western theater commander Joseph Johnston; and had lost the costly Battle of Stones River (or Murfreesboro) in Tennessee in late December 1862 and January 1863. All of these missteps and setbacks gave fuel to the "western concentration bloc," including generals Johnston and P. G. T. Beauregard, in the Confederate leadership, calling for devoting more resources to western campaigns and for putting someone other than Bragg in charge of them. With Rosecrans bearing down on Chattanooga, a vital rail center known as the "gateway to the Deep South," Davis and Lee opted to meet the crisis in Tennessee by reinforcing rather than replacing Bragg—sending Longstreet and two divisions to the beleaguered general's aid.[3]

The historian Alexander Mendoza has argued convincingly that "Longstreet ultimately failed to commit to the western concentration bloc" and "remained dedicated to serving under Lee and fighting for the Confederate case in the East." Longstreet foreshadowed this in a September 12, 1863, letter to Lee, saying of his move west: "If I can do anything there, it shall be done promptly. If I cannot, I shall advise you to recall me." "If I did not think our move a necessary [one]," Longstreet continued, "my regrets at leaving you would be distressing to me. . . . All that we have to be proud of has been accomplished under your eye and under your orders." But Mendoza also notes that Longstreet preferred Joe Johnston's tactics to Lee's aggressiveness and relished the chance to be reunited with Johnston.[4]

Bragg's fortunes continued to plummet. In deft flanking maneuvers, Rosecrans compelled Bragg's Army of Tennessee to fall back toward Chattanooga in the summer of 1863; determined to avoid getting trapped in a Vicksburg-like siege, Bragg and his forces abandoned the city in early September. Bragg headed south toward the mountains of North Georgia, and Rosecrans sent his army, divided into three columns, probing after him. Bragg called for reinforcements and received them, welcoming regiments from Mississippi and eastern Tennessee—and, just in the nick of time, elements of Longstreet's corps from Virginia. On September 9, the very day Bragg was relinquishing Chattanooga, troops in Longstreet's corps departed from their camps in central Virginia to undertake their urgent journey toward Bragg's army in northern Georgia. The journey itself became an ordeal, as the Confederate withdrawal from Knoxville in East Tennessee that August (to redirect those forces to the Chattanooga front) disrupted rail travel from Virginia to Georgia and consigned Longstreet to taking an indirect route of some 800 miles through the Carolinas.[5]

In mid-September Bragg and Rosecrans clashed south of Chattanooga along the Chickamauga Creek, in northwestern Georgia's hill country. After initial skirmishing on September 18, the battle began in full the next day as Bragg targeted the Union left, hoping to push the Northern army into the mountains to the south, deeper into enemy territory and away from its supply base. This plan unraveled in part because some of Bragg's subordinates, such as Lieutenant General Leonidas Polk, were skeptical of his orders and failed to carry them out properly. Over the course of a vicious day of combat in heavily timbered terrain, both commanders poured new arrivals into the fight, but neither made decisive progress.[6]

On the 20th, Longstreet "reached the front at daybreak to conditions that can only be described as chaotic," according to historian Peter Cozzens. Bragg's plan for the day was to mount a two-pronged assault, with Polk on the right wing and Longstreet on the left, to push Rosecrans southward, further cutting him off from the Federal base at Chattanooga; Longstreet was to enter the fray once Polk's wing had rolled up the Union right. Polk's thrust fizzled, due partially to poor communication with Bragg, but this set the stage for Longstreet to act as the Confederacy's savior at Chickamauga. With Federal forces concentrated in the Brotherton Woods, Longstreet chose tactics adapted to the terrain, in which he could use the forest as cover: he massed his forces in a deep narrow column, packing eight brigades in tight. This was in keeping, Jeffry Wert explains, with Longstreet's view that an attack "required depth to preserve its momentum" and overcome the advantages held by defenders. The ensuing blow leveled by Longstreet devastated the Union center and right and scattered a third of the Federal army. Were it not for the stubborn resistance of General George H. Thomas, the Union forces would have been overwhelmed completely. "Indisputably, Longstreet's presence on the battlefield on September 20 was the decisive factor on the Confederate side," Wert has concluded, crediting him not only for the column tactics but also for "send[ing] additional units into the fighting at timely intervals." Confederates had repelled the Federal army from Georgia, sending it falling back into Tennessee.[7]

This banner victory—the only major Confederate triumph in the western theater—prompted Lee, from his headquarters back east, to write Longstreet a warm letter of praise. "My whole heart and soul have been with you and your brave corps in your late battle. . . . Finish the work before you, my dear general, and return to me. I want you badly, and you cannot get back too soon," Lee confided, showing no lingering bitterness about the men's disagreements during the Gettysburg campaign. Longstreet evinced considerable pride in the Chickamauga triumph; he issued a ringing congratulatory order to his troops, for public dissemination through the press, in which he exalted that "the enemy, late so defiant and exulting, has been driven from his chosen positions with slaughter," and predicted that "Tennessee and Kentucky, with their rolling fields and smiling valleys, are to be reclaimed to freedom and independence." He described the battle in similar terms in a September 26, 1863, letter to Confederate secretary of war James Seddon as "the most complete victory of the war, except perhaps the first Manassas."[8]

But in that same letter to Seddon, Longstreet also struck a sobering and sour note, calling out Bragg for failing to capitalize on the victory. "I am convinced that nothing but the hand of God can save us or help us as long as we have our present commander." Seeking to place himself on the high ground of patriotism, Longstreet added, "In an ordinary war, I could serve without complaint under any one whom the Government might place in authority, but we have too much at stake in this to remain quiet under such distressing circumstances." Longstreet's worries and disappointments were visible to some observers. As reported in the *Richmond Daily Dispatch*, Longstreet was no longer the exuberant character he had once been; his eyes were "marked with care," and he was "watchful [and] wary," as though his very nature had "gone into mourning for the war." He turned to religion for some solace, confiding to D. H. Hill the hope that "a kind and infinitely merciful Providence will not abandon us. And that we shall, after all, be successful."[9]

Longstreet, who felt that the Confederacy squandered its advantage on the evening of September 20 and in the days after the battle, was angry that Bragg refused to reinforce him so that he could pursue and finish off Thomas. "I suggested crossing the river above Chattanooga, so as to make ourselves sufficiently felt on the enemy's rear to force his evacuation of Chattanooga and, indeed, force him back upon Nashville," Longstreet explained in his October 1863 after-action report. But Bragg, rejecting

Longstreet's call for aggressive action, instead permitted the Union forces to strengthen their defensive works at Chattanooga and to tempt the Confederates into laying siege to the town, in what Bragg hoped might be a Vicksburg-in-reverse. The Confederates seized the imposing Lookout Mountain and Missionary Ridge, which girded the city to the south, leaving the Federals only a tenuous supply line through the mountains to the north. Recognizing that the Union forces would have to spring this trap or face starvation, the Union War Department sent in reinforcements: General William Tecumseh Sherman from Mississippi, Joseph Hooker from Northern Virginia, and Grant, who would command all the Union forces in the West.[10]

Meanwhile, as his letter to Seddon revealed, Longstreet, in the aftermath of Chickamauga, placed himself at the head of the anti-Bragg faction in the Confederate high command. Historians have regarded Longstreet's maneuvering for Bragg's ouster as self-aggrandizing, duplicitous, and even mutinous, and these are fair characterizations, although it should be noted that Longstreet felt that his views were widely shared. "Bragg was the subject of hatred and contempt, and it was almost openly so expressed," wrote Moxley Sorrel.

Longstreet was now both critiquing Bragg in public and undermining him in private. He went so far as to declare Bragg incompetent to Jefferson Davis, who visited the Tennessee front the second week of October in order to hold a council with his senior commanders. The president of the Confederacy hoped to quell dissension in the ranks, but in an ensuing private meeting with Davis on October 10, Longstreet ran down Bragg again and provocatively sang the praises of Joseph Johnston, which "only served to increase [Davis's] displeasure," as Longstreet would later recall. When Davis and Longstreet parted company, the president "gave his hand in his usual warm grasp and dismissed me with his gracious smile; but a bitter look lurking about its margin . . . admonished me that clouds were gathering about head-quarters of the First Corps." Davis confirmed in an October 12 speech that he was going to support and stick with General Bragg.[11]

III

Clouds did indeed gather. In early November Bragg ordered Longstreet to depart his base of operations at Lookout Mountain and to lead a detached force against Ambrose Burnside's Union army in Knoxville, East Tennessee, in what would prove to be a doomed mission. There were compelling reasons, in Bragg's view, for sending Longstreet away. Even as he continued to second-guess Bragg, Longstreet had performed poorly during the Chattanooga siege, failing to hold Lookout Valley and to prevent the surrounded Federals from opening supply lines there. And Knoxville, an important rail juncture, was a logistical prize, the retaking of which would open up lines of supply and reinforcement from the eastern theater to the West. "Your object should be to drive Burnside out of East Tennessee first, or better, to capture or destroy him," Bragg urged Longstreet in his marching orders of November 4, 1863, adding, "[T]he success of the plan depends on rapid movements and sudden blows."[12]

There would be no rapid movements and sudden blows. From the start of the campaign, Longstreet was in a funk, complaining to Bragg, Assistant Adjutant General G. W. Brent, and Major General Simon Bolivar Buckner of short rations, inadequate rail transportation, bad weather, feeble animals, and poor maps and guides. Most of all, Longstreet was angry that his detached force was not large enough to take on Burnside. "We thus," Longstreet wrote on November 5, "really take no chance to ourselves of great results." The Confederates' initial success at crossing the Tennessee River only raised the stakes. As the historian Earl Hess explains, from then on, Longstreet could no longer be easily recalled by Bragg, and his "only hope of success lay in meeting Burnside's force in the open field and defeating it early in his campaign." But Longstreet's forces repeatedly frittered away opportunities to intercept and cut off Burnside as the Union army effected a retrograde movement back toward its Knoxville fortifications. Burnside successfully drew Longstreet farther away from the Army of Tennessee and the Chattanooga front—and bogged him down in a quasi-siege.[13]

The attempted siege of Knoxville commenced on November 19, and although each general had roughly 12,000 men, Burnside's defenders enjoyed some structural advantages: they possessed the high ground in a strong defensive perimeter anchored by superior artillery; they received some support from local civilians, as Unionism was relatively strong in East Tennessee; and they were able to keep supply lines open to the south of the city. After some reconnaissance, Longstreet determined to target Fort Sanders, the key to the city's western defenses. But nearly everything went wrong that could: Longstreet muddled his orders and hesitated and then postponed his attack. In addition, he underestimated how formidable the walls and ditches of the fort were; his men lacked the proper entrenching tools and ladders; and the Confederates failed to prepare the way for their final assault by sufficiently softening the Union defenses through skirmishing and artillery fire. To make matters worse, on the day of that assault, November 29, the twelve-foot earthen walls of the fort were encased in sheets of ice, confounding Southern soldiers' efforts to scale them. The well-prepared and provisioned Yankees drove Longstreet's men into retreat.[14]

Longstreet's communications to his commanders on the eve of the Fort Sanders assault have a desperate quality, as evidenced by this November 19 note to Major General Lafayette McLaws: "If the troops, once started, rush forward till the point is carried, the loss will be trifling; whereas if they hesitate, the enemy gets courage; or, being behind a comparatively sheltered position, will fight the harder. Besides, if the assaulting party once loses courage and falters, he will not find courage probably to make a renewed effort."[15]

This was not a confident commander's summoning the indomitable will of Confederate troops, but instead a gloomy wish that a burst of odds-defying brazenness could counteract the structural strategic and tactical failures of Confederate leadership. It was also a form of cover: after the fact, Longstreet blamed not only Bragg for the doomed Knoxville campaign but also McLaws and other subordinates, whom he charged with mismanaging their assignments and failing to carry out his orders.[16]

The timing could not have been worse, as the defeat at Fort Sanders came in the wake of Bragg's own defeat at Chattanooga, where Grant, now in charge of the Federal army in the West, planned and executed a successful Union breakout. Hooker, Sherman, and Thomas drove the rebels off Lookout Mountain and Missionary Ridge on November 24 and 25, avenging their September loss at Chickamauga. The Battle of Chattanooga was not unusually costly in terms of casualties: 5,800 Federal and an estimated 6,000 to 8,000 Confederate. But it was nonetheless a humiliating setback for the Confederates. Bragg had again displayed his weaknesses, including an inability to work well with subordinates and poor tactical decision-making. After Chattanooga, Bragg was done for. Jefferson Davis turned to Joseph E. Johnston to command the Army of Tennessee. Longstreet, after the Fort Sanders debacle, went into winter quarters in the East Tennessee region before being reassigned back to Lee's army in Virginia in the spring of 1864. Meanwhile, Ulysses S. Grant, whose star was rising ever higher, assumed command as general-in-chief of the entire Union army.[17]

Longstreet, chastened by his time in Tennessee, felt a keen sense of responsibility for the disheartening outcome of the campaign. On December 30, 1863, with his personal confidence at its nadir, Longstreet wrote to Samuel Cooper, adjutant and inspector general of the Confederacy, asking to be relieved of duty. Citing the "combination of circumstances" that prevented the "complete destruction of the enemy's forces in this part of the state," Longstreet conceded that "it is fair to infer that the fault is entirely with me" and that "some other commander [should] be tried." While James Seddon accepted this logic, Jefferson Davis refused Longstreet's resignation. Longstreet would have to think and fight his way out of his slough of despond.[18]

This was a daunting task, as Longstreet felt not only that he had failed, but also, and more persistently, that others had failed him. A fatalism crept into his thinking about the war. He had not lost faith in "the cause," but he was coming to believe that if it prevailed, it would be in spite of the Davis administration's and high command's conduct of the war effort. More than anything, the Confederacy's logistical failings preoccupied Longstreet; during the bitterly raw winter of 1863–64, he wrote a steady stream of letters from East Tennessee back to Richmond bemoaning the lack of food, forage, clothing, shoes, and other necessities. The absence of supply lines, passable roads, and railroad access through the mountains meant that there was seemingly no hope for relief. "This army is in great distress. . . . The weather is now extremely severe, and our service very hard," Longstreet lamented to Samuel Cooper on January 2, 1864. In other such letters, Longstreet revealed that half of his men and nearly half of their horses were without shoes. "We have been making shoes since we left Knoxville, but with all of our workmen can only make one hundred pairs a day. As our shoes are all old, they wear out faster than we can make them," he explained. Hospitals filled up with sick and wounded men as short but sharp clashes with the enemy took an additional toll that winter.[19]

Along with logistical failings, it was a kind of moral failing that worried and demoralized Longstreet: the Confederates' propensity to underestimate their foes. "It is a bad principle in war to despise your enemy," Longstreet wrote to one of Bragg's aides-de-camp at the start of the Knoxville campaign, upon being informed, erroneously, that Burnside's Federal troops were in a "demoralized condition." This dictum—that one should not underrate the opposition—became a staple of Longstreet's writing about the war from this point on. It is no coincidence that he struck such a despondent note at this juncture, for it was the first time he found himself in the same theater of war as Grant. In Longstreet's view, Grant, who "was not lightly to be driven from his purpose," could make the Confederates pay for their blunders and dysfunction more than any other Federal commander. On the eve of the Knoxville campaign, Longstreet asked Bragg for more troops not because he particularly feared Burnside but because he knew that Grant had arrived at Chattanooga to take on Bragg, and the Union general would capitalize on any extended absence by Longstreet.[20]

Decades later, in his memoir *From Manassas to Appomattox*, Longstreet reflected, "In my judgment, our last opportunity was lost when we failed to follow the success at Chickamauga, and capture or disperse the Union army." This was not only an indulgence in hindsight and another dig at Bragg, but also a tribute to Grant, whose arrival in the Chattanooga theater Longstreet noted in that same memoir passage. Longstreet's own confidence was shaken both by Grant's presence and by his own powerlessness to prevail upon Davis or Bragg to comprehend the grave threat that Grant posed.[21]

IV

While modern-day historians generally see the Tennessee phase of the war as a bitter chapter for Longstreet, revealing his weaknesses, Alexander Mendoza has a different view, praising the general's ability to somehow maintain the morale of his corps as "a significant achievement considering the dire situation his troops faced."

Longstreet certainly worried about morale and tried to attend to it. On December 16, 1863, he promulgated his General Order No. 11 to his troops, in which he presented to them a letter captured from a Federal soldier, as a window into Union army morale. The letter referred to the short rations, severe marches, and other hardships endured by the Northern troops, and evinced "endurance, patience, & hope" in the face of such adversity. If the Yankee invaders could "carry out their work under such trials," Longstreet told his men, then surely the Confederates, who were "resisting tyranny" and fighting to defend their homes, could match that spirit. "Let it not be said that the heart of the invader is stronger & stouter than the determination of you, who fight for your all," he cautioned. Referencing the terrible supply shortfalls of his army, Longstreet added, "Your wants are known to your Gen and every effort has been made to relieve them."[22]

But even as he sought to motivate his men, Longstreet recognized that the Union leadership was seizing the momentum. In the wake of the Knoxville campaign, on December 8, 1863, President Abraham Lincoln introduced his Proclamation of Amnesty and Reconstruction. It tendered forgiveness and a restoration of political rights to any white Southerner who took a loyalty oath, accepting abolition and pledging future allegiance to the Union. The amnesty plan also offered readmission to seceded states that could form an electoral core of such oath-taking loyalists, equal to 10 percent of a given state's 1860 electorate.[23]

Union authorities sought to blanket the Confederacy with announcements of the proclamation and hoped that they would reach not only wavering civilians but also war-weary Confederate soldiers, to induce desertion. When handbills announcing Lincoln's amnesty offer appeared among the Confederate ranks in East Tennessee in January 1864, Longstreet wrote a caustic letter of complaint to his Union counterpart in the region, General John G. Foster, commander of the Department of Ohio and stationed in Knoxville. Foster should have communicated the Union's new policy to Longstreet rather than underhandedly appealing directly to Longstreet's men. Lincoln's policy, Longstreet warned, was both dishonorable and impractical. "The few men who may desert under the promise held out in the proclamation cannot be men of character or standing," he insisted. "If they desert their cause, they disgrace themselves in the eyes of God and of man. They can do your cause no good, nor can they injure ours."

Longstreet's letter begged the question: If the policy was doomed, why protest so vociferously? According to the historian Jeffry Wert, scores of men deserted during Longstreet's East Tennessee camps that winter. Surely Longstreet felt that his own troops' dire condition might make some receptive to the Yankees' clemency.[24]

Upping the ante, Foster responded provocatively, sending Longstreet an additional twenty copies of the Amnesty Proclamation for him to personally distribute in his army. In a livid rejoinder, Longstreet chastised Foster for "trifling over the events of this great War" and descending into a "contest of jests and jibes." He charged, "Step by step, you have gone on in violation of the rules of civilized warfare. Our farms have been destroyed, our women and children have been robbed, and our houses have been pillaged and burnt. You have laid your plans and worked diligently to produce wholesale murder, by servile insurrection, and now, most ignoble of all, you propose to degrade the human race by inducing soldiers to dishonor and forswear themselves."

This was a remarkable degree of high dudgeon, given that all of the Confederates who had formerly served in the United States Army, Longstreet included, had been induced to forswear themselves in accepting secession. But that irony was lost on Longstreet and on the Confederate press, which reprinted the Longstreet-Foster correspondence approvingly.[25]

Indeed, Southern newspapers and other periodicals continued to hold Longstreet in very high regard, the *Richmond Dispatch* calling him "one of the most sagacious and indefatigable of our military leaders" in March 1864. Longstreet's surrogates, too, clung to the idea that their commander had absolved himself with honor in the Knoxville campaign. "If Genl. Bragg had held his position at Chattanooga for *one* week longer, we would have taken Knoxville together with Burnside and his army," Thomas Goree wrote home to his mother on February 8, 1864, in a campaign postmortem. "Although the campaign failed in great results, yet, we have many minor successes. Not during the war has a campaign been carried on under such adverse circumstances as was ours." He closed by observing, "Many people throughout the country are somewhat despondent as to the final result of this struggle, but I free the greatest confidence in our success." Such musings reveal the perils of measuring morale, as Goree provided evidence in the space of a single sentence both of demoralization and of resilient fighting spirit.[26]

Longstreet's own resilience comes through in a series of letters he wrote in late February and early March to Lee, Seddon, and Beauregard, proposing that the Confederates retake the initiative by moving Longstreet's command, as mounted infantry, over the mountains and into Kentucky, to strike at the enemy's lines of communication. Committed as ever to victory at all costs, Longstreet held out hopes of being a strategic savior for the cause. In the service of this proposed move, Longstreet not only asked to be supplied with the requisite horses, mules, saddles, bridles, and so on, but also he suggested that the Confederate government ratchet up its policy of impressment. His troops could only be properly supplied with food-stuffs and other essentials, Longstreet wrote Lee, if all the railroads were impressed, and passenger service stopped for forty days, so that the cars could be used exclusively by the military. In making such a bold demand, Longstreet was revealing his close philosophical affinity with Lee, who favored, as the historian Gary W. Gallagher has explained, "the expansion of national power at the expense of state authority or individual liberties . . . to achieve military victory and independence." Longstreet, like Lee, believed that "all the Confederacy's war-related resources should be brought to bear against the enemy." But in this case, Lee and the Davis administration refused to concentrate resources on Longstreet's army, lest they deprive, in a zero-sum scenario, Confederate armies in other theaters.[27]

V

In early March Longstreet was summoned away from his command, east to Virginia, to confer with Lee and Davis over further operations in Tennessee. In a strategy session in Richmond and then again in letters he penned as he traveled back to Tennessee, Longstreet reiterated to Lee, Davis, and Joe Johnston his view that the "strongest and most effective move" for the Confederates was not a new campaign into Middle Tennessee but instead "to concentrate an army near Abingdon, Va. and throw it into Kentucky." Longstreet's pleadings for this plan reveal his deep preoccupation with public opinion in the North and with the impending Northern presidential election of 1864. Again and again, Longstreet's letters from March 1864 expressed his view that if the Confederates moved decisively, they could "get an honorable peace in a short time," as he put it to Confederate quartermaster general Alexander R. Lawton. "If we can break up the enemy's arrangements early, and throw him back, he will not be able to recover his position nor his morale until the Presidential election is over, and we shall then have a new President to treat with," he continued.

However, if the Republican incumbent rode military successes to re-election, Longstreet feared, the war would be prolonged for another four years, "and no one can tell what may be the result." Sensing that his proposed Kentucky offensive had been rejected, he offered this same grim prophecy to Lee: that "another four years" would "possibly result in our entire destruction." Longstreet added bluntly, "I have entire confidence if our affairs are properly managed, but I have none if they are not well managed. Hence my great anxiety and concern at our present inaction."[28]

Longstreet elaborated this point in a March 27, 1864, letter to Beauregard's chief of staff, Brigadier General Thomas Jordan. Emphasizing the high stakes of the 1864 presidential contest, Longstreet mused,

> The political opponents of Mr. Lincoln can furnish no reason at this late day, against the war, so long as it is successful with him, and thus far it has certainly been as successful as any one could reasonably expect. If however his opponents were to find at the end of three years that we held Ky., and were as well to do as at the beginning of the war, it would be a powerful argument against Lincoln, and against the war.... If he is elected, the war must continue, and I see no way of defeating his reelection except by military success.

With this analysis, Longstreet straddled two opposing Confederate schools of thought on the upcoming election—and provided an early signal of his political iconoclasm. Some Confederates, most notably Vice President Alexander Stephens, argued that the Davis administration should actively support the so-called Copperhead Democratic faction in the North in calling for an armistice and negotiated peace, and also that Confederates should refrain from offensive fighting during the election campaign season, so as not to galvanize Northerners into forming a united front against invasion. (Copperhead was the derogatory nickname Republicans gave antiwar Democrats who opposed Lincoln's policies, especially emancipation and conscription.) Stephens and his ilk imagined that a Democratic Party victory in 1864, unseating Lincoln, would pave the way for peace on the Confederacy's terms: guaranteeing independence, or, as a fallback position, a reunion with slavery restored. Other Confederates, including President Jefferson Davis himself, took a hard line that for the South to offer a peace proposal would be seen as a sign of weakness and would be greeted with contempt by the North; hard-liners held that the Northern Democratic Party could not be relied upon and that only military victories could secure Confederate independence.

Longstreet adopted his own distinct position in this debate: he agreed with Stephens that a Lincoln defeat at the polls would bode very well for the Confederacy, but he took Davis's view that Confederates could influence the election outcome only on the battlefield and not by political machinations. Most surprisingly, Longstreet broke with both camps in his positive assessment of Lincoln's effectiveness as a commander in chief: while Copperheads and Confederates alike generally missed no opportunity to call Lincoln both a tyrant and a failure, Longstreet, determined not to underestimate the enemy, saw the sixteenth president as a success.[29] Lincoln's Democratic opponent come November would turn out to be none other than George McClellan, the general who had so frustrated the president with his timidity on the battlefield that he'd replaced him with Ambrose Burnside two years before.

Jeffry Wert has praised the "astuteness" of Longstreet's own strategic thinking at this stage: Confederate gains in Kentucky could indeed have amounted to a huge political setback for Lincoln. But all of Longstreet's calculations and lobbying were for naught. In early April Longstreet's First Corps was ordered to return to Virginia, where it would help Robert E. Lee in his long-anticipated faceoff with Grant. Longstreet still strove to visualize victory. "I think that we should take the shortest line of march for Washington City . . . [to] be able to get between the enemy and his Capitol," he wrote Lee from Charlottesville, Virginia, on April 1, 1864, in a burst of optimism. Longstreet's men reveled in being reunited with Lee's army, as well as taking part in the grand review—a procession of the troops, before a crowd of admiring civilians—conducted on April 29 near Gordonsville in central Virginia. As Lee and Longstreet rode along the "long gray lines," E. P. Alexander remembered, "the effect was that of a military sacrament, in which we pledged anew our lives." Alexander was eager to take the fight to Grant, to "let him have a smell of our powder." But it was the Union general who would seize the initiative, trying to get between Lee and Richmond.[30]

VI

"The Armies here seem to be quietly looking at each other," Longstreet wrote his uncle Augustus on May 2, 1864, on the eve of the seismic Overland campaign of that spring. "I don't know yet that we have adopted any plan or policy except it be to wait till the enemy is entirely ready." This diffident outlook reflected Longstreet's lingering pique over the Tennessee campaign. "I opposed the move into E. T. [East Tennessee] as too weak to accomplish the results hoped for," he stressed to Augustus, confiding that he had made such a prediction in a missive to Confederate general Simon Bolivar Buckner and preserved the letter—sending it to Louise Longstreet for safekeeping—as proof that Longstreet had prophesized the Knoxville debacle. Longstreet ended his letter to his uncle with an attempt at reassurance. "I sincerely hope that we may be able to destroy Grant as readily as we have the other Yankee Generals. We have never met one who has been able to stand against us yet."[31]

In the company of his fellow soldiers, at Lee's headquarters, Longstreet offered a less encouraging assessment. "I know him through and through," he said of Grant, "and I tell you we cannot afford to underrate him and the army he now commands. . . . For that man will fight us every day and every hour till the end of this war." Grant, it would soon be confirmed, was fundamentally different from his predecessors. He was determined that the Federal army's superior numbers would at last prove decisive—and his Overland campaign in Virginia in the spring of 1864 kept relentless pressure on the Confederates, as part of a multipronged offensive in Virginia. Meade's Army of the Potomac would take on Lee; Ben Butler's army would move up the James River to threaten Richmond from the south; and General Franz Sigel would occupy Confederate forces in the Shenandoah Valley to keep them from reinforcing Lee.

Union soldiers under Grant and Meade crossed the Rapidan River on May 4, 1864, aiming to lure Lee into battle. On May 5–6, 1864, the opposing forces clashed in the Wilderness, near where the Battle of Chancellorsville had taken place the previous spring. Lee attacked Grant, although outnumbered two to one, hoping that the heavy underbrush of the woodland would neutralize the Union general's artillery and cavalry advantage. Lee's plan was for Richard Ewell's Second Corps and A. P. Hill's Third Corps to intercept the Federals in a pincer movement, so that Longstreet's First Corps—rushing to the front from central Virginia—could then deliver the crowning blow. But Longstreet did not get to enter the fray on May 5, as the Confederates' initial movements met with a strong counterattack, at a ghastly cost to both sides. Both armies fought amidst brush fires, which erupted as the dry woods were ignited by muskets and the explosion of shells, and then raged into the night, burning wounded men alive.[32]

The following day, though, Longstreet's presence was crucial, as his corps came on the scene with an expertly executed flank attack (after an initial frontal attack using conventional alignments) along the Orange Plank Road just in time to save the rest of Lee's army from being overwhelmed by a Federal offensive. Longstreet's men were so effective because he used atypical tactics—arranging his men into skirmish lines followed by supporting lines—well suited to the thickly wooded terrain. "By dispersing the front units as skirmishers," Jeffry Wert explains, "the troops delivered a continued fire into the massed ranks of the enemy and were elusive targets to their opponent's volleys."

But just as Longstreet was planning a follow-up blow against the shaken Federals, disaster struck: in an eerie echo of Stonewall Jackson's wounding at Chancellorsville a year earlier, Longstreet was hit by friendly fire and had to be carried, bleeding profusely, from the field. As he would put it later, succinctly and sorrowfully, in his 1889 Confederate pension application, he was struck "through the throat and right shoulder, paralyzing the right arm and shoulder to such extent to render the right arm a painful burden." The bullet's trajectory and the tracheal damage it caused accounted for the "weak, breathy voice" that "persisted for the rest of [Longstreet's] life," as a modern medical analysis notes: "His voice, which once could be heard all along the lines, was gone. He was barely able to speak above a whisper." Staff officer Francis Dawson, present at the scene, gauged Lee's reaction, writing, "I shall not soon forget the sadness in his face, and the almost despairing movement of his hands, when he was told that Longstreet had fallen." Longstreet's wounding, just after he had "saved the day on the right," as the *Richmond Dispatch* reported, robbed the Confederates of momentum and gave the Northern troops time to regroup and halt Lee's progress. In two days of savage fighting, the Union army, which started the campaign with 119,000 men, suffered 18,000 casualties, and the Confederate army, which numbered 66,000, incurred 11,000.[33]

Longstreet recuperated slowly over the course of six long months, spending time with his family in his wife's hometown of Lynchburg, Virginia, and then with his own relatives in Georgia. He was mentally as well as physically depleted. When Susan Leigh Blackford, the wife of the First Corps' judge advocate Captain Charles Minor Blackford, visited Longstreet in Lynchburg in mid-May, she found him "very feeble and nervous.... He sheds tears on the slightest provocation and apologizes," Blackford wrote in a letter home. A letter of condolence Longstreet wrote in July, mourning the death of General Micah Jenkins (who had been killed in the same friendly fire that wounded Longstreet), hints at the difficult road to recovery: Louise Longstreet signed her husband's name for him and added a postscript explaining that "he has not sufficiently recovered the use of his arm to sign himself." Gradually, Longstreet taught himself to write legibly with his left hand, and the use of his right arm was "partially restored in later years," Moxley Sorrel would note, observing that Longstreet "was forever pulling at the disabled arm to bring back its life and action."[34]

During Longstreet's spring 1864 convalescence, the Confederates' military prospects went from bad to worse. Grant clashed with Lee in a costly series of battles in which, again and again, the Union general tried to move his left flank around Lee's right flank, to get between the rebels and Richmond, only to find Lee waiting for him, entrenched behind hastily constructed earthworks. The futile Federal assault on Confederate entrenchments at Cold Harbor on June 3 was "sickening," Sorrel remembered, "heartrending to the stoutest soldier. Nothing like it was seen during the war." The Northern side endured roughly 13,000 casualties "and that awful mortality was inflicted in but little more than an hour!" he marveled.

Undeterred, Grant decided that the best course of action was to join forces with Butler's army and take the vital rail junction of Petersburg, twenty-three miles south of Richmond, thereby cutting off the rebel capital from its lines of supply. To that end, Grant dislodged his vast army from the scene of the bloodletting at Cold Harbor and moved it south, across the James River.[35]

Federal forces tested Petersburg's defenses in mid-June, but the outnumbered Southern forces held them in check. Grant's army, which had suffered 65,000 casualties since the Overland campaign began, faced the prospect of a protracted siege. But the Confederates' defenses had been compromised: the carnage of May 5 through June 18 amounted to nearly 36 percent of Lee's total force. The ensuing summer of trench warfare along the Richmond-Petersburg front further whittled down the Army of Northern Virginia, which had to contend with constant sharpshooting and shelling, blistering heat and drought, and short rations. Desertions spiked in August amidst complaints about poor pay and scanty supplies.

In the three months of fighting after the July 30 debacle at the Crater, in which Union troops had tried to blow a hole in the rebel lines only to get trapped and mowed down in the massive gap created by the blast, Grant launched a series of offensives aimed at capturing the railroads that supplied Petersburg from the south and at hooking the southernmost part of his own line around Lee's rightmost flank. At the same time, Grant extended his lines to the north and probed at Richmond, above the James River, largely to draw Lee's attention and his troops away from defending Petersburg's railroads. In mid-August, on the south end of the siege line, Grant succeeded in seizing the Weldon Railroad, leaving Confederates to rely on the South Side Railroad. Meanwhile, although the Federal attacks at Deep Bottom, above the James, failed to break the Confederate defenses of Richmond, they imposed casualties that Lee could not afford.[36]

Confederates seemed briefly to regain the momentum with two victories. At Reams Station, on August 25, they drove off Federals who were busy destroying the Weldon Railroad, twelve miles south of Petersburg. And in mid-September Confederate general Wade Hampton's "Beefsteak Raid" on a Union supply corral in Northern Virginia captured more than 2,000 cattle and brought desperately needed rations to Lee's men. But Grant resumed the offensive in late September, as Ben Butler's army attacked the Confederate works at New Market Heights and then captured Fort Harrison, above the James. Meanwhile, Federals breached the Confederate outer defenses at Poplar Spring Church, south of Petersburg. And in late October, Grant again launched coordinated assaults on rebel lines both north and south of the river, with the Confederates successfully fighting on the defensive and clinging to their last tenuous transportation links.[37]

With the two armies at an impasse, and with Lee fearing that his army would be starved into submission during the coming winter, Longstreet resumed command of his First Corps in October 1864, to hold down the Confederates' positions north of the James River. Sorrel would recall the "happiness of welcoming our chief back to his command," but also the lingering effects of Longstreet's Wilderness wound, writing, "His right arm was quite paralyzed and useless." Longstreet himself questioned "the propriety of being assigned, in my crippled condition, to positions now filled by officers of vigorous health." But Lee deemed his presence indispensable, and he dutifully reentered the fray.[38]

Longstreet's image in Confederate eyes remained strong, as an anecdote in the Georgia *Sumter Republican* illustrates. On his way to report for duty, Longstreet was complimented for his heroic services to the cause. He replied: "I have some little reputation, but my men made it all for me." Likening this response to Lee's magnanimous accepting of the blame for the Gettysburg defeat, the *Republican* editorialized that "the great and good Generals always think of the *men*." The paper also quoted from Longstreet's new general order rallying his First Corps to action. "We have in the past a brilliant, an unsurpassed record. Let our future eclipse it in our eagerness for glory, our love of country, and our determination to beat the enemy," Longstreet intoned, sounding very much like his old self. But his cup of glory was running dry.[39]

VII

"Siege of Richmond & Petersburg, lasting 11 months, with lines in places 80 yards apart, assaults, sorties & 'affairs' daily,—bombardment and picket firing continuous, night & day. Mines exploded, &c., &c., Losses about 35,000." This was how Longstreet's new chief of staff, Osmun Latrobe, who replaced the promoted Moxley Sorrel in the fall of 1864, described the war's end game in Virginia. Watching starvation and desertion eating away at the army, Longstreet seesawed between a fatalistic despair and a defiant hope.

He wrote Lee's aide, Colonel Charles Marshall, on October 31, 1864, that, given the way his meager force was strung out over a long line of defense, "the safety of my position must in a great measure depend upon chance."

Two months later, on the first day of the new year, Longstreet argued in a letter to Lee that the Confederacy could still control its own destiny, if only "we should leave nothing undone which may tend to improve the efficiency of our armies." Among the measures Longstreet continued to push was impressment. He was convinced that there were abundant foodstuffs both in the Confederate countryside and within enemy lines that Southern civilians would bring forth to feed the rebel army—if only they could be paid in gold ("they wont go to that trouble for confederate money," he noted). Longstreet suggested further, "If the Govt has not the gold, it must impress it; or if there is no law for the impressment, the gold must be taken without a law. Necessity does not know or wait for laws." Lee agreed in principle with Longstreet, but objected that this particular plan was impractical. Nonetheless Longstreet doubled down, writing to Lee in late February, "The gold is here, and we should take it."[40]

To justify targeting resources of wealthy civilians, Longstreet continued grimly, "We have been impressing food and all the necessaries of life from women and children, and have been the means of driving thousands from their homes in destitute condition. Should we hesitate, then, about putting out a few who have made immense fortunes at our expense to a little inconvenience by impressing their gold?" The fate of Richmond and the cause was staked on feeding and clothing the army. "We have expended too much of blood and treasure in holding [Richmond] for the last four years to allow it to go now by default," he insisted. This revealing passage dramatizes the evolution in Longstreet's thinking over the course of the war. He had moved from a focus on the Yankees' depredations against women and children to a recognition that the Confederates, too, victimized innocent civilians, including their own. In November 1864 Longstreet issued General Orders No. 21 to the First Corps, decrying the "extent of the depredations" committed by his troops "upon the stock, gardens, and other property of the citizens around Richmond." The troops' excesses called "for the most rigid measures of correction"—thus, Longstreet informed them that roll calls would be held at "irregular hours, to detect absentees, who will promptly be brought to trial." Longstreet feared that wanton misconduct would "demoralize" the army, by which he meant erode both its morals and morale. The appeal of impressing gold from the wealthy so that foodstuffs could be purchased rather than seized was that such a policy might at least distribute civilian sacrifice more evenly. As long as victory was possible, Longstreet could and did cling to the idea that some targeted victimization of Confederate civilians was a necessary evil.[41]

While determined to save Richmond, Longstreet was decidedly ambivalent about a controversial new Confederate proposal for rejuvenating the war effort: enlisting enslaved men in the Southern army and offering them freedom as a reward. The idea was first pushed forcefully in the winter of 1863–64 by General Patrick R. Cleburne after the reverses in Tennessee. Confederates faced the dilemma of choosing "between the loss of independence and the loss of slavery," as Cleburne put it. He hoped that "every patriot will freely give up the latter—give up the negro slave rather than be a slave himself." After Abraham Lincoln handily defeated George McClellan in the 1864 presidential election—winning the Electoral College by a ten-to-one margin—Jefferson Davis, who had previously rejected the idea of Black enlistment, came around and endorsed bringing some enslaved men into the army in order to try closing the growing manpower gap between the Confederacy and the Union. A heated public debate followed, with opponents arguing that it would alienate the Confederate rank and file, undermine agricultural production, encroach on property rights, threaten a race war if armed Blacks turned against their former masters, and, most important, undermine slavery—the very institution Confederates were fighting to defend. Longstreet lent his voice to this chorus, objecting that Black enlistment would "involve the necessity of abolishing slavery entirely in the future" without "materially aiding" the Confederate cause in the present.[42]

Defenders of Black enlistment, Lee prominent among them, argued that the policy would preserve what was left of plantation slavery. "Their plan would not emancipate and arm *all* of the South's slaves but only a relatively small proportion of them," the historian Bruce Levine has observed. "These black soldiers would then, by salvaging the Confederate military effort, secure Confederate independence—and, in the bargain, secure the continuing enslavement of all the rest." Crucially, advocates noted that the limited freedom granted to recruits would fall far short of full equality, for only white men would have political rights; Blacks would be relegated to a perpetual serfdom, as a subordinate laboring class, akin to slaves. These arguments made Longstreet willing, despite his reservations, to give the experiment a small-scale, provisional try: he approved moving some unarmed Black hospital workers, who had been attached to a local defense corps of convalescing patients, into Richmond's trenches to shore up his manpower.[43]

Those favoring Black enlistment won an empty victory in the form of an equivocating bill that the Confederate States Congress passed in March 1865. The bill, H.R. 367, "An Act to Increase the Military Force of the Confederate States," invited slaveowners to offer up their slaves for service—while still retaining legal title to them—and slaves themselves could now enlist in the Southern military on the shaky promise of a conditional, limited freedom. Not surprisingly, masters and slaves alike were uninterested in accepting these terms, and the measure produced negligible results. After the bill's passage, Longstreet's own doubts resurfaced, as he felt that scheming Confederate officers might use the call to raise companies of Black troops as an excuse to leave the front and head home indefinitely, thus exacerbating the manpower crisis.[44]

Escapes and resistance by the enslaved remained major preoccupations for Longstreet in the war's final phase, as they had all along. Tantalizing clues in the historical record reveal that a stream of fugitives fled Longstreet's lines for Union lines and lived to tell the tale. For example, a Union soldier named Washington Roebling (later to become the chief engineer behind the building of the Brooklyn Bridge) recounted in a letter dated March 30, 1864, that a man claiming to have been Longstreet's camp servant made his way to the Union army at Culpeper, Virginia. The man tendered his services as a spy, professing to be "well acquainted with the country on the other side" of the Rapidan River. A year later, in April 1865, Andrew J. Tabb, an enslaved waiter on Longstreet's staff on the Petersburg front, escaped to Union lines and enlisted in the 115th Regiment of the US Colored Troops (USCT). The Union army would by the war's end enlist 150,000 Black soldiers and sailors from the South. Longstreet continued to try to roust out and discipline such Black Unionists: in March 1865 he ordered the arrest and imprisonment of "Alexander, slave of William B. Randolph" on the charge of "aiding soldiers to desert." But there was no rolling back the tides of slave flight and Confederate desertion.[45]

VIII

With the Confederate army eroding along the Richmond-Petersburg defenses, Longstreet and Lee alike explored, in the three months before Appomattox, the prospects of an honorable negotiated peace. The two men did not doubt each other's rock-ribbed commitment to victory. Lee wrote Longstreet on February 25, 1865, "I am much gratified by the earnestness and zeal you demonstrate in our operations; and were our whole population animated by the same spirit, we should be invincible." But the morale of Southern soldiers and civilians alike was ebbing, and both Lee and Longstreet puzzled over how the Confederacy might leverage whatever power it had left to extract concessions and bring peace on favorable terms. Both clung to the hope that conservative Northerners might yet be persuaded to come to the negotiating table and recognize Confederate sovereignty—or, failing that, offer peace with amnesty and the restoration of Southerners' property and political rights.[46]

Such hope persisted even after the Hampton Roads Peace Conference near Fort Monroe, Virginia, on February 3, 1865, where Lincoln categorically rejected the idea that peace could come without reunion and emancipation. Jefferson Davis, ever the hard-liner, in turn rejected Lincoln's conditions for peace as insulting. But Lee and Longstreet opted to test the waters a second time. After the Hampton Roads conference failed, Longstreet responded to a February 20 entreaty from an old West Point friend: Major General E. O. C. (Edward Otho Cresap) Ord, commander of Yankee forces on the James. Ord asked Longstreet to meet him between the lines, ostensibly to discuss the topic of "irregular" bartering and fraternization between rank-and-file soldiers of the two armies. The conservative Maryland Democrat believed that soldiers, rather than politicians, were best suited to forge an honorable peace. The two men met on February 25, and Ord, requesting a "side interview," shared his hope that military commanders might come together as "former comrades and friends" and broker a cease-fire and peace negotiations. He suggested to Longstreet that perhaps Generals Grant and Lee "should meet and have a talk," and that simultaneously a second channel of communication should be opened between Longstreet's wife, Louise, and Grant's wife, Julia Dent. After all, the two women were old friends, and Ord imagined that they could enact women's traditional role as social mediators and represent the potential rapprochement between North and South. Longstreet signaled that he was receptive, but also told Ord that he was not authorized to begin such a process. He would need to check with his superiors.[47]

On February 26 Longstreet presented Ord's proposal to Davis, Lee, and Secretary of War John C. Breckinridge in Richmond. Lee and Breckinridge were approving, and even Davis offered his grudging permission. Although the Confederate president "still refused to entertain any thoughts of restoring the Union," the historian Terrianne Schulte points out, he was "willing to support a military convention, believing that it might somehow lead to Southern independence." Davis authorized Lee to reach out to Grant, pursuant to a second Longstreet-Ord meeting, this time on the purported topic of exchanging civilian political prisoners. Meanwhile, Ord looped in Grant, who, cryptically, tendered his approval of a plan for Louise Longstreet—and Longstreet's entire family, if necessary—to be sent to Grant's headquarters and then northward, even though Grant also made it clear that he disapproved of Julia's playing any role in negotiations. Ord portrayed Longstreet as a man fed up with the "hopeless and unnecessary butchery" of the Confederate war; critical of Davis as the "great obstacle to peace"; and interested, as Lee was, too, in securing some eleventh-hour concessions for the South, such as "compensation for the loss of their slaves and an immediate share in the Gov't." What Grant made of all this is uncertain, but it seems he saw no harm in a consultation among military leaders that could set the stage for Confederate surrender. Revealingly, both Grant and Longstreet expressed their desire to meet with each other—but they also recognized that it was more politic to have Longstreet follow up first with Ord.[48]

On February 28 Longstreet and Ord met again between the lines. According to Longstreet's recollections, Ord "asked to have General Lee write General Grant for an interview," and Ord also "indicated a desire on the part of President Lincoln to devise some means or excuse for paying for the liberated slaves, which might be arranged as a condition and part of the terms" of a putative "military convention." As Longstreet and Ord reported this meeting up their respective chains of command, their scheme unraveled. Following Ord's lead, Longstreet assured Lee and Davis that Grant was open to peace terms that were "equally honorable for both sides," including remunerating Southerners for their liberated slaves. On the basis of such assurances, Lee then wrote to Grant on March 2, 1865, expressing his desire to "leave nothing untried which may put an end to the calamities of war." But the overture went nowhere, as Grant had consulted with Union secretary of war Edwin Stanton and with Lincoln, and received stern orders not to negotiate with Lee or to let up the military pressure on the rebels. Political questions lay beyond Grant's jurisdiction; he could address only subjects of "purely a military character." Grant then wrote Lee on March 4, throwing cold water on the military convention idea and suggesting that Longstreet and Ord had misconstrued Grant's meanings and intentions. Ord and Longstreet returned dutifully to the business of fighting.[49]

Although the armistice scheme fizzled, it spawned some significant consequences, the most momentous being Jefferson Davis's response. The president of the Confederate States of America saw the twin failures of Hampton Roads and the proposed military convention as vindicating his view that the Confederacy must fight it out to the last ditch. He said so explicitly in his March message to the Confederate Congress, recounting the whole Ord episode and suggesting that Longstreet, as go-between, had acted in good faith, only to be spurned. Painting a dystopian picture of Yankee victory and reconstruction, Davis concluded that Confederates would never agree to "live in a country garrisoned by their own negroes and governed by officers sent by the conqueror to rule over them." President Davis handed over to the Confederate press the March 2–4 correspondence between Grant and Lee, ensuring extensive coverage in both the South and the North. Southern newspapers cast Longstreet as a credulous victim: Ord had misled him into thinking "there really was an opening for a peace discussion between Lee and Grant," as a New Orleans paper mused. In contrast, Union papers charged that it was Longstreet, not Ord, who had initiated the peace overtures. For instance, the *Philadelphia Inquirer* theorized that the duplicitous Davis authorized Lee to explore such negotiations in order to buy time and secure an armistice during which "the sorely pressed rebels might have an opportunity to readjust their military strength, [and] recuperate" for another round of fighting. But Lincoln and Grant, the paper crowed, had not been "bamboozled" by this ruse.[50]

This coverage brought Longstreet a great deal of publicity as a man in the thick of the peace process. The episode was an occasion for him to signal that his friendship with Grant set him apart from other Confederates— and the primary audience for that signal was Grant himself. In the months after the surrender at Appomattox, Grant would confirm that he received the message loud and clear. But in the short term, the central takeaway of the Longstreet-Ord encounter was the directive it sent from Lincoln and Stanton to Grant: that there must be no military conference or cease-fire with Lee's army intact. Grant must disable that army and force Lee to capitulate and leave the subsequent political negotiations to Lincoln.[51]

The end was nigh. On March 25, 1865, Lee made one last attempt to break Grant's line, with a predawn attack on Fort Stedman near Petersburg. But the dramatic assault, led by Major General John B. Gordon's Second Corps (he had assumed command in December 1864), was a costly failure. Grant countered by launching yet another of his offensives, aimed at turning Lee's right flank and cutting the South Side Railroad, the last functioning supply and communications line out of Petersburg. As panic gripped Richmond, and its residents prepared for evacuation, Confederates lashed out in vain at the Union army's Fifth Corps and General Philip H. Sheridan's mounted troops, in what turned out to be Lee's last counter-offensive maneuvers of the Petersburg campaign. The North's success at fending off Lee's blows set the stage for the decisive developments of the following day. On April 1, Federal forces smashed at the Confederate-entrenched position at Five Forks, which Lee had ordered Pickett to hold at all hazards. Despite spirited Confederate resistance, the line gave way, and, by nightfall, Five Forks was in Union hands.[52]

Grant, concerned that Lee would mount a counterattack on Sheridan and escape the closing Federal trap, ordered the final Union offensive of the prolonged Petersburg campaign, unleashing a punishing artillery barrage on the night of April 1–2. The North blasted away at Lee's lines from the Appomattox River to Five Forks with the heaviest bombardment of the entire war, literally shaking the ground beneath Richmond. The morning of Sunday, April 2, brought a massive Federal onslaught on the Petersburg defenses, intended to flush the rebels out of their forbidding layers of entrenchments, rifle pits, and abatis. The dramatic breakthrough of the Union Sixth Corps forced Lee to recommend to the War Department that both Petersburg and Richmond be abandoned. Federal forces entered Petersburg in the predawn hours of April 3, raising an American flag above the courthouse there and preparing the way for Abraham Lincoln's triumphant visit to the newly occupied city later that day. Jefferson Davis directed government officials to prepare to depart Richmond for Danville, to the southwest, hugging the North Carolina border, via the last working rail line; Davis himself would leave the beleaguered capital on the 7:00 p.m. train.

With Confederate statesmen on the run, control over the city devolved upon the municipal authorities. Those authorities set fire to resources such as warehouses, mills, and bridges, to keep them from falling to the Yankees; it took Union soldiers, who entered the city as the liberators of its enslaved population, to douse the flames that engulfed Richmond.[53]

After abandoning the defenses of Richmond and Petersburg, Lee's army began its flight west. Grant's goal was to cut off Lee and prevent him from veering south and joining the Confederate army of Joseph Johnston in North Carolina. Lee planned for his fleeing columns to concentrate at Amelia Court House, where they would meet awaiting supply trains and pick up the tracks of the Richmond & Danville Railroad, leading south. But the provisions never arrived, and the Confederates wasted a day in fruitless foraging, even as desertion ate away at their ranks. Lee's men undertook a desperate night march westward on April 5, but the Federals caught up with them at Sailor's Creek, a tributary of the Appomattox. In a series of clashes there on April 6, the celebrated cavalry commander Sheridan led the Union forces to a crippling victory.

General Lee decided to divide his army: he and Longstreet moved south of the river to Farmville, while Gordon and General William Mahone crossed the High Bridge in Cumberland County to get north of the river. On the morning of April 7 in Farmville, Longstreet's depleted men fell upon their first rations in four and a half days. But soon they were ordered to move out as one of Sheridan's cavalry divisions and Ord's Army of the James swarmed in. Lee directed his columns back across the Appomattox, using the river as a protective cordon as they moved north toward Appomattox Station, where supplies sent from Lynchburg awaited them. Union troops that had also crossed the High Bridge were north of the river. The Federals attacked Lee's flank at Cumberland Church, five miles away from the bridge crossing. Confederate troops under Longstreet and Mahone beat back a wave of attacks, but this was another hollow victory. "The beginning of the end was now at hand," Longstreet would later recall in his memoir.[54]

However, in the moment, there were still contingencies at play. Grant arrived in Farmville on April 7 and set up headquarters at Randolph House, a hotel, where he conferred with Ord. Late that afternoon, Grant penned a two-sentence overture to Lee, invoking the "hopelessness of further resistance" and asking him to surrender "that portion of the C.S. army known as the Army of Northern Virginia." Lee, in Cumberland County, received Grant's note at around 9:30 p.m. on April 7. Longstreet, who was with Lee, recalled the scene: "I was sitting at his side when the note was delivered. He read it and handed it to me without referring to its contents. After reading it, I gave it back, saying, 'Not yet.'"[55]

In the hours before Grant's message arrived, Confederate brigadier general William N. Pendleton had met with Lee, on behalf of some fellow officers, to delicately broach the subject of surrender. A classmate and close friend of Lee's from West Point, Pendleton (an Episcopal priest) sought to absolve Lee of the shame of proposing surrender himself. Lee abjured any such martyrdom, telling Pendleton, "General, we have yet too many bold men to think of laying down our arms." Years after the war, when Pendleton emerged as one of Longstreet's most caustic critics, Longstreet would cast this meeting as "pathetic" and even "mutinous"—proof of Pendleton's faintness of heart and Longstreet's own steadfastness.[56]

IX

Like Lee, Longstreet was not yet willing, on April 7, to accept the futility of negotiations or the inevitability of defeat. Both men still believed that something—national pride, personal honor, and the ability to shape public opinion as well as extract some concessions from the Yankees—could still be defended by continuing the fight. Lee instructed his aide-de-camp, Colonel Charles Marshall, to answer Grant with the following: "Though not entertaining the opinion you express of the hopelessness of further resistance on the part of the Army of Northern Virginia, I reciprocate your desire to avoid useless effusion of blood, and therefore, before considering your proposition, ask the terms you will offer on condition of its surrender." Lee did not show the response to Longstreet, but Longstreet surmised, based on the orders Lee soon gave for another night march, that the commanding general had rejected Grant's overture. The Confederate army moved out toward Appomattox Station, where, if all went according to plan, it would reprovision and then make its way to Campbell Court House, thirty miles south of Lynchburg, and from there to Danville.[57]

The April 7 exchange inaugurated a correspondence with Lee leading to the April 9 meeting at Appomattox. As those letters passed back and forth between the two men, Grant was carefully laying a trap, with Federal armies converging on Appomattox north and south of the river, while Lee was maneuvering to somehow slip that trap. Knowing full well his army had one final chance to forestall surrender, Lee summoned Longstreet, Gordon, and General Fitzhugh Lee, his nephew, to his headquarters north of Appomattox Court House late at night on April 8. Lee shared with them his exchange of letters with Grant and reviewed their predicament. Together they decided that Fitz Lee and Gordon, with Longstreet in support, would try to break a hole in the Federal line at sunrise. If it was only the Union cavalry obstructing the way, the men stipulated wishfully, Lee and Gordon were to clear the foe from their path and open an escape route to Campbell Court House. But if they came upon Federal infantry massed in force, they were to notify Lee, "in order that a flag of truce should be sent," Fitz Lee recalled, "to accede to the only alternative left us."[58]

On April 8 the final battles of Lee's retreat were joined, with the Federal cavalry seizing the Confederate supply trains at Appomattox Station, occupying the high ground west of Appomattox Court House, and blocking the Richmond–Lynchburg Stage Road. This set the stage for Lee's last breakout attempt on the morning of the 9th. When it failed, Lee was forced at last to agree to Ulysses S. Grant's proposal that he capitulate. During the tense cease-fire that preceded the two opposing generals' meeting at the McLean House, James Longstreet's state of mind was revealed by a brusque exchange with the Union general George Armstrong Custer. Longstreet sent Major Robert Sims of his staff to inform John Brown Gordon of the cease-fire, and Gordon then dispatched Sims to take the news to Sheridan's lines, under the flag of truce (a towel wrapped around a stick). Upon reaching his destination, Sims encountered the twenty-five-year-old Custer, who told him brusquely, "We are behind your army now, and it is at our mercy." The Union general then insisted on riding back to Confederate lines, brandishing a handkerchief wrapped around his sword as his own flag of truce, to confront Longstreet with this grim message. In Longstreet's account, Custer, with his "flaxen locks flowing over his shoulders," demanded the "unconditional surrender of this army." Longstreet reminded Custer that Lee was its commander, and that he was at that very moment on his way to Grant to negotiate a surrender.

But Custer would not relent. Thomas J. Goree vividly reveals what happened next: "Finally, Genl. Longstreet seemed to lose his patience, and in substance told Genl. Custer that he could not and would not surrender the army, that he (Longstreet) was not half whipped yet, and if he (Custer) was not satisfied to await the result of the conference between Genl. Lee and Genl. Grant, he could return to his command and commence hostilities again as soon as he pleased, and he would see that he met with a warm reception." Custer stood down, knowing full well he would soon have the satisfaction of seeing Longstreet yield.[59]

As for Lee, his "brave bearing failed to conceal his profound depression," as Longstreet recalled in his memoir. While waiting for Grant's response, Lee had confided to Longstreet that he feared his earlier rebuff to Grant might "cause him to demand harsh terms." Longstreet tried to dispel Lee's forebodings: "I assured him that I knew General Grant well enough to say that the terms would be such as he would demand under similar circumstances." But this did not assuage Lee's fear that Grant aimed to humiliate him. Longstreet suggested to his chief that if Grant's terms were harsh, "Lee should break off the interview and tell General Grant to do his worst." "The thought of another round seemed to brace him," Longstreet observed, for the reckoning that lay ahead.[60]

Longstreet's reading of Grant's intentions was vindicated. On April 9 at the McLean House at the village of Appomattox Court House, Grant offered Lee surrender by parole. In exchange for their pledge that they would never again take up arms against the United States, Confederates would effectively be set free. "Each officer and man will be allowed to return to their homes, not to be disturbed by United States authority so long as they observe their paroles and the laws in force where they may reside," the terms stipulated. Grant permitted Confederate officers to keep their sidearms and horses and baggage. And at Lee's request, Grant provided food for the starving Confederate troops; 25,000 Union rations would be directed from Sheridan's commissary to Lee's. When news of the surrender reached the Union lines, the jubilant soldiers commenced firing a salute of a hundred guns in honor of their victory. But Grant "sent word . . . to have it stopped." "The Confederates were now our prisoners," he explained later, and there was no need to "exult over their downfall."[61]

In Longstreet's view, the parole conditions were essentially "as liberal terms as General Lee could expect." But from the very moment the surrender agreement was signed, debates took shape over the implications of Grant's liberality. His "immediate concern," the historian Caroline E. Janney has explained, was the military objective of avoiding "protracted and irregular-style war" and a cycle of "reprisals and retaliation" of the kind that had so often followed civil wars. Grant believed that generous terms were essential to pacification. His longer-term goals reflected his political philosophy. In Grant's eyes, the surrender was a triumph of right over wrong: proof of the moral and material superiority of the North's free-labor democratic society over the South's slave-labor autocratic one. Grant's hope, in extending clemency, was to change hearts and minds—to effect Confederate repentance and submission.[62]

In Lee's view, by contrast, the United States' victory was one of might over right, attributable to brutal force, not to skill and virtue. Although Lee rejected the option of guerrilla warfare as impractical and dishonorable, he did not admit moral defeat or counsel submission. Lee's Farewell Address to his army on April 10, 1865, copied and circulated among his commanders as General Orders No. 9, to be read to the troops, trumpeted the Confederacy's righteousness in defeat, declaring that "after four years of arduous service, marked by unsurpassed courage and fortitude, the Army of Northern Virginia has been compelled to yield to overwhelming numbers and resources." In the wake of the surrender, Lee's officers developed this might-over-right theme, churning out speeches, articles, and memoirs designed to disseminate the idea that Lee had faced insurmountable odds of five to one or worse in the final campaign. This doctrine referred not only to the size but also the social composition of the Union army. Lee's lieutenants lamented that they had been compelled to surrender to a mercenary army—"German, Irish, negro, and Yankee wretches," as Brigadier General William N. Pendleton put it—of their social and racial inferiors. Scholars have since established that Lee faced odds of two to one at Appomattox, no worse than odds he had beaten before. But in its day, the numbers game had a distinct political purpose. By denying the legitimacy of the North's military victory, former Confederates hoped to deny the North the right to impose its political will on the South.[63]

Lee moved decisively at Appomattox to cast the surrender terms in the most useful light. Hoping their paroles could confer on his men a measure of immunity from reprisals at the hands of the victorious Federals, he requested of Grant at their April 10, 1865, meeting on horseback that each individual Confederate be issued a printed certificate, signed by a Union officer, as proof that such a soldier came under the settlement of April 9. Grant assented readily. In keeping with the language of the surrender terms, a parole certificate vouched that if a soldier observed the laws in force where he resided, he was to "remain undisturbed." This seemingly simple phrase would prove to be deeply problematic. In Confederate eyes, the paroles represented the promise that honorable men would not be treated dishonorably—namely, forced to yield to new political realities.[64]

Northerners viewed Appomattox as the effective end of the Confederacy: with Lee's army neutralized, independence was a dead letter. It seemed to be only a matter of time until Joseph Johnston's army in North Carolina would succumb to the relentless General Sherman. Jefferson Davis and his government were in flight, but could not long elude the grasp of the Federals; the same was true of the remaining Confederate forces, scattered throughout Alabama, Mississippi, and the Trans-Mississippi theater.

Tragedy quickly disrupted Northern reveries of peace when the famous actor John Wilkes Booth assassinated Abraham Lincoln on the evening of Friday, April 14, 1865, at Ford's Theatre in Washington, DC. Booth, an ardent Maryland secessionist, was enraged that the president had, in his last speech, on April 11, endorsed limited Black suffrage, or voting rights. While Lincoln sat in the presidential box with his wife, Mary, and another couple, Booth walked up behind him, aimed his pistol, and fired a bullet into the back of Lincoln's head. The sixteenth president of the United States died the following morning at the age of fifty-six.

Among Northern civilians, the assassination brought forth a tidal wave of grief and calls for stern retribution against the South. Trying to salvage Lincoln's own vision of a reunion characterized by "malice towards none," the new president, Tennessee Unionist Andrew Johnson, promised clemency to "the unconscious, deceived, conscripted—in short, to the great mass of the misled" and harsh penalties to the "conscious, intelligent, leading traitors."[65]

The Confederate military effort collapsed within a matter of weeks: Johnston surrendered to Sherman near Durham Station, North Carolina, on April 26; General Richard Taylor capitulated to Union major general Edward Richard Sprigg Canby in Citronelle, Alabama, on May 4; Union forces captured Jefferson Davis in Irwin County, Georgia, on May 10; and, finally, General Edmund Kirby Smith surrendered to Canby at Galveston Harbor, Texas, on May 26.

In the aftermath of the war, Longstreet would stake out a distinct and unusual position on the Appomattox surrender. Longstreet personalized the surrender terms, viewing them through the lens of his and Grant's long-standing bond. In Longstreet's view, a brief encounter between him and Grant on April 10, 1865, was broadly symbolic of the promise of national reunion. The two men crossed paths at the McLean House. Longstreet was there in his official capacity as one of the commissioners Lee had appointed to hash out the details of the parole process. When Grant saw Longstreet, he extended his hand in friendship "with his old-time cheerful greeting," and they embraced. "Grant acted as though nothing had happened to mar the ties that had existed between us before the war," Longstreet recalled later. "He put his arm within mine ... and said with the same affection as of old: 'Pete, let's go back to the good old times and play a game of brag as we used to.'" This act of personal grace had a profound and enduring impact on Longstreet, who would go on to argue that he took part in Reconstruction out of gratitude to Ulysses S. Grant.[66]

Longstreet left no in-the-moment reflections, from the surrender spring, on the demise of slavery. In time, as he experienced the transformations of Reconstruction, he would come to accept fully an influential Unionist interpretation of emancipation—that "an overruling Providence had ordained that slavery in these states should cease forever in the year 1865," as he would put it in a letter to Thomas Goree ten years after Appomattox. This narrative, with its emphasis on 1865 as slavery's death knell (and not 1863, the year of Lincoln's Emancipation Proclamation), highlighted that it was the capitulation of the Confederate military that brought de facto freedom to the enslaved.[67]

At the moment of Lee's surrender, however, Longstreet was not yet prepared to regard Black freedom as providential. Over the course of the war, he had grudgingly recognized the impact of Black Southern Unionism on the Confederate war effort, and he sought, from the war's first days until its very last, to punish and suppress that Unionism. At Appomattox, Longstreet regarded the end of slavery with wary resignation. He evinced no willingness whatsoever to accept emancipation as a positive good or to consider the possibility of Black citizenship.[68]

Indeed, although the themes of gratitude and acceptance would come to dominate Longstreet's postwar accounts of the surrender, neither was uppermost in his mind at Appomattox. A Northern army correspondent on the scene during the surrender portrayed Longstreet as "very morose and taciturn." The dispersal of Longstreet and other parolees involved sorrowful leave-takings. Longstreet did not issue a Farewell Address, but he did, in other kinds of communications to his troops, echo Lee's sentiments. "The deplorable events of yesterday will cause for a time, at least, our speedy separation," Longstreet lamented in an April 11 note to his chief of staff, Osmun Latrobe. "I seize a moment of leisure to express my profound regret at leaving you." Longstreet went on to thank Latrobe for his "distinguished services . . . to the cause of the Confederate states" and his "courage and devotion to principle." Robert E. Lee added a postscript to the note, "concurring in the commendation" of Latrobe's "merit and worth." He and Longstreet wrote as if recommending Latrobe for future promotions. But as the issue of amnesty loomed over the surrender, it was now up to the Union, and not the Confederacy, to determine who would be punished and who would be rewarded.[69]

PART II

Reconstruction

Chapter 5

BURYING THE PAST

I

James Longstreet construed the Appomattox terms in the way that Grant had hoped and intended: as conferring a conditional freedom on the defeated Confederates and incentivizing their compliance with the new political order. Confederates had "appealed to the arbitrament of the sword" and now had to live with the results. "The decision was in favor of the North, so her construction becomes the law, and should be so accepted," Longstreet would write in 1867 as he launched a new life in New Orleans. Such were the "obligations under which we were placed by the terms of our paroles."[1]

More so than any other prominent Confederate, Longstreet accepted the war's verdict as final. Abundant testimony from the men in Lee's army, officers and rank-and-file alike, reveal that many held out hope that the war was somehow not yet really lost. They made their way to their homes, the historian Caroline Janney has noted, "awaiting a renewed call for battle." Longstreet, by contrast, would pivot very quickly to building a future for himself and his family in the restored Union.[2]

After Appomattox, Longstreet headed south with Thomas Goree, his aide. Goree was returning home to Texas, and Longstreet intended to scout out the Lone Star State, where he had been posted before the war, as a possible new home for his family. They were accompanied by a former slave named Jim, presumably a body servant in the Confederate army, who had been owned by a Mr. Frierson in Shreveport, Louisiana, and was returning there in search of his own kin. The men's drawn-out journey began in Lynchburg, Virginia, where Longstreet was reunited with his wife, Louise, and their sons, sixteen-year-old Garland, now a cadet at the Virginia Military Institute, in Lexington, and Robert Lee, one and a half years old, at her parents' home. Louise was pregnant, and Longstreet stayed with her in Lynchburg for the birth of their son James Jr. at the end of May and for a month thereafter.[3]

During his Lynchburg sojourn, Longstreet wasted no time in trying to avail himself of the very amnesty offer, promulgated by Lincoln in December 1863, that Longstreet had so scorned in his testy exchange during the East Tennessee campaign with the Union general John G. Foster back in the winter of 1864. On May 26, 1865, the provost marshal in Campbell County, Virginia, administered to Longstreet the amnesty oath, whereby the former rebel swore allegiance to the Union. Lincoln's policy required that certain categories of Confederates take a second step in order to obtain full immunity from prosecution and restoration of rights: they would have to apply directly to the president for a pardon. As a high-ranking Confederate military officer and a former US Army officer who had resigned his commission to join the rebellion, Longstreet belonged to two of the excepted classes—and thus he would need to throw himself on the mercy of Lincoln's successor, Andrew Johnson, a pro-war Democrat from Tennessee whom Lincoln chose as his running mate on the National Union Party ticket in 1864 in order to widen the Republican coalition.[4]

Immediately after taking the amnesty oath, Longstreet telegrammed Brigadier General Lorenzo Thomas, adjutant general of the US Army, seeking permission to visit Washington, DC, on "important private business." U. S. Grant promptly endorsed the request, writing, "Longstreet is really one of the least objectionable officers lately engaged in rebellion & would no doubt be willing himself to return to citizen ship [*sic*]." Whether Longstreet intended on this visit to ask Johnson for a pardon is unclear—

Grant suggested that Longstreet's principal aim was to request passage through the North for his family in advance of their relocating to Texas. But, revealingly, rumors circulated through the press in early June 1865 that Longstreet was to visit the capital to ask for a presidential pardon. A Washington, DC, newspaper wrote of him, "He accepts the conditions of things as irrevocable, and we are glad to say will devote all his energies and efforts personally to a restoration of the Union." Soon Northern papers were opining that Longstreet's pardon bid would be a test case of whether US-Army-officers-turned-Confederates could win clemency from President Johnson. Some commentators were sanguine: Longstreet had "been a very great sinner but claims to have experienced a change of heart," the *Cleveland Daily Leader* noted. Others, such as the *Weekly Republican,* from Plymouth, Indiana, were diffident: "We do not think it would be just or politic to restore any forfeited rights to officers who basely deserted their flag at the hour of the nation's peril."[5]

As it turned out, the test case would have to wait. Longstreet did not apply to Johnson for a pardon until November 1865. The fact that some Northerners—Grant, most notably—were disposed to seeing him as repentant reflects the lasting effects of the earlier Longstreet-Ord exchange. Grant seems to have interpreted it as evidence of Longstreet's good-faith interest in peace. In hastening to take the oath in May 1865, Longstreet had taken his first steps in his journey back to citizenship.

But, as Grant had surmised, Longstreet's priority in the summer of 1865 was finding a new home for his family. On June 28 he, Garland, Goree, and Jim were "Off at Last" toward Texas, as Goree noted with anticipation in his diary. They made their way toward North Carolina, stopping for a "splendid dinner" at the plantation of Samuel Hairston of Pittsylvania County, Virginia, on the border. Before the war, Hairston had a reputation as the "richest man in Virginia," for his extensive holdings of thousands of slaves and his huge estates in the region. Wending their way through the Carolinas, the party's next notable stop was at Fort Hill, South Carolina, the plantation home of the late John C. Calhoun and of his descendants. Goree relished a tour of the Calhoun mansion, but Longstreet took a pass: "The Genl. Would not consent to spend the day with the good people at Fort Hill," Goree wrote in his July 11 diary entry. Whether Longstreet's choice is attributable to fatigue or to some discomfort at paying homage to Calhoun is unclear, but Goree captured the melancholic aura of John C. Calhoun's library, "arranged just as it was at his death." Goree mused wistfully, "I could but think while here how fortunate this great man was not to live to see the disgrace and ruin of his country which he strove so hard to prevent."[6]

In Georgia, the party's destination was a residence of Longstreet's older brother, William, in White County, northeast of Atlanta. As executor of their late father's will, William had assumed control over the family properties in Georgia and Mississippi following their mother's death in 1855 and had since augmented those holdings. Tom Goree and Longstreet were met at William's Cleveland, Georgia, home by James's former slave Maurice, who had been sent south from Appomattox with the general's horses for this rendezvous. Both William and Maurice joined the group of travelers as they proceeded farther south. In early August, as they moved through Alabama toward the Longstreet family's cluster of homes in Noxubee County, Mississippi, Goree parted ways with the others and headed to Texas.[7]

Noxubee County, where Longstreet's mother, Mary Ann Dent, had settled in 1843 after nearly a decade in Alabama, was home to James's extended family: William had his own principal residence there, and their younger sisters Rebecca Longstreet Ruff, Maria Longstreet Dismukes, and Sarah Longstreet Ames lived there, too, with their husbands, all of whom were in the legal profession. The Mississippi Longstreet clan had been wealthy and prominent before the war. Together they owned dozens of enslaved persons. James would end his 1896 memoir of the Civil War by remembering that "most of the family servants were discharged after the war at Macon, Mississippi," Noxubee's county seat. He recalled that among them was his "old nurse" Daniel, who continued to reside in the Macon region after the war and "still claims the family name, but at times uses another."

It seems likely that Daniel was the same person whom Augustus Baldwin Longstreet had deeded James in 1832, and who Longstreet "called for" to act as his body servant when the Civil War began; the 1880 census for Macon, Noxubee County, shows a sixty-year-old Dan Longstreet, born in Georgia, as living there. A kinship network of Black Longstreets (and Dismukeses) resided in Noxubee after the war and struggled to weather a storm of anti-Black violence during Reconstruction. General Oliver Otis Howard, named commissioner of the newly established Bureau of Refugees, Freedmen, and Abandoned Lands in May 1865, designated Noxubee as one of the three worst counties in the state in terms of Ku Klux Klan depredations. The Black Longstreet family would give rise to an influential Republican Party activist and minister, Joseph "J. W." Longstreet, who fought back ardently against the tide of Jim Crow violence and discrimination.[8]

James Longstreet, for his part, would not cast his lot with his siblings in rural Mississippi, nor forge on to Texas, as initially planned. Instead, he decided to head to Mobile, Alabama, on the Gulf Coast, and from there to New Orleans. He arrived in the Crescent City in September 1865 and found it hospitable: the city, the largest in the former Confederacy, had drawn other prominent Confederate veterans such as John Bell Hood and P. G. T. Beauregard, and was a bustling hive of moneymaking. Longstreet quickly linked up with two former comrades in arms, brothers William Miller Owen and Edward Owen of New Orleans, and partnered with them in starting a cotton brokerage firm. "We predict for the new house immense success, and cordially recommend our friends to them," declared a Shreveport newspaper, in a benediction on the former general's new venture, Longstreet, Owen & Co.[9]

II

Longstreet knew his efforts to establish some financial security for his family would be hampered if he did not reestablish his own citizenship rights, and so he turned in earnest to securing a presidential pardon from Andrew Johnson. On May 29, 1865, just a few days after Longstreet took his oath of allegiance under Lincoln's plan, Johnson formally proclaimed his Reconstruction policy. Like Lincoln's, Johnson's Amnesty Proclamation required Confederates to take an oath of allegiance to the United States government as the condition for restoring their individual political and property rights. Johnson's plan also enumerated the exceptions to this rule: high-ranking Confederate civil and military officials and members of the antebellum elite would have to apply personally to the president for their pardons. Johnson believed that his amnesty policy struck a balance between clemency and sanction.[10]

Longstreet was surely alarmed by the news that he, along with Robert E. Lee and thirty-five other upper-echelon Confederates, was indicted for treason by a Federal grand jury in Norfolk, Virginia, on June 7, 1865. But Lee managed to obtain immunity by appealing personally to U. S. Grant to intervene, invoking the Appomattox promise that surrendered Confederates who observed their parole terms would avoid reprisals. Grant persuaded Johnson to drop the case against Lee and the others rather than go to trial. Meanwhile, Longstreet cultivated Grant's trust further, to lay the groundwork for a pardon appeal to Johnson. In the summer of 1865 Longstreet wrote two letters to Grant, asking for the release of some Confederate prisoners of war and for the pardon of a fellow Southern officer on the grounds that such acts of clemency "would do much good toward restoring order & tranquility." In his second letter, Longstreet asked rhetorically, "Let me appeal to you then to determine whether there is justice or honor in pursuing a fallen foe, whose only crime is error of judgment." In Longstreet's view, the "terms granted by you at the surrender of Gen'l Lee, extended to all of us the benefit of the Amnesty Proclamation of President Lincoln of 1863."[11]

Grant found this line of reasoning persuasive. But would Johnson? In November 1865 Longstreet left New Orleans and headed north to Virginia, to reunite with Louise and the children and help them prepare to resettle in New Orleans. He proceeded on to Washington, DC, in search of his pardon. Longstreet called on Grant first, asking for his endorsement, and Grant complied readily, penning a note that vouched for Longstreet's honor as a former West Point cadet and testified to their own close personal acquaintance. Longstreet included this note in his November 7 pardon application. The application again pledged his allegiance to the US Constitution (he retook the amnesty oath) and also revealed that his family's well-being was his paramount consideration: "Your petitioner further states that he is the head of a family—wife & children, who are dependent upon him to a great extent for the means of their support & education—that he is anxious to engage in business for the purpose of accumulating additional means . . . but is advised that it is unsafe & impolitic to enter into any business engagements until he shall have received the pardon of the President."

Johnson was unmoved by this plea, telling Longstreet, "There are three persons of the South who can never receive amnesty: Mr. Davis, General Lee, and yourself. You have given the Union too much trouble." Secretary of War Stanton took a similar tack, reportedly telling Longstreet "that he was regarded as rebel No. 3—only Davis and Lee outranking him," according to a Washington, DC, correspondent of the *New Orleans Picayune*.[12]

In the fall of 1865, as Longstreet appealed for amnesty, press reports and rumors coming out of Washington, DC, portrayed him as "disposed to accept the issues of the war." He was receiving, newspaper coverage suggested, a warm welcome in "military circles" and among "old friends"—most notably Grant, whose endorsement of Longstreet's application was public knowledge. This was folded into a popular narrative that cast soldiers as disposed to bury the hatchet and politicians as the sources of ongoing strife. Thus, a Cleveland paper supplied an anecdote in which a defiant politician claimed that Confederates were "not whipped, though outnumbered," only to draw this rejoinder from Longstreet: "You were not in the army, I believe, and may not be whipped, but I am." The account is revealing, whether or not Longstreet actually spoke these words. Northerners already saw him as a potential ally in reunion.[13]

While visiting the capital, Longstreet began for the first time to opine in public about Southern defeat. He was interviewed by William Swinton for the former war correspondent's forthcoming tome *Campaigns of the Army of the Potomac* and was critical of Lee's offensive tactics at Gettysburg. Though his comments attracted little attention at the time, they were seeds for later conflict. More conspicuously, Longstreet shared with reporters his view that the "rebellion could and would have succeeded had it not been for the incapacity of Jeff Davis, whose intermeddling destroyed all their hopes, and . . . prevented the rebels from taking Washington." Why Longstreet thought this a good moment to make such a pointed comment is unclear, but it seems he was beginning to try to distance himself from Davis, who was a figure of scorn and contempt in Northern eyes.[14]

Longstreet took his initial pardon rejection in stride, relieved that Johnson promptly granted a pardon to Louise. Longstreet's wife was required to apply to the president for amnesty, as her family's wealth landed her among the exempted classes. Her pardon application complained that some of her familial landholdings in the state of Michigan had been confiscated on the grounds that she was a "public enemy"; she defended herself by saying that while she supported her husband during the war, she had not committed "any personal act . . . [of] rebellion or treason against the United States." In her appeal to Johnson, Louise held up James's May 1865 oath of allegiance as proof that the couple were now loyal citizens committed to peace. Grant, for his part, reassured Longstreet that his own pardon would surely come through eventually, and that in the meantime, he could "engage in any business without fear of molestation." Longstreet returned to New Orleans with his family, to get down to business in his brokerage firm, and in his roles as insurance company president and railroad developer.[15]

But there was no avoiding politics, which suffused every aspect of Southern life as "Presidential Reconstruction" took hold. Johnson's rebuffing of Longstreet's pardon bid was an exception to the rule of extreme leniency on the president's part. After some initial tough talk about punishing the rebel leaders, the volatile Johnson soon abandoned his wartime alliance with the Republican Party and reasserted his identity as a Southern Democrat. He proved susceptible to the entreaties of his former foes and granted them pardons gladly, issuing at least 15,000 to individual rebels over the course of his four turbulent years in office; among those he pardoned were the Confederate vice president, Alexander Stephens, and two of Davis's Cabinet members.[16]

Johnson's policies permitted former Confederate leaders to return to power in the South and emboldened them to reassert racial dominance. Johnsonian state governments, through a harsh regime of "Black Codes" and extralegal violence, pushed the freedpeople into a state of subordination as close as possible to slavery. As conditions deteriorated, President Johnson essentially went to war with the Republican Congress, vetoing its efforts to grant freedpeople the basic rights and protections of citizenship. In 1866 Johnson's erratic behavior alienated the Northern electorate, and Republicans secured the power they needed in congressional elections that year to institute their own policies.[17]

These developments at first confounded Longstreet, who struggled to stake out his own position. In December 1865 he was involved in an incident that dramatized what a political tinderbox the Deep South was. According to newspaper reports nationwide, Longstreet, while visiting the Aberdeen, Mississippi, home of his former staff officer, Peyton Manning, was the target of an attack by freedpeople. "Upon the very night of his arrival, the house in which he slept was set on fire," the report ran. "When an alarm was given, it was found that the chain of the well had been broken and all the buckets carried off, so that it was with extreme difficulty that the house was saved from total destruction." Longstreet escaped unscathed, and the local citizens, to "make some amends," gave a public dinner in his honor a few days later. Conservative Southern papers cast this as evidence of the lawlessness and vengefulness of former slaves, while some Northern papers saw it as evidence that Blacks were fighting back against the "incendiarism" of Southern whites. Longstreet did not comment on the incident, but it surely served to remind him that while Grant was willing to absolve him, he was still "rebel No. 3"—a symbol of slavery and the Confederate war—in the eyes of Southern Blacks.[18]

In the ensuing months, Longstreet tested the waters with some public comments on the challenges of Reconstruction. In February 1866 the *Cincinnati Gazette*—a Republican newspaper—printed a section of a private letter of Longstreet's, in which he pledged his loyalty and that of most of his fellow ex-Confederates to the Union. "We are willing and anxious to do anything that is wanted of us, provided we are allowed to get on some constitutional platform," he wrote. By this, Longstreet meant that he wanted political "terms of equality" for the Southern states and was willing to offer "further guarantees" of his goodwill in order to secure them. That June, on a trip to Natchitoches, Louisiana, Longstreet took a more ambivalent posture, giving a speech in which he declared that since both the conservative Johnsonians and the Radical Republicans looked askance at him, he must "be content to remain on the fence." He portrayed himself not as rebel No. 3 but as a "humble citizen, in fact, only a prisoner of war on parole," who must restrain his voice for the time being. That November, Longstreet gave an interview with two Texas reporters in which he urged "moderation, forbearance, and submission" on his fellow Southern whites, so that they would not "be made the objective point of Northern fanaticism." Too much defiance, he warned, would play into the hands of those Radical Republicans who wanted to thoroughly remake the South.[19]

None of these statements tarnished his stellar reputation among former Confederates. Longstreet was widely "loved and venerated" by whites in New Orleans, both as a "famous warrior" and one of the city's "most influential merchants," as the local press put it. Nothing he had said or done in his life had prepared the public for what came next.[20]

III

In March, April, and June 1867 Longstreet published four letters express-ing his support for the newly announced program of congressional Recon-struction. Congress's Reconstruction Acts were a dramatic turning point in the nation's history; they were also a crossroads for Longstreet, who in the spring of 1867 very consciously chose a different path than most former Confederates. Longstreet's letters changed the course of his life forever.

In writing the letters, Longstreet chose not only to weigh in on na-tional policy but also to wade into the turbulent waters of Louisiana's highly factionalized politics. Divisions there dated back to the wartime oc-cupation of New Orleans and the surrounding southeastern parishes by the Federal army in the spring of 1862. The Lincoln administration regarded the state as a promising test case for a policy of amnesty that would draw Southerners back into the Union. Louisiana featured, in New Orleans, the South's largest, wealthiest city. It also had a unique blend of inhabitants: a strong core of prewar white Unionists (former Whigs and pro-tariff sugar planters) and a large, well-educated, French-speaking, mixed-race Afro-Creole freeborn population, centered in New Orleans. In the Louisiana context, *Creole* referred to those with French and French Caribbean roots, descendants of a "French and Spanish colonial culture that tolerated inter-racial relationships," as the historian Michael A. Ross has explained. These *gens de couleur libres* occupied a liminal social tier between enslaved Blacks and white enslavers: they had some of the prerogatives of citizenship, such as the right to make contracts and own property, but they did not possess voting rights or access to public schools. Elite Afro-Creoles "took great pride in the francophone identity they shared with white Creoles" and pride, too, in their "place in the martial lore of Louisiana," as their ancestors had fought against the British in the American Revolution and the War of 1812. Seeking to tap this wellspring of Unionism, the Republican Party fervently battled to establish political control over the state.[21]

During the war, Republicans in Louisiana fought not only against conservative Democrats and Confederates but also against each other, as the state pursued readmission to the Union under Lincoln's 1863 Amnesty Proclamation, which stipulated that once 10 percent of a state's 1860 electorate had taken an oath of loyalty to the Union, the state could set up a new, loyal government. Two Republican factions grappled over the state's future: a moderate group led by Lincoln's right-hand man, General Nathaniel Banks, and by Michael Hahn, Banks's choice for governor; and a radical one led by New Orleans attorney Thomas Durant and New Hampshire–born teacher Benjamin F. Flanders. Both factions were committed to ending slavery and to granting citizenship rights to Blacks, but they differed over how quickly change should come. Hahn's group hoped that a deliberate pace of change and conciliatory language would allow them to win over conservative whites; Flanders and Durant thought conservatives to be irredeemable and spoke in uncompromising terms about the need to extend education, suffrage, and economic opportunity to former slaves. Lincoln publicly favored Hahn, who soundly beat Flanders in the February 1864 gubernatorial election.[22]

A third Republican cadre, the leadership class of New Orleans's *gens de couleur libres*, was the key variable in Republican politics within the state. It included the physician Dr. Louis Charles Roudanez, founder of the bilingual Black newspaper the *New Orleans Tribune*; the artisan-class community leader Oscar Dunn; and Union army veterans Captains James H. Ingraham and P. B. S. Pinchback. Ingraham and Pinchback represented the numerically small but symbolically powerful vanguard of Black commissioned officers in the Union army, the vast majority of whom were drawn from New Orleans's Afro-Creole milieu and served in Louisiana regiments. General Benjamin Butler, the initial commander of Union-occupied Louisiana, initiated an experiment in Black military leadership by commissioning Afro-Creole line officers; this defied the widespread opposition among whites to according command roles to Blacks. Butler's successor in Louisiana, General Banks, was part of that opposition and rolled back Butler's experiment, purging Black officers from the Union army rolls—but not before they had proved their bravery and skill in battles such as the May 1863 Union assault on the Confederate stronghold of Port Hudson, Louisiana, where Ingraham's combat leadership earned him a hero's status.[23]

The approximately 110 African American men who were commissioned at the rank of lieutenant or above in the Union army made their mark, leveraging their collective military experience into political activism. The purged officers of the Louisiana Native Guards formed a political phalanx, leading the charge for Black suffrage and civil rights. In the spring of 1864 they petitioned Lincoln and the Congress to grant voting rights to Black men in Louisiana, insisting that "as slavery is abolished, with it must vanish every vestige of oppression." The president followed up by writing his now-famous March 13, 1864, letter to Louisiana governor Hahn suggesting that Black veterans could perhaps be granted the right to vote. Hahn in turn quietly lobbied for Black suffrage during the 1864 Louisiana constitutional convention, only to find that there was not sufficient support, even among liberals, to pass the measure. Louisiana's new state constitution abolished slavery, without compensation, and opened up schools, militias, and courtrooms to Blacks. But the fact that Blacks remained disfranchised rankled Radical Republicans.[24]

Lincoln's assassination and Andrew Johnson's ascendancy in the spring of 1865 derailed the Ten Percent Plan and changed the course of Louisiana's Reconstruction. The man who succeeded Hahn as governor, former planter James Madison Wells, embraced Johnson's permissive policy of pardon and amnesty, seeking to build a coalition of conservative Unionists and former rebels. The statewide elections of November 1865 brought the Democrats back into power. They promptly instituted racially discriminatory laws that came to be known as Black Codes, intended to deprive freedpeople of basic legal rights, turn back the clock on emancipation, and undermine the status of Creoles of color. The historian Ted Tunnell has written of this period of Johnsonian restoration, "For two long years in Louisiana and the South, rebels vilified, purged, and massacred loyal citizens." When, in July 1866,

Louisiana Republicans tried to reassert power by reconvening the 1864 state constitutional convention to introduce universal suffrage, a white supremacist mob, including the New Orleans police, attacked a peaceful pro-suffrage demonstration, murdering forty-six Blacks. "[T]he New Orleans violence was essentially a continuation of the Civil War," writes the historian Douglas R. Egerton, pointing out that "more than half the whites involved were Confederate veterans, while just less than half of the African Americans had served in the U.S. Army." Shockingly, President Johnson sided with the rioters, blaming the violence on Radical Republicans.[25]

Republicans in the US Congress recoiled at the New Orleans massacre and other such anti-Black violence in the South and pushed through their Reconstruction Acts in the spring of 1867. Their goal: to override Johnson's policies, invalidate his state governments, and create a new body politic, with former slaves as voters. The US military presided over this process, and Louisiana became part of the Fifth Military District (one of the five federal jurisdictions, under War Department control, into which the former Confederate states were divided by Congress); the Fifth District was commanded by General Philip Sheridan. He replaced Wells with Benjamin F. Flanders, as provisional governor, and in the "registration summer" of 1867, a massive campaign of registering loyal voters set the stage for the next phases in Louisiana's Reconstruction: the election of delegates to a new constitutional convention, and their drafting a new state charter. Congress was establishing, in essence, new biracial, Republican governing coalitions for the South.[26]

"A deep gloom spread over the white South" when Congress's program went into effect, the historian George C. Rable has noted. Southern Democrats "insisted that the party condemn the usurpations of Radical Republicans in unequivocal language." Confederate veterans such as Jubal Early, vowing never to be reconstructed, expressed their unremitting bitterness at defeat. In a March 1867 letter to former Confederate secretary of war John C. Breckinridge, Early cast the Republicans in Congress as "infernal demons" and maintained that he would "like to begin the fight over right now.... I think I could scalp a Yankee woman and child without winking my eyes," he hissed, while fulminating against abolitionism and defending the "propriety, advantages, and justice" of slavery.[27]

These developments were the backdrop and context for Longstreet's controversial letters. His new course was charted in March 1867 when a prominent New Orleans Democratic newspaper, the *Times*, solicited the view of the city's leading citizens on the dominant question in Southern politics: Should former rebels comply with Congress's new Reconstruction program, or should they resist it? On March 18, Longstreet wrote to the *New Orleans Times* the following: "There can be no discredit to a conquered people for accepting the conditions offered by their conquerors. Nor is there any occasion for a feeling of humiliation. We have made an honest, and I hope that I may say, a creditable fight, but we have lost. Let us come forward, then, and accept the ends involved in the struggle.... Let us accept the terms, as we are in duty bound to do."[28]

Longstreet developed this theme in a second letter to the *New Orleans Times*, on April 6. Again he spoke of the need to accept defeat, only this time he enumerated what exactly he felt Confederates had staked in the war and lost: "The surrender of the Confederates armies in 1865 involved, 1. The surrender of the claim to the right of secession. 2. The surrender of the former political relations of the negro. 3. *The surrender of the Southern Confederacy.*" The South's duty, as he put it, was to "speed the work of reconstruction and put our people [in a] condition to make their own laws." He acknowledged the prevailing Southern opinion that "we cannot do wrong, and that Northerners cannot do right." But he urged that "each should extend charity if they expect it in return."[29]

Among former Confederates, reactions to Longstreet's initial letters were muted; his sterling military reputation gave him the benefit of the doubt. As the *Richmond Dispatch* put it, military commanders were "presumed to be men of chivalry and honor" and "practical in all cases." Longstreet, it seemed, was simply advising the South to face reality: it no longer had the power to fight and so must "frankly and manfully" conform to the law. Longstreet's letters were interpreted as a plea that Southerners assert themselves in Reconstruction politics in order to "make the best of a bad bargain," as none other than Confederate naval hero Raphael Semmes stated in an op-ed entitled "Longstreet's Epistles." This early press coverage often aligned Longstreet with others, such as Robert E. Lee and P. G. T. Beauregard, each of whom urged Southerners to be law-abiding and to rebuild their political influence within the Union.[30]

Even newspapers that were critical of Longstreet's early letters refrained from writing him off altogether. Pronouncing his first letter to the *Times* a "curiosity," the *Augusta Constitutionalist* stipulated that because of his wartime "deeds of valor," Longstreet deserved a "respectful hearing." The paper then chided him for knowing "little of politics or statesmanship" and went on to declare that the South should not sacrifice its principles by accepting the "degrading" terms of the Reconstruction Acts. Longstreet's letter was "unfortunate," it concluded, and might in time "prove pernicious." The *Memphis Public Ledger* took a similar tack, reminding Longstreet that Congress's plan was "punitive and mandatory," and scolding that his letters filled the minds of his admirers with "regret" (at his having gone public with his unorthodox views).[31]

IV

Regret soon turned to rage. On June 3, 1867, Longstreet wrote a third letter, which appeared in the *New Orleans Times* and was reprinted with extensive commentary across the country. This letter was addressed to a former Union soldier and staunch New Orleans Republican named John M. G. Parker, the brother-in-law of Union general Benjamin Butler. Parker was one of a number of Republicans who made overtures to Longstreet in the spring of 1867, reflecting their sense that he had already begun to distance himself from his fellow Confederates and was receptive to new ideas. Parker invited him to attend a Republican rally in May that was to feature a speech from Massachusetts senator and abolitionist Henry Wilson.

Longstreet accepted the invitation and was hailed at the ensuing rally with acclaim and applause. His June 3 letter began by saying that he was "agreeably surprised to meet such fairness and frankness in a politician [Wilson] whom I have been taught to believe uncompromisingly opposed to the white people of the South." Longstreet again professed to offer a "practical" approach to Reconstruction, with the aim of peace and prosperity. But then he made an altogether arresting rhetorical pivot: "It matters not whether I bear the mantle of Mr. Davis or the mantle of Mr. Sumner, so [long as] I may help to bring the glory of 'peace and good-will toward men.'" This was highly provocative, as the Radical Republican Massachusetts senator Charles Sumner was heartily loathed by Confederates.[32]

The letter would get more provocative still. Longstreet offered the "self-evident" proposition that "the highest of human laws is the law that is established by appeal to arms," and he then deduced that since the "sword has decided in favor of the North," Northern principles had become the law. It was the duty of the defeated South, he insisted, to "abandon ideas that are obsolete." Among the things he classed as obsolete was the Democratic Party itself, which was nothing more, he said, than a vehicle for old "prejudice." Sounding a whole lot like a Republican, Longstreet described Congress's Reconstruction Acts as "peace offerings" that the South should accept as starting points "from which to meet future political issues." Moreover, he addressed directly the issue of race relations, casting Black suffrage in the South as a fait accompli and arguing that the experiment of Black voting should be extended to the North and "fully tested."[33]

On June 7 Longstreet submitted a fourth letter as a coda to his June 3 offering. He reiterated his claim that the "war was made upon Republican issues . . . [and] that the settlement should be made accordingly." The "object of politics," Longstreet observed, "is to relieve the distress of the people and to provide for their future comfort." In his view, Republicans shared his desire for peaceful reunion, while recalcitrant Southern Democrats, determined to wage ideological war on the North and to resist change with violence, did not. Peaceful reunion was only possible, he reckoned, if those white Southerners willing to concede defeat stepped forward to assume some of the burdens of leadership.[34]

Longstreet's June letters ignited a political firestorm. Southern newspapers opposed to Reconstruction dissected them in a spirit of mounting wrath and incredulity. Raphael Semmes, lamenting that Longstreet's letter writing had "become chronic," commented archly, "It is a very difficult thing to know when to speak, and how often to speak." Semmes found Longstreet's characterization of the Reconstruction Acts as a "peace offering" to be ludicrous and chided him with a suitably nautical metaphor: "In accepting the reconstruction acts, we are accepting a hard bargain, driven . . . by a heartless and unrelenting enemy, who would be glad to sink us many fathoms deep in mid ocean, if the thing were possible." Referring to the likes of Charles Sumner, Semmes charged that the Republicans were led by "ranting, raving New England Puritans."[35]

Such views were common among Southern Democrats who were appalled that Longstreet had jumped ship. The *Louisiana Democrat* explicitly targeted the passage in which he had declared that "it matter[ed] not" whether he bore the mantle of Davis or of Sumner. "If it matters not with General Longstreet, it matters a great deal with those who fought under him," the paper objected, adding, in a coup de grâce, "Just imagine General Lee classing the mantle of Sumner with that of Jeff. Davis!" Longstreet was, the *Democrat* charged, no more than a tool of Radical Republicans; he was feeding on "Federal pap" and would be "left to starve by his new allies" as soon as they had taken advantage of his "enviable reputation." No longer, after the June letters, did Democratic papers liken Longstreet's postwar advice to Lee's. Instead, they cast him as "alone in his apostasy," comparing him to Benedict Arnold for his "wanton, wicked desertion of his friends and his country."[36]

Southern papers took particular umbrage at Longstreet's "sword as arbiter" proposition. "According to [the] Radical logic of General Longstreet," the *Charleston Mercury* suggested, "when our Lord was crucified, Christianity should have died. Force had settled that [Christ] was an imposter;

and if General Longstreet had been one of his disciples, he would ... have joined [Christ's] murderers, and have helped them to prosecute his other disciples and to crush his cause." Not content with this insult, the *Mercury* added that Longstreet would have sided with the Inquisition against Galileo. "The man who asserts that force settled truth," it concluded, "is hardly worthy to have either a conscience or a God." Some of his Southern critics expressly cast Longstreet as a race traitor. The *Mobile Daily Tribune* wished Longstreet dead: "It has become a subject of regret that the wound he received at the [Battle of the] Wilderness was not mortal. We would then have been spared the mortification of seeing him in the bum-boat of radicalism, side by side with the enemies of his country and race."[37]

This rhetoric tapped into the dominant Confederate interpretation of Appomattox. At the very moment of surrender, Confederates began laying the building blocks of the Lost Cause ideology: claiming that the North's victory was one of might over right, and that Southerners had fought flawlessly for a still-righteous cause. The Lost Cause take on defeat was designed to preempt social change: by denigrating Northern victory as a mere show of force, Southerners hoped to deny Northerners a political mandate for Reconstruction. Longstreet's letters seemed to his critics to be a wholesale rejection of this Confederate position and a wholesale embrace of the heretical idea that the Union had won a moral as well as military victory in the Civil War.[38]

In reality, Longstreet was not as much of an outlier as his critics made him out to be. There were other Southern whites willing to affiliate with the Republicans. Most, such as Louisiana Republican leaders Michael Hahn, Benjamin F. Flanders, and James Madison Wells, belonged to the beleaguered but tenacious white minority that had remained loyal to the Union during the war. Some of Louisiana's white Republicans, by contrast, claimed to have been reluctant rebels who fought for the Confederacy under pressure and without enthusiasm. Others still, such as the lawyer George W. Carter, a former Confederate cavalry commander, had been eager Confederates, and, like Longstreet, converted to Unionism and Republicanism only after the South's defeat. Whatever their wartime loyalties, most white Southern Republicans saw the party as the means to the end of peace and prosperity. Relatively few made an abiding commitment to racial justice and equality.[39]

From the start, opponents of Reconstruction nonetheless vilified these so-called scalawags as traitors, for the willingness of white Republicans to form a governing coalition with Black voters and with Northern "carpet-bagger" transplants to the South threatened the racial caste system and the Democratic Party's traditional grip on Southern politics. In a relent-less divide-and-conquer campaign, conservatives used propaganda, fraud, and violence to try to draw Southern whites away from the Republican coalition and into the Democratic fold. Demonizing Longstreet was an essential element of that project, as he was the most prominent former Confederate to join the Republican ranks and was setting a potentially dangerous example.[40]

The anti-Longstreet ire of conservative Southerners was stoked by Northern enthusiasm for the rebel general's letters. Republican newspa-pers lavished praise on Longstreet and held him up as a bellwether. The *New York Times* saw Longstreet's missives as proof that Southerners would respond positively to a "tolerant and practical" defense of Reconstruc-tion. The *San Francisco Daily Evening Bulletin* went even further, seeing in Longstreet's letters evidence that a "revolution in opinion has begun in the late slave states," and that the Reconstruction Acts had "opened the way for national ideas" and for the organization of the Republican Party in the South. Naturally, Northern Republicans relished Longstreet's critique of the Democratic Party. As the Philadelphia *North American and United States Gazette* put it, the war had weakened the Democrats in the South as well as in the North, so much that "as a national party and political power, they [were] irretrievably lost." Longstreet's letters were hailed by Republicans because they represented a best-case scenario: that some of the old rebel elite would see the light and exert benign influence. Again and again Northern coverage played up Longstreet's exalted military stature to amplify his potential political influence. Precisely because Longstreet displayed such "firmness and devotion to the South," the *Milwaukee Daily Sentinel* urged, the Southern people could "safely follow [his] lead and guidance" during Reconstruction.[41]

Perhaps the most revealing endorsement by a Northerner came from Benjamin Butler. The Union general reached out privately to Longstreet in a June 19, 1867, letter expressing his "high appreciation" for Longstreet's brave stance. Writing in reply, Longstreet thanked Butler for his "magnanimity," seeing him as representative of "the great minds of the north." "I sincerely hope and believe that we shall meet the wishes of Congress in due time and present ourselves in acceptable form for admission into the Union," Longstreet attested, closing his missive, "I am sir with great respect, Your Most Obt Servt." This exchange was altogether remarkable, given that Butler was one of the most loathed Yankees in the entire South, notorious in Confederate eyes for his stern wartime administration of Union-occupied New Orleans and for his ardent support for Black enlistment; Jefferson Davis had designated Butler, known to white Southerners as the "Beast," as "an outlaw and common enemy of mankind." Butler had undergone his own political transformation from prewar Democrat to postwar Radical Republican and had recently been elected to the US Congress, representing Massachusetts. Butler and Longstreet clearly saw each other as fellow political mavericks, willing to weather the storm of public vilification.[42]

Crucially, debates over Longstreet's stand broke down over partisan, not sectional, lines: Northern and Southern Republicans who backed Reconstruction defended Longstreet, and Northern and Southern Democrats opposed to Reconstruction derided him. The small cadre of Republican newspapers taking root in the South joined the Northern chorus of praise for Longstreet. The *New Orleans Republican*, for example, used a military metaphor to argue that his letters had exposed the "masked batteries" of unrepentant rebels: "General Longstreet's battery shelled the woods where these people were lying in ambush: he drew their fire and enabled us to see just what is their position. And it is simply this—what they failed to accomplish by war they now seek to accomplish by political stratagem." Some Southern Unionist papers were every bit as breathless as their Northern counterparts in characterizing Longstreet's conversion as a hopeful sign. The *Union Flag* of Jonesborough, Tennessee, declared, "We look upon this change in his political course as a bright promise of a corresponding change in the sentiment and feelings of the entire Southern people."[43]

Just as Longstreet had some Southern supporters, he had critics in the North, and they offered some of the most overblown invective hurled at the general. Conservative Northern Democrats, who had opposed emancipation and now opposed Black citizenship and voting, joined with Confederates in condemning him. The *New Hampshire Patriot and Gazette*, for instance, cast Longstreet as a dupe who debased himself in order to receive "absolution from the hands of the radicals." "He eats dirt with a hearty relish. It evidently agrees with him—seems to be his natural diet," the paper sneered. "Did the gallant rebel ever hear of the spider's invitation to the fly?" No Northern paper came close in its anti-Longstreet vitriol to the *Old Guard*, the New York Copperhead monthly journal edited by the acerbic Charles Chauncey Burr. A dogged defender of slavery, Burr quoted with glee the Mobile editor who had wished that Longstreet had died in the Wilderness, and offered his own indictment of Longstreet for siding with the "Mongrel" Congress and the "enemies of the Caucasian race." Dismissing Longstreet's professed desire for peace, and insisting that all white men must oppose Reconstruction to their final breath, Burr seethed, "In the grave there is peace and honor; but in the blended society of white men and negroes, there is eternal unrest and dishonor." Longstreet, Burr concluded, had "miserably tarnished a once bright and honored name."[44]

V

All of this turmoil raises the question: How can we explain Longstreet's actions in the spring and summer of 1867? His modern biographers Jeffry

Wert and William Garrett Piston have argued that Longstreet, politically inept and misunderstood, was in over his head. In his four controversial letters, he did not mean to repudiate his Confederate identity or his commitment to white rule in the South. But, hampered by political naïvete, he did an ineffectual job of explaining to his fellow Southern whites what his true intentions were: namely, to preserve as much as possible of the old order and to reestablish the white South's power in regional and national politics. This scholarly interpretation has some merit: Longstreet did believe that elite whites should govern the postwar South. As he put it in a July 1867 private letter to Confederate veteran R. H. Taliaferro, joining the Republican Party was the best way for Southern whites to "influence" the Black vote: "We should do the work [of politics] ourselves, & have it white instead of black & have our best men in public office." Revealingly, the *New Orleans Tribune*, which represented the city's free Black population, argued in 1867 that Longstreet was not to be trusted as a true ally and real Republican: he cynically hoped (so the *Tribune* suspected) that the experiment of Black suffrage would fail so that both North and South would reject it forever. "[Longstreet] is the man who looks for the best mode of disfranchising the colored people . . . a leader who would look forward to the taking back of our rights," the paper editorialized. If Longstreet had communicated his true intentions to his fellow Southern whites more clearly, Piston and others suggest, perhaps he would not have been branded a traitor.[45]

But the image of Longstreet as inept and misunderstood does not fully capture his political views or their evolution. Longstreet was emerging as an iconoclastic and dogged critic of his own society, motivated by three primary factors: a sense of duty to his "people" (his family and region); a set of pragmatic calculations about which political leaders to trust; and his exposure to the unique political milieu in New Orleans.

Reflecting the first of these factors—a sense of duty—Longstreet's published letters on Reconstruction blended the personal and the political. The April 6 letter contains a passage deeply revealing of Longstreet's mindset:

The soldier prefers to have the sod that receives him when he falls cover his remains. The political questions of the war should have been buried upon the fields that marked their end. Our most cherished objects of this earth, blood of our blood, life of our life, if not duly deposited as ordained by an All-wise Providence, become offensive. So it must be with this dead matter. If the last funeral rites of the Southern Confederacy have not been performed, let us, with due solemnity, proceed to the discharge of that painful duty, and let us deposit in the same grave the agony of our grief, that we may the better prepare ourselves for a return to the duties of this life.[46]

Longstreet was channeling a very intimate agony: the crushing blow he had endured in the winter of 1862, with the deaths of his three young children. (Of the ten children born to him and his wife, only five would live to adulthood.) His reference in the April 6 letter to "our most cherished objects of this earth, blood of our blood, life of our life" is a window into his lasting trauma and how he soldiered on and discharged his duty: by burying the dead and the past. "I think now that war is a great folly," Longstreet wrote to the former Confederate general John G. Walker in May 1866, reflecting on the "gloomy" state of the postwar South and the need to "stay at home" and do everything possible to "reconcile matters."[47]

Longstreet saw his stance on Reconstruction as an extension of his Southern identity, not a repudiation of it. He believed he owed the Southern people (whom he defined, in the spring of 1867, as his fellow whites) counsel "in their hour of need." As he wrote his sister Sarah in June 1867, he had prayed to God for guidance, to help him "devise honorable means by which our people might be saved from the extremity of distress." The war had illustrated the power of the North's free-labor society; only an acceptance of defeat and of change—including the North's aid—could bring the South peace and prosperity. Longstreet yearned, in short, to pivot toward a serene, secure future for his family and his former comrades in arms.[48]

Longstreet was keenly aware that he was risking his personal reputation, but he believed the risk worth taking in order to banish forever the specter of civil war. Before releasing the June 3 letter, Longstreet ran it by his surrogate father, Augustus Baldwin Longstreet. The old man found the draft "certainly too direct for the time," warning, "It will ruin you, son, if you publish it." Longstreet, undeterred, sought the approval of a second mentor, writing an imploring missive to Robert E. Lee on June 8 in which he confided both the personal and political impetus of his support for Reconstruction. "I am established and must live in the U.S., and my children must inherit the good or evil of the condition of the country," Longstreet wrote. The war had unleashed a "revolution," the hatreds and excesses of which would have to be "excised or palliated." Otherwise "anarchy" would be the result, for "such is the nature and history of revolutions," he warned. He told Lee, "Your opinion in support of my views will satisfy the people, and we shall have the states back and our best people in position in six months more." One side or the other must make concessions, he continued, and that fell on the conquered rather than the conquerors. But Lee was having none of it. He replied to Longstreet: "I cannot think the course pursued by the dominant political party the best for the interests of the country, and therefore I cannot say so, or give them any approval."[49]

Even as his uncle and former commander rebuffed him, Longstreet's wife seems to have embraced his new politics. While Louise largely kept a low profile, the extant press coverage of her suggests that she "did not long hold out," as an 1869 article put it, against Longstreet's efforts to "reconstruct his own household." The only remnant of political commentary that remains from Louise comes courtesy of the remarkable African American author and activist Elizabeth Keckley. Written from her vantage point as seamstress and confidante to Mary Todd Lincoln, Keckley's 1868 memoir, *Behind the Scenes. Or, Thirty Years a Slave, and Four Years in the White House*, provided readers with an insider's view of the Lincoln household. Louise and Elizabeth knew each other from before the war: Louise Longstreet was the cousin of Ann Garland, the mistress from whom Keckley had purchased her freedom in St. Louis in 1855. The women's paths crossed again in the fall of 1865, as Louise called on Keckley at her apartment in Washington during one of James's visits to push for pardon. As Keckley reflected on the vast changes the war had brought, Louise responded, "Well, we must take a philosophical view of life. After fighting so long against the Yankees . . . we propose to live in peace with the United States again."[50]

Blended in with this "philosophical view" was the hope, which both James and Louise had expressed in their pardon applications, that the restoration of the family's citizenship rights might ease their way economically and make it possible for them to achieve financial security in the restored Union. But that, too, was a gamble: the backlash against Longstreet's political conversion initially hurt him economically, as he felt it necessary to withdraw from his cotton brokerage as well as a second venture in an insurance firm, lest the controversy damage his business partners.[51]

While a sense of duty to "his people" was a powerful motivator, at the heart of Longstreet's political conversion was his admiration for Ulysses S. Grant. From 1867 on, Grant was Longstreet's political polestar. The lenient terms at Appomattox had reflected the victorious general's moral courage, in Longstreet's view, and had required of the defeated Confederates that they display moral courage, too: the courage to change their convictions, and to accept the death of slavery and of the Confederacy. Rewarding this reading of the terms, Grant provided Longstreet the very approval that Lee withheld. "I have seen with great interest your two letters on the duties of the South in the present circumstances," Grant wrote Longstreet on April 16, 1867. "These ideas freely expressed by one who occupies a position like yours have to exercise a beneficial influence." Grant continued to advocate amnesty and pardon for Longstreet, writing Radical Republican congressman Thaddeus Stevens of Pennsylvania in April 1868 that the political disabilities imposed on rebel leaders by the Reconstruction Acts and the Fourteenth Amendment (such as barring them from government employment) should be removed in Longstreet's case. The course he had pursued since the rebellion, as well as his "high character," entitled him to the "confidence of all good citizens," Grant urged. Grant's support helped Longstreet secure such congressional amnesty, removing his disabilities, in June 1868—Longstreet was now cleared to hold state or federal office.[52]

Grant represented, for Longstreet, the alternative to the reckless divisiveness of Andrew Johnson. Johnson was the very antithesis of Grant: a vain and volatile politician who possessed none of the discipline, composure, honor, and courage of the war hero. Johnson's comportment in office—his bitter defiance of the Republican Congress, truckling to the old Southern Democratic element, and sputtering, inebriated rhetoric—was reviving rather than dispelling the old hatreds of the war. Seeing Grant's Appomattox terms as an extension of Lincoln's own desire for the swift reintegration of the South into the Union, Longstreet lamented Lincoln's passing and saw Johnson as an unworthy heir—a view shared by the Republican-controlled Congress, which tried in vain to remove Johnson from office through the impeachment process.

Longstreet also folded his disgust at Johnson into his wartime critique of politicians as a class. Like Jefferson Davis, Johnson was, in Longstreet's eyes, a self-aggrandizing figure at cross-purposes with honorable men in the ranks who yearned for peace. Grant and his magnanimity represented the prospect that "the South, purified from the blight of human slavery . . . would grow, and flourish," as Longstreet put it in an interview with a Northern reporter. "The dallying policy of Andrew Johnson," by contrast, "fed the spirit of the South with false hope of recovering the supremacy they had lost." Longstreet bemoaned the "infernal tyranny of politicians, who will hold on as long as a breath of popularity remains to the most fossilized or exploded political theories."[53]

Increasingly disgusted by Johnson's incompetence, Grant himself had come to see congressional Reconstruction and Black voting as the means to safeguard the Union's victory at Appomattox. With his embrace of the congressional program, Grant moved to center stage as the man designated to unseat Johnson. Chosen as the Republican Party nominee in 1868, Grant campaigned as the candidate who stood for "*both* sectional harmony *and* the guarantee of the freedpeople's newly gained political and economic freedoms," as the historian Joan Waugh has put it. Longstreet publicly endorsed Grant during the presidential race of 1868, describing him as "my man," adding, "I believe he is a fair man" who would bring a "complete and prosperous restoration of the Union." This endorsement further alienated Longstreet politically from Lee, who saw Grant's election in 1868 as a tragic and humiliating setback for the South. And it drew Longstreet closer to a new set of allies in New Orleans.[54]

Longstreet's commitment to Reconstruction was conditioned, to no small extent, by the singular political environment of New Orleans itself. The city, with its cosmopolitan culture, entrepreneurial energy, and demographic diversity, seemed fertile soil for political transformations to take root—should the federal government and Union army provide the necessary support and protection. As the historian Caryn Cossé Bell has noted, the Afro-Creole intelligentsia's undaunted "activism and republican idealism" meant that Louisiana would draft "one of the Reconstruction South's most advanced blueprints for change." That intelligentsia, with its cadre of former Union officers, was uniquely positioned to challenge Longstreet's views on race and to reform them. Longstreet's June letters appeared at the very moment Republicans were registering and mobilizing Southern Blacks to vote, for the first time ever, for delegates to the constitutional conventions that would dismantle the old racial caste system. In Louisiana, Union general Phil Sheridan registered 83,000 Blacks and 45,000 whites (temporarily disfranchising some recalcitrant rebels) in the summer of 1867. This electorate chose a nearly equal number of Black and white delegates to the fall 1867 constitutional convention; the delegates included Black Union veterans such as Pinchback and Ingraham. The convention produced, in early 1868, a bold new state constitution that proclaimed the equality of all men, required the state to establish integrated schools, and prohibited segregation in public transportation and some public spaces.[55]

In April 1868 the former Union army officer Henry Clay Warmoth was elected governor, soundly defeating a conservative challenger, James G. Taliaferro. A Midwesterner who decided to settle in New Orleans after being posted there during the war, Warmoth affiliated with the fledgling state Republican Party and rose quickly through its ranks. Only twenty-six years of age at the time of his nomination for the highest state office, Warmoth was a political prodigy: magnetic, unabashedly ambitious—and overconfident. Sharing Warmoth's ticket, as candidate for lieutenant governor, was the formerly enslaved artisan Oscar J. Dunn. Although not part of the francophone class of prewar free Blacks, Dunn made a name for himself after the war as a champion of Black suffrage and workingmen's rights. Dunn's sober civic-mindedness was a counterpoint to Warmoth's prickly self-regard and opportunism.

A third key figure, State Senator P. B. S. Pinchback, had an equally unlikely rise to power. He was born in Macon, Georgia, in 1837, the son of a white Mississippi plantation owner and formerly enslaved mother. After moving to Ohio with his brother, Pinchback plied his trade as a steamboat steward on the Mississippi River. Making his way to New Orleans, he served during the war as an officer and recruiter in a Native Guards regiment. Charismatic and irrepressible, Pinchback rose through the party ranks rapidly thereafter as a delegate to the 1868 constitutional convention, an influential legislator, and, later, the editor-publisher of the Black newspaper the *Weekly Louisianian*.[56]

Casting aside some initial skepticism, leading Republicans in New Orleans, such as Warmoth and Pinchback, accepted Longstreet into their ranks and tendered him respect and acclaim. Their endorsement reflected the fact that Longstreet was proving himself willing to challenge Southern orthodoxies on slavery and race. He was not yet a Radical Republican— Longstreet remained committed to white domination of Southern society and was drawn primarily to Grant's message of sectional harmony. But a crucial dynamic was emerging that would shape Longstreet's political evolution: the more his white Southern critics treated him as an apostate on the issue of race, the more receptive he became to Republican ideology. The fierceness of the backlash against him confirmed his view that Southern Democrats did not desire peace.

The reactions to an August 1868 Longstreet interview with the *New York Tribune* illustrate this dynamic. In this interview, Longstreet both praised Grant and mused about race relations in the South. The reporter asked him about whether freed Blacks would be a reliable and productive laboring class in the South. Longstreet said they would; that he had found them, in his own experience, to be compliant. The reporter then asked whether Black men should serve on juries. Longstreet began by saying that perhaps they could, but not in all instances. He then claimed that Blacks were "generally . . . ignorant upon intricate matters of business" and therefore not suitable as to constitute juries in cases involving complex business accounts. He went on to propose what he took to be a compromise position: "[I]f a district is disposed to do right with them, the jury may be divided—white and black. They (the negroes) soon learn, and appreciate the position."[57]

The next question posed was "about negro supremacy." Longstreet replied, "Ah, that can never be; it is silly to think of it. . . . The whites of the South know it, but they are misled by the politicians." Clearly, Longstreet was disavowing radicalism. But he was also pointedly rejecting a major tenet of Lost Cause politics. President Johnson and the Southern Democrats repeatedly argued that any Black political participation would lead inexorably to "Black rule" or "negro supremacy": they cast race relations as a zero-sum game in which any gains for Blacks would result in losses and, indeed, abject subjugation for whites. Longstreet flatly repudiated this form of racist propaganda. He was coming to believe that a limited kind of biracial politics was possible—that Blacks could be constituents in the South and even exercise some authority and leadership, in alliance with and deference to the right whites.[58]

Such a view was at odds with the reactionary politics of Longstreet's uncle Augustus, who refrained from publicly criticizing James by name but did take aim at Republican policies and at Grant. Unreconstructed and unrepentant, Augustus continued—until his death in the summer of 1870—to defend slavery, states' rights, and the Lost Cause. In a pair of frothing essays, published in 1869–70 by the Charleston journal the *XIX Century*, Augustus characterized the Union war and Grant's generalship as forms of fratricidal "barbarism." Not stopping there, he railed against Northerners for making "slaves freemen and freemen slaves" and putting the "bright Caucasian under the stupid African," and defended Calhounian states' rights doctrine and Calhoun himself as a moral paragon. Augustus, in short, trafficked in zero-sum-game thinking and sounded alarms about supposed Black rule.[59]

The unreconstructed rebels in the South assailed James for racial radicalism and for endorsing Grant. The *Mobile Daily Tribune*, for example, described Longstreet in September 1868 as "in full communion with the Radicals" and scorned the idea that one could simultaneously be a loyal Confederate and a Republican. "A man should be one thing or the other," the paper pronounced. Longstreet fired back, insisting in a published November 1868 letter to a relative in Georgia that his critics had "lost sight of . . . the interest of the people" in "their zeal to maintain their ideas of consistency . . . adhering to old truths whether they work for weal or woe."[60]

At the Democratic National Convention in New York in July, the party jettisoned the politically wounded Johnson in favor of that state's governor, Horatio Seymour. Ulysses Grant won the presidency in November 1868 with an electoral vote margin of 214 to 80; the ballots cast by newly enfranchised Southern Blacks helped to provide Grant's edge in the popular vote, 52.7 percent to 47.3 percent.

The Republican press further cultivated Longstreet's loyalty by praising the "brave and noble stand" he took in Grant's presidential campaign. "Grant is said to be very friendly to him and will show his friendship next March in some unmistakable manner," the *New Orleans Republican* predicted. The editors of the venerable Black newspaper the *New Orleans Tribune* wrote of Longstreet in February 1869, "Il se fit l'apotre des idees de tolerance et de progres, sans se preoccuper des clameurs qu'il pouvait soulever autour de lui"—that he was an apostle of progress despite the controversy that swirled around him. The paper urged others to follow his "wise example." In contrast with the "extreme harshness," as Longstreet put it, of his Confederate critics, the Republicans seemed willing to let him finesse the issue of loyalty. They commended Longstreet's military prowess and his political courage, reckoning that the more prominent he had been as a soldier, the more significant he could be as a symbol of repentance.[61]

Longstreet took another step as a politico when he visited Washington in December 1868 and was introduced by William Pitt Kellogg, Louisiana's new Republican senator, to his fellow legislators. Knowing of Grant's "pronounced partiality" for Longstreet, the senators "greeted him with pride," as the *New Orleans Advocate* reported. The stage was set for Longstreet to join the ranks of officeholders.[62]

VI

The Republican coalition's leadership ranks in Louisiana were impressive. But could these men govern, and enforce the new constitution, in a state where so many parishes (those that had not been occupied by the Union during the war) were firmly in the hands of ex-Confederate white supremacists? Even New Orleans had a large white majority. White conservatives mounted a swift backlash against the emerging new order through an extensive network of secret paramilitary political organizations, such as Louisiana's Knights of the White Camellia. These groups, awash in a culture of paranoia and hatred, believed that "the need to restore white rule justified every means, every sadistic impulse, every enormity," as Ted Tunnell has explained. They mobilized in the presidential campaign season of 1868 to perpetrate violence that would intimidate, suppress, and punish Republican voters, so as to help deliver the Democrat Seymour to the White House. Though a Northerner, Seymour ran an aggressively racist national campaign, promising to secure white supremacy and painting Grant as a radical. White supremacist terrorists committed over a thousand political murders in Louisiana in 1868, enabling Seymour to defeat Grant in the state, and undercutting the Republicans' claim that Grant's overall victory in the election constituted a mandate for congressional Reconstruction.[63]

The stakes were thus dauntingly high when, on March 11, 1869, just one week into his presidency, Grant appointed Longstreet to the plum patronage position of surveyor of customs for New Orleans. In this era, before civil service reform, presidents selected the main officers for Custom Houses in the major ports of entry in the United States. These officials—collectors, surveyors, appraisers—collected federal customs duties on imported goods; in the era before the income tax, customs duties were a major source of federal revenue. Customhouse positions, like postmasterships, were major sinecures of the partisan spoils system and much sought after. Grant's nomination of Longstreet received extensive press coverage, as a wide range of stakeholders debated whether this was an act of nepotism (given that Longstreet was distant kin to Grant's wife, Julia), an olive branch to the South (heralding conciliatory treatment to ex-Confederates), or a recognition of Longstreet's own moral courage in defying the South's unreconstructed rebels.[64]

His supporters portrayed Longstreet in a wide range of ways. Moderates and conservatives in the Republican Party cast Longstreet's nomination as a rebuke by Grant of the Radical wing of the party: Longstreet represented reunion and "the cause of nationality" rather than the prospect of "terrible vengeance," the *Boston Daily Advertiser* editorialized. Some Republican papers offered only qualified support: they commended Longstreet, but saw him as singular and did not want ex-Confederates, as a matter of policy, favored over more deserving white and Black Southern Unionists. The Democratic press, for its part, used the nomination as an occasion to flay Republicans for hypocrisy, claiming that if an ex-Confederate Democrat was seeking a patronage post, the Republicans would have howled in protest.[65]

After a flurry of initial coverage, the appointment seemed to founder, as the US Senate was slow to weigh in. A concerned Longstreet wrote Grant on March 31, 1869, volunteering to take on a different post, perhaps as a commissioner adjudicating issues between the United States and Mexico. He surmised that "most of the Senators who cause delay, in my case, desire that I should be assigned a national position, so as to avoid the great influence that I might have in a particular locality." The ensuing contentious meetings in executive session of the Senate revealed deep opposition to Longstreet, led by fervent Tennessee Unionist William G. "Parson" Brownlow, who objected that he was "in favor of rewarding those who had stood by the flag in the hour of peril, and not those who had endeavored by every means in their power to wipe it out of existence." Brownlow was countered by Louisiana senator Kellogg, who boasted that Longstreet's "character and standing" in the South gave him more influence in securing Reconstruction "than all the laws of Congress."[66]

On April 3, 1869, the Senate confirmed the appointment by a vote of 25 to 10, only one more than a quorum. The fact that a majority of Southern senators ultimately favored Longstreet demonstrates that he still symbolized, for many, the hopes for Southern restoration and sectional reconciliation. This vote, however, did not quiet the debate over the New Orleans surveyorship, but instead led to another round of analysis over whether Longstreet's confirmation was justified and what it betokened. His advocates seized on a report that circulated in the press in April, claiming that Longstreet had, in the spring of 1867, entered a pact of sorts with some other former Confederate officers to publicly "accept the situation," but that the others had then "slunk from our loved General and left him alone to bear the brunt of the reproach"; here was proof of Longstreet's moral courage and of Confederate perfidy. In a bold show of magnanimity, the *Christian Recorder*, the Philadelphia-based organ of the African Methodist Episcopal Church, commented, "Of our white fellow-citizens, we ask not the question 'What *were* you? Union or rebel?' We simply ask, 'What *are* you? Are you for Union? For liberty?'" Since Longstreet had answered the last two questions in the affirmative, he received the paper's "hearty congratulations." Some newspapers noted approvingly that Longstreet's appointment to federal office coincided with that of another Southern maverick: the Union spy Elizabeth Van Lew of Virginia, whom Grant chose, illustrating his "personal good judgment," to be postmaster of the city of Richmond.[67]

From the start, the fate of Longstreet's nomination was linked not only to those of white Southern Republicans such as Van Lew but also to the nominations of Black Republican office seekers from Louisiana. For example, as Louisiana's senators pushed Longstreet, Congressman and former general Benjamin Butler successfully promoted Blanc F. Joubert for the position of New Orleans assessor of internal revenue. He was a propertied freeman of color, a grocer by trade, who had spent much of the war living in Paris, France. According to the press, Joubert sought to "test whether his race were to have equal rights under the new administration." Southern Democrats saw Van Lew, Longstreet, and Joubert alike as the vanguard of a stampede of Radical Republican office seekers who would corrupt Southern politics. It was one thing for Longstreet to express his heretical opinions; it was a far greater offense for him to accept the enemy's patronage and let himself be bribed into submission by the lure of office. In accepting the surveyorship, Longstreet had, in the eyes of recalcitrant rebels, consummated his treason.[68]

While Longstreet's critics would repeatedly charge that he converted to Republicanism for financial gain, the economic implications of his conversion were far more complicated than that. An extended controversy over debts he owed to the Virginia Military Institute (V.M.I.) is instructive. In February of 1865, in the Civil War's final months, Longstreet sent his eldest son, Garland, to V.M.I., a prestigious Southern academy in Lexington, Virginia. The fall of Richmond and Confederate surrender interrupted Garland's studies, but the young cadet resumed his training in February 1866, and graduated in July 1869. Bizarrely, nearly three years after Garland's graduation, the state of Virginia brought a lawsuit in Louisiana's Seventh District Court against James Longstreet, for his failure and refusal to remunerate V.M.I. for an overdue tuition bill, covering years of expenses for Garland's room, board, food, clothing, instruction, and related costs.[69]

The court considered as evidence extensive correspondence between V.M.I.'s superintendent, Francis H. Smith, and James and Louise, charting the deterioration of a once-cordial relationship. Garland's education had begun, back in 1865, promisingly enough—Superintendent Smith had showered James with praise, as a great hero of the war, and "esteemed[ed] it a privilege" to care for Garland (calling him an "unusually fine youth"). Longstreet, for his part, had made regular payments to V.M.I., drawing on the comfortable earnings of his cotton brokerage partnership with William Owen and his insurance company, which netted him roughly $10,000 a year. But in early 1868, after Longstreet's embrace of Reconstruction, signs of trouble appeared. Smith wrote to Louise and James that Garland's academic performance had fallen off precipitously and that the young man was accumulating demerits, and making excuses: Garland claimed that he was being politically persecuted—that some professors were "visiting upon him their feelings for the course his father had taken." Meanwhile, Smith ratcheted up the pressure on James Longstreet to pay the debts he owed the school, and Longstreet demurred, begging that he was in financial straits—he had closed out his cotton brokerage and insurance enterprises after his political conversion, and was struggling to get by, "seeking some employment that may enable me to live." Even after he landed the federal surveyor position in 1869, with its salary of $2,500 per year, Longstreet still claimed that he had insufficient funds to pay the "extravagant" sum of more than $1,200 that V.M.I. was unfairly charging. The relations between Longstreet and Smith devolved further, with V.M.I. reaching out to the prominent New Orleans lawyer T. J. Semmes—a staunch Democrat and confidant of Jefferson Davis—to force Longstreet, in court, to pay up. In short, Longstreet could not and did not simply cash in on federal patronage: he took an economic hit when he became a Republican in 1867 and felt the financial ripple effects of the attendant political backlash for years to come.[70]

VII

As it turned out, white and Black Republican officeholders would not only work side by side in the New Orleans Custom House, where Longstreet, Joubert, and other political appointees were based, but they would make common cause. As Longstreet took office, factional lines within the state Republican Party were sharpening. Governor Warmoth, although he garnered support from Radicals early on through his support of universal suffrage, was a "political pragmatist, not an ideologue," explains the historian Justin Nystrom. Warmoth sought to build a centrist coalition by appealing to the "substantial mass of black and white voters who yearned for stability as they went about reconstructing their private lives." To that end, he began to court some moderate Democrats through patronage, showing a willingness to appoint them to important posts. He hoped his message of economic modernization and infrastructure improvement would appeal to some of the white commercial elite.[71]

Warmoth's most notable innovation was the creation in July 1868 of the biracial Metropolitan Police Force as the primary law enforcement agency in Orleans, Jefferson, and St. Bernard Parishes, to replace the existing all-white police force and dislodge its most recalcitrant Democratic Party and Confederate elements. The advent of the Metropolitans was part of a broad national movement toward modernizing police forces by screening, training, arming, and better compensating them, and also a reflection of local imperatives: Warmoth wanted to create a security branch at his own disposal to protect the state government. The Metropolitans' racial composition, with 243 white and 130 Black policemen in 1868, mirrored the city's own social composition: 62 percent white and 38 percent Black. Working-class white men, including many Irish immigrants, made up the bulk of the new force, while Blacks who joined came overwhelmingly from the mixed-race francophone Creole community; their inclusion was in part a response to lobbying efforts from activists such as Louis Charles

Roudanez of the *New Orleans Tribune*, who had demanded Black representation in law enforcement.

In 1870 Warmoth installed Algernon S. Badger, a Union veteran from Massachusetts, as the commanding superintendent of the force. Like Warmoth, Badger had enjoyed a position of authority at a young age, as the twenty-four-year-old commander of a loyalist regiment of white Southern Unionists, the First Louisiana Cavalry, during the war. After leading his men with distinction, he settled in New Orleans, seeing it as a land of economic and political opportunity. Badger threw himself into his new role as police superintendent, working tirelessly to professionalize the force.[72]

Even as Warmoth took a stand against entrenched interests by reconceiving the police, he held the line against radical change by opposing the efforts of some legislators to pass and enforce laws fully desegregating public accommodations. In 1868, much to the disappointment of Radicals, Warmoth vetoed "Isabelle's bill" (sponsored by an African American veteran and legislator named Robert H. Isabelle), which would have made it a criminal offense to deny Blacks access to public transportation and to "licensed places of business, or of public resort," such as restaurants and theaters. This stance suggested that Warmoth might prove to be a "little Andy Johnson," warned the *New Orleans Tribune*. The fraught issues of social and political equality would confound the governor's effort to tilt toward the center and alienate him from key allies—including his own lieutenant governor, Oscar Dunn.[73]

James Longstreet, early in his tenure as New Orleans Custom House surveyor, seemed committed to Warmoth's attempted fusion of moderate Republicans and Democrats. Longstreet was widely quoted for commending the state of Virginia's own moderate Republican coalition, which came to power in 1869 pledging "universal suffrage and universal amnesty." Longstreet believed Virginians were "adopting the very class of ideas and very line of action" he had proposed two years earlier in his tendentious letters of 1867.[74]

But Longstreet soon courted controversy. The first signs that he intended to challenge the status quo came in the summer of 1869 when—as newspapers around the nation reported—he nominated Black men for positions in the surveyor's office. By the end of August, the press was marveling that "Longstreet has employed fifteen negroes in the New Orleans customhouse." It was no foregone conclusion that white Southern Republicans would favor the integration of civic institutions such as the police force or Custom Houses. In Mobile, Alabama, for instance, the Republican Custom House collector, William Miller, initially appointed only white employees, reckoning that the "key to (white) social respectability for federal officials was in distancing themselves from blacks and their demands." It was not until 1871, when Miller was replaced by a collector receptive to the demands of Black constituents, that the federal service in Mobile was integrated. Such employment in federal patronage positions was a "tangible civil rights victory," the historian Michael W. Fitzgerald has observed. Longstreet's bold move to employ Blacks in his office generally won praise from Republican papers and prompted some wonderment in the North: "Has any Northern surveyor acted in the same just and liberal manner?" the *Burlington Free Press* of Vermont asked leadingly.[75]

Supporters of integration were well aware that a federal post could be an economic stepping-stone. Among those Longstreet hired, as a messenger earning a salary of $660 a year, was James B. Combs, who, decades later, would tell his story to a W.P.A. (New Deal) interviewer gathering the narratives of ex-slaves in the 1930s. Combs, who was born in Georgia and moved to New Orleans after the war, would go on to attend Straight University in New Orleans and embark on a long and distinguished career as a schoolteacher and principal in Mississippi.[76]

Southern Democrats fumed at these appointments. Some accused Longstreet of using his Black employees as pawns: of cynically hiring them in order to have scapegoats ready "when the defalcation comes," as one Alabama paper put it, predicting that Longstreet's tenure in office would prove corrupt. Other commentators warned of something they regarded as even more pernicious than corruption: the specter of social equality between the races. Under the heading "Political Chit-Chat," a Democratic paper in West Virginia reported in the fall of 1869, "General Longstreet and the nigs are having a mutual admiration society at New Orleans." The Democratic press in Louisiana confirmed worriedly that Longstreet was not only "appointing plantation negroes to office" but also "associating with them." As the historian Hannah Rosen has explained, the term "social equality" in this era "referred broadly to forms of association between white and black people that did not convey a hierarchical meaning for race and that did not serve to mark racial difference." Southern whites used "social equality" to refer to Blacks' new access both to public and private spaces that had previously been white domains. In the eyes of ex-Confederates already incensed by Longstreet's position on Reconstruction and acceptance of Republican patronage, Longstreet's integrating of the Custom House bureaucracy proved further that he was a race traitor. A newspaper in Fayetteville, North Carolina, fumed that Longstreet had "promised Grant to make a vile n***** of himself to get the appointment," and was now fulfilling that promise.[77]

As was expected of a high-level political appointee, Longstreet increasingly played a prominent leadership role in the state Republican Party. At the end of January 1870 he was elected president of the Central Republican Club of Louisiana. Thereafter, the club's announcements would go out over his name and that of his recording secretary, the Black war hero and activist James Ingraham. For example, in March 1870 the club sent a series of resolutions to the *New Orleans Republican*, from Longstreet and Ingraham, pledging their support for Governor Warmoth and Senators Kellogg and John S. Harris and their commitment to "equality before the law, without distinction of race, color, or political opinion."[78]

More surprising still was Longstreet's willingness to play a subordinate role to Black leaders and to join them in celebrating milestones in the freedom struggle. On April 30, 1870, he participated in the grand gala celebration of the Fifteenth Amendment's adoption, marking the enfranchisement of Black men. Longstreet helped plan and raise funds for the widely publicized event, consisting of an elaborate procession through the city and speeches during the day, capped off by meetings at the Mechanics' Institute and other gathering places that night. Longstreet rallied the party faithful to attend, posting notices in the *New Orleans Republican* explaining that any Republicans who were not members of the city's various ward clubs could assemble with his Central Republican Club, at the Custom House, to partake in the procession. At the evening meeting in Mechanics' Hall, chaired by Lieutenant Governor Dunn, Longstreet was again prominent, included among the twenty vice presidents on the Committee of Arrangements, alongside Black leaders as Ingraham, Joubert, and Isabelle.[79]

The event was a high-water mark for the Warmoth regime, but also a harbinger of the troubles that lay ahead. The *New Orleans Republican* offered breathless coverage of the celebration, recounting how Warmoth and the State Central Committee led the procession, in their carriages, followed by three wagons filled with "beautiful young ladies" representing the states and territories of the Union; then by Custom House and postal employees; then ward clubs, benevolent associations, university students, and scores of others who "from first to last . . . bore themselves as became good citizens." Banners festooned the scene with mottoes such as "Washington—Independence. Lincoln—Emancipation. Grant—Universal Suffrage." Adjutant General George A. Sheridan, a Union veteran (unrelated to Philip H. Sheridan) who had served on Warmoth's staff, delivered a speech in which he both hailed the Fifteenth Amendment as a great sign of progress and opined that it should be paired with "universal amnesty" to ex-Confederates, as the people of the South had endured "full and ample punishment for the wrongs they have committed." The event, the *Republican* crowed, had seen contributions "from every quarter—from white, colored, poor, rich, Democrat, and Republican."[80]

The Republicans challenged the South's hierarchies related to gender as well as to race. Black women from the city's politically elite families, such as Mary Anne Antoine, the wife of USCT veteran and state senator Caesar Carpentier Antoine, joined together with reformers such as the Freedmen's Bureau teacher Carrie Satchell in helping to organize the tableau in which women represented the states and territories of the Union. The day's grand procession was "well filled with citizens, of both sexes," the *Republican* reported approvingly, while, by contrast, the conservative press scorned women's participation in the event.[81]

Southern Democratic papers emphasized that "many gentlemen of Radical proclivities" were seen in the procession, among them Longstreet: he conspicuously rode in a carriage "literally covered with stars and stripes." Northern Republican papers commented in turn that "unsubdued rebels" were "in a rage" over Longstreet's behavior. Much of the negative coverage had gendered overtones, casting Longstreet as "weak-kneed" and cringing in his submission to the Radicals; Northern papers countered by explicitly defending Longstreet's manhood. Longstreet was "never braver," a Massachusetts paper declared, than when he stood up to the "forces of Southern prejudice" by attending the Fifteenth Amendment celebration. That bravery would face a stern new test when Warmoth called on Longstreet to assume a controversial new role.[82]

Chapter 6

RADICAL REPUBLICAN

I

While his support for Black voting was the central feature of Longstreet's Republicanism, his support for Black soldiering was his boldest, most radical contribution to Reconstruction. On May 13, 1870, two weeks after the Fifteenth Amendment gala, Warmoth appointed Longstreet as adjutant general (chief of staff to Warmoth, who as governor was commander in chief) of the newly constituted Louisiana State Militia (LSM). Warmoth had pushed for a reorganization and expansion of the state force to compensate for the limited reach of his Metropolitan Police and for the reduction in federal occupying troops and of army posts in the state. He envisioned a statewide biracial force of 5,000 militiamen segregated by race that could effectively protect Republican voter turnout and defend the state government from insurgency.[1]

As the historian Justin Nystrom has noted, Warmoth also "hoped that by inviting prominent members of both black and white New Orleans society to accept command in the militia, the force might convert political adversaries into friends." But such hopes were dashed by the recalcitrance of whites, who condemned Black militarization and sought to deny African Americans the right to bear arms and to self-defense. Black militiamen, for their part, were not content to wheel in behind Warmoth as he maneuvered the state Republican Party to the center. The Black men who served as officers in Warmoth's militia were experienced, visionary leaders accustomed to using all the tools at their disposal—lawsuits, legislation, conventions, speeches, petitions, processions, print culture, and so on—to advance their agenda of full equality. They saw their role in the militia not only as deeply symbolic of Blacks' leadership capacity but also as essential to the survival and security of their communities. They backed Warmoth only so far and so long as he was a perceived ally in their broader freedom struggle.

Warmoth seems to have calculated that Longstreet, as adjutant general, would help to keep both former Confederates and the Black leadership class in line. And Longstreet seemed willing and able to play that role. But only for a time, before he felt the need to break from Warmoth and ally with the Radicals.[2]

II

Warmoth's enlistment of Black militiamen was authorized by Congress's 1868 Militia Act, which permitted reconstructed Southern states to create such forces once they had been readmitted to the Union. Some Republican governments, in Arkansas and South Carolina, for example, seized the opportunity to incorporate Black militiamen into the defense of the state, while Georgia and Alabama, to name two, refused to do so for fear of white backlash. As the historian George Rable explains, the general hostility of Southern whites to arming and serving alongside Blacks was reflected in the racial composition of these state forces: while some whites were willing to join biracial state forces (in Tennessee and North Carolina, for instance), Blacks dominated militia companies in Arkansas and South Carolina.[3]

In Louisiana, the LSM embodied Warmoth's belief in including repentant rebels in his moderate Republican coalition; the militia attracted roughly 2,500 former Confederate soldiers, most of them Democrats, into its ranks, or about half the total force. The other half consisted principally of New Orleans Blacks, drawn from both the Creole elite and the working class, and augmented by some white Southern Unionists and Northern transplants to the South (generally Union veterans). Warmoth, confident that Longstreet shared his desire to widen the governing coalition, turned to him to help lead the militia in part as a gesture of outreach to rebel veterans. To symbolize political balance, the governor and Longstreet chose as commanders of the militia's two initial divisions a former Union officer, Hugh J. Campbell, and a onetime Confederate, J. Frank Pargoud. Campbell, a major general, outranked Pargoud, a brigadier general.[4]

In some respects, the LSM was clearly segregated by race. It had three core regiments: a white one and two Black ones, based in New Orleans. These were the first three regiments to fill; additional regiments would eventually be formed in the interior of the state. The 1st Regiment of Infantry, together with some artillery and cavalry companies consisting mostly of Confederate veterans, were designated as the all-white Louisiana Legion—named after one of the city's oldest, most storied volunteer militia companies. The Legion was assigned to the Louisiana State Militia's Second Brigade, which was led by former Confederate officer A. P. Mason.[5]

The 2nd and 3rd infantry regiments, consisting largely of Black Union veterans, had both white and Black officers, with two prominent African Americans serving as regimental commanders: Colonel James Lewis, a former captain in both the Native Guards and the Metropolitan Police, was assigned the 2nd Regiment, while Port Hudson hero Colonel James H. Ingraham commanded the 3rd. As the historian James K. Hogue has noted, these Black militia units "incorporated several distinct advances over the [US] army in terms of racial equity and mobility": advancement to higher rank was open to Blacks in Warmoth's force (at least ten held ranks above captain), and there was no discrepancy in pay between white and Black recruits.[6]

Notably, although its white ex-Confederate regiment was separate from its Black Unionist ones, the Louisiana State Militia's command hierarchy and command staffs were not entirely segregated either by Civil War allegiance or by race. The Confederate veteran Mason and the Legion reported to the First Division commander, the Union veteran General Campbell, five of whose nine staff officers were Black. Campbell's commissary general, for example, was Colonel Charles S. Sauvinet, a former Native Guards quartermaster and prominent Republican civil servant and critic of segregation. Blacks served as staff officers for white commanders at the brigade level, too. The aides-de-camp of First Brigade head Edward S. Meyer included Jordan B. Noble, a legendary figure who, at age fourteen, had been a drummer boy in Andrew Jackson's forces at the 1815 Battle of New Orleans, and who remained a symbol of Black patriotism in the decades that followed.[7]

The most remarkable feature of the LSM's hierarchy was that it featured a Black brigadier general, Alexander E. Barber (sometimes spelled Barbour), who was assigned to the militia's Third Division and eventually given command, in 1872, of the First Division's First Brigade. A native of Louisville, Barber had been enslaved before the war and eventually found an occupation working on Mississippi River steamboats. During the war, he served in the Union army and settled in New Orleans. Barber was active in the very first conventions in which Black leaders in Louisiana demanded universal suffrage, and in civic organizations such as the Progressive Literary Lyceum Association, and a public charity hospital. A gifted leader of "strong character and agreeable personality," in the words of historian Charles Vincent, he was appointed as a Custom House official (harbor master of New Orleans) and was elected to the Louisiana State Senate in 1870, where he served as an outspoken proponent of civil rights legislation and causes such as education. Barber was the chairman of the organizing committee for the April 1870 Fifteenth Amendment celebration and the grand marshal on the day of festivities. His appointment in the LSM made Barber "one of the first commissioned militia generals of African descent in American history."[8]

Press coverage of the formation and composition of the LSM foretold future conflict. The conservative press approved of the inclusion of ex-Confederates—the "tried and true element" of society and "gentlemen of the first standing," as the archconservative *New Orleans Picayune* put it. Former Confederates were the social group, the paper claimed, most deeply interested in the "tranquility of the state" and in hedging against "chaos." That paper also asked, ominously, whether Confederate veterans would prove willing to be "made subordinate in the Louisiana militia to Major Gen. Hugh J. Campbell." Before long, the *Picayune* began sounding the alarm about the dangers of including Black units in the LSM, reporting on some tense interactions and exchanges between militiamen and private citizens as "very unwelcome portents" of the Black militiamen's "insolent, not to say bloodthirsty, bearing toward white people," and calling for "prudent white officers" to be assigned to the "deluded creatures."

Ironically, the *Picayune* furnished ample evidence of white people's insolence and implacable hostility toward Black militiamen—reporting, for example, that some of them were assaulted during a march through the city in July by a "number of half-grown boys, who threw rocks into their ranks." The paper also noted that "a number of parishes have held meetings of remonstrance against the organization of colored militia." Across the South, ex-Confederates cast Longstreet's willingness to accept the militia post from the "Radical" governor Warmoth as another sign of his "downfall and degradation."9

III

To his credit, Longstreet was undaunted by such opposition. During the summer of 1870 he took conspicuous steps to publicly promote the Black regiments, their leaders, and their mission. On July 20, 1870, he promulgated his General Orders No. 17, requiring all militia members to pledge that they would "accept the civil and political equality of all men, and agree not to attempt to deprive any person or persons on account of race, color, or previous condition, of any political or civil right, privilege, or immunity enjoyed by any other class of men." That fall, he organized and presided over some mustering in and regimental review ceremonies, each of which further challenged the old racial caste system. In October he reviewed three of the Louisiana Legion's Confederate-filled white artillery companies, and—provocatively—included among the reviewing officers the Radical Republican mayor Benjamin Flanders *and* a Black municipal official, Administrator of Public Buildings the Honorable L. T. Delassize. The scene, according to the *New Orleans Republican*, was breathtaking: "the spectacle of these ex-Confederate soldiers reviewed by the distinguished Confederate general who once led them into battle . . . now flanked by the Radical Mayor of New Orleans . . . and by one of the representative men of the colored race, now an honored Administrator of the city," was so stunning that the "review in Lafayette Square last night deserves to take a place in American history."[10]

Black-led units in the LSM were mustered in by Longstreet with equally great fanfare, as in a fall 1870 ceremony for the 2nd Regiment, commanded by USCT veteran James Lewis. Barber joined Longstreet in the reviewing stand to watch General Campbell present the state colors to Colonel Lewis—"for the first time ever was the flag of the State received by a Republican colonel from the hands of a Republican general," the *Republican* crowed. Longstreet was well aware of the symbolic importance of standing shoulder to shoulder with Black leaders, and he continued to meet with men such as Lewis as allies on political turf as well as through the LSM. In a November 1870 Republican gathering at the city's Mechanics' Institute, for example, Longstreet served alongside Colonel Lewis, and other Black militia officers such as Sauvinet and Isabelle, as one of the vice presidents of the meeting.[11]

Perhaps the most striking evidence of Longstreet's commitment to the militia's integration was his first annual report as its adjutant general, delivered to Warmoth, dated December 31, 1870. The report proudly detailed the recruitment, training, arms, organization, regulations, and purposes of the militia, with no overt references whatsoever to the race of any of the soldiers. Longstreet simply listed the men and their ranks matter-of-factly and reprinted his series of general orders to them, including one that required all militiamen to swear oaths of allegiance to the United States, pledging to defend it against all "enemies or opposers whatsoever." He noted that "about one half our force is composed of officers and soldiers who were in the military service of the Southern States during the late civil conflict," and expressed the hope that "their voluntary action in placing themselves in the position of protectors and supporters of the law" would give "greater moral tone and effect to our organization ... paralyzing at once the energies of such as may have been disposed to conspire against the honor and prosperity of the State." The only mention of race in the forty-seven-page document was Longstreet's reprinting General Orders No. 17 mandating that militiamen swear to accept the civil and political equality of all men.[12]

Warmoth's choice of Longstreet seemed to have paid off: the former general threw himself into leading the LSM and building its legitimacy. The governor's bid to build a centrist Republican Party seemed vindicated when the Republicans gained seats in the 1870 midterm election over the demoralized Democrats. His security apparatus and a series of election laws he pushed through to combat election fraud and violence made the 1870 contest the "freest election of the decade" and also the Republicans' "most sweeping victory," enabling them to consolidate their control over the legislature, over New Orleans, and various other statewide offices, as the historian Ted Tunnell has noted. The Republican press credited Longstreet's conspicuous show of force by the militia—which included stationing seven companies of infantry and two Gatling machine guns at the Custom House—with deterring any mob violence and election interference.[13]

IV

The militia and the Republican Party were not the only vehicles through which Longstreet promoted Reconstruction. He also worked closely with

Black leaders in his capacity as a member of the municipal school board. The state education system was in the midst of a remarkable transformation. The Union army and the Freedmen's Bureau had established federally funded schools for Black children during the war, and this laid the groundwork for the opening of the first public school for African Americans in New Orleans in 1867–68. With the Black leadership class in the city championing school integration to strike a blow at the foundations of white supremacy, the new 1868 state constitution provided for mixed public schools. But white hostility, including on the part of the sitting state superintendent and school board, delayed de facto desegregation. In early 1871 the Republican administration and state legislature finally took decisive steps to implement integration. In compliance with a new law authored by Robert Isabelle that disbanded the existing local school board and provided for appointing integrationists, the city was divided into school districts, each with its own director. Longstreet was named director of the tenth district, with Pinchback and Joubert leading the fourth and seventh districts, respectively; Longstreet would eventually be reassigned to the fourth district.[14]

The directors vetted and hired teachers, kept accounts and strategized about funding, secured and maintained facilities, conducted visiting days and inspections, and procured and disbursed supplies, along with many other such tasks. Longstreet threw himself into these activities with gusto and was a proactive, outspoken participant in school board meetings. He served on numerous specialized committees of the board, such as the Committee on Rules and Regulations (with Pinchback), and he proved a stickler on such rules, arguing that no teacher or other official should be fired or reprimanded without a fair hearing.[15]

In the midst of ongoing debates about integration, a school board appointment was a profoundly political role, and one that kept Longstreet in the public eye, as the board's monthly meetings were covered in detail in the city papers. In an April 1871 article, Pinchback's *Weekly Louisianian* hailed Longstreet's inclusion on the board, praising him as "a man of cultivated mind" who had shown "moral courage ... in his manly acceptance of the results of the war." The job took moral courage because the integration-ist school board operated in the midst of immense hostility from unrecon-structed whites in the Democratic Party. Opponents of integration found a variety of ways to forestall or undermine it, starving the schools of tax support, sending white children to private schools, setting up segregated zones within ostensibly integrated schools, and insisting that Black teachers not teach white children (though whites did teach Blacks). Despite these obstacles, the city school system achieved some degree of integration, with roughly one-third of the public schools having a mixed student population.[16]

Even as he worked for school integration, Longstreet tried to main-tain a political balancing act, defending the Republican Party while denying charges that Radicals held him in their sway. In early November 1870 a cri-tique of Longstreet began circulating in conservative Southern papers for his allegedly having refused to fly the flags of the New Orleans Custom House at half-mast after the death of Robert E. Lee on October 12, 1870. (Lee died at his home in Lexington, Virginia, due to complications from a stroke, at the age of sixty-three.) Here was more damning evidence, Longstreet's crit-ics fumed, that the "renegade" was in the thrall of "Grant's Radical adminis-tration." Longstreet denied the "scurrilous" charge, writing to the offending editors to set the record straight. To an ally in Kentucky, he complained, "I have no more to do with the flag over the Custom House at New Orleans than I have to do with the flag over the national Capitol," going on to con-demn the "conduct of those who without cause . . . keep in circulation such wicked falsehoods." Longstreet remained hopeful that he could, by example, win some Democrats and Confederates over to the Republican side. In mid-December 1870 he presided over the presentation of a regimental flag to a newly organized all-white artillery unit under the command of Confederate veteran Colonel C. W. Squires. Longstreet's speech on the occasion credited the artillerymen for "overcom[ing] deeply rooted sentiments and prejudices" to enlist in the Louisiana State Militia on "the side of peace and order."[17]

But no such incantation could keep chaos and division at bay. There would be no lasting peace in the Crescent City.

V

In January 1871 Longstreet visited President Grant in Washington, DC, to gauge his degree of support for the recently reelected Warmoth. When attending a White House reception with a delegation from Louisiana, Longstreet attracted much attention, according to the *Philadelphia Inquirer,* "there being great curiosity to see one who had been a prominent Rebel and who had the courage and manliness to again become a faithful servant of the Union." While some commentators saw Longstreet's presence in such settings as signs that sectional hostility was fading, others were more doubtful. The reformist New York journal the *American Missionary* praised Longstreet for his principled Unionism but also warned that "the bulk of the whites in the South are as rebellious as ever at heart. The 'lost cause' is still to them the just cause." For its part, the conservative Southern press evinced more alarm at Longstreet's crossing the color line than at his mingling with former military foes. When Longstreet turned up at a dinner honoring Union general and former military commander of Louisiana Philip H. Sheridan in New Orleans in late February, the press objected that he had "chosen to set an example of social equality by mingling socially with the negroes" and thus plunged into a "lower depth of shame and degradation" than ever before.[18]

Longstreet served as a go-between for Grant and Warmoth, deciphering the complex factional politics of Louisiana for the president, and conveying Grant's state of mind to the governor. Portentously, opposition to Warmoth was coalescing from within the Louisiana Republican Party in the form of a "Custom House ring" led by Grant's brother-in-law James F. Casey, collector of customs, and US Marshal Stephen B. Packard. While Casey and Packard presented themselves as the Radical Republican alternative to the fusionist governor, and cast Warmoth as a self-serving demagogue who had betrayed his Black constituents, each faction claimed some support from prominent Black leaders. Warmoth's own lieutenant governor, Oscar J. Dunn, sided with the Custom House ring, while the president of the state senate, P. B. S. Pinchback, supported the governor.[19]

The two competing Republican factions grappled over federal and state patronage. Longstreet, aligned with the governor and Pinchback against the Casey ring, tried to persuade Grant that Warmoth was a "staunch friend" and that some of Casey's allies, such as the New Orleans postmaster, Charles W. Lowell, should be removed in favor of Warmoth men. Longstreet back-channeled to Warmoth that Grant was prepared to follow the governor's recommendations provided that Warmoth "only select the best men for the positions." However, the president, who was clearly irritated by the factionalism, vacillated, and Lowell remained in office even as dissension within the party escalated.[20]

By July 1871, Longstreet was begging Grant to intervene and to demand that Casey and the anti-Warmoth Republicans stand down. Longstreet lamented the "unsettled and unsatisfactory condition" of political affairs in Louisiana, and invoked the larger stakes, as he saw them: if the Louisiana Republican Party could only reunify, he explained, that would give it vital "prestige and influence" with other Southern state delegations when Republicans gathered at their national convention. More than anything, Longstreet worried that if the "disaffected element" led by Casey did not yield to the Warmoth administration, "a division will be made which will probably defeat both."[21]

The stage was set for a showdown at the Republican State Convention in August 1871, during which Packard posted federal troops and deputy marshals armed with a Gatling gun at the convention site—the Custom House itself—seemingly to ensure the delegates' safety, but really to keep Warmoth and his followers out. This appalled Longstreet, who objected that there was "no excuse" for the federal presence and insisted that the Louisiana State Militia was sufficient to "preserve peace if by chance there had been violence."

In the aftermath of this standoff, Pinchback gave a remarkable interview to the *Cincinnati Commercial* in which he commented extensively on Longstreet's role in Louisiana politics. He confirmed that Longstreet found the convention's federal show of force to be "impolitic and unnecessary." And he praised Longstreet as a reliable ally to Black Republicans. When the interviewer asked Pinchback, "The rebels look a little cross-eyed at [Longstreet], don't they?" he replied, "Yes. But they look cross-eyed at everybody who don't do what they want them to." When the interviewer asked, "Is Longstreet popular with the colored people of Louisiana?" Pinchback answered unequivocally, "As popular as any man in the state."[22]

The Custom House faction's next move was an attempt to "engineer a quorum in the Louisiana Legislature to impeach the governor and seat Lieutenant Governor Dunn in his stead," explains historian Justin Nystrom. Dunn's untimely and sudden death from a mysterious illness in November 1871 vitiated the impeachment scheme, and Warmoth moved quickly to replace him with Pinchback. The Custom House group then tried allying, out of pure opportunism and expediency, with New Orleans Democrats, including some defiant Confederate elements, to undermine the Warmoth administration's power in the upcoming state legislative session of January 1872.[23]

Chaos ensued, with literal brawling between the legislators, and the mobilization of rival forces. In the first act of a two-part street battle, on January 4 Packard's deputies arrested Warmoth, Pinchback, Metropolitan Police commander Algernon S. Badger, and other Warmoth loyalists. After posting bail, the embattled governor retaliated by using the state militia and the municipal police to seize the statehouse and the Mechanics' Institute, where the House of Representatives, purged of Casey factionalists, was meeting. Warmoth commissioned Longstreet as a major general and directed him to supervise the "entire militia, police, and all civil forces of the state," and to coordinate the defense of the administration with Major General William H. Emory, commander of the US troops in the city. Longstreet had to improvise politically to maximize the turnout of the LSM, as some of its officers belonged to the Custom House ring. He proved more than willing to replace those men with

Warmoth supporters—for example, handing James Ingraham's regiment to Warmoth loyalist A. E. Barber.[24]

In act two of the January drama, the Custom House ring tried to convene its own legislators under Colonel George Washington Carter. A former Confederate cavalry officer, Carter joined the Republican ranks after the war and served as speaker of the state legislature, only to turn his back on Warmoth. Carter proved to be a man of "feral cunning . . . greedy for power and the spoils of office," as the historian Frank J. Wetta has noted. Carter's career illustrates that white Southern Republicans were both a powerful element of the party's governing coalition, but also the weak link, susceptible to Democratic pressure and appeals to racial solidarity. The Carter forces held an alternate assembly in the French Quarter's Gem Saloon and went so far as to try to forcibly round up some Warmoth legislators so as to obtain a quorum.

With both sides appealing in vain to an exasperated President Grant, this posturing took a lethal turn when one of Carter's henchman murdered a Warmoth Republican. On January 10, 1872, Warmoth ordered Longstreet, Badger, and the Metropolitan Police—three hundred strong and armed with Winchester rifles—to arrest Carter and to disperse the Gem Saloon assembly. They failed in the first task, letting Carter slip away, but succeeded, peaceably, in breaking up his rogue legislature. The menaces and violence could have escalated even further were it not for the presence of federal troops in the city under General Emory, who sent the signal that he would not abide the overthrow of the Warmoth administration.[25]

Longstreet played a central role in communicating Warmoth's wishes to Emory. Such communications revealed Longstreet's fear and suspicion that the Democrats who colluded with anti-Warmoth Republicans were "the violent element of the democracy," as he put it, "composed of Ku Klux Klans, or other organizations of a similar type," intent on "precipitating riot" and the "violent destruction of the state civil authority." Longstreet implored Emory to use his "moral influence on the side of law and order," the general proved willing to hold the line, and the January crisis subsided.

Longstreet, too, held the line, showing himself to be impervious to the pressure and cajoling of unreconstructed whites. On January 8, 1872, a delegation of six conservative Democrats claiming to "speak for three or four thousand citizens" visited his office to complain about the Metropolitan Police. Because the police had been used as a strike force and were concentrated in certain areas of the city rather than walking their usual patrol beats, the "citizens" claimed they felt unsafe and unprotected. Longstreet called their bluff. He asked the men pointedly when and where they had been delegated to represent the people of New Orleans; they dodged his question. He told them sternly that he knew best "where and how the police should be placed." And he threw the onus of danger and disorder back on them: "If every citizen would use his best efforts to frown down and discourage the banding together of citizens for the purpose of overturning the legal government," he noted, "there would be no trouble."[26]

In a final rhetorical coup de grâce, Longstreet invited the delegation to join in defending the state: "If you want to carry arms, join the militia, and then you will move under the direction of proper officers," he said archly. "Squads of men parading the streets with arms in their hands is only an armed mob." This provocative stance dramatizes how deeply implicated Longstreet was in fierce debates over "who would legitimately wield the means of organized force in the South." Opponents of Reconstruction invoked a "racially encoded reading of the Second Amendment," as the historian Carole Emberton has explained, to assert their own right to bear arms while denying that right to freedmen and delegitimizing Republican coalition governments. In calling their bluff, however, Longstreet only further stoked their resentment.[27]

VI

Warmoth had survived, but his days as governor were numbered. With the 1872 state and national elections looming, the Republican Party splintered further: Warmoth joined the Liberal Republican movement, whose presidential candidate, the influential newspaper editor and publisher Horace Greeley, challenged the Grant administration on a platform of amnesty for former Confederates, civil service reform, anti-corruption measures, and the abandonment of Radical Reconstruction policies. Warmoth's Radical Republican allies, such as Pinchback, repudiated him in turn and supported U. S. Grant's national ticket. Pinchback implored Warmoth not to turn his back on Black voters. In September 1872 he wrote the governor: "All you have politically you owe to the Republican Party and especially the colored people of Louisiana, and I hope & trust that a sense of obligation will prevent you from putting their enemies in power merely to get your revenge upon Packard Casey Kellogg and Company." But Warmoth was deaf to such pleas.[28]

Meanwhile, the Custom House faction forsook its brief, and failed, strategy of colluding with the Democrats, focusing instead on building support among Black voters and coalescing behind Senator William Pitt Kellogg as their gubernatorial candidate, with Black Union veteran Caesar C. Antoine as lieutenant governor. As Warmoth drifted further to the right, throwing his support in the governor's race to the Fusion ticket headed by conservative Democrat John McEnery, a former Confederate officer, Pinchback closed ranks with the Kellogg faction, completing his circuitous journey from the Warmoth camp to the Custom House ring.

The ensuing election for the governorship was mired in controversy and fraud, as the incumbent Warmoth had unseemly power over local registrars and a willingness to use corrupt tactics such as ballot box stuffing. The election tallies were so disputed that the returning board appointed to certify the contest itself split in two, with half the members declaring McEnery the winner and the other half crowning Kellogg. A federal court ruling on the disputed returns, together with the Grant administration's and federal army's support for Kellogg, enabled him to be installed in January 1873 (after a brief stint in which Pinchback had served as interim governor).

The tug-of-war over the governorship was by no means over, however. The defeated Fusionists refused to see the Republican regime as legitimate, setting the stage for more bitter conflict. "While Kellogg may have actually polled the greatest number of votes, his means of victory smacked of federal tyranny to white Louisianans, who believed that President Grant had used the judiciary to sustain an unpopular Republican government in the South," Justin Nystrom has explained. "That Kellogg's political base was almost entirely black amplified this outrage and unified a previously divided white electorate."[29]

How did Longstreet navigate these shifting currents? The infighting among Republicans disillusioned him initially, and he resigned his post as surveyor of customs in March 1872 as the Custom House faction maneuvered for that office. He also resigned as major general of the militia in April, citing his discomfort at mixing a military office and a political role. In his letter to Warmoth tendering his resignation, Longstreet invoked his desire to be "untrammeled in the approaching political canvass." Warmoth asked Longstreet to reconsider, assuring him, "No attempt will be made to control or influence your political course." But Longstreet was not persuaded. His trust in the beleaguered governor was wavering.[30]

Later that spring, Longstreet flirted briefly with the idea of following Warmoth into the Liberal Republican movement, telling the press that he supported law and order and was disappointed with the lawlessness of the Custom House ring; Longstreet implied that Grant's support for the Custom House clique tainted the president in his mind. But in October 1872 Longstreet, with some fanfare, rededicated himself to Grant, publishing a letter in the *New Orleans Republican* declaring that there was "more liberality in the Republican Party than has been developed by the move that has been called the liberal move." Longstreet had come to conclude that the Liberal Republican movement in Louisiana was a ploy to lure unwitting Republicans "to enter the Democratic ranks as recruits"—and he had no intention of falling for such a ruse. The major national organs of the Republican Party, such as the *New York Times*, rejoiced in Longstreet's pro-Grant stand and expressed hope that it would lead to further such defections from the group of defectors.[31]

In short, Longstreet, rather than casting his lot with Warmoth, followed the path of Pinchback into a rejuvenated Republican Party led by former internecine rivals such as Stephen Packard. He did so conspicuously: on the eve of the election, for example, Longstreet took his place alongside Black Republicans such as Pinchback, Barber, Sauvinet, and Lewis as one of the ceremonial vice presidents at a "Republican Mass Meeting" in New Orleans, called to order by Packard and presided over by Mayor Flanders. Longstreet's choice at this critical juncture reflected the faith he had invested in Grant and also his growing respect for these Black politicians: Pinchback, Longstreet told a reporter in the summer of 1872, "possesse[d] the coolest brains and the shrewdest faculties of any public man in the State." And it reflected, too, the resilient hope that somehow the fractured party could present "an unbroken front and closed ranks" and "march forward to glorious Victory," as James Lewis put it in an August 1872 letter to Pinchback, using a military metaphor.[32]

Longstreet played a prominent role not only in Republican voter mobilization in 1872 but also in the adjudication of the election results, as he served on the election returning board that declared the Kellogg-Antoine ticket victorious and confirmed Republican majorities in the statehouse and senate; those majorities made it possible for the legislature to impeach and suspend Warmoth and install Pinchback during the short lame-duck period before Kellogg was sworn in. The returning board drama was bitter and convoluted: Longstreet was appointed to the board by Louisiana secretary of state Francis J. Herron late in the game, when Pinchback and one other board member for office were disqualified, as they were candidates in the election; Warmoth refused to recognize the new appointees and chose his own replacements. Longstreet then acted on behalf of the anti-Warmoth board in demanding that the governor and his allies turn over the election tallies so that they could be verified and certified. Longstreet invoked his position as a "Deputy United States Supervisor" of elections under the purview of the congressional Enforcement Acts of 1870–71 that provided for federal supervision of local polling places in federal elections in Southern states that were defying the Reconstruction Acts. Warmoth refused to recognize Longstreet's authority, and it took a federal court order on December 6, 1872, to force the outgoing governor to turn over "each and every paper, document, affidavit, tally-sheet, list, sworn statement, certificate, letters, communication or proof" pertaining to the election and to authorize the Custom House faction to take possession of the statehouse.[33]

The election controversy involved endless procedural disputes about the legitimacy of appointees, jurisdictions, ballots, court rulings, and so on. Republicans who testified in the ensuing congressional hearings on Louisiana politics tried to keep the congressional investigators and politicians focused on the big picture: the pervasive, systemic violence and intimidation and fraud perpetrated by the Warmoth-McEnery conspiracy against the Black voters of the state. Depositions and other documentary evidence from a wide range of Republicans—from Kellogg himself, to federal election supervisors, to state and local officials, to individual Black voters protesting their disfranchisement—described for Congress the playbook of voter suppression. Warmoth had appointed "the worst characters" as parish registrars, and such officials had stuffed, lost, hidden, moved, and tampered with ballot boxes; ejected federal supervisors; relocated and shut down polling places to deny Blacks access to them; refused valid registrations or changed parish boundaries so that new registrations were required; and generally charged registrars with "the especial duty of disfranchising as many Republicans as possible." In some places, as an official from Webster Parish in North Louisiana testified, "the Klan, acting ostensibly as constabulary, under the commission of Governor Warmoth, carried the election by pure and open force." Economic intimidation was another tactic: as customs collector James Casey explained, "Our members are poor and adversaries are rich, and offers are made that are difficult for them to withstand," referring to how white and Black voters alike might be bribed or threatened with job loss or other economic penalties for defying wealthy employers and landowners.[34]

This political fraud and economic pressure went hand in hand with a relentless propaganda campaign, carried out by conservative organs such as the *New Orleans Times*, "to array the people against us," as Casey put it. Such propaganda described U. S. Grant as a "boorish soldier" and "military dictator" whose presidency had reduced Louisiana to a "state of revolution and anarchy." Invoking the specter of "Black rule," conservatives claimed that the new Republican legislature was dominated by "uneducated" former slaves and included only a "small minority of whites"—when, in fact, whites dominated both the statehouse and the Senate, and the Black delegates from the Afro-Creole elite were generally well educated.

Cross-referencing the census records and previous election returns with various forms of witness testimony, the Republican State Central Executive Committee concluded that Henry Warmoth's tactics had disfranchised more than 31,000 Black voters. His dubious claim that some Black voters had supported McEnery for governor was flatly rejected by the committee, which noted that "the whole Democratic campaign was denunciative of the negro and a class appeal to the whites."[35]

As it had during the strife-ridden January 1872 legislative term, this "turmoil in the state government produced turmoil in the state militia," to quote the historian James K. Hogue. In December 1872 acting governor Pinchback "bolstered his authority by purging the officer ranks of the militia of the disloyal," removing the former ally-turned-Fusionist Hugh Campbell from command of the LSM's First Division in New Orleans and asking Longstreet himself to take over that role. Longstreet accepted. These maneuvers led to a December 1872 mutiny among some of the ex-Confederates in the militia, with a few hundred of them refusing to obey Longstreet and instead forming a rival, conservative militia led by Confederate veterans. One of them, James B. Walton, had served as an artillery commander for Longstreet during the war, while William M. Owen, also an artillerist, had been Longstreet's postwar business partner in the cotton brokerage Longstreet, Owen & Co.

As members of the storied militia unit the Washington Artillery of New Orleans—which was organized in 1838 and served in the Mexican War and then in the Confederate army—these men had significant reputations in the city. In a tense standoff in December, the Pinchback forces, with the support of the Grant administration and of the federal troops in the city, preempted the mutinous militia from seizing one of the city's armories; the mutineers dispersed, but were poised for further mayhem.[36]

Together, these developments at the end of 1872—Warmoth's demise, Kellogg's election, Pinchback's interim tenure, Grant's endorsement of the Pinchback-Kellogg forces—all raised Longstreet's standing among Radical Republicans and Black voters, and damned him further among conservative whites. In their interactions with the Republican Party's national leaders, Kellogg's backers traded on Longstreet's public visibility and prestige, lauding his "invincible probity" and noting that "in personal integrity, in caution, and a most painstaking regard for the rights of all," Longstreet was "beyond reproach." Unreconstructed Southerners, by contrast, unleashed another wave of vituperative commentary, deeming Longstreet the "blackest of all traitors," wallowing in the "political filth into which he has tumbled," as the *Shreveport Times* put it. Northern Democratic papers joined in, deeming McEnery the legitimate victor and describing Pinchback as a "revolutionary usurper" and Longstreet as a "rebel scoundrel." Northern and Southern Democrats alike leveled the charge of a "corrupt bargain": that the returning board members received lucrative public offices in exchange for supporting Pinchback and Kellogg. Longstreet was appointed as a commissioner on the Board of Levees by Governor Pinchback in November, but the returning board vehemently denied that there was any quid pro quo involved.[37]

VII

The January 1873 swearing in of Kellogg as governor resolved nothing. The defeated McEnery forces refused to stand down, and instead set up a shadow government in New Orleans, with McEnery's inauguration taking place on the very same day as Kellogg's. Pinchback stepped down as interim governor, in frustration. No African American would serve as governor of a state for more than another century. In his view, the Grant administration's support had not been robust enough: Grant forbade Pinchback from using federal military force to forestall the formation of a McEnery legislature. As James K. Hogue has explained, "Grant and his cabinet believed McEnery's government would fade away after a few days of excitement if Louisiana Republicans simply ignored it." Congress fell short, too: its Democratic and Liberal Republican members were unsympathetic to the Kellogg forces, and even congressional stalwart Republicans seemed content with a policy of "masterly inactivity" on the dauntingly complex Louisiana problem. Thus the Forty-Second Congress refrained, before its third session ended on March 4, 1873, from endorsing either governor's administration.[38]

McEnery was both disappointed in the lack of federal support for his rump government and eager to go on the offensive. At the end of February, he called up his conservative militia and instructed Commander Frederick N. Ogden (or so Ogden would later claim), a former Confederate officer, to strike at and seize the Kellogg administration's militia arsenals and police stations. On March 5 Ogden led a few hundred men (estimates range from two hundred to six hundred)—the core of whom had mutinied against Longstreet in December—in attacking the Metropolitan Police Station and arsenal on Jackson Square; as the station was located in the city's old Spanish Cabildo (which had served as city hall during the Spanish colonial era), this street fight came to be known as the "battle of the Cabildo."

Kellogg immediately telegraphed President Grant: "An organized mob claiming to be police of McEnery have taken forcible possession of one of our outside police stations where we had a small force," adding, "I propose to immedy move a body of police under the Command of Genl Longstreet with orders to retake that station at any Cost." The ensuing battle was a debacle for the Ogden forces, as Longstreet's municipal and state forces and Emory's federal troops converged on the scene, outmanning and outgunning McEnery's followers and forcing them to disperse. The two sides exchanged sporadic fire, but only one fatality occurred, as the Kellogg forces showed restraint, and fired blanks and warning shots above the heads of the furious crowd to scare them off. The failure of the Ogden offensive emboldened the Kellogg forces in turn to seize the hall where the McEnery assembly was meeting and to scatter its ersatz legislators.[39]

Once again Longstreet was at the center of the action. The March 5 attack coincided with a Kellogg order mustering the Metropolitan Police into the state militia as the Metropolitan Brigade, so that "thereafter not a man was moved except with the knowledge and under the instructions of General Longstreet," the *New Orleans Republican* reported on March 7. The national press covered the Cabildo clash at length. Republican journals credited Longstreet with having outfoxed McEnery and Ogden—Longstreet had gleaned his opponents' plans and "by his prudent disposition of the armed police," had saved the day, according to *Harper's Weekly* magazine. Even the unsympathetic Democratic newspapers in the North had to concede the Kellogg victory. "Evidently the backbone of the McEnery government is broken," the *New York Herald* reported, adding that Kellogg "spent the morning at the statehouse in company with General Longstreet and the leading radical politicians, all of whom are much elated."[40]

Such elation would be short-lived, however, for the conflict between the dueling Kellogg and McEnery administrations spread ominously across the state. Now Kellogg found himself in a position akin to President Grant's: receiving desperate calls from the hinterlands for state intervention and peacekeeping, but unsure whether deploying troops would ratchet tensions up or down. The March 1873 mustering of the New Orleans municipal police into the state militia was part of a broader effort by Kellogg to consolidate his control over Louisiana's armed forces and to make them more disciplined, reliable peacekeepers who could be posted in any part of the state. Kellogg and his adjutant general, Henry Street, rebranded the militia as the National Guard of the State of Louisiana. Over the course of 1873, they worked to procure it uniforms and better weapons, including Gatling guns, howitzers, Springfield rifles, and Spencer carbines. Most important, they entrusted its revamped and expanded First Division, consisting of more than 2,000 officers and men, to Longstreet. The division was made up of four brigades: the First Brigade, commanded by A. E. Barber; the Metropolitan Brigade under A. S. Badger (made up of the Metropolitan Police), replacing the old Second Brigade, which had mutinied; and the Third and Fourth Brigades, commanded, respectively, by Louis J. Souer, a Republican politician from Avoyelles Parish, and T. Morris Chester, a Black military recruiter, militiaman, and war correspondent originally from Pennsylvania. Adjutant General Street's published annual report on the year 1873 included his many orders asking Longstreet to deploy National Guard detachments in sites of conflict in various parishes, "to enforce the laws, to suppress domestic violence, and to aid the civil authorities . . . in the discharge of their duties."[41]

But the most tragic and notorious outbreak of domestic violence, the Colfax Massacre of April 13, 1873, dramatized the limits of the National Guard's reach and of its legitimacy. The slaughter took place in Grant Parish in north central Louisiana, where Black militiamen, led by US Army veterans William Ward and Levin Allen, were under siege as they tried to retain control of the county seat of Colfax in the face of attacks by McEneryite paramilitary companies. Violent attacks on Black families in the parish had led those families to converge on the Grant Parish courthouse, seeking the protection of the roughly 150 Black troops there. White supremacist paramilitary companies, numbering nearly three hundred and led by a Confederate veteran named C. C. Nash, menaced Colfax from a position north of town and prepared for an assault. Black militiamen tried to shore up the courthouse defenses by digging trenches and preparing earthworks. They also sent two spokesmen, Ward and Eli Flowers, to New Orleans to beg for military aid.

On Easter Sunday, April 13, Nash demanded the group's surrender. When Allen, commanding the courthouse defense, refused, Nash's forces launched a brutal assault. The Black militiamen were able to bravely hold them off until Nash's paramilitaries wheeled a cannon into action and over-

whelmed the courthouse defenses. Carnage ensued, as the white supremacists burned down the courthouse, consigning those inside to surrender
to the flames, mowed down those who fled, and executed survivors who
were taken prisoner. With a death toll of at least 150 Blacks and 3 whites,
the Colfax Massacre was the single bloodiest day of Reconstruction. The
next day, April 14, Longstreet's adjutant general, Colonel Theodore W. De
Klyne, and inspector general, Colonel William Wright, arrived at the scene
to find the parish "in a most deplorable state": dead, decomposing, disfigured bodies littered the ground, bearing silent witness. The interviews the
men conducted with local Blacks confirmed that the Nash paramilitaries
had perpetrated a merciless massacre.[42]

The Colfax Massacre sparked a new round in the war of words between the defenders and detractors of Reconstruction, with Republicans
in Congress and the press calling for convictions of the perpetrators and
greater resources for the embattled Republican governments in the South;
conservative Democrats, however, blamed the violence on "bayonet rule"
and the corruption of the likes of Kellogg. Once again Longstreet was
deeply implicated in a national debate over the fate of Reconstruction,
as Congress and the press scrutinized the Colfax chain of events and
demanded to know why Longstreet's National Guard had not been dispatched to the scene in time to forestall the violence. Republicans, including Kellogg himself, insisted that Longstreet had been willing and eager to
send a detachment of troops to Grant Parish in early April, but had been
stymied by a far-reaching conspiracy on the part of the McEnery forces to
throw up every obstacle possible, including restricting access to steamboats
that might take troops from New Orleans to Colfax. Democrats countered
that Kellogg and Longstreet had conspired to prevent the National Guard
from being sent to the aid of the beleaguered white citizens of Grant Parish, whom, Democrats claimed fraudulently, were under threat of attack
from Blacks such as the Radical Republican William Ward. In the eyes of
Democrats, Ward was a "negro incendiary," and his so-called militia were
"banditti" intent on "robbery, pillage, and outrage."[43]

Democrats went one step further in implicating Longstreet by contending that he (during Warmoth's term) was to blame both for commissioning Ward as a captain in the state militia back in 1871 and for then shipping Enfield rifles to Grant Parish for the militia's use. When Ward's militia company had tried to fight back against vigilantism in the parish, whites there raised a hue and cry, claiming the Black troops were "parading with their arms in a semi-military organization," and "committing deeds highly prejudicial to good order." Although Longstreet took a series of measures—enjoining Ward from conducting drills without obtaining authorization first, and then discharging him, and, finally, retracting the militia's affiliation with the LSM in 1872—conservatives insisted in the Colfax aftermath that Longstreet had been too permissive and had "emboldened" Ward, to quote the *New Orleans Picayune*.[44]

In truth, it was leniency toward Nash and to the other Colfax perpetrators that emboldened white terrorism. Federal troops who arrived at Colfax after Longstreet's men were able to round up some suspected paramilitaries and indict them for conspiracy under the 1870–71 Enforcement Acts, but only nine went to trial. Despite searing testimony from Allen and other Colfax survivors, only three of the accused perpetrators were convicted. Furthermore, in a bitter blow to Reconstruction, those few guilty verdicts were overturned in June 1874 by US Supreme Court justice Joseph P. Bradley while he was riding circuit (visiting the federal courts in the Deep South) in New Orleans. The justice maintained that the Fourteenth Amendment—which granted citizenship to all men and women born in the United States and, in principle if not practice, guaranteed all Americans equal protection under the law—offered protections only against the discriminatory actions of a *state* entity, not against the actions of individuals or a private entity like Nash's mob. Although the three defendants could have remained in custody until the Supreme Court itself heard the case, Bradley ordered them released on bail. His reasoning was then upheld in the US Supreme Court's ruling, voiding the Colfax indictments and gutting the Enforcement Acts, in *United States v. Cruikshank* (1876).[45]

As the historian James K. Hogue has noted, Bradley's 1874 decision "fanned the flames ignited by the spark at Colfax into a wildfire blaze of paramilitary mobilizations across Louisiana." Summoned to arms by inflammatory appeals in white supremacist newspapers such as the *Caucasian* of Alexandria, Louisiana, paramilitary units calling themselves White Leagues exploded in rural parishes, gathering some 14,000 men under their banner in the summer of 1874. These groups forced Republican officials out of office and terrorized Black communities in hit-and-run strikes and murderous sprees. The White Leaguers' shocking Coushatta Massacre in northwest Louisiana in August 1874—the execution, torture, and mutilation of six white Republican officials and as many as twenty Blacks—was intended to serve notice that neither Longstreet's National Guard nor the meager federal force in Louisiana under Emory (only 130 strong) could protect Republicans, Black or white, from the White League onslaught.[46]

Longstreet, for his part, worked assiduously in the period between the Colfax and Coushatta tragedies to shore up his state militia's strength and public image, and to deny resources and legitimacy to the burgeoning New Orleans White League. He lobbied the legislature for appropriations and made the most of every opportunity for public displays of the National Guard's readiness and respectability. For example, on Sunday, February 22, a parade of the state troops was the centerpiece of the city's annual celebration of George Washington's birthday. A. E. Barber's First Brigade of the First Division led the way. The *New Orleans Republican* described the scene laudatorily: "Brigadier General Alexander E. Barber, sitting [on] his magnificent stallion, rode on in front, proud of his command and every inch a soldier. He had discarded the regulation army hat and adopted the more tasty chapeau de bras, decorated with flowing black plumes, which added to the magnificence of his tout ensemble. His presence rendered him the cynosure of all eyes and excited the admiration of thousands of lookers-on."

Barber's troops were followed by the "gallant boys" of Badger's Metropolitan Brigade. Longstreet presided from the reviewing stand on Canal Street alongside Governor Kellogg and other dignitaries, including Brigadier General T. Morris Chester. "All in all, the parade was one of the most magnificent demonstrations New Orleans has ever witnessed," the *Republican* concluded, and "the Governor was given new cause to be proud of the material that composes, and the men who command the citizen soldiery of Louisiana." The national press offered some sympathetic coverage of the militia, and particularly of the Metropolitan Brigade. "We see colored men acting under white officers, and sometimes white men under colored officers," a correspondent for the *Baltimore American* noted with surprise, adding, "They are a fine looking body of men," led by "the platoons of mounted police, white and black intermixed."[47]

Longstreet continued in this period to conspicuously align himself with Black politicians and military officers and with the Radical Republican cause. In late 1873 he was caught up in a frenzy of attention and activity regarding Cuba. The United States had a long-standing preoccupation with the island as a possible target of annexation. Before the Civil War, slaveholders had promoted such a policy as part of an agenda of Southern Manifest Destiny; some Southern filibusters—those soldiers of fortune conducting rogue military expeditions—had launched failed bids to establish an American beachhead on Cuba. When Cuban rebels rose up against their Spanish imperial overlords in 1868, launching a Ten Years' War that was the first phase in a prolonged independence struggle, Americans watched with interest. The fate of plantation slavery on the island was at stake, as rebel leaders promised to dismantle the institution if they came to power. But it was not until 1873 that the American public fixated on the conflict. In November of that year, the US steamer the *Virginius*, which had been hired by Cuban rebels to carry men and arms to the island, was captured by the Spanish, and its captain and crew summarily executed as pirates. A shocked American public called for punishment of the Spanish perpetrators, and New Orleans, with its geographic proximity and cultural ties to Cuba, led the way in fervor for intervention, with many advocating occupation. In November and December 1873 war fever gripped the city.[48]

Crucially, although both Democrats and Republicans joined in the

"Free Cuba" chorus, they had very different reasons for doing so. While Democrats were eager to project US military power and establish commercial connections to the island, Republicans, led by Black politicians such as P. B. S. Pinchback, argued that America should intervene to liberate Cuba's enslaved population. They believed that "the United States had a duty to promote the principles it had vindicated in the Civil War—free labor and republican government—throughout the world," as the historian James M. Shinn Jr. has explained. Pinchback, Barber, Lewis, Joubert, and other Black leaders, together with Longstreet, held public meetings to execrate Spanish tyranny and express solidarity with Cuba's rebels. Longstreet went one step further, offering to organize and lead a military expedition himself. In the end, the *Virginius* crisis was resolved by diplomacy and the war fever in New Orleans subsided: by the end of December, the national press was reporting that "the legions which expected to go under the leadership of General Longstreet and capture Cuba have disbanded."[49]

But the interlude of excitement over Cuba deepened Longstreet's alliance with Black Republicans. The grand National Convention of Colored Men that assembled in New Orleans in November 1873 nominated him as part of a ten-man delegation to go to Washington, DC, along with Flanders, Ingraham, Lewis, Joubert, and other Radicals, to plead the case of Louisiana's people of color to U. S. Grant and the Congress. Although Longstreet did not ultimately make the trip (Lewis and Barber led a delegation to attend the National Civil Rights Convention in DC), the appointment was nonetheless a clear vote of confidence. Longstreet reciprocated this support. He participated, for example, in a March 1874 meeting to honor the recently deceased abolitionist icon, Senator Charles Sumner of Massachusetts, and served with Pinchback, Antoine, Lewis, Joubert, and other Black leaders as a vice president of the gathering, with General Barber as one of the speakers. Longstreet's influence within the Louisiana Republican Party, and his commitment to Reconstruction, were at a peak. But his hopes for lasting change were about to come crashing down.[50]

Chapter 7

THE CANAL STREET COUP, 1874

I

The Republican Party's displays of cross-racial alliance only further infuriated the McEneryite opposition in New Orleans, which ramped up a propaganda campaign centered on fears of Black militarization. The state militia parades and maneuvers that Longstreet saw as signs of progress and sources of pride were mocked by hostile whites. "Look at them as they pass through our street on parade days," the *New Orleans Bulletin* wrote of the Black police and militiamen. "Every movement proclaims the vanity, egotism, and love of display of the African race."[1]

Barber and Chester, the highest-ranking Black military officers in the state, were favorite targets of the conservative press. The two commanders were at the peak of their influence. Barber led efforts to obtain proper uniforms for Black-led companies in the state militia; initiated a lawsuit against the Louisiana Jockey Club (a prestigious horse-racing association) for denying him equal treatment; and presided proudly over Black militiamen on memorial days marking the anniversaries of the 1815 Battle of New Orleans and the Union victory in the Civil War. In 1872, when Barber provided Frederick Douglass with a military escort during the famed abolitionist's April visit to New Orleans, Douglass praised the general as "one of the most agreeable gentlemen we met in New Orleans—a man we are proud to call our friend." Barber used his voice in the Louisiana State Legislature and on speaking tours of the North to decry white terrorism and hold whites accountable for having sparked and perpetrated the violence at Colfax. Chester, for his part, was an accomplished lawyer, journalist, and activist. After relocating from Pennsylvania to New Orleans in 1871, he played a leading role in representing civil rights litigants who invoked Louisiana's equal public rights laws to challenge discrimination in saloons, theaters, and other "places of public resort." While Barber was giving speeches in the North in 1873, Longstreet assigned Chester to temporarily lead Barber's First Brigade; Longstreet then reinstated Barber upon his return to New Orleans.[2]

Conservative sheets such as the New Orleans *Picayune* and *Bulletin* rained down contempt and vituperation on these men, deriding them as "oleaginous" (obsequious) tools of Kellogg—"military puppets, who exhibit their brass buttons and asininity on high days and holidays." When Black troops decorated the graves of the Union dead on Memorial Day, May 31, 1874, the *Bulletin* and *Picayune* derisively claimed that Barber's "Senegambian Brigade" had marched "with the majestic regularity of a flock of sheep" and had then attempted "to create a riot" when several militiamen entered a local drugstore and "demanded" some soda water and ice water. Such "outrages" were the consequence, the *Bulletin* editorialized, of "misguided negroes" being "fed the pap of civil rights by political demagogues."[3]

With their claims that the Republican regime was intent on race war, conservatives were setting the stage, deliberately and systematically, for a coup d'état.

II

In the summer of 1874 this toxic rhetoric took on a portentous urgency, as the *Picayune* spread false rumors that so-called "Black Leagues" were poised to wreak havoc on New Orleans, with July 4 as a target date for an assault in which "negro militias" would enter white businesses, demand service, and then kill white proprietors who refused their demands. As the *Picayune* put it on July 1, "The demeanor of a certain class of negroes has been for some months past significantly insolent and overbearing.... Have we not observed in the cars, on the streets, at the saloons and places of public resort, a growing persistency of assertion, and a manifestation of resolve which could only spring from a settled and well-defined purpose?" The paper singled out General Barber for condemnation, arraigning him for participating in the "avalanche of civil suits" by Black leaders against segregation, and for continually assuring the Black masses, "by example as well as precept, that the privileges in question are rightfully and inalienably theirs."[4]

In newspaper interviews of their own (with a paper, the *New Orleans Times*, that purported to be neutral), Barber and Longstreet emphatically denied the existence of any "Black Leagues" and tried to tamp down rumors of a July 4 uprising by noting that the one company of Black militiamen who would march in the city's festivities that day would do so as "picknickers" with unloaded muskets; Longstreet added, with some bitterness, that the state militia did not have the necessary funds for a grand parade on the Fourth, as the attorney general had enjoined the state funds appropriated to the militia. The stalwart *New Orleans Republican* defended the veracity of Barber and Longstreet, noting: "Their habits as officers and their character as gentlemen place them above the suspicion of being guilty of such a high crime as knowing of a projected massacre." But the conservative press shot back that as the ones most "responsible for the acts of the negro militia," Barber and Longstreet were "the very men whose interest it was to deny the existence of any such plot."

Revealing the sinister purpose of its misinformation campaign, the *Picayune* cynically summoned whites, in early July, to form their own "Crescent City White League," in the guise of self-defense against an imaginary uprising that whites had concocted. When no Black League riot materialized on July 4 after all, the *Picayune* insisted that the holiday's rainstorms had dampened the "rage" of Barber and Chester—and that the whites' preparations had averted disaster.[5]

The roughly fifteen hundred men in New Orleans who answered the insurrectionist call in the summer of 1874 were led by combat-toughened Confederate veterans such as the Crescent City White League's president, Frederick Nash Ogden. Some were very well known to Longstreet, most notably J. B. Walton, a former auctioneer in New Orleans's slave trade markets who became First Corps artillery chief during the war. An ardent Democrat who nursed a grudge against Longstreet for having snubbed him (in favor of E. P. Alexander) at Gettysburg, Walton became a prominent White Leaguer, on the staff of Ogden's rogue militia. But the rank-and-file recruits, the historian Justin Nystrom has noted, were disproportionately young men, who were born too late to enlist in the Confederate army and who relished the chance to "prove their worth to their fathers, their older brothers, and themselves." After the July call to action, the White League organized itself into military-style companies and "regularly drilled, sometimes with arms and sometimes without," as General Algernon Sydney Badger of the Metropolitan Brigade observed with growing alarm.[6]

By late summer, arms were "constantly arriving" in New Orleans for the White League's use. The August Coushatta Massacre of Republican officials further stoked the blood lust of Crescent City white supremacists, and their determination to strike while the iron was hot. Badger played into their hands by conducting raids to confiscate arms shipments, which only served to raise an alarm about the Kellogg administration's abridgement of Second Amendment rights. In September rumors circulated among worried Republicans that the White League was planning to seize a recently arrived arms shipment that was under police surveillance at a city dock, as a prelude to launching mob attacks on police stations.[7]

III

"Generals Longstreet and Badger entertain the gravest apprehensions as to the peace of the city," the Radical Republican newspaper the Chicago *Inter Ocean* reported on the fateful day of September 14. The entire nation was transfixed by the unfolding crisis in Louisiana. The previous day had witnessed an ominous escalation of tensions in New Orleans, as White Leaguers led by Ogden and McEnery's running mate and self-styled "acting governor," David B. Penn, planned for a mass meeting at the Henry Clay statue—a prominent landmark on the central thoroughfare, Canal Street—on September 14, to demand the abdication of the "usurping Government." (McEnery himself was a nonfactor, as he was out of the state at the time.) The *Picayune* published an inflammatory rallying cry over the names of fifty prominent businessmen, to signal the elite's solidarity. "One by one your dearest rights have been trampled upon," its address declared, invoking aggrieved whites' right to "keep and bear arms." The mass meeting would test, so the paper claimed, whether the First Amendment rights to assemble and to petition the government for a redress of grievances remained intact. As the *Inter Ocean* noted, what made the situation "extremely critical" was the absence of federal troops from New Orleans: the US Army forces that were usually posted there had been sent to Holly Springs in northern Mississippi to wait out yellow fever season, leaving Longstreet's state forces especially vulnerable.[8]

The fuse was thus lit—and the events of September 14 exceeded Longstreet's grimmest fears. By 11:00 a.m., the rally at the statue teemed with a crowd of some 5,000. They had been whipped into a frenzy by orators such as R. H. Marr, a lawyer who had defended the Colfax Massacre perpetrators. Marr headed a small delegation who went to the statehouse to convey their demands directly to Kellogg; they were met instead by his representative, US District Court judge Henry Dibble, who explained that the governor would listen to peaceful petitions but would not be bullied into abdicating. Reporting back to the Clay statue assemblage at around 1:00, Marr literally instructed the crowd to go home, fetch their weapons, and reassemble at 2:30 on Canal Street. At that time, they would be provided with military commanders and weapons and White League companies to help them to consummate their coup d'état. Meanwhile, as war cries of "Hang Kellogg!" echoed from the crowd, White Leaguers were already at work, between 2:00 and 4:00 p.m., occupying city hall and the telegraph office; erecting barricades—composed of streetcars, barrels, logs, and billboards—all along Poydras Street, from city hall to the levee; cutting the telegraph wires, to isolate the city; and positioning pickets and snipers in buildings along their defensive line.[9]

Longstreet and his National Guard staff were at the statehouse as this drama unfolded. Governor Kellogg, who had abandoned the statehouse that morning, fearing that it would be a White League target, was hunkered down on federal property at the Custom House, a few blocks away from the assembled mob, hoping to find relative safety with the company of US soldiers posted there. The federal troops had arrived from Jackson, Mississippi, after having been requisitioned the previous night by a panicked US Marshal Stephen B. Packard. Four other companies of General Emory's men were on their way to New Orleans from Holly Springs, but not expected to arrive until the late afternoon. Packard telegrammed US Attorney General George Henry Williams in Washington, DC, that the local forces were "exercising the utmost discretion, in order that if blood be shed, it will be precipitated by the White League." Kellogg, in testimony he would later provide to Congress, claimed that he was determined not to "provoke any collision," and that he had sent Judge Dibble to the statehouse with the message that Longstreet was in charge of the military defense of the besieged government and "must use his own judgment in regard to the disposition of the local force."[10]

At this crucial moment, at around 3:00 in the afternoon, Longstreet implemented the second of two plans that he, Kellogg, and Badger had agreed to earlier in the day. The state forces were arrayed in a defensive posture, with roughly 475 Black state militiamen at the statehouse (in the former St. Louis Hotel in the French Quarter), and the 500 men in General Badger's Metropolitan Brigade (about 85 percent of whom were white and 15 percent men of color) at Jackson Square. The initial strategy, according to an "official memorandum" written by Longstreet and published in the *New Orleans Republican* on September 20, was "to hold these positions until the insurgents came out and attacked at Jackson Square, as we had learned that they had arranged to do." A second backup plan, for "active operations with State troops, in case it became necessary," was to go on the offensive, leaving the Black militia under Generals Barber and Campbell as a reserve force at the statehouse, and moving Badger's better armed and more experienced troops, with their cavalry and artillery, in two columns "from Jackson Square up the levee" to protect the Custom House and disperse the insurgents. According to Longstreet's memorandum, it was clear by 3:00, as armed White Leaguers gathered menacingly along Canal Street, that the initial passive plan was obsolete—so "the Governor then ordered the State forces to move out in accordance with the plan for active operations."[11]

Longstreet thus directed Badger, at about 3:30, to move the bulk of the Metropolitan Brigade in a "leading column" to the vicinity of the Custom House; Longstreet would head the supporting column of Metropolitans in "echelon" (at a diagonal angle to the main column) to the corner of Chartres and Customhouse Streets. Badger's column marched from Jackson Square to the corner of Canal and St. Peter Streets, and a small mounted force was then "ordered forward to the Clay statue to warn noncombatants to clear the street," as Longstreet put it, so that Badger could "read the riot act and order the insurgents to disperse." This plan, too, was obviated, as the advance squad was fired upon by a sniper; moreover, Badger learned that the mass of White Leaguers had left the vicinity and were streaming down Poydras and Canal Streets to the levee. As soon as Longstreet received updates, he immediately ordered Badger to change his front to meet the movement of the White League and establish a line of battle at the base of Canal Street, at a right angle to the levee, anchored by an imposing building there made of cast iron.[12]

As the insurgents advanced on this newly established position, Badger's men opened fire. Although they were armed with artillery that included a Gatling gun and two Napoleon cannons, the Metropolitans' left flank was very vulnerable, Badger recalled, while the White Leaguers had fashioned a "very effectual barricade" from cotton-bale freight along the levee. "They were almost completely sheltered, while we were completely exposed," Badger continued, adding that his troops also received severe fire from sharpshooters in "buildings in the vicinity." Badger sent a plea to Longstreet for reinforcements, but it was too late. As his artillerists were mowed down by White League fire, Badger himself was shot four times, thrown from his horse, and taken into White League custody. The rout was on: the loss of Badger, and a ferocious charge by White Leaguers letting loose the "rebel yell," broke the Metropolitan Brigade's lines and sent its men streaming back toward the Custom House, the statehouse, and Jackson Square. Longstreet met some of the retreating troops at the Custom House and tried in vain to rally them, so that they could at least conduct an orderly retreat, but by that time, their spirit was broken.[13]

Badger and other witnesses clearly credited Longstreet as the source of the major tactical decisions during the hour-long battle on Canal Street. But Longstreet's exact disposition during the fighting is difficult to pinpoint. Some contemporary accounts have him riding up and down Canal Street, ordering the mob to disperse. Others emphasize that he remained to the rear of the iron building–levee battle line, and that his aide-de-camp, Colonel John W. Fairfax, carried his orders back and forth to Badger. Still other reports have Longstreet advancing with reinforcements toward the Canal Street firefight, only to turn back when he saw Badger's men in retreat. Longstreet's memorandum of September 20, 1874, makes no reference to his own movements on September 14, focusing instead on his orders to Badger. Fortunately, an 1885 account that Longstreet provided to the press confirms that he was on the move during the battle, at times riding forward along Canal Street to break up the crowd, to advise Badger in person, and to spur on the troops.[14]

At some point, Longstreet was in the line of fire and wounded—possibly hit by a spent bullet, and either thrown from or pulled from his horse, reinjuring the arm that had been wounded in the Wilderness. Some reports claimed dubiously that Longstreet was briefly taken prisoner by the White Leaguers; others noted, more plausibly, that he was conveyed, after being injured, to the refuge of the Custom House—one of the last major redoubts, full of Republican officeholders, in the possession of the Kellogg forces by day's end. Neither Badger's nor Longstreet's accounts of the battle mention Longstreet's being wounded or captured. Debates over Longstreet's whereabouts during the firefight would linger on, as his defenders and detractors embellished their competing stories.[15]

Although the Metropolitan Brigade lost only thirteen men, and killed sixteen White Leaguers while injuring dozens more, the firefight on Canal Street was a tragedy for Kellogg forces. Scores of people, including bystanders, were injured. Badger was gravely wounded, and the LSM overwhelmed and unnerved. Having gained the momentum, White Leaguers proceeded to seize arms from police stations and militia arsenals, and fan out across the city, imposing martial law and controlling virtually all of its terrain save the Custom House and state arsenal. On the following day, September 15, what was left of Kellogg's demoralized police and militia either dispersed, surrendered (the White League cannily offered "amnesty" to those who laid down their arms), deserted, or were compulsorily disarmed, yielding the statehouse and arsenal to the insurrectionists. The Crescent City White League declared its coup a success and installed David Penn as governor of Louisiana.[16]

Penn ruled his stolen kingdom for three days, until General Emory and his federal troops intervened, at President Grant's direction, and made it clear that the US government would use force to return Kellogg to power. On September 17, knowing they could not fight off the US Army, the White Leaguers agreed to Kellogg's restoration as governor. But the battle on Canal Street had nonetheless presaged the demise of Reconstruction in Louisiana. As the historian Justin Nystrom explains, the US troops who took control of the city "failed to pursue those who had just days earlier mounted [a] coup against the lawfully recognized civil government of the city," and thus "not a single political leader, officer, or soldier of the White League ever faced criminal prosecution for his role in the bloodshed."

The White League's propaganda coup proved successful. The League congratulated itself for refraining from widespread vigilante violence against Black noncombatants—taking this posture in order to avoid rousing Northern ire. And it recast the Canal Street firefight as the heroic "battle of Liberty Place"—the defense of an aggrieved citizenry against overweening federal tyranny and rampant social radicalism. These tactics worked. "Overwhelmingly, white America saw the League's rebellion as the justifiable actions of a wronged people," Nystrom has noted. After September 14, 1874, the National Guard iteration of the state militia was obsolete, with its remaining brigades relegated to an auxiliary role secondary to that of the dominant federal troops; the Metropolitan Police would be a shadow of its former self; and the Republican state government was living on borrowed time.[17]

IV

In the fall and winter of 1874, as the nation struggled to make sense of the bloodshed in New Orleans, Longstreet was once again front and center, both as a screen onto which various political agendas were projected and as an active agent pressing his own narrative. Longstreet's detractors accused him of craven cowardice during the battle on September 14. Some claimed that he had ignominiously retreated as soon as the fighting got sharp—that he "came out with the police and directed their movements up to the time of the first shots, then disappeared," as the *Vicksburg Herald* put it. In a variation on that theme, other conservative outlets claimed apocryphally that when Longstreet heard the "rebel yell" emanate from the White League ranks, he "ingloriously fled the field," as the *Memphis Appeal* reported; the *Appeal* described Longstreet as "a bad man—the worst of the entire Kellogg regime." For added effect, some Southern papers reprinted Longstreet's 1862 speech rallying Confederate troops to defend Richmond, and asked incredulously how it was possible that the author of that address was "the same individual who has been riding along the streets of New Orleans at the head of negro militia, with a negro staff by his side ... [and] who recently ordered his negro outlaws to fire upon some of his old comrades of the Confederate army?"[18]

Conservative papers seized the opportunity to argue that the racially integrated police force had been disgraced at the Canal Street battle. "Before the fight, Longstreet boasted of the Metropolitan Brigade as the finest and best disciplined body of troops he had ever seen," the *New Orleans Bulletin* observed. "When Badger fell and his routed men sought refuge in the Custom House and in flight, the great usurpation balloon collapsed. . . . Gone was Longstreet and his noble army of metropolitans," the paper gloated. Such rhetoric was the culmination of a relentless, bitter campaign to discredit Black policemen. From the moment New Orleans first integrated its police force in 1867, the conservative press routinely heaped disdain on Black policemen, accusing them of corruption and negligence. The *Bulletin* was the most egregious slanderer of the police, prompting the *Weekly Louisianian* to complain archly in the spring of 1874: "We suggest that the *Bulletin*, in lieu of damaging innuendoes and vicious assaults upon the poorly paid but faithful officers who now protect the city, should turn its attention to the denunciation and detection of the criminals themselves."[19]

Despite the hostile atmosphere in which it operated, the integrated police force "had a fair claim to distinction as the best force the city had fielded at any time during the nineteenth century," the historian Dennis Rousey has demonstrated: it was "less abusive of civil liberties than either its predecessors or successors, and its officers were held to a strict accountability." Due to public scorn, low pay, and daily dangers, the percentage of

Black policemen in the New Orleans force fell steadily over the course of Reconstruction, from a high of 38 percent in 1868 to 15 percent in 1874. But the declining numbers did little to mollify hostile whites. Their racial animus only grew fiercer once the Metropolitans were incorporated into the state militia in early 1873; the police, the *Picayune* fumed, had been turned into "janissaries, a pretorian band, to . . . maintain the authority" of "remorseless plunderers."[20]

At issue was not only the participation of Blacks in law enforcement but also the visibility of Black police officers in politics. Whites infuriated by the activism of the state militia commanders such as Generals Barber and Chester were no less infuriated by that of Black police captains Eugene Rapp, Octave Rey, and Peter Joseph, who were in the front lines of protests against racial discrimination. Rapp and Rey had long careers of leadership, having been in the delegation that first offered the services of New Orleans Native Guards to Union army general Benjamin Butler in the summer of 1862, and they were active, influential Republican politicians during Reconstruction. Joseph was captain of the Metropolitan Brigade's Company E when he, in the spring of 1874, became a prominent litigant seeking legal redress for discrimination by public facilities (in this case, denial of access to the Academy of Music); he won his case and was awarded damages of $1,000. In other words, like Barber and Chester, Joseph very consciously leveraged his respectability and public position to strike a blow against segregation.[21]

But such moral courage only stoked white scorn. Ubiquitous press reports that "the colored men, of which the Metropolitan Brigade was largely composed, broke and ran upon the first fire" on September 14 worked to undermine the remaining public support for an integrated force. By 1880, the percentage of Black officers on the force would fall to 7 percent. The state militia, as well as the Metropolitans, came in for withering criticism in the aftermath of the September 1874 clash. The *New Orleans Bulletin* concocted and circulated rumors that General Barber had run in fear from the statehouse, cast off his uniform, and disguised himself as a stable hand so that he could hide out during the battle. The French-language sheet *Le Carillon* asked mockingly, "Ou donc est passe le gros Barber avec ses epaulettes et son plumet? Et Morris Chester l'avocat sans causes . . . a l'heure du danger"? It answered this question—where were the vaunted Barber and Chester in the hour of danger?—by repeating the charge that the two generals had fled "aux premiers coups de feu," with the first shots.[22]

Black leaders in New Orleans countered these slanderous accusations of cowardice. Pinchback's *Weekly Louisianian* stated that "the charge that the colored Metropolitans ran at the first fire is unqualifiedly false," and maintained that Black casualties from the day's violence were higher than whites let on. Its account of the firefight emphasized that a few hundred Metropolitans had been outnumbered and "entrapped" by a force of more than 2,000 insurgents, and demoralized by the "murderous volleys" from White League sharpshooters and snipers. Thomas Morris Chester, although he was in Harrisburg, Pennsylvania, on September 14, shared his controversial views with reporters, off the record, only to have them published, without his authorization, in the *Harrisburg Patriot*. "The statement that the colored police beat a hasty retreat must be taken *cum granio salis*," Chester observed, according to the *Patriot*. The initial dispatch out of New Orleans reporting on the alleged retreat had likely been written, Chester surmised, by "an associated press agent whose sympathies were with the Penn party." When asked if he knew anyone who fought in the street battle, Chester replied, "I was well acquainted with Corporal Claremont, one of the negro police killed. He was a client of mine, and a braver man never lived." John Frank Claremont (whose name is sometimes spelled Clarmont or Clermont in historical records) was roughly thirty-five years old, and the father of two, when he was killed in action, shot in the skull and ribs, during the White League uprising. Newspaper lists of the September 14 police casualties did not specify the race of those named, and thus readers could not easily glean that men of color had been killed and wounded in the fighting. But coroners' inquests and Metropolitan Police pension fund ledgers detail the toll the fighting took on Black officers and their families—for example, Edward Simonds, a patrolman who was killed on September 14 by a gunshot wound to the head, left behind a widow, Ophilia, and four young children. Among the sixty policemen wounded was a young patrolman named Rodolphe Lucien Desdunes, who would go on to become a literary spokesman, journalist, and community chronicler for New Orleans's Creoles of color; he would help mount the landmark *Plessy v. Ferguson* legal challenge to segregation in 1896.[23]

In the press account of his views, Chester took pains not only to shine a light on Black sacrifices but also to hold whites to account. "The metropolitans are divided into white and colored troops, the former having about two-thirds of the force," he noted. Thus "If the negroes broke and fled, the whites must have done the same, as they were all together." Chester critiqued Kellogg both for fleeing fearfully from the statehouse to the Custom House on the morning of the 14th, and for never giving the Black state militia units, held as they were in reserve, the chance to participate in the firefight alongside the Metropolitan Brigade. Chester was echoed by James Lewis in congressional testimony in December 1874. Lewis emphasized the interracial makeup of the Metropolitan Brigade and the fact that it took its orders from a white man—namely, Longstreet. But despite such protestation that Blacks were not to blame for the day's defeat, the damage to the militia's reputation was done. In his 1874 annual report, Adjutant General Street concluded morosely that his hopes of organizing a "good and efficient division of National Guard during the past year, has been entirely overthrown."[24]

Refuting the White League claim that Blacks had not been targets of wanton white violence during the Canal Street coup, African Americans' testimony emphasized the great harm, in the loss of life and security, the uprising had done to their communities. When asked during Congress's investigation that winter on "the effect of the 14th of September on the colored people," the Black state senator T. B. Stamps answered, "The effect of it was, the colored people all over my district felt their lives were insecure, and that if they dared to open their mouths in any way, expressing themselves dissatisfied at what had been going on in the interest of this White League organization, that they would suffer death, like a great many of their friends did on the 14th of September."[25]

In a different sort of testament to the trauma of September 14, participants in the séances of spiritualist Henry Louis Rey channeled spirit messages from the martyrs of Canal Street, including the murdered Black officer E. R. Monat, who "cried out" in "acute pain" for "[d]eliverance from his body." Spiritualism, which emerged as a force in American religion in the 1850s, gained popularity as those who lost loved ones in the Civil War were drawn to the promise of communicating with them in the afterlife. Rey came from a prominent Afro-Creole family and served as a political as well as religious leader in the community; he joined Longstreet on the school board in 1873, for example. Henry's brother Captain Octave Rey was a stalwart of the police force.[26]

As the press churned over rumors and reports about the September 14 uprising, Kellogg and Longstreet stepped forward with their own public accounts. In testimony before Congress, Kellogg painstakingly traced the "concerted, systematic effort" of the White League's leaders, between June and September, to rile up the mob with sensationalist reports that armed "Black Leagues" were planning to massacre whites and impose "African supremacy." Laying out his own cautious policy, the governor explained that although he was authorized to arm Black militiamen, he had refrained from doing so—they were issued arms only on parade days, for temporary use, without ammunition, "to be returned after the parade to the arsenals." Kellogg pointed up the chilling mendacity of White League's propaganda campaign. Its leaders, he was sure, knew perfectly well "that there was no such thing as the Black League, and that they were not furnished with arms." Kellogg expressed considerable bitterness that this propaganda had vitiated his efforts to recruit white men for the state militia: applying social pressure and threats, the White League fiercely denounced any whites who considered signing on with Kellogg's force.

The White League's invocation of the Second Amendment also struck

Kellogg as self-serving and hypocritical. The League emphasized the "right to a citizen to bear arms," he noted, while "ignoring the language of the clause, 'that a well-regulated militia being necessary to the security of a free State, the right of the people to keep and bear arms shall not be infringed.'" In Kellogg's view, he, Longstreet, and the state militia were the guardians of the people's security and freedom, and the ones whose right to bear arms the amendment was designed to protect.[27]

While Kellogg's account accorded broadly with James Longstreet's views, one crucial detail of the September 14 clash became a subject of bitter, lasting contention between the two men: namely, who had given the order to move the Metropolitan Brigade forward toward the Custom House and the Canal Street front on that fateful day. Kellogg reiterated, in his January 1875 testimony, a claim he had staked on September 15, 1874, in an interview with the *Picayune*: that he "did not order the disposition of the metropolitans," but "Gen. Longstreet did." Not being a military man, Kellogg had decided to entrust Badger and Longstreet—"discreet and experienced officers"—with authority as to "what course to pursue." "I gave no specific order," Kellogg insisted to Congress.[28]

This was a transparent attempt by Kellogg to throw the blame for the day's bloodshed and defeat on his subordinates. Longstreet's own "official memorandum," published by the *Republican* on September 20, emphasized that the governor had explicitly "ordered the state forces to move out" and that they did so in order to counter an "evident" impending attack by the White League. Longstreet added that the relinquishing of the statehouse on September 15 was necessitated by the lack of firepower possessed by the militia troops there, and that "the want of ammunition and military supplies in state arsenals was due to the Attorney General of the State, who had enjoined the militia appropriation of twenty thousand dollars, made by the legislature in its last session." This austerity measure had cost the state dearly, as "there was not ammunition enough to resist more than one assault," Longstreet complained.[29]

On September 21 Longstreet granted an extensive interview with a correspondent for the *Indianapolis Journal* who was on the scene in New Orleans; the interview was first published on September 24 and reprinted widely thereafter. The interviewer was quite taken by Longstreet, describing him as a "handsome, military-looking gentleman," with "more of the qualities of true statesmanship, and a better understanding of the general situation . . . than any one of all those who are denouncing him." When asked to comment on the "military operations made by the State Government to meet the White League," Longstreet took Kellogg to task. Explaining that he himself had been away from the city for several weeks prior to the September 14 uprising, attending to his duties as levee inspector, Longstreet opined that Kellogg's preparations for the defense of the government were "very meager," and repeated that the militia lacked ammunition. Then Longstreet pivoted to the general mood in the region. "The state of feeling in the South is very unsatisfactory and very discreditable to the Southern people," he commented. Musing on the ostracism he had experienced, Longstreet reflected,

> Men can't all think alike, and the trouble with the Southern people always has been that they won't tolerate any difference of opinion. If God Almighty had intended all men to think just alike, He might just as well have made but one man. . . . My opinion is that the only true solution for Southern troubles is for the people to accept cordially and in good faith all the results of the war, including the reconstruction measures, the acts of Congress, negro suffrage, etc., and live up to them like men. If they would do this, and encourage Northern immigration, and treat all men fairly, whites and blacks, the troubles would soon be over, and in less than five years, the South would be in the enjoyment of greater prosperity than ever.

The Southern people, Longstreet continued, were "their own worst enemies."[30]

Given that Longstreet spoke these words one week after risking his life in defense of Reconstruction, they constitute perhaps his bravest and boldest endorsement of transformative, radical change in the South. But, tellingly, they were followed in this interview by a rhetorical retreat to a posture of gradualism. When asked about civil rights legislation pending in Congress to outlaw discrimination in public accommodations, Longstreet hedged his bets, saying that "Its passage at present would be unwise," as in "matters of statesmanship" it was sometimes best to "make haste slowly." The government should prove it could enforce the Reconstruction laws that had already passed and make good on its existing "promises to the negro" before making new promises, he counseled. Moving too quickly would "exasperate the Southern people" and "endanger the lives of the blacks." Longstreet turned to a military metaphor to drive home his point. "In making soldiers . . . we first teach men how to stand straight and to look right and left, then to march, etc., and, finally, by gradual discipline, they are brought to move with the precision of machinery." So, the government, he concluded, ought to accomplish the great end of Reconstruction "by gradual steps." The *Indianapolis Journal* reporter ended his interview by noting that Longstreet's views deserved "consideration as representing the sincere views of an able man."[31]

If Longstreet's interview was an attempt at damage control, it fell far short. He had some Northern defenders, such as the newspaper from Concord, New Hampshire, that called his *Indianapolis Journal* interview "the truth in a nutshell." The Chicago *Inter Ocean* went so far as to suggest that Grant install a military governor in Louisiana to maintain order, and it nominated the "noble and patriotic" Longstreet for the position. But such encomiums were fewer and more muted than in past controversies. In the weeks and months after the White League uprising, Longstreet's reputation among white conservatives hit a new low. It was an unfortunate thing for Longstreet, a Georgia paper mused, reflecting on September 14, "that he was not one of the victims of Gettysburg."[32]

Perhaps even more discouraging than such predictable criticism was the continued infighting among New Orleans Republicans. Not only Kellogg but also Badger blamed the September 14 defeat on Longstreet. The general did not explicitly call out Longstreet in public—initially. But in a December 1874 letter to his father in Massachusetts, Badger disclosed privately his resentment at the incorporation of the Metropolitans into the militia, and his resultant loss of command autonomy. Badger insisted that Longstreet's "bad generalship" had lost the battle of Canal Street: if Longstreet had only ordered the Kellogg forces directly to the levee, as Badger claims to have suggested, rather than moving them to the Custom House first, the Metropolitans could have bought precious time and established a strong defensive position. Referring to the January 1872 Gem Saloon fracas and the March 1873 battle of the Cabildo, Badger wrote that on "previous occasions when I encountered this mob element, I was in command, with no one to dictate or interfere in my arrangements, and each time, we were victorious, with little loss of life." In the same letter, Badger disparaged the Black militia as "poorly disciplined" and "unreliable," and praised his White League captors for conveying him to the hospital after they shot him full of lead.[33]

Whether Badger had, in fact, objected to Longstreet's orders and been overridden by him is unclear. When Badger went public with this claim in an 1885 interview, Longstreet pushed back in an interview of his own. Badger had chosen a faulty, vulnerable position on Canal Street, and Longstreet had ridden forward to urge Badger to "hold closely to the Levee with his left column . . . and [avail] himself of the river to cover his rear," Longstreet maintained. While the debate made good copy, the two men were essentially arguing a moot point. Even if the Kellogg forces had moved with more alacrity to the levee on September 14, they would have still been outnumbered and outgunned. Badger himself conceded in his letter to his father that the insurgents were "no ordinary mob but a well armed, organized and drilled White League officered by experienced Confederate soldiers and outnumbering my little command at least 8 to 1." He went on to say that restoring Kellogg to the governorship had not neutralized the danger, lamenting, "The mob spirit yet prevails and controls the State & city to a certain extent."[34]

On that point, Republicans could agree. In a January 13, 1875, executive message on the troubles in New Orleans, President Grant noted ominously that the White League insurgents had not "in any sense disarmed. On the contrary," he warned, "it is known that the same armed organizations that existed on the 14th of September, 1874, in opposition to the recognized State government, still retain their organization, equipments, and commanders, and can be called out at any hour to resist the State government." Grant was, in effect, conceding a major point to the conservative opposition: that white Southern Republicans, the men Democrats had maligned as scalawags, were at this point leaders without followers. Over the course of the early 1870s, the state militia and the Metropolitan Police and the Republican Party had hemorrhaged support among whites, in the face of a ruthless Democratic campaign of ostracism, scare tactics, and force.[35]

"It seems the special pleasure of the democratic party to assault the character and impugn the motives of all white men who act in concert with the policy of the republican party in the Southern States," intoned Congressman Charles E. Nash in an 1876 speech in the US House of Representatives, in a sort of requiem for Longstreet's career in Louisiana politics. Nash, hailing from Opelousas, Louisiana, was a disabled Black Union veteran who lost a leg in the war, and who served afterward as night inspector in the New Orleans Custom House while Longstreet was surveyor. Nash singled out Longstreet for praise—for having the "political sagacity and independence of character to be among the advance guards in this patriotic labor of reconstruction." But he knew that such sagacity had been unavailing in the face of the "ostracism and menaces," and the "many glaring misrepresentations" of conservative whites. Nash tried to strike a note of optimism in his speech—to conjure a future in which "malice and hate shall give place to brotherly love"—but there were few reasons for Republicans to be hopeful. The only African American to represent Louisiana in Congress during Reconstruction, Nash would lose his congressional seat in 1876 to a former Confederate Democrat, making him the last Black congressman from the state for more than a hundred years (until 1991).[36]

In the aftermath of the Canal Street battle, Longstreet shared in the Louisiana Republicans' pervasive sense of gloom. He was not only demoralized but in ill health—his chronic rheumatism had been made worse by his physically demanding travels, as levee commissioner, through the region's bayous and swamps. Heeding the calls of his brother William, who had settled near Gainesville, Georgia, Longstreet contemplated leaving behind city life and starting anew in his former home state. In the winter of 1874–75 Longstreet began an extended, deliberate process of "switching his political power base from Louisiana to Georgia," as the historian William Garrett Piston has explained. He stepped down from the state returning board after another disputed election, in November 1874, that resulted in an electoral deadlock, more White League terrorism, and another round of federal military intervention. Longstreet continued to play a nominal role as commander of the state militia's First Division, and to serve on the school board, and as a levee inspector, and on the Republican Central Executive Committee of Louisiana, and as a trustee for the University of Louisiana. But he spent large stretches of time on furlough from these responsibilities, so that he could scout out new opportunities in northeastern Georgia.

He continued to be a favorite target of Louisiana conservatives. The Democratic press complained in 1875 that it was "illegal" for him to still serve simultaneously as militia commander, levee commissioner, and school board member. Increasingly, though, the press portrayed Longstreet as a man forsaking the turbulent Louisiana scene and assuming a new role as a "prodigal son" returning to his ancestral homeland. "If we cannot fall on his neck and kill the fatted calf to welcome his return," one Georgia paper opined, "we can at least bury in oblivion the past few years of his career, and believe it was an error of his head and not of his heart." Another paper predicted: "His return will, after a long probation of good behavior, partially restore him."[37]

V

In the late summer of 1875 Longstreet bought a picturesque farm, located on a "beautiful eminence" with commanding views of the mountains, on the outskirts of Gainesville, to serve as his family's principal residence, and as a vineyard and orchard. That fall he purchased the Piedmont Hotel in town, under construction roughly two miles from his farm, and, by the summer of 1876, his family had relocated to Georgia, with his son Garland in charge of running the newly completed hotel. From that point on, Longstreet's public image was inextricably linked to that of Gainesville. A "little hamlet of wooden residences" when Longstreet first settled there, the community grew exponentially in the ensuing decade into an "attractive, thrifty, and prosperous" town of 4,000 inhabitants, graced, so its boosters bragged, by "handsome public buildings," "extensive manufactories," and "excellent schools, churches, and newspapers." The completion of an Air Line railroad had jump-started this development, making the town an important hub for the shipment of cotton and a marketplace for farm produce. At the same time, the town retained a reputation for homespun hospitality, crystal clear water, and cool mountain breezes. Gainesville's image proved malleable: it could represent the enterprising commercial development of the New South or a quaint refuge from big cities such as Atlanta, fifty miles to the southwest. In his nearly three decades based in Gainesville, Longstreet's desire to promote its fortunes would tie him ever more closely to the economic development agenda of the Republican Party—even as he cultivated an image as a "Cincinnatus" who "revel[ed] in his rustic surroundings and farm duties."[38]

Longstreet told the press that he was "attracted to Gainesville by the healthfulness of the place," but, in truth, he also sought to reboot his political career by securing the federal patronage post of US marshal for northern Georgia. As U. S. Grant's second and final term as president came to an end, and the Republican Rutherford B. Hayes assumed office in the bitterly contested election of 1876, Longstreet maneuvered to get in the good graces of the incoming administration. Hayes ran as a reconciliationist candidate who would replace the "bayonet rule" of military governments in the South with "home rule" by local elites and parity between the Northern and Southern states.

The election yielded no clear winner: although the Democratic candidate, Samuel J. Tilden, claimed the popular vote edge, the returns from three key states—Louisiana, South Carolina, and Florida—were disputed, and Republicans charged, with good cause, that the Black vote had been heavily suppressed in the South. An electoral commission established by Congress resolved the dispute in Hayes's favor. The new president's removal of the remaining federal troops from the South, and his overtures to conservative Southern Democrats, suggested that he had come to power through a quid pro quo, or "corrupt bargain," with his foes. A decade after Longstreet's letters favoring the Reconstruction Acts, Hayes's ascendance effectively ended congressional Reconstruction.[39]

In Louisiana, another contested gubernatorial race marked the final days of Reconstruction there, as the Republican candidate, Stephen Packard, faced off in 1876 against Francis T. Nicholls, a former Confederate general representing a "Conservative" coalition that was willing to reach out to some moderate Republicans and to some Black voters. In an atmosphere of fraud, violence, and profound mistrust, both sides claimed victory: as Packard took office and convened his legislature, Nicholls prepared the White League forces to besiege the Republican government and depose it in a bloodless coup. With Hayes making it clear that federal military intervention would not be forthcoming to save the Packard regime, the Republicans were forced to abdicate, and Nicholls assumed control over Louisiana in the spring of 1877.[40]

Evoking the lost promise of Reconstruction, and the massive scale of anti-Black violence in Louisiana, William Murrell, a former slave and Union veteran from rural Madison Parish, testified in Congress in 1880 that white conservatives had established a "reign of terror." Murrell, who had served as a lieutenant colonel in Longstreet's National Guard in 1874 (commanding its 4th Regiment), reported: "[T]he white people in Louisiana are better armed and equipped now than during the war, and they have a better standing army now in the State of Louisiana than was ever known in the State, and I defy any white man in Louisiana, Democrat or Republican to deny that assertion.... You see them parade the streets of New Orleans with their gray uniforms on, and with their improved Winchester rifles and their Gatling guns, and they have now got everything except the rebel flag." Events like the Washington's Birthday parade in New Orleans on February 22, 1874—at which Murrell had stood alongside Governor Kellogg and Longstreet, to review the troops of the interracial militia—were a distant dream.[41]

Longstreet navigated these events by shelving his principled defense of Reconstruction and opportunistically tacking to the political winds. In the 1876 governor's race, he allied with Packard early on, when it looked like Republican victory might open up Packard's US marshal position for Longstreet to fill. But as Packard's fortunes waned and Hayes's rose, Longstreet pronounced publicly, in January 1877, that Nicholls was the legitimate victor in the governor's race. Revealing his lingering resentment of Kellogg, Longstreet conceded that the Democrats might have committed "irregularities" to suppress the vote, but added that those "were fully balanced by the irregularities practiced by the Kellogg administration." Longstreet was not alone in conciliating the Nicholls force—P. B. S. Pinchback, too, abandoned Packard and acknowledged Nicholls as governor. Longstreet was not at this moment repudiating the Republican Party but instead detaching himself from its failed Louisiana leaders and looking ahead to the prospect of patronage rewards from President Hayes.[42]

Even as he stepped away from Louisiana politics, Longstreet sealed his commitment to a powerful institution that had provided him refuge and solace during his time in New Orleans: the Catholic Church. In March 1877 he formally converted from Protestantism to Catholicism, at St. Patrick's Church in New Orleans. As his second wife, Helen Dortch Longstreet, would explain later, this conversion had been a long time in the making and was a direct outgrowth of his political conversion. After he embraced the Republican Party, his ostracism by his fellow Protestants led him to "wonder if there was any church broad enough to withstand differences caused by political and sectional feeling." He discovered that

New Orleans's Catholic priests "extended him the treatment he longed for." And he was drawn to Catholicism, too, for its messages of redemption, in the face of the personal tragedies he had endured. The Catholic Church seemed to him designed for the "sorrow-laden of earth," as Helen Longstreet would poignantly put it.[43]

Although this conversion was a lasting legacy of Longstreet's time in Louisiana, by the spring of 1877, newspapers were routinely describing him as a resident of Gainesville who made occasional trips to New Orleans, rather than the other way around. And they reported, too, on Longstreet's desire to land a position as US marshal for Georgia. Reconstruction was a dead letter, but Longstreet's fighting days were far from over. In a sense, they were just beginning. For even as he moved through the dangerous terrain of Louisiana politics, he ventured deeper into the battlefield of Civil War memory.[44]

VI

In the early 1870s Longstreet was pulled into an escalating debate over his wartime record. Tellingly, this struggle over Civil War memory took shape in the very years that Longstreet was most visible and active in New Orleans politics.

The opening salvos in this conflict were attacks on Longstreet by Jubal Early, one of Robert E. Lee's lieutenant generals, and Reverend William Nelson Pendleton, Lee's former chief of artillery. In a January 19, 1872, speech in Lexington, Virginia, commemorating the birthday of Lee (who had died two years before, and for whom Washington College in Lexington was soon named Washington and Lee), Early pinned the Confederate loss at Gettysburg on Longstreet, charging him with delaying the crucial attack on the Federal left flank on July 2, 1863.

A year later, in another Lexington speech that became the centerpiece of an ensuing lecture tour of the South, Pendleton piled on, indicting

Longstreet for failing to obey Lee's order for a sunrise attack on July 2. These men were soon joined in the anti-Longstreet faction by Lee staffers Walter H. Taylor, A. L. Long, Charles Marshall, Charles Venable, and by Lee's nephew Fitzhugh Lee and the Reverend John William Jones, the latter of whom edited the influential *Southern Historical Society Papers*, a pro-Confederate journal, beginning in 1876. They saw themselves as champions of the Lost Cause—the creed, dominant among Southern whites, that proclaimed that the Confederate cause was righteous and would be vindicated; that Reconstruction was a travesty; and that the racial caste system must persist. Early and his ilk positioned Lee as the symbolic embodiment of the Lost Cause, and they worked relentlessly to immortalize him as a saintly, faultless marble man.[45]

The public reception of the 1872–73 Lexington lectures reveals the toll that Longstreet's political career in New Orleans took on his military reputation in the South. The Democratic Southern press praised Early and Pendleton for exposing not only Longstreet's failures at Gettysburg but also his allegedly treacherous motives: his delay was not simply a question of poor execution but instead an act of "criminal negligence and disobedience," as one North Carolina paper put it. Northern Republican Party papers saw such critiques of Longstreet's military record as brazenly political. Longstreet was paying the "penalty a prominent Southerner has to pay for being honest, for being a Republican," editorialized a Vermont paper. "If he was less prominent," it added, "they would 'ku-klux' him, or, perhaps treat him as the aristocratic Southerners did the poor republican negroes at Colfax."[46]

Longstreet regarded Early's and Pendleton's attacks as a smear campaign, but he was reticent at first about countering them. At the time of Early's 1872 speech, Longstreet had twice, fleetingly, questioned Lee's judgment at Gettysburg; once, in an interview with journalist William Swinton, as part of the research for Swinton's 1866 book, *Campaigns of the Army of the Potomac*; and a second time in an 1871 interview with the noted war correspondent George Alfred Townsend (who used the pen name "Gath") for the Republican newspaper the *Chicago Tribune*. In both, Longstreet revealed that he thought the Confederate assaults on July 2 and 3 ill-advised and had hoped Lee would stick to defensive tactics during the Gettysburg campaign. Longstreet claimed, in a "full and free conversation" with Swinton, that Lee had lost his "equipoise" (sense of balance) on the second day at Gettysburg after having "gotten a taste of blood" and of success on the battle's first day. These comments, in the immediate aftermath of the war, caught Early's attention, but were not enough to unleash his wrath; revealingly, the memoirs Early completed by the end of the 1860s evinced nearly no anti-Longstreet bias. But as Longstreet's political influence rose, his musings on the war seemed, to the likes of Early, more pointed and provocative. In his 1871 interview with Gath, Longstreet explained that he had "advised the turning of the Federal position on Cemetery Ridge," and that if Lee had only permitted him to flank Round Top to the right, Longstreet would have marched "directly upon Washington city." Longstreet mused "philosophically" that "both sides, in the civil war, committed mistakes when they put engineer officers at the head of large armies"; this was a dig at George McClellan, but also, more leadingly, at Lee. While politics was not the focus of the 1871 interview, it was the subtext: Gath closed the interview by noting Longstreet's admiration for Grant.[47]

Once Early and Pendleton escalated the debate over Gettysburg by impugning Longstreet's motives and honor, Longstreet knew he would have to marshal a substantial array of documents and allies in order to mount a sustained counterattack. In the summer of 1873 he let it be known to the press that as soon as he could "collect the facts and figures," he would prove that he was not responsible for the Gettysburg loss. He began reaching out to former comrades in arms for support. In a revealing letter of July 1873, Longstreet wrote John Bell Hood asking for "information and data as you may be able to furnish regarding the Gettysburg campaign." At this early stage in the imbroglio, Longstreet was able to effect a wry, confiding tone: "I have always thought that Gen Lee spoke the truth when he said of Gettysburg, 'It is all my fault.'" Since Lee had "so generously made this admission, I have not been inclined to say anything that might make the error more glaring," Longstreet added. He did not yet burn with anger at his critics or feel that they had done his reputation great damage, and he assumed that Hood would read such comments in the spirit of the two men's shared admiration for their former chief. Longstreet's role in Louisiana politics was, at that time, his main focus, and he was ambivalent about relitigating the past. He told a reporter from the *St. Louis Globe* in May 1874 that it was "better to look to the welfare of the country than to speculate upon the reasons the South, or this or that exponent of its principles, got whipped."[48]

But there was no avoiding this war of words. As the White League planned and then perpetrated its September 1874 uprising, Longstreet's detractors explicitly connected his wartime failings and postwar conduct in Louisiana—indeed, the more deeply Longstreet became implicated in Republican politics, the more receptive white Southerners became to the criticisms of his war record. Referring to Pendleton's 1873 speech, the *Dallas Herald* editorialized in October 1874 that it had not believed the charges against Longstreet at first. But since his appearance "at the head of the metropolitan police, prepared to hurl his messengers of death upon the citizens of New Orleans," the editors proclaimed, "we withdraw our incredulity and are prepared now to believe that no deed of infamy could be named or conceived that [Longstreet] would not gladly be a party to." The publication, that fall, of the Reverend Dr. Jones's "personal reminiscences" of Robert E. Lee fueled the fire, as the volume reprinted Lee's October 1867 private letter to Longstreet, in which Lee sternly chastised him for accepting the Reconstruction Acts.

The Early clique was trying to suggest that Lee himself mistrusted Longstreet—and to retroactively deny Longstreet his standing as Lee's trusted "war-horse." A sharp exchange between Longstreet and Pendleton in the spring of 1875 lays bare the political nature of their debate over the war. Longstreet regarded the Reverends Pendleton and Jones with contempt, referring to them derisively as the two "Parsons," highlighting their sanctimony. When Longstreet expressed his shame at ever having served alongside Pendleton, the right reverend shot back: "You say that you would never consent to my representing you on the field of battle. To that honour I could no means aspire, especially since your exploits in the last '*Battle* of New Orleans.'"[49]

The controversies over Longstreet's roles in the war and in Reconstruction followed him to Georgia and became entwined with a new phase in his political career. Preoccupied with the attacks on his military reputation, Longstreet stepped up his appeals to former Confederate officers and aides for their recollections, and traveled to Washington, DC, to gain access to War Department archives containing official records. He was gratified to find that some of his former First Corps staff were willing to defend his military performance while setting aside or rejecting his politics. This was partly self-interest. They understood that, whatever their partisan leanings, their own reputations were at stake: defending Longstreet's wartime performance meant vindicating the First Corps. For example, when Longstreet wrote his former aide-de-camp, Thomas Goree, a Democrat, in May 1875, asking for his recollections of Gettysburg with which to counter Pendleton's charges, Goree offered his support for Longstreet's account, noting, "Although we may differ in our political opinions, yet I have always given you credit for honesty and sincerity of purpose." In a passage that must have delighted Longstreet, Goree also declared it "preposterous" that "such an old *granny* as Pendleton" would presume to know anything about Gettysburg, as he had spent the battle "miles in the rear." Echoing Longstreet's own take, Goree noted, "Pendleton has presumed upon your present unpopularity to make charges which he otherwise would not have dared to utter." Perhaps most important, Goree suggested that Lee himself had admitted, after Gettysburg, the merits of Longstreet's plan; he recalled having heard Lee say, in the winter of 1863–64, that if Longstreet had made his proposed flank attack on July 3, instead of the ill-fated Pickett's charge on Cemetery Hill, it would "have met with but little opposition."[50]

Longstreet deeply appreciated such support, writing back to Goree, "I presume that the difference in our politics is not so great as it appears, if sifted to the bottom. The end that we seek, I know, is the same, the restoration of the Southern people to their natural and proper influence. The best and speediest means of arriving at this end has been [the] only difference." Showing his impulse to get the last word, however, Longstreet pressed this point, defending his own conduct in New Orleans as "the best policy for that state" and, in a remarkable passage, suggesting that he not only accepted Confederate defeat but also welcomed it retroactively as divine intervention had ruled "that slavery in these states should cease forever in the year 1865, and it is hardly possible that it should have ceased if we had been made an independent nation." Goree chose not to engage over politics, and the two men remained friends.[51]

This May letter illuminates both the extent and limits of Longstreet's political transformation during Reconstruction. His condemnation of slavery was an attempt to occupy the moral high ground—to suggest that there was more at stake in these debates about the war than individual military honor. By invoking the workings of "overruling Providence" in bringing emancipation and Union victory, Longstreet grasped at a way to exonerate Lee—and any mortal man, including himself, from the "awful burden" of responsibility for Confederate defeat. But Longstreet could not hold that high ground, for he was too keen to win the battle over reputation. And so his letter to Goree developed a claim that would be a staple in Longstreet's self-defense in the coming decades: that Lee admitted, during the war itself, that Longstreet had been right at Gettysburg. Seizing on Goree's brief mention of Lee's regrets over July 3, Longstreet cited the 1872 magazine article of Francis Charles Lawley, a *London Times* correspondent who had traveled with the Confederate troops. Lawley quoted Lee as having said, in the winter of 1863–64, "If I had taken General Longstreet's advice on the eve of the second day of the battle of Gettysburg . . . The Confederates would today be a free people." Adding his own gloss, Longstreet told Goree, "It has often been reported to me just before Gen. Lee's death that he often, and in the most poignant distress, referred to that occasion as the one on which the cause was lost, with a full sense of his own responsibility in the matter." In the space of one letter, Longstreet had both absolved and condemned Lee.[52]

Longstreet's missive signaled his hope that there were other former Confederates willing to take his side. Men who served under Longstreet did occasionally come forward with public statements to counter the Early-Pendleton critique. Their defenses either distinguished Longstreet's wartime record from his postwar politics or distinguished between his heroic combat leadership and his performance as a tactician (praising the former as untainted by the latter). Thus, in May 1873 an article by "One of Longstreet's Foot Cavalry" circulated through the press, in which the writer exclaimed,

> Gen. Pendleton may lecture and create a sensation that will put money in his pocket, but he will never convince the fighting men who are left of Longstreet's corps that the grim commander at whose word they so often threw themselves against the battalions of the north, was a traitor to the cause he sacrificed for. No matter what his politics may be; no matter how much derided, vilified and abused, Longstreet's name will go sounding down the corridors of time as one of the best, bravest, and most unassuming officers the southern confederacy produced.

Longstreet was also defended by a former brigadier general in his corps, Benjamin G. Humphreys. Though a conservative Democrat—and governor of Mississippi under Johnsonian Reconstruction—Humphreys believed that when an "impartial history" of the Civil War could one day be written, the "military fidelity and heroic record" of Longstreet would "shine among the brightest ornaments of the Confederate struggle."[53]

Unfortunately for Longstreet, the men whose endorsements he needed most—those in Lee's inner circle—generally hedged their bets rather than offer him unqualified support. Charles Marshall, Lee's former aide-de-camp, denied the existence of a sunrise order by Lee on July 2 at Gettysburg, but did get in a swipe, observing that Lee felt "there was not proper unity of action that day," and also that Lee had hoped that Longstreet's attack on the 3rd would begin earlier than it had. Pendleton had perhaps confounded the 2nd and the 3rd, Marshall observed, but was not wrong to note that Lee's battle plans were poorly executed. A. L. Long, also of Lee's staff, took a similar tack, writing Longstreet that while he had no recollection of a sunrise order, he did believe that "it was Gen. Lee's intention to attack the enemy on the 2nd of July as early as practicable." Lee's former adjutant general, Walter H. Taylor, for his part, wrote Longstreet that he either "never knew" of a sunrise order, or perhaps it had "strangely escaped" his memory.[54]

While such equivocating boded poorly, Longstreet could take encouragement from the Northern press, which covered his research trip to Washington with some fanfare and speculated that he had commenced writing a book about the war. Republican papers expressly cast his task as that of defending himself against the "batteries of social hate" aimed at him by "the White League press of the South," to quote the Chicago *Inter Ocean*; the paper editorialized that "the scars of the men who faced him at Gettysburg, and on many other fields, is all the vindication that he requires." Longstreet would find reconciliation with his Confederate detractors to be more elusive than reunion with his former Yankee foes.[55]

PART III

Reconciliation

Chapter 8

RETURN OF THE PRODIGAL

I

In January 1876 Longstreet began in earnest to defend his war record by providing the *New Orleans Republican* with a copy of the letter he had written to his uncle A. B. Longstreet from Culpeper, Virginia, on July 24, 1863, just three weeks after the Battle of Gettysburg. Longstreet, it will be recalled, had confided to Augustus that "the battle was not made as I would have had it. My idea was to throw ourselves between the enemy and Washington, select a strong position, and force the enemy to attack us." Professing his abiding loyalty to Lee, Longstreet added, "As we failed of success I must take my part of that responsibility. . . . As General Lee is our commander, he should have all the support and influence that we can give him." Longstreet closed the letter with the prediction "The truth will be known in time." The *Republican* printed the letter in full, editorializing that Lee was responsible for the "rash policy" that resulted in defeat, and saying of Longstreet that although he "was overruled by his commanding officer," he "did the best he could to turn the mistake into success." Longstreet fed the paper a second claim: namely, that in January 1864 Lee had written him a letter confessing regret at having not chosen defensive tactics. Lee's letter purportedly told Longstreet, "Had I taken your advice at Gettysburg, instead of pursuing the course I did, how different all might have been."[1]

It is unlikely but not inconceivable that Lee wrote such a letter to Longstreet. On the one hand, as historian Earl Hess has put it, "It is quite possible that there is a germ of truth in the notion that Lee went through a period of analysis and concluded, too late, that a flanking movement might have been worth trying." In an 1889 private letter to Longstreet, a former staff officer named Erasmus Taylor vouched for the existence of the January 1864 letter, recalling that Longstreet received Lee's missive while in winter quarters at Morristown in East Tennessee, and that Longstreet had called Taylor into his tent and read him the letter, "saying that it some time might be important for some other than [Longstreet] to remember it." On the other hand, the fact that Longstreet never produced the text of the entire letter, and that he relied initially, in 1875, on hearsay (Lawley's and Goree's reports) rather than citing a Lee letter militate against the existence of such a document. Longstreet's references to the letter were sporadic and tentative, suggesting a lack of confidence in his own memory of it.[2]

The conservative Southern press called the *Republican* article "a vain attempt" by Longstreet to restore his damaged reputation, and Jubal Early and Fitzhugh Lee led the way in assailing Longstreet for slandering Lee. Both cast doubt on the existence of the January 1864 letter. Early suggested that if Lee wrote something like "Had I taken your advice," he was doing so to humor or console Longstreet, as he often did junior officers, or perhaps being self-abnegating and generous in his noble fashion. Fitzhugh Lee demanded that Longstreet produce "the whole of the letter said to have been written in January 1864, of which only one short sentence has been published."[3]

Longstreet explained in early March 1876, in the pages of the *Republican*, that his effort to collect "all the facts in the case of Gettysburg" had been interrupted by "severe sickness" and that he still intended to collect such evidence and publish his own account. Longstreet accused Fitzhugh Lee, in a charge he would level repeatedly during the controversy, of exploiting current "political prejudices" to rewrite the history of the war. Fitzhugh Lee replied, "I cannot see what politics has to do with the matter at issue"—a claim that was plainly disingenuous, as the partisan press was the vehicle for the war of words over Gettysburg, with Republican papers taking Longstreet's side and conservative Southern Democratic ones condemning him. Erasmus Taylor, in a mid-March private letter of support to his former commander, lambasted Fitzhugh Lee for "self-exaltation." He went on: "Thrusting himself forward continually as the exponent of Southern, and especially Virginian opinion, his hope and aim is for political preferment." Longstreet surely agreed. In late March, in a long, caustic piece published in the *Republican*, he staked another claim that would become a staple of his writings on the war: namely, that Early and his critics were attacking him and exonerating Lee so that "the drippings of [Lee's] robes may remove blemishes that hang about their names." From here on out, Longstreet's defense of his own performance would be coupled with arch attacks on the military failings of his critics.[4]

Meanwhile, new literary and political alliances were taking shape for Longstreet, in both the North and the South, which raised his hopes that he could counter his negative public image as a partisan placeman and craft a new image as a national statesman and promoter of sectional reconciliation.

II

Longstreet found a key literary ally in Alexander K. McClure, editor of the *Philadelphia Weekly Times*. The paper was in the process of commissioning a series of accounts of the war by Union and Confederate veterans, in what historian David Blight has described as "an initial effort at reconciliation through recollection ... aiming at providing a forum for healing, accuracy, and multiple points of view." McClure was in the vanguard of an ascendant national cult of reconciliation, which submerged the difficult unresolved political and racial conflicts of the war era and enshrined a narrative of shared heroism and sacrifice on the part of the blue and the gray. As

Blight has shown, the cult promoted fraternal feelings among white veterans while marginalizing Black ones. Articles of the kind commissioned by McClure, and then gathered together and published in the popular 1878 book *The Annals of the Civil War*, frequently pitted soldiers' competing accounts of military events against one another—but they nonetheless served the purpose of reconciliation by diverting public attention away from politics toward military history, and by channeling "embittered emotions to the pursuit of facts and accuracy."[5]

McClure had been following the controversy over Longstreet and Gettysburg, and upped the ante by commissioning Walter H. Taylor to write an anti-Longstreet account of Gettysburg in March 1876 for the *Times*. Taylor's charges that Longstreet had delayed on July 2 and failed to use the forces at his disposal on July 3 had the predictable result of goading Longstreet into action. As he explained to Henry B. Dawson, a New York editor-historian, it was not the criticism per se but its disproportionate nature that was so objectionable. "Those of us who bore prominent parts in the struggle should recognize its failure. And should submit to the responsibilities of that failure, as belonging to us all in proportion to our positions," Longstreet conceded. But, he added, he resented being singled out as solely to blame for Confederate defeat.

McClure swept in, offering Longstreet the chance to vindicate himself in the pages of the *Times*, and even sending the rising journalistic star Henry W. Grady to Gainesville to assist in the writing and editing process. The Georgia-born Grady was serving at the time as an Atlanta-based correspondent for the *New York Herald* as well as taking on freelance assignments like the one offered by McClure. Grady would go on to become a journalistic legend and icon of reconciliation in his own right, but at this stage, in 1876–77, his duty was a simple one: to make sure Longstreet finished his article in a timely fashion so that the *Times* could claim to offer its national readership "Longstreet's first public defense of his movements at Gettysburg," as McClure put it.[6]

Longstreet's article in the November 3, 1877, edition of the *Philadel-*

phia Weekly Times, and a follow-up piece that the paper published a few weeks later, were responses not only to McClure's bait but also to provocations coming from another influential source: the pages of the recently established *Southern Historical Society Papers* (*SHSP*). An outgrowth of the Southern Historical Society, which had been founded in New Orleans in 1869 to promote a pro-Confederate history of the war and that relocated to Richmond, Virginia, in 1873, the *SHSP* series was a forum for the anti-Longstreet faction. Under its head, the Reverend J. William Jones, it proclaimed, as a central tenet of the Lost Cause creed, the "military and moral infallibility of Lee." The *SHSP* printed or reprinted (from sources such as the *Philadelphia Times*) a slew of anti-Longstreet articles by Early, Taylor, and others; these included an August 1877 offering from Early accusing Longstreet of having a "constitutional inertia, mental and physical, that very often delayed his readiness to fight."[7]

With such slanders ringing in his ears, Longstreet provided, in his first *Philadelphia Times* essay, the detailed argument the public had awaited, addressing his own behavior and his relationship with Lee. He led with his July 24, 1863, letter to his uncle and then pivoted to his precampaign deliberations over strategy with Lee. His "close personal and social relations" with Lee permitted Longstreet to propose to his superior that the Confederates concentrate their forces under General Joseph Johnston at Tullahoma, Tennessee, for a march through Tennessee and Kentucky into Ohio; this would surely, Longstreet reckoned, take the pressure off Vicksburg, the key Mississippi River stronghold that was under siege by Grant. Lee agreed that the time was right for an offensive that would relieve Vicksburg by drawing the Union army north to protect its own territory, but he proposed an invasion of Maryland and Pennsylvania instead. After some back-and-forth, Longstreet "finally assented that the Pennsylvania campaign might be brought to a successful issue if [Lee] could make it offensive in strategy, but defensive in tactics."[8]

Of the many key points and phrases in the *Philadelphia Times* article, this "offensive in strategy, but defensive in tactics" formulation has attracted the most attention from modern scholars, and justifiably so. Here was the key to all that followed: Longstreet went on to describe how he pressed this argument on each day of the Gettysburg battle, clinging to the hope that Lee would dislodge the army from the unfavorable low ground it occupied and throw it between Meade and Washington, inviting a defensive battle, akin to Fredericksburg, on terrain favorable to the Confederates. Lee failed to take this advice, Longstreet explained, because he had been thrown off balance and lost his "matchless equipoise," due both to the "deplorable absence" of his cavalry chief J. E. B. Stuart and to Lee's own overexcitement at the prospect of another underdog victory. Longstreet's men gave their all in their attacks on July 2 and 3, he maintained, despite the fact that they had lacked the necessary support from Lee's other two corps and had been asked to do the impossible. Longstreet was willing, he professed in the closing section of his second article, to accept his share of the blame for the Gettysburg "disaster," but not to take on "the whole burden of that battle."[9]

Longstreet's articles created quite a public stir. "I have this day read your letter in the *Phila. Weekly Times*, Nov. 3, which I have been trying to get for a week or more; the letter was so sought after, I had to send to the office in Phil'a [Philadelphia] for a copy," Longstreet's devoted former aide-de-camp John W. Fairfax wrote him on November 12, 1877, from Prince William County, Virginia. Fairfax had literally followed Longstreet's lead during Reconstruction, as a staff officer in the New Orleans–based National Guard and secretary of the Republican State Central Committee. Fairfax noted, accurately, that the *Times* article was "favorably received" by much of the public, and he chalked that up to the spirit of reconciliation ushered in by Republican Rutherford B. Hayes's election to the White House. Fairfax endorsed Longstreet's account of Gettysburg as truthful and declared his war record to be "faultless."

A few other prominent former Confederates who had served under Longstreet—most notably the colorful Texas politician Tom Ochiltree and the Louisiana officeholder W. B. Merchant—joined the Republican Party and defended both Longstreet's wartime service and his postwar politics.

They shared his belief that Southern white Republicans should be the dominant element within the party coalition, with Northern transplants ("carpetbaggers") yielding their leadership roles, and Black voters serving as a subordinate rank and file. They promoted Longstreet's standing with Republican administrations, and he promoted theirs.[10]

But such men were rarities. If Longstreet had imagined that the *Philadelphia Times* articles would blunt the opposition of his Virginia critics, he was sorely mistaken. Early led the way in the *SHSP*'s new round of counterattacks. For Longstreet to suggest that "he was the self-constituted 'council' of General Lee," and that Lee sought his "assent," was proof, Early charged, of Longstreet's "impudence, arrogance, and presumptuous self-conceit." Early also noted that Longstreet had still not produced the full text of the retrospective January 1864 letter ("Had I taken your advice . . .") from Lee. The Lost Cause faithful across the South rallied to the beloved Lee's defense. Longstreet's article could "not disturb the imperishable fame" of Lee, as a rebuttal that circulated in Deep South newspapers put it: Longstreet had merely shown that "Lee's matchless strategy failed to be executed by his lieutenants." The *Times* pieces could "add nothing to Longstreet's reputation," sniffed the *Daily Enquirer-Sun* from Columbus, Georgia, "shadowed as it has been by late years by his reception into the ranks of Radicalism." In New Orleans, Longstreet had "joined the worst foes of his section," the paper reminded readers, and "had his course been followed," Louisiana would "have still been under the rule of carpetbaggers and ignorance." He should not have dared to "attack the memory and reputation of the noble leader of the most gallant army the world had ever seen."[11]

Union generals, like Confederate ones, found that military reputations were perennially subject to dispute. In 1879 Longstreet played a prominent role in exonerating General Fitz John Porter, who had been court-martialed back in 1863 for failing to follow his commander John Pope's orders at Second Manassas in August 1862. Porter, leading the Army of the Potomac's Fifth Corps, had declined to launch an assault against the Confederate right on the grounds that the rebel lines there—reinforced by

Longstreet—were too strong. Porter shared the excessive caution and tendency to overestimate enemy strength that characterized General George McClellan; the two men were confidants who also shared a Democratic Party affiliation and a distrust of the Lincoln administration. McClellan, while he led the Army of the Potomac, viewed Porter as his right-hand man. Both McClellan and Porter were under a cloud after the Union loss at Second Manassas, as McClellan was suspected of failing to send reinforcements to Pope, and Porter became the scapegoat for Pope's tactical failings. McClellan's and Porter's political leanings, particularly their recalcitrance toward Lincoln's emancipation policy, stoked the suspicion of Radical Republican politicians, and Porter was cashiered from the army for disobedience. The Porter controversy garnered major press attention, with Democrats maintaining that he'd been "sacrificed solely as a political blow at McClellan," as the historian William Marvel has explained.[12]

Porter spent a decade and a half after the war seeking vindication, lining up allies who could vouch for his version of the story. Longstreet was among them—he wrote Porter privately in 1866 that Confederate forces were indeed strong enough on August 29, 1862, to repel any Union assault. The implication was that Porter had exercised sound judgment in choosing not to attack. Porter finally got his shot at public redemption when an army commission reconsidered his case in 1879. Longstreet served as a witness, traveling from Georgia to West Point in New York for the retrial and confirming in his testimony that "most of his wing of Lee's army, at least twenty-five thousand strong," faced down Porter on the 29th. The review board found that Porter's delay had been justified and his court martial of 1863 unjustified, and the general was exonerated and restored to the army's rolls.

Longstreet's role in this drama was yet another occasion for him to find the media spotlight. Surely he saw parallels to his own scapegoating over Gettysburg: like Longstreet, Porter was accused in the court of public opinion not only of tardiness but of treachery and even treason. For Longstreet, the Porter retrial was a chance to posture as the objective truth teller, beholden to the facts, and not, as his critics charged, merely a pawn of the Radical Republicans.[13]

Longstreet continued to press his own case before the public, giving an extensive interview to the *Philadelphia Times* in the summer of 1879 purporting to be a "frank criticism of the military men and of the operations on both sides," as the interview's subtitle ran. He called the war "a grievous error—an error of both sections and for which both sections have deeply atoned." But he then focused on the causes of Southern defeat. "[I]n a protracted war," Longstreet mused, "everything depends upon organization." Confederate forces, he continued, "were never properly organized or disciplined." Longstreet attributed the Confederates' failure to concentrate troops to none other than President Jefferson Davis and his faulty perimeter defense strategy, which sought to "protect our soil as much as possible." The Union forces, by contrast, "moved like machines" under the leadership of Grant, who "understood the terrible power of concentration and persistency." Longstreet praised Lee as a "wise, deep, and sagacious" leader, but also observed that Pickett's charge on July 3, 1863, was ill-considered and that Lee was operating "under great excitement" on that day. Even as he assessed Grant, Lee, and other leaders, Longstreet's main argument was that systemic factors and grand strategy counted for more than individual valor or genius in a drawn-out war of attrition.[14]

Longstreet received an endorsement for the 1879 interview from D. H. Hill, a former Confederate corps commander and South Carolinian, who shared Longstreet's antipathy to the Early-led Virginian clique. Hill felt unfairly criticized for his efforts during the Maryland campaign of 1862, as the Virginians blamed him for having lost Lee's famous Special Orders 191 (which revealed that Lee had divided his forces). Hill praised Longstreet for having provided the "correct" account of the Gettysburg campaign, and they corresponded and commiserated regularly thereafter. "They have made me the scapegoat for the Maryland campaign and you the scapegoat for the Pennsylvania campaign," Hill wrote Longstreet in a series of letters decrying the "vanity of the Virginians," who "glorify their own prowess to deify Lee." Such support was encouraging. But Longstreet's quest for military vindication was about to take a back seat, as his political career experienced a revival.[15]

III

When Longstreet bought property in Gainesville in 1875, some of the Democratic newspapers in Georgia had initially expressed hope that the move betokened a retreat from the political arena. The *Savannah Advertiser* observed that while Longstreet's postwar "sins against the south [were] most grievous and never to be forgotten," there was, in the form of his wartime heroism, "a large credit side to the account." Now that he had "retired from . . . the most serious strife of public civil life," the *Advertiser* suggested, the public should give him a chance to show his repentance.[16]

Such hopes that Longstreet would forsake the political arena were soon dashed. While he no longer led and trained Black militiamen and police officers, he continued to relish a role he had played during Reconstruction: as a spokesman for white Southern Republicans to presidential administrations and to the Northern public, using his influence—especially over patronage appointments—to try to build the Republican Party in his state. At the time of the Longstreet family's move east, the Georgia Republican Party was in steep decline. It had enjoyed a brief ascendance during the early phase of congressional Reconstruction, with the 1868 election of Radical Republican governor Rufus Brown Bullock. But moderate anti-Bullock Republicans and Democrats soon joined forces in rejecting the Fifteenth Amendment, expelling duly elected Black legislators from the general assembly, and using violence and intimidation to suppress Black voting. Congress, deploying the US military, tried to restore the Republicans and to bring the state into compliance with its readmission procedures, but the state elections in 1870 gave Democrats control over both houses of the state legislature and the majority of federal congressional seats, and the Republicans struggled to shake the "stigma of corruption" they had acquired under the unpopular Bullock.

In 1872, with disillusioned moderate Republicans flocking to the Liberal Republican movement and to the Democratic Party, and with anti-Black intimidation and violence rampant, the Democrats regained the governorship, leaving the Georgia Republicans with a minimal presence in the legislature, and mired in competition with one another over federal patronage appointments.[17]

From the start of his time in Georgia, Longstreet sought political office. He lobbied the Hayes administration, avowing that if he held a prominent Republican post, he could "Southernise the party and regain its lost morale and strength." The president finally obliged him in September 1878, appointing Longstreet as a deputy collector of internal revenue for Georgia and Florida, and then, in December, as postmaster of Gainesville. The conservative press had a field day with the image of Longstreet, who once "licked Yankees," now "licking postage stamps." "How are the mighty fallen!" a Texas paper proclaimed of the Gainesville appointee. But Longstreet refused to go gently into the political night. Instead, he remained a vocal commentator on partisan politics, uniquely positioned to explain the South to the North. Longstreet took issue with the White House's over-conciliation of Democrats. For example, Hayes had appointed a Democrat to the US marshal job that Longstreet coveted. Although the president's goal of fostering national unity was the right one, it "could have been more gracefully reached through judicious selections from the republican party," Longstreet explained in an October 1877 letter to a Midwestern newspaper. He had himself in mind—he felt he had earned a prominent federal patronage job.[18]

In a steady stream of interviews, letters, and speeches spanning his transition from Louisiana to Georgia, Longstreet expressed the hope that "political intolerance, the band that now holds the solid South together, will be broken," as he told the Chicago *Inter Ocean* in February 1880. While Longstreet's main goal was to augment the relative power of Southern whites within the Republican coalition, what is most striking about his political commentary was his consistent support for Black voting. In the same 1880 interview in which he decried political intolerance, Longstreet called attention to the ways that economic pressure and vigilante violence were used to suppress the Republican vote:

> You must know, if you know anything of Southern politics . . . that at election times, the Republicans here, both white and colored, are subjected to peculiar inconveniences. The businessman who votes the Republican ticket sacrifices thereby his business interests and loses the patronage of the Southern people. The negro laborer—well, six-shooters are the inconveniences that he sometimes meets with in the exercise of his suffrage . . . [and] it is impossible for him to find an honest way of earning his bread after he votes contrary to the wishes of the men who employ him.

Longstreet clearly hoped, for his own part, to change this, saying wishfully, "Why, in a free and fair election, I believe that the colored and white Republican vote would amount in Georgia to a clear majority." Longstreet also looked ahead to the 1880 presidential contest and asserted that U. S. Grant, alone among Republicans, could carry some Southern states because only he could command the united support of Black voters. "They will risk their lives to vote for him," Longstreet maintained.[19]

Longstreet's resilient Republicanism paid off when, in May 1880, Postmaster General David Key resigned. The Tennessee Democrat and former Confederate general had been appointed by Hayes as a gesture of sectional reconciliation. In line to replace Key was the US minister to Turkey, Horace Maynard, a wartime Tennessee Unionist. That opened up the foreign posting, and Hayes appointed Longstreet to fill it. To be sure, the position of minister to Turkey was not an especially high-profile one. American diplomacy in this era was focused on expanding foreign markets and trading rights in Latin America and the Far East, and the State Department still viewed the Ottoman Empire and the Mediterranean largely as beyond its sphere of influence.[20]

Nevertheless, the posting in Turkey appealed to Longstreet. His minister's salary would be more robust than the paltry pay he earned as postmaster of Gainesville. He had a genuine interest in his diplomatic brief, which was to improve commercial relations with Turkey. As part of his postwar political conversion, Longstreet fully embraced the project of economic modernization and the view that "successful domestic and international commerce can only be reached through Republican policy," as he put it. Moreover, Longstreet had long taken a keen spectator's interest in the so-called "Eastern question" involving the fate of the Ottoman Empire in its competition with European Great Powers. The US press closely followed the Russo-Turkish War of 1877–78 and the ensuing Treaty of Berlin, which stripped the Ottoman Empire of vast swaths of its provinces in the Balkans. In a fall 1877 interview with a reporter from a newspaper in Macon, Georgia, Longstreet noted that he tracked the war between the Turks and Russians intently; he analyzed "every movement with interest, and [could] detect an error as quickly as any one, in the maneuvers of the armies." Three years later, as Longstreet set sail for Istanbul, that same newspaper speculated that Longstreet would find "much to interest him in the East" on "all matters relating to the organization of armies." Most important, the appointment as minister was a chance for Longstreet to revamp his political reputation and prove wrong the critics who had gleefully mocked his fall from grace. Whatever its challenges, a diplomatic post could elevate Longstreet to the rank of statesman: a representative of the United States government on the world stage.[21]

Longstreet's 1880 nomination as minister immediately yielded yet another surge of press interest. He was not the first or only former Confederate-turned-Republican to serve in the diplomatic corps: James Lawrence Orr had been the US minister to Russia, and Thomas Settle, minister to Peru in the early 1870s; John Singleton Mosby was US consul in Hong Kong from 1878 to 1885; Henry Washington Hilliard represented the United States in Brazil as envoy and minister from 1877 to 1881; and George Earl Maney would serve as minister to Colombia, Bolivia, Paraguay, and Uruguay in the 1880s. But as the highest-ranking Confederate to ally with the Republican Party, Longstreet exemplified more than anyone the North's commitment to Southern deliverance: the view, as Massachusetts senator George F. Hoar put it in an 1877 speech, referring to Longstreet, that "the great victory of the Union arms was achieved not to make the men of the South dependents, but only equals." While Northern deliverance rhetoric focused on the redemption of the nonslaveholding white Southern masses, it always held out hope of redeeming some elite slaveholding whites, too, who could lend prestige to the project of national reunion. In that spirit, the Republican press lavished praise on Longstreet, hailing his nomination as minister and predicting for him great success in his new role. The "graceful and courtly" Longstreet would be "an honorable acquisition to our diplomatic service," according to the *Weekly Louisianian*, the New Orleans newspaper published by Longstreet ally P. B. S. Pinchback. Periodicals such as *Frank Leslie's Illustrated Newspaper* added that Longstreet's fame as a soldier would reflect well on America and secure him a "cordial welcome abroad."[22]

There were dissenting voices—for example, a Grand Army of the Republic post in Ohio, consisting of veterans who had faced Longstreet's Confederates at Chickamauga, forwarded to President Hayes a resolution declaring that the United States had "dishonored itself and insulted the Loyal Soldiers of the Nation" by elevating the "Rebel General Longstreet." But such critics failed to get traction. Unlike in the case of Longstreet's earlier federal patronage appointment in the New Orleans Custom House, his Democratic opponents this time did not wage a bitter campaign against his confirmation. The Senate, in which the Democrats held a majority, confirmed him on June 14, 1880, by a resounding margin of 39 to 3. The vote reflected long-term political calculations. Southern Democrats were ambivalent, rather than uniformly hostile, about Longstreet taking on the mantle of ambassador. Predictably, some howled that he was unfit for office and a tool of the Radical Republicans, or rued the fact that Longstreet's ministerial appointment had brought him back into public life after his relatively obscure spell in Georgia. Others, however, viewing him as a political independent rather than a Radical Republican, tentatively abided the appointment: a former Confederate was better than a Northern carpetbagger or Southern Unionist, they reckoned, and perhaps Longstreet could do less harm "away off in Turkey" than at home in the South. It was possible to interpret Hayes's appointment of Longstreet as a way of "honoring the South" and opening the door to a greater role for ex-Confederates in the federal government.[23]

Northern Democrats, for their part, acquiesced in Longstreet's diplomatic appointment because it could be ammunition in the 1880 presidential election. Hayes chose not to seek reelection. With both parties holding nominating conventions that June, the contest would pit Ohio Republican James A. Garfield against Pennsylvania Democrat Winfield S. Hancock. While some Republicans emphasized Garfield's antislavery reform credentials and hoped the race would return the party, after Hayes's conciliatory policies, to a bold defense of freedpeople's rights, others cast Garfield as a moderate on the Southern question and favored a campaign strategy that would consolidate Republican power in the North rather than breaking the resurgent Democrats' grip on the Solid South. Moderate and Radical Republicans alike claimed to be defending the sanctity of the Union against Democrats who harbored the South's disloyal elements.[24]

Northern Democrats used the Longstreet appointment to turn the tables: How dare the Republicans—"high-toned hypocritical God and morality snivelers" as a Kansas paper fumed—wave the bloody shirt while also rewarding "red-handed traitors" like Longstreet? The Democratic candidate, Hancock, was a Union hero of the war and of Gettysburg in particular, and Longstreet was the man that Hancock's army had whipped. Even as they arraigned Republicans for hypocrisy, however, Democrats noted with palpable satisfaction that Republican patronage of former Confederates set a precedent that Democrats could use to their own advantage, to bestow federal office on the legions of former rebels in their ranks. It "set us the example to put these men into power," as a West Virginia newspaper editorialized.[25]

The British press took a keen interest in Longstreet's political fortunes. The very fact of his appointment struck British commentators as utterly remarkable. That a man who had "contributed so powerfully to the protracted maintenance of the fratricidal struggle should now be selected by the Government against which he fought as its representative in a diplomatic post," marveled the *London Telegraph*, was "very unusual" and a "significant exemplification" of the Union's "clemency and forgiveness." The *Telegraph* thus captured succinctly the broad implications of Longstreet's tour in Istanbul: a mere fifteen and a half years after the end of the Civil War, members of the Confederate elite had insinuated themselves into the federal government, not only as representatives of states and localities, but also as symbols of the nation and its interests. The *Telegraph* mused that Longstreet was ill-prepared to enter the "hotbed of diplomatic intrigue" in the Ottoman capital and predicted that he would treat his job as "little more than a sinecure." But this prediction underestimated Longstreet's savvy and ambition.[26]

IV

James Longstreet's sojourn abroad took place at a tense moment of transition in US-Ottoman relations, with regard to the treatment of missionaries, and provides a new perspective on that transition. Moreover, Longstreet's performance as minister illustrates the limits of the Republican Party's reach in the aftermath of Reconstruction. Longstreet had remarkable success in landing positions of influence and trust within the US government. But he struggled to project power on the government's behalf, either in the American South or on the international stage. There were simply not enough Longstreets in the South to sustain the Republicans' ambitions for asserting national power, at home or abroad.[27]

Once his diplomatic nomination was assured, Longstreet made arrangements to step down from his Gainesville postmastership. Then he traveled to Washington in early September 1880 to receive his formal instructions from Secretary of State William M. Evarts. A correspondent for the *Baltimore Sun* interviewed Longstreet during this visit to the capital and found him "looking in fine health" and confident that "he would be abundantly able to manage any diplomatic questions which are likely to arise between our government and that of Turkey." Longstreet undertook his Atlantic crossing that fall (without his family), arriving in Liverpool, England, in October and making his way to Istanbul by mid-December.[28]

At the time of Longstreet's ambassadorship, the vast Ottoman Empire, which in the early nineteenth century had reached into Eastern Europe, North Africa, and the Arabian peninsula, was confronting "dual threats of external pressure from ascendant Western imperial powers and internal pressures from emergent nationalist movements," as the scholar Mary Roberts has explained. In a decades-long period of reform, or Tanzimat (1839–1876), intended to reinvigorate the contracting empire, the ruling elite preached Ottomanism: an outlook and set of policies meant to bind together the empire's diverse and restive ethnic and religious elements through administrative, fiscal, legal, and infrastructure modernization. It resulted in new tax and penal codes; the spread of factories, railways, and the telegraph; the restriction of slave trading; improvements in education; and mounting debt to European powers, among other changes. This first wave of reforms had a secular flavor and promised legal equality to Ottoman subjects regardless of sect. But under Sultan Abdulhamid II, who reigned from 1876 to 1909, Ottomanism had a stronger Muslim emphasis, as the sultan advanced Pan-Islamism centered in his supremacy as caliph, or the leader of the faith. His Pan-Islamism was intended to bind together Muslim groups such as Arabs, Albanians, and Kurds in Ottoman lands, and to preempt proto-nationalist activities among them. This was also an era of intense Ottoman focus on diplomacy, as strategic alliances, especially with Britain against Russia, became essential for safeguarding the empire. But European powers premised such alliances on the Ottomans' willingness both to give more latitude to Christian missionaries and to improve the treatment of the Christian subjects within the Ottomans' domains; the persecution of Armenians in Anatolia was an especially tendentious topic.[29]

The Ottoman image in American eyes was complex. The United States' formal diplomatic relations with Turkey were focused on trade, under the parameters of treaties signed in 1830 and 1862 that gave US merchants free passage to the Black Sea. But the United States had an outsized footprint in the Ottoman Empire through its Protestant educational missions: with a far-reaching network of missionaries and schools serving thousands of Ottoman students, the American presence outpaced that of any of the European powers. Missionaries were typically affiliated with the New England–based American Board of Commissioners for Foreign Missions; the ABCFM poured more resources into its Ottoman missions than in any other part of the world, seeing the ancient Holy Lands as a field of future converts to Christianity. Missionaries established influential institutions in Istanbul, most notably the Bible House, a center for publishing and disseminating religious materials produced in a variety of languages, and Robert College, the first American-sponsored university founded outside the United States.[30]

Missionaries also collaborated with diplomats and merchants to advance—sometimes without the US government's authorization—what they considered America's "sacred interest" in reforming the Ottoman Empire. Americans promoted commerce and modernization on the premise that Muslims could not advance without Western guidance and that the United States had achieved, after the Civil War, the "moral legitimacy . . . to spread its crusade of freedom to the world." For example, the US consul in Crete, William J. Stillman, appealed ardently to the American people to aid Cretan revolutionaries during their insurrection against Ottoman rule in 1866–69; the public responded sympathetically, with the Republican press in particular stressing the "barbarity" of Ottoman rule and the bravery and intelligence of the Greeks. The US State Department tried to rein in officials like Stillman, but their rhetoric contrasting American civilization and Turkish depravity invariably antagonized the Ottoman authorities.[31]

Sultan Abdulhamid was, to Americans, a forbidding figure of mystery. The New York journal the *Christian Union* described him in November 1880 as a man of "invincible obstinacy" whose purpose was to "restore the lost glory and power of the Caliphate, [and] to make himself the real successor of the Prophet." But it added that the sultan had a "fear of assassination which at times amounts to monomania" and also a desire to impress upon the outside world "the idea that he is a good man, who is anxious, above all things . . . to strengthen and improve his government." This portrait was largely accurate. Fearful that he, like his two predecessors, would be deposed, Abdulhamid tried to keep threats at bay through censorship and spying, and sequestered himself in his Yildiz summer palace. As he confronted threats from insurgent elements and foreign rivals, the sultan suspended the reformist constitution of 1876 and the Parliament in order to give himself monarchical sway, and portrayed himself, the British historian Caroline Finkel has noted, as "a proud autocrat in the mould of the German kaiser or the Austrian emperor."[32]

Given this context, it is somewhat surprising that Longstreet's first interactions with the sultan received very favorable coverage in the United States. The new US minister presented his credentials to the sultan on December 14, 1880, in Istanbul (or Constantinople, as the Americans still called it). According to the *New York Times*, Longstreet "conveyed to the sultan the friendly greetings of President Hayes, who desired to cement the present amicable relations between the United States and Turkey," while the sultan, in reply, "expressed readiness to do all in his power to draw closer the existing friendly relations." After the formal audience, the sultan invited Longstreet and US consul general Gwinn Harris Heap, along with thirteen officers of the US man-of-war naval vessel the USS *Nipsic*, to dinner. One US paper speculated that the sultan would take special pleasure at Longstreet's company precisely because Longstreet was a diplomatic ingénue who would not press the sultan about "the payment of the interest on his bonds . . . [or] about that Berlin Treaty."[33]

Longstreet did, it seems, make a good first impression. A midshipman on the *Nipsic*, Albert Gleaves, wrote back home to Nashville a wry, detailed account of the reception and ensuing dinner, which was published under the heading "In the Land of the Sultan." The initial audience took place at the sultan's summer palace at Yildiz. Longstreet and his fellow attendees were conveyed there in state carriages and then ushered into the palace amidst crowds of Turkish officials. After being offered what Gleaves described as "bad coffee in tiny china cups, resting in gold-lined silver holders, incrusted with diamonds, some of them quite large," the Americans were ushered into the audience chamber to meet "the most interesting monarch of all Europe." Longstreet, presented to the sultan first, gave an address that was "very happy and charmingly delivered." Gleaves gushed: "The truth is, we are all in love with the old soldier, and feel very proud of America's representative. He was the finest looking man at the palace, and the most finished courtier could not have borne himself better." The Americans were then presented to Osman Pasha, the hero of the 1877 siege of Plevna, in which he repulsed a series of Russian assaults. According to another eyewitness account sent to an American newspaper, "Osman Pasha particularly seemed very much pleased to make the acquaintance of Gen. Longstreet." Presumably, as fabled commanders and heroes of lost wars, they had much to discuss. Amid all the pomp and rhetorical flourishes, Midshipman Gleaves could not shake the impression that the sultan himself was a "painfully nervous" man, with a "restless, unsteady eye," and that the empire itself was only a "relic of former prosperity."[34]

Longstreet's ministerial responsibilities soon proved, however, to be more than ceremonial. Indeed, he prided himself on the finesse he showed in handling some "delicate" issues that arose on his watch. At the request of Harvard professor Charles Eliot Norton, president of the Archaeological Institute of America, Secretary Evarts directed Longstreet to lobby for a firman (sultan's decree) permitting American excavations at the ruins of the ancient Greek city of Assos, on the island of Cephalonia, and also at sites in Crete. These Greek-speaking territories remained under Ottoman rule even after Greece's war of independence in the 1820s and were the subject of prolonged boundary disputes. For reasons of timing as well as geography, the firman request was no easy ask. The Ottomans had begun in 1869 to "systematically regulate archaeological activities within Ottoman territory and prohibit the unfettered export of antiquities to the West," as Mary Roberts observes. Longstreet met with the sultan's prime minister on January 16, 1881, to request the firman, and was assured that it would be granted. "We cannot refuse these concessions in the interest of the arts and sciences," Longstreet was told. But he then "found himself met with indefinite postponements and courteous excuses," as the provincial governors who had to tender their permission dragged their feet.[35]

The Turks suspected, given the tense relations between Greece and Turkey and the Americans' historic support of the Greeks, that the expedition's purpose was more political than archaeological. Longstreet gleaned, and reported to Evarts, that while the Assos request was viable, the Crete request faced major headwinds: the Archaeological Institute's agent, W. J. Stillman, was the former American consul who had provoked Ottoman officials by openly promoting Cretan independence. This left such an "unfavorable impression upon the minds of the State and Provincial authorities," Longstreet explained, that it seemed "injudicious" to press the matter of the firman with Stillman still in the picture.[36]

Following up in the spring of 1881 with Evarts's successor as secretary of state, James Blaine, Longstreet philosophized on the best way to handle the Ottomans. As he faced further delays from provincial officials, he described the Turkish authorities as "too polite to refuse anything, yet knowing better how to do nothing than any other enlightened people." This was a typical Western view, ascribing to Turks an "Oriental tranquility of mind and evasion of work," as the historian Tarik Tansu Yiğit has explained. But Longstreet also showed some tactical savvy, advising that it "may be better to press one subject at a time" than to overplay the American hand. Longstreet persisted and prevailed, obtaining the necessary permission for excavation in Assos (but not Crete)—the firman was enough of a break with previous policy that it was widely noted as a diplomatic achievement.[37]

Longstreet also showed sound judgment in his response to a "fearful catastrophe": a deadly earthquake, with an estimated magnitude of 7.3 and casualties exceeding 7,000 and protracted aftershocks, that befell the north Aegean island of Chios, near the Turkish coast, on April 3, 1881. Longstreet dispatched an American naval vessel, the USS *Galena*, docked at Istanbul, to the island to provide humanitarian aid. Given the "probable confusion of authority" after the quake, he reasoned, "it seemed proper" that the United States should leap to the "aid of the sufferers." The plight of Chios was a major news story, and Longstreet's decision to send the *Galena* was duly noted by the press.[38]

The "unsettled condition of the relations of Turkey and Greece" was at the heart of a third issue Longstreet tried to finesse: the question arising in February 1881 of whether an American citizen (a Mr. A. Eutychides) residing in Thessaly, another Greek region under Ottoman rule, could fly the American flag from his dwelling as a protection from marauding Turkish troops. As Eutychides put it in an imploring letter to Longstreet, the Turkish authorities were "sending a great many soldiers to Thessaly . . . preparing for war." Eutychides added: "The Turks in previous wars have done atrocities to the peaceful men, women, and children with impunity." If he could only fly a US flag at his house, it might protect him, "as the Turks generally are more afraid to injure the people under the flag of a powerful nation." As Eutychides was formerly an Ottoman citizen who went to the United States and then returned claiming to be a US citizen, one of the contexts for this seemingly minor matter was the fraught issue of "extraterritoriality": the right of foreign governments to "exercise direct jurisdiction over their citizens or subjects in [a] host country." In the American case, the degree of extraterritorial immunity and protection US citizens could claim was unclear, as the exact terms of the 1830 treaty between the two nations were in dispute. Longstreet enclosed the Eutychides letter in his own missive to Evarts, explaining what he had decided to do: namely, to authorize Eutychides to fly the flag "as a symbol of nationality only, and with the understanding that it shall bear no political significance." "It is my opinion that any citizen may, in time of great danger, hoist his national colors, without in any wise, compromising the General Government," Longstreet continued, hoping this rationale would protect Eutychides without antagonizing the Turks.[39]

Longstreet tried, in handling his various diplomatic duties, to maintain a balancing act: to be receptive to appeals from American citizens in the provinces but also mindful of official protocols. Yet the main source of contention in US-Turkish relations—the status of American missionaries—confounded Longstreet's efforts to remain diplomatic. As he explained later in an interview, the principal duty of the US minister to Turkey was "to look after the missionaries." He elaborated:

> There are in Turkey a number of persons, lay and clerical, sent out by the American Missionary Society, who are constantly getting into trouble with the Ottomans. As a rule, they are all right so long as they stop in Constantinople, but they persist in running into danger by going into the interior to teach Christianity to fanatical Mohammedans. Frequently they are arrested and thrown into prison, and their Bibles and papers destroyed. The only wonder is that they do not lose their lives. Of course their complaints are frequent, and it is to settle these that the Minister's services are called in.[40]

Reflecting such complaints, Longstreet's central preoccupation as minister was the fate of a claim for indemnity on behalf of the American Bible House in Istanbul. The claim was for restitution after a provocative October 1880 incident: the seizure by provincial authorities of some 860 books—copies of the Old and New Testaments—from a Bible House agent named George Klonares, who was plying the missionary trade in

Gallipoli (the peninsula extending from the European part of Turkey into the Dardanelles Strait). As revealed by Longstreet's indignant exchanges with the Turkish minister of foreign affairs, Assim Pasha, much was at stake in this affair. The Bible House wanted recompense for the lost value of the books and lost time of Klonares (who waited in vain, for months, for the books to be returned); Longstreet used the occasion to demand guarantees for the future protection and safety of missionaries "against molestation." Longstreet reminded Assim Pasha that the American missionaries had been at work in Turkey for a half century; that Klonares and his sponsors had obtained all of the proper permissions from Istanbul authorities and had paid all the requisite fees; and that confiscating the Bibles was "inconsistent with the stipulations of recent treaties"—by which he meant commerce and navigation treaties of 1830, 1862, and 1874 that granted the United States "most favored nation" status. Finding that his appeals fell on deaf ears, Longstreet grew indignant, telling Assim Pasha in a letter of February 11, 1881, that his "patience and moderation" had "reached their limit."[41]

Climbing up on a moral high horse, Longstreet proclaimed, "My government and its citizens regard civil liberty as a priceless jewel." He then issued a veiled threat, invoking the "unpleasant necessity of referring the matter to my government." When Assim Pasha summarily rejected the claim for indemnity, calling it unprecedented, Longstreet upped the ante. In a March 21, 1881, response, Longstreet, no doubt drawing on his experience as a Custom House official back home, doubled down on his claim that commercial rights—the "unmolested movement and sale of goods"— were at stake. American missionaries had sent "millions" of books into the interior while doing "business" in Turkey, as he put it; it was the seizure of their goods that had "no precedent." Longstreet observed archly that "a Government that fails to command the attention of its own officials, to its own decrees, may lose somewhat of that high esteem that should be maintained between friendly powers."[42]

Assim Pasha flatly denied Longstreet's premise, insisting: "An enterprise which by public notoriety is within the purely religious province cannot take a commercial character." The provincial authorities in Gallipoli had every right to seize and inspect the books to make sure that they "did not offer any danger." Longstreet refused to yield, emphasizing yet again that the books had passed "a thorough and satisfactory examination" by the Istanbul authorities and that the provincial officials were defying their own government.[43]

This testy exchange resolved nothing: the books were never returned, and neither side backed down. But it is a revealing window into the deterioration of US-Ottoman relations on the missionary issue. The early 1880s were, the historian Emrah Sahin has explained, a moment of marked transition: a long-standing Ottoman policy of tolerating "peaceful coexistence" with American missionaries gave way to a new "strategy of containment." Worried that the burgeoning missionary presence was fueling sedition, especially among susceptible rural populations, Ottoman officials at the provincial and state administrative levels increasingly treated missionaries as a threat, ramping up regimes of censorship, surveillance, and regulations, and resorting to "coercion, relocation, and punishment."[44]

Longstreet's performance as minister is not only a window into US-Turkish relations but also, more broadly, into the shortcomings of American foreign policy in this era and the limits of diplomacy on the cheap. As the historian Robert L. Beisner has explained, the US diplomatic service itself was still, in the early 1880s, woefully underdeveloped, with ministers and consuls lacking both training and instructions. Although Longstreet was hailed by the missionaries as a stalwart defender of their interests, his own frustration at his lack of leverage, resources, prestige, and support is palpable in his accounts of his Istanbul tour of duty. Longstreet had been forewarned by Secretary of State Evarts that while the government would pay him a decent salary, it would not fund the kind of lavish hospitality that Europe's diplomatic corps practiced in Istanbul. Just what a handicap that was became apparent immediately: the ministers of the Great Powers hosted grand parties and charity events to which Longstreet was sometimes invited, but he could not reciprocate. The American consulate's invisibility on the social calendar meant that Longstreet was not privy to the informal diplomacy that took place in social settings. With the United States having no say in weighty issues such as the Ottoman Empire's debt renegotiations with its European creditors, America was truly marginal to the main diplomatic intrigues in Istanbul. Accordingly, while the English- and French-language press in Istanbul covered Longstreet's receiving of his credentials from the sultan in December 1880, they ignored him thereafter.[45]

Longstreet's keener frustration came from the ways that wrangling missionaries detracted from his main goal of promoting trade and commerce. He regarded as a "farce" the endless, futile cycle in which missionaries got into trouble; the US minister intervened to help them; Ottoman authorities made "all sorts of good promises"; and those promises were promptly broken. The fact that Longstreet emphasized commercial rights rather than religious freedom in his handling of the Klonares case is revealing—he showed little zeal, as minister or after the war more broadly, for religious evangelizing and reforms, but great enthusiasm for economic modernization and expansion. In Beisner's typology of American imperialists, ranging from "market expansionists" who wanted "nothing more than to empty the warehouse of America's productive surplus," to jingos who wanted to initiate the world in the "wondrous workings of Anglo-Saxon political institutions," Longstreet was somewhere in the middle, leaning toward the market expansionist end of the spectrum. In a series of interviews he did about his tour in Istanbul, Longstreet marveled at the economic potential of Turkey. Given Istanbul's favorable geography, he opined, it "might be at once the Chicago and New York of Europe," if only the Turks would develop more railroad access to the city. (With this, Longstreet had identified a genuine issue: Istanbul was not connected to the European railway system via the Orient Express until 1883.) When asked by the reporter whether any country had the capacity to "get into Turkey and instruct the Turks on these advantages," Longstreet denigrated the "mercantile energy" of Europeans and riffed that the only ones who could do it were "Yankees" from the United States. "The Yankee moves things quicker than any other kind of man. They would get to work and do something, and that would be the best model for the Turks."[46]

Longstreet's admiration for the North's "mercantile energy" was a recurring theme in his postwar speeches and writings. It manifested as praise for the North's prewar industrial development, which made the New England states a "land of opulence, power, and beauty"; awe at the Union army's machinelike efficiency during the war; and appeals to Southerners to "attract northern capital to develop our great industrial and mineral resources." "Investments in commercial enterprises by each section in the other" would make the bond of union between the North and South "indissoluble." And "with this accomplished," Longstreet predicted, "the United States must become one of the greatest of world powers." The 1890s would bring some of the developments Longstreet hoped for: US diplomacy would turn in earnest to the project of extending American markets, with the Ottoman Empire as a "specific commercial objective." And a new paradigm for the US diplomacy would emerge, replacing passivity and drift with systematic efforts to assess America's place in the balance of power and "tip the balance for the sake of American interests." But in the early 1880s, diplomats such as Longstreet still typically reacted to incidents rather than implement coherent policies.[47]

Although Longstreet was frustrated by the ways missionaries and diplomats were at cross-purposes, and by the limits on his influence, it was not these frustrations that ended his diplomatic tour abruptly in the spring of 1881. Instead, he was drawn back into the domestic fray as the Republican Party summoned him to lead the party's "home mission" in the South.

V

Rumors of Longstreet's removal from the minister post and reassignment to a domestic patronage position began to circulate nearly as soon as he landed in Turkey. The rumors were traceable to Longstreet himself. One of the first major communications he sent home from the Ottoman seat of imperial power was a December 1880 letter to his former Confederate aide Thomas P. Ochiltree, on the prospects of a Republican revival in the South. A colorful columnist, editor, entrepreneur, and politician from Texas, Ochiltree, like Longstreet, had supported congressional Reconstruction after the war. In his letter, Longstreet maintained that "the only way to build up the Republican party in the South was through the influence of the Southern Republicans." By Southern Republicans, he meant white men like himself and Ochiltree; the letter was a critique of both the Grant policies and the Hayes policies, which had relied too heavily, Longstreet believed, on Black voters and Northern carpetbaggers (in Grant's case) and on overtures to Democrats (in Hayes's). In a blatantly racist piece of paternalist pandering, Longstreet argued that the "colored man" as a voter had been "put in the hands of strangers who have not understood him or his characteristics." Carpetbagger misrule of the Republican Party had driven some Black voters into the arms of the Democratic Party, Longstreet maintained.[48]

Was there a contradiction between Longstreet praising Yankee ingenuity in the context of international affairs while ruing carpetbagger domination of the Republican Party in the South? In his mind, there was not. He had adopted the Republican message of economic development, but believed that white Southern Republicans were the best messengers for that message. In Longstreet's view, Democratic propaganda had succeeded in falsely equating Republicanism with corrupt "negro rule," and the challenge was thus to "show the white people of the South that republicanism here means the same good government as Republicans have at the North." Ochiltree, who agreed heartily with Longstreet, saw to it that excerpts from Longstreet's letter were published in a friendly Republican newspaper, the Chicago *Inter Ocean*, in the immediate aftermath of James Garfield's election. The letter was widely reprinted and framed as a bid by Longstreet for a Cabinet position in the incoming administration, and as an appeal to the president-elect to formulate a Southern strategy that would break the

Democratic grip on the region. Behind the scenes, Ochiltree sent the letter directly to Garfield on January 12, 1881, with a letter of his own imploring him to recall Longstreet from Turkey and give him a "place of honor and responsibility near your person, where his wise council would avail to give you accurate and unprejudiced versions of matters and things in the South." Ochiltree included a paean to Longstreet's "heroic spirit of honor," which had "forbade him breaking his plighted troth to his generous conqueror given on the field of Appomattox."[49]

This angling worked: by late March 1881, after being lobbied by Longstreet surrogates such as Georgia congressman Emory Speer, President Garfield made it known that he intended to recall Longstreet and appoint him US marshal for Georgia. Although some Southern Unionists and Northern Democrats objected to an ex-Confederate assuming the marshal post, most of the press coverage was positive, noting that Garfield would strike a blow at the Solid South by favoring the "native Republicans" over the "carpetbag element."

"If Longstreet is brought from Turkey to be United States Marshal in Georgia," the *New Orleans Picayune* quipped in April 1881, "it is because he will have a Republican home mission to attend to." While that conservative Democratic newspaper generally served up anti-Longstreet invective, in this instance it captured something of the political dynamic at play. A home mission was by definition one conducted within the national territorial boundaries of the sponsoring church. Longstreet and his allies did see the goal of building a white Republican base in such a light—as a kind of political proselytizing that ideally should be carried out by a vanguard of white Southerners. As Congressman Speer put it, Longstreet's "renown has been won among our people and by their valor," and thus it was far better for him to fill the marshal office "than that it should be filled by a man from another section."[50]

VI

Longstreet's emphasis on bolstering white Southern Republicanism in no way signaled a retreat from his criticism of the Lost Cause ideology. His June 1881 return to America from Turkey coincided with the publication of Jefferson Davis's memoir, *The Rise and Fall of the Confederate Government*, in which the former Confederate president joined the chorus of critics blaming Longstreet for the loss at Gettysburg. Reporters started asking Longstreet about the book as soon as he arrived on US soil in New York, and he did not hesitate to opine on published excerpts of it even before he had read the entire volume. In an extensive interview with the *New York Herald*, Longstreet took issue with Davis's harsh criticism of General Joseph Johnston and contradicted Davis's claim that he had not sought the Confederate presidency, but had accepted it only when bestowed. He went on to blame Davis for the Confederates' failure to pursue the defeated Yankees at Bull Run and held him responsible for the poor appointments of generals who then failed, such as Pemberton at Vicksburg. Longstreet criticized Davis for the "cruelty of continuing a hopeless war" in late 1864 and early 1865, when the Union's superiority in manpower and resources had become decisive under Grant's leadership. Even more pointedly, Longstreet renounced the "extreme state's rights doctrine" that started the war and had since "proved a fallacy." He distanced himself, too, from the postwar overcorrection: the "reactionary tendency . . . to the opposite extreme—to consolidation." He predicted that the moderate, mainstream states' rights theory—"of local self-government in the union"—would in the end prevail. In a pair of July interviews about the book, Longstreet further elaborated, calling Davis's account of the war "stinted and prejudiced," and accusing Davis of having a petty "mania for criticism" and faultfinding.[51]

The Northern press noted gleefully that some of the sharpest criticisms of Davis's book were coming from Southern soldiers, and it took

Davis to task for his politically motivated scapegoating of Longstreet. This coverage suited Longstreet's purposes to a tee: his emphasis as he pivoted back to Georgia politics was on how to motivate white Southerners to reject the traditional Democratic leadership, and how to take "progressive ideas" and "present them to the average voter," as he put it in the winter of 1881. Longstreet would find that his role as marshal in Georgia, no less than his posts as surveyor in New Orleans and minister in Istanbul, was a test of whether a Republican administration and appointee could protect American citizens and promote their interests in the face of vigilante violence and lawlessness.[52]

Chapter 9

KEEPING THE PEACE

I

Longstreet's appointment in June 1881 as US marshal for the Northern District of Georgia installed him in Atlanta, at the heart of the action, and emboldened him to use his federal position to advance Republican fortunes in the state. He would fall short. The Republican Party's efforts to project power and implement assertive policies were thwarted by the difficulty of forging sustained political coalitions that could harness the energies of a wide enough range of stakeholders. Longstreet's vision of a biracial Southern polity—one in which Blacks exercised the franchise and held some limited patronage positions, subordinate to white Southern Republican leadership—not only clashed sharply with the Southern Democrats' vision of whites-only governance but also ran aground on the shoals of Republican factionalism.

On the national scene, the decades after Reconstruction witnessed a battle over the identity of the Republican Party, with advocates of social reform and civil rights, who favored an activist role for the government in addressing societal ills, often at odds with the ascendant big business wing of the party, which embraced laissez-faire "trickle down" economics and prioritized generating prosperity and protecting property rights. Against this backdrop, regional and local rivalries further split the party, playing into the hands of Democrats.[1]

Longstreet's embattled three-year stint as US marshal has been overlooked by historians and biographers, who have briefly noted that he was drummed out of office for corruption but have failed to recognize the importance of the marshalship in Georgia politics and race relations. Like the other major federal posts, the office of marshal gave its holders the opportunity to dispense patronage of their own and to build their state's party apparatus. Longstreet was certainly expected to do so, by his friends and foes alike. Right after accepting the post, he was asked by a Savannah journalist whether he intended to "organize the Republican party in Georgia on the Mahone plan"—by forming a coalition, as Virginia politician William Mahone had, of Republicans and Democrats, including Black voters and white farmers and workingmen. Longstreet replied pointedly, "I am not a follower of General Mahone. He is a Democrat. I am a Republican. I am fourteen years ahead of Mahone and am firmly fixed in my Republican principles." "As to the building up of the Republican Party in Georgia," Longstreet continued, "I would be very glad to see some advance made in that direction." Increasingly, Longstreet tried to harmonize his Republican principles with his Confederate identity and the ascendant cult of sectional reconciliation—only to face persistent skepticism and resistance from those who believed white Southern Republicans could not be trusted.[2]

II

Longstreet returned to the political scene in Georgia hoping to revive the Republicans by forging an alliance with "Independents," such as former Confederate vice president Alexander Stephens, who sought to challenge the dominance of "Bourbon" Democrats. (*Bourbon* was a nickname for the Southern reactionaries who overthrew Reconstruction; the term alluded to the restoration of monarchy after the French Revolution.) The Independents had growing traction among yeoman farmers in the mountainous regions of North Georgia, such as Longstreet's Ninth Congressional District, where resentment against low-country planters had translated into some wartime Unionism and had furnished the state's small core of white Republicans. A hybrid platform of protective tariffs, fair elections, public schooling, and internal improvements might, Longstreet reckoned, unite disparate anti-Bourbon voters. But the Independents proved unreliable and too susceptible to Democratic Party pressure and appeals. The Democratic press branded the new movement a "second attempt to Africanize the South for the benefit of the Republican Party," and criticized Longstreet for trying to lure unwitting voters into a trap. After a failed bid to recruit Stephens to head a "fusion" ticket in the 1882 gubernatorial contest—Stephens rejoined the Democratic fold and ran as its candidate—Longstreet and other Republicans endorsed Independent candidate Lucius J. Gartrell for governor, only to see him go down to a crushing defeat. This spelled the end of the Republican-Independent fusion bid in the state.[3]

The inability of Georgia Republicans to compete for state office only raised the stakes of federal patronage: Longstreet and his allies would have to rely on Republican presidents to bestow appointments upon them. In Georgia, as in other Southern states, the quest for federal spoils gave rise to endemic factionalism among Republicans, as the demand for offices exceeded the supply, and those on the outs maneuvered, in ever-shifting combinations, for preferment. Longstreet headed the so-called syndicate faction of the Georgia Republican Party, which controlled the federal patronage game and the dispensing of offices to whites and Blacks alike.

The Black electorate in Georgia, which made up 90 percent of Republican voters, had a complex relationship with Longstreet, and he with them. African American leaders were understandably resentful of the ways that whites generally monopolized the best posts, and in the early 1880s, an anti-syndicate faction made these resentments known. While the two factions were often referred to as the "black and tan" and "lily white" factions (with Longstreet in the latter), those labels obscured the fact that Blacks themselves were divided over tactics, with some choosing the syndicate camp out of cautious pragmatism or ambition for federal office. Longstreet selectively promoted the careers of a number of African American federal office seekers, such as John H. Deveaux, the founder and editor of the influential *Savannah Tribune*. Longstreet's Black allies in turn supported him for important positions within the party. Ishmael Lonon, a Black legislator who had survived the white supremacist Camilla Massacre in southwest Georgia in 1868, explained in a letter to James A. Garfield why he supported Longstreet for US marshal: "We want a man that has our confidence and respect. . . . We recognize in General Longstreet an ardent, true, and unselfish Republican." Reflecting that view, some Black Georgians reached out to Longstreet once he took office as US marshal, to provide them with federal protection against vigilante attacks.[4]

The office of US marshal was not only a patronage plum but also a vital arm of federal law enforcement. Technically, marshals came under the purview of the executive branch, and were commissioned by the president (though temporary marshals could be appointed by the courts); they reported to the attorney general and the Department of Justice. Marshals and their deputies were tasked with enforcing federal revenue and tax laws, and with hunting down counterfeiters, illicit whiskey distillers, and other unsavory characters. The work of arresting moonshiners and seizing their untaxed whiskey and destroying their illicit stills was dangerous and controversial, especially in places that actively resisted the whiskey tax, such as North Georgia.

The work was also poorly compensated. Marshals like Longstreet earned a minimal annual salary for their administrative work. They "supervised the work of the deputies, made the assignments, kept the books, [and] hobnobbed with the local power brokers," as the historian Frederick S. Calhoun has noted. Their deputies—the ones taking all the risk in the field—earned only fees for official acts such as serving process in lawsuits. Those fees, one-quarter of which was owed to the US marshal, were generally too meager to cover the expenses involved in tracking down lawbreakers, transporting and remanding prisoners, and other such duties. The system was vulnerable to abuse: marshals and their deputies came under frequent scrutiny by the Department of Justice for the pervasive practice of falsifying their expenditure accounts and skimming some money off the top.[5]

US marshals were also entrusted with protecting African American voting rights in the South and enforcing the anti-Klan legislation passed by Congress in 1870–71 during U. S. Grant's presidency. During congressional Reconstruction, marshals and their deputies, using US troops stationed in the South as posses, arrested more than 7,000 Southern whites for violating civil rights laws. After the withdrawal of federal troops and the resurgence of Southern Democratic rule, marshals were increasingly isolated in the South, facing the hostility of Democratic state officials who actively sought to prosecute them on charges of corruption, or of overstepping their authority and privileging federal law over state law. The comportment of federal marshals became a battleground in contests over states' rights, and generally the federal government did not do nearly enough to protect marshals from harassment and punishment by state authorities.[6]

On Longstreet's watch as US marshal for North Georgia, a major Ku Klux Klan case roiled the state, culminating in the US Supreme Court decision in *Ex parte Yarbrough* (1884). The case resulted from a series of violent attacks carried out in July 1883 by a group of white Georgians, led by Jasper Yarbrough, against African Americans in North Georgia's Banks County. As it wound its way through the courts, the case came to be known in the press as the "Banks County Ku-Klux" case; although it is not clear whether the perpetrators were formally affiliated with the Ku Klux Klan, their gang was clearly Klan-like and engaged in "kukluxing"—a commonly used verb describing white supremacist terrorism. On the night of July 13, masked marauders had perpetrated a brutal spree of terrorism against African American men, meant to punish them for voting for the Republican-endorsed Independent Emory Speer in the 1882 congressional election and to discourage their casting Republican ballots in the future. Speer had lost the 1882 election to the Democrat Allen D. Candler in part because of the widespread violence and fraud against Black voters during the campaign. But Speer had caught the eye of the Republican national

Above left: "Rebel No. 3": Longstreet during the Civil War.

Above right: Robert E. Lee described Longstreet as his trusted "warhorse." Longstreet was brokenhearted when Lee rejected his military advice at Gettysburg.

Below: Chickamauga, Georgia: The scene of Longstreet's triumph on September 20, 1863.

Above: Fort Sanders, Tennessee: Confederate defeat at the nadir of Longstreet's doomed Knoxville campaign, November 1863.

Below: Robert E. Lee's surrender to Ulysses S. Grant, April 1865. Longstreet would say of Appomattox, "the surrender of my sword was my reconstruction."

Above left: "It will ruin you, son": Longstreet's uncle Augustus Baldwin Longstreet, a prominent defender of slavery, warned his nephew not to support the 1867 Reconstruction Acts.

Above right: "The man who was to eclipse all": Ulysses S. Grant's friendship and postwar patronage shaped Longstreet's political career.

Right: Longstreet's wife Maria Louise Longstreet Garland and their sons Robert Lee and James Jr. in 1870. Of the ten children the couple had together, only five lived to adulthood.

Left: Longstreet ally P. B. S. Pinchback of Louisiana, the first African American state governor. Longstreet said Pinchback had "the shrewdest faculties of any public man in the state."

Below: Chaos on Canal Street: Longstreet's interracial militia battles against the White League in New Orleans on September 14, 1874.

Left: Longstreet the officeholder and politician. His career as a staunch Republican lasted more than three decades.

Right: Nemesis: Jubal Early led a clique of Confederate veterans who scapegoated Longstreet for their loss at Gettysburg and their ultimate demise in the war.

Above: The Piedmont Hotel in Gainesville, Georgia, which Longstreet and his family ran and used as a residence in the 1880s and 1890s.

Below: Yildiz Palace in Istanbul (upper left), where Longstreet, as US minister to Turkey, met Sultan Abdulhamid II in December 1880.

Right: Judson W. Lyons, a leader of Georgia's Black Republicans, collaborated with Longstreet in the dispensing of patronage.

Left: Longstreet's second wife, Helen Dortch Longstreet, lays a wreath at his gravesite. After Longstreet's death in 1904, his widow worked relentlessly to defend his reputation.

Above: The James Longstreet equestrian statue at Gettysburg, erected in 1998, was unveiled from behind a giant Confederate flag.

leadership, and, at the urging of Longstreet's syndicate faction, he was subsequently appointed US attorney in North Georgia—the very jurisdiction in which the Yarbrough case unfolded—by President Chester A. Arthur, who had succeeded James Garfield following his assassination in 1881, just six months into his term.

Speer prosecuted the case in October 1883, bringing a bill of indictment against eight offenders (four Yarbrough brothers and four of their neighbors), charging them with violating Congress's anti-Klan Enforcement Acts of 1870–71. He argued that the perpetrators of the July violence had formed a conspiracy to abridge the victims' constitutional right to exercise the franchise in a federal election.[7]

The victims' testimony, delivered over five days in a packed Atlanta courtroom before a grand jury consisting of seven white Democratic and five Black Republican jurors, was vivid and shocking. Calvin Bush, who recalled being dragged from his bed by a "shrieking mob," ordered to strip, and then whipped with 175 lashes, testified that "he knew he was struck 175 lashes because one of the mob counted them aloud as they were hit." During the trial, Speer asked him to remove his shirt to "show the scars these lashes had made." Warren Bryson, another victim, recounted a mob of fifteen swarming his house, shouting threats, and then pistol-whipping him. A third victim, Elisha Brooks, fought the mob in vain, only to be dragged outside his home and beaten with brass knuckles. Berry Saunders, as he tried to escape the mob, was shot three times and left for dead, but survived. Matilda David was stripped and lashed twenty-five times each by nearly a dozen different men.

It came to light that the July 13 incidents were part of a broader series of midnight raids perpetrated by the Yarbrough gang in Banks, Jackson, White, and Hall Counties in the summer of 1883. The assailants were angered by the economic success of some Blacks in the region and intent on enforcing racial subordination. Jasper Yarbrough told a Northern interviewer as he was being transported to New York for incarceration that one of the attacks sought to punish "Cad Bush" for brushing up against a white girl on the road in their presence and then getting "sassy" when confronted about it. Bush had had the temerity to say "he was a taxpayer, worked on the roads, and had a right to walk on 'em." Wreaking vengeance, his assailants, armed with hickory sticks, had "dressed him up right smart," Yarbrough bragged. "No light dressin', but one he would remember." The common thread in the series of attacks was their political motivations, the victims recalling that the mob vowed vengeance against anyone who'd voted for Speer.[8]

Speer, an impressive orator, handled the case expertly, urging the grand jury to uphold the rule of law and emphasizing that the sanctity of federal elections was at stake. The judge in the case, Henry K. McCay, a former Confederate veteran turned Republican, did not mince words in his charge to the jury, describing the behavior of the accused as a disgrace to the South. The jury found the eight accused men guilty, and McCay, after a delay in which some additional evidence came to light, sentenced six of them to two years of hard labor at the Albany penitentiary in New York and a fine of $500 each. (Two of the eight were released on bond.) At the sentencing, McCay sternly lectured the convicted men: "Of what avail is the form of a republic, the machinery and parade of ballots and elections, if the voter may not cast his vote without fear? . . . The acts of which you have been found guilty are not therefore mere acts of violence; they are attacks upon the very vitals of the republic and if permitted to continue would make the right to vote a sham and a snare." The defendants in turn filed writs of habeas corpus questioning the legality of the trial, conviction, and sentence, and appealed to the US Supreme Court to have the decision overturned.

With the cases now consolidated and Berry Saunders standing in for the other victims, the court upheld the convictions, rendering a unanimous decision in *Ex parte Yarbrough* that denied the writ of habeas corpus and affirmed Congress's right to secure federal elections from fraud as a means for the government's self-preservation. Justice Samuel Freeman Miller, who delivered the opinion of the court, insisted that the government "must have the power to protect the elections on which its existence depends from violence and corruption. If it has not this power, it is left helpless before the two great natural and historical enemies of all republics, open violence and insidious corruption." He warned that "no lover of this country can shut his eyes to the fear of future danger from both sources."[9]

As a legal case, *Ex parte Yarbrough*, by sustaining the federal government's power to punish private persons for obstructing voting rights, was somewhat anomalous: it ran counter to earlier decisions that limited the scope of the Fifteenth Amendment and was followed by cases reverting to the position that the amendment did not prohibit private individuals from disenfranchising African Americans. But at the time it was handed down, the *Yarbrough* ruling was a "major doctrinal victory" for the Arthur administration, which sought "new ways to build Southern Republicanism" through alliances with Independents like Speer; the case represents, legal scholar Pamela Brandwein explains, the "joint judicial-executive development of voting rights" under Republican administrations in the aftermath of Reconstruction. And with its emphasis on the constitutionality of the enforcement acts, the decision raised "the possibility of future federal enforcement legislation," notes the historian Eric Foner.[10]

Longstreet and his deputy marshals were integral to the prosecution of the Yarbrough gang and to the rendering of the Supreme Court decision. In July 1883, Deputy Marshal J. B. Gaston rounded up and arrested the Yarbrough gang under a United States warrant for conspiracy, tracing the hoofprints made by their horses from the victims' homes to the Yarbrough settlement, and finding a key incriminating clue—a calico baseball hat worn by Jasper and identified by his victims—at the scene. Indeed, Gaston tracked down Jasper Yarbrough, who was released on bond a second time, in September 1883, for brazenly perpetrating further attacks on African Americans. Longstreet's marshals were responsible for conveying the accused to court and then to prison in Atlanta's Fulton County jail. And after the December sentencing, Longstreet directed his chief deputy marshal, O. E. Mitchell, to convey the indicted men to Albany. (Their numbers were whittled down, as two had their sentences withheld in a follow-up ruling by Judge McKay, and one, Neal Yarbrough, was too sick in the Atlanta jail to be moved.) Longstreet, in a controversial move reported by the Associated Press, "made a requisition to the Department of Justice for authority to appoint an additional force of guards" to accompany the prisoners to New York, as he feared there would be attempts to rescue them en route. Under the heading "Afraid of a Rescue," the *Atlanta Constitution* editorialized that an escape was unlikely and that there were "no sufficient grounds" for Longstreet to request a heavy guard. It is unclear whether Longstreet received such reinforcements, but Deputy Marshal Mitchell completed the journey by mid-January; the prisoners, "by close watching, were prevented from accomplishing anything," the *Constitution* reported on the transfer.[11]

Once the case went to the US Supreme Court, Longstreet was asked to weigh in: the first sentence of Justice Miller's Supreme Court opinion referred to Longstreet (although not by name), as he in his capacity as US marshal of the Northern District of Georgia was required to "show cause" why the writ of habeas corpus should not be issued for their release. Longstreet duly submitted those returns in January 1884, confirming that the men had been held in Atlanta and then transferred to Albany because they were convicted of conspiracy in the US Circuit Court of the Northern District of Georgia.[12]

The entire *Yarbrough* case was covered closely by the national press. Republican papers emphasized the political nature of the terrorism, with headlines such as "Reviving the Kuklux: Democratic Outrages in Georgia and South Carolina," as per a *Cincinnati Commercial Gazette* piece in December 1883. The *Gazette* obtained the official verbatim stenographic report of the district court proceedings in Atlanta and printed it in four long columns, editorializing in literary allusions that Victor Hugo and Harriet Beecher Stowe could not have exceeded the vividness or the horror of the testimony by the Black victims of the Yarbrough gang, and that none of the many tragic episodes of political violence in the South could exceed the Georgia case in "cold-blooded barbarity." Northern newspapers expressed an incredulous horror at the interview Jasper Yarbrough gave with a reporter in Cincinnati as the convicted men were being transported to New York. Yarbrough was sneeringly defiant, telling the reporter, "I ain't ashamed of what I've done," and adding, "with a smile": "When I was first arrested they had me charged with whipping an old colored woman down in Madison county . . . but they couldn't bring politics against me as the cause of that, and so they didn't try me on it." Yarbrough cynically denied that his violent acts were political, but the Northern press saw through this ruse and charged his gang with "midnight ravages on inoffensive colored people who did not vote to suit them," as the *New York Times* put it succinctly.[13]

In the Georgia press, conservative Democrats generally expressed some degree of distaste for the seedy Yarbroughs themselves, but took the position that their actions, while regrettable, were not political in nature and therefore not punishable by federal courts. The *Atlanta Constitution* did not dispute that the Yarbrough gang was guilty of committing assault, but it insisted that there was "no kuklux in Georgia" and that the state was "as orderly and law abiding as any in the country." The Yarbroughs, it claimed, were avenging themselves after some Blacks had accused them of burning down a church because its presence interfered with the selling of whiskey from the Yarbroughs' grocery store. The *Constitution* editorialized: "Granting that Mr. Yarbrough and his friends whipped the negroes, this is just such a piece of disorderly conduct as occurs in New York or Pennsylvania a dozen times, where it occurs in Georgia once." Calling the district court trial a "mockery of justice," the Athens *Banner-Watchman* editorialized in December 1883 that the prisoners were "answerable only to the state courts, for they were entirely innocent of any transgression of national laws." It followed up in January 1884 by taking Longstreet to task for refusing to allow the prisoners to remain in Atlanta while their habeas corpus appeal was in process; his decision to quickly send the convicted men to New York rather than having them linger in Atlanta ran counter to the notion that the case was a state, not federal, matter. Longstreet, the paper insinuated, was also looking to line his pockets: "The prospect of mileage and fees . . . to Albany and back for half a dozen retainers, was too great to be resisted, hence the prisoners were hustled away."[14]

This scrutiny of Longstreet's motives in the Banks County case coincided with an acrimonious campaign by his rivals within the Georgia Republican Party—Speer among them—to push Longstreet out of the marshal's office to make way for new syndicate member J. E. Bryant. Speer combined forces with State Party Chairman Alfred E. Buck (a Union veteran from Maine who had resettled in Georgia after the war) in striking a deal whereby President Arthur would bestow patronage on them in exchange for their delivering the Georgia delegation at the 1884 Republican National Convention. Bryant initially favored Senator James G. Blaine as the Republican presidential candidate in 1884, but he eventually got on the bandwagon of Arthur's reelection campaign and lobbied him for Longstreet's removal. The Arthur clique looked to exploit the fact that Longstreet's predecessor, O. P. Fitzsimmons, had flagrantly mismanaged the marshal's office, and that Longstreet had inherited his dodgy financial accounts and some of his corrupt deputies. Longstreet was vulnerable on another score: the conduct of his son John Garland, whom he had named as a deputy and who continued, so Bryant's clique charged, Fitzsimmons's fraudulent practices. A prolonged, painstaking Department of Justice investigation into Longstreet's tenure in office produced the finding, by the investigators, that Longstreet himself was inefficient and largely ignorant of the day-to-day operations of the office, which he had yielded to his alcoholic and extortionate son, resulting in total disarray: "services were charged for which had never been performed, travel charged for which had never been made, transportation of prisoners charged for when no prisoners had been transported and charges made for expenses in endeavoring to arrest when none were incurred or paid," as the *Washington Times* put it in a summary of the alleged transgressions.[15]

The relentless campaign against Longstreet succeeded eventually, with Arthur asking for his resignation in July 1884 and then replacing him with

Bryant. But not before Longstreet mounted a spirited defense, one that belies the claim by his biographers that this episode was yet more proof that he "possessed little political skill or insight." In extensive testimony before the Department of Justice's Committee on Expenditures, Longstreet patiently took up and rebutted every accusation made against him. To his DOJ examiners' charge that he was a doddering old man "given to the vaporings of a mind in second childhood" and at the mercy of unscrupulous younger men, Longstreet countered: "To be 'old' is not recognized as a violation of law nor a fraud upon the Government, but it is probably as much so in the estimation of these agents as anything connected with this office. Among *honorable* men, advanced age in good repute is a jewel of the first water, more to be prized than gold."

Turning the tables, Longstreet charged that one of the examiners in his case, Ralph Ballin, was in cahoots with Bryant. When the examiners called on witness Homer Wallace, an African American janitor in the Atlanta Custom House, to testify that John Garland Longstreet was a dissipated drunkard who frequented a "house of ill-fame," Longstreet's side produced its own Black witness, Robert Martin, the porter at that very establishment. Martin insisted that Garland Longstreet never attended it and that Wallace himself was a "man of bad repute among his own color." In response to testimony from Emory Speer that Longstreet had refused to assign enough guards to manage the Yarbrough prisoners in court during the October 1883 trial, Longstreet countered that "all the officers allowed by laws were there in court" and that they were working very effectively to keep order. What is more, he had asked two of his deputy marshals who were on the scene to act as officers of the court, "giving the weight of their moral influence" to the proceedings, though he could not technically pay them for their presence. If he had known Speer was concerned about security, Longstreet protested, he would have telegraphed the US attorney general himself, "asking for greater force in the case."[16]

Most important, Longstreet embedded his defense in a broader critique of the system governing US marshals—a critique very consistent with modern historians' assessments of that system. Longstreet conceded that his financial accounts and his deputies' paperwork were not always in perfect order, but chalked that up to the structural difficulties that marshals faced. "It should not be a matter of surprise that deputy marshals, whose labors are severe, working night and day, through mountain fastnesses, in pursuit of violators of the law, should sometimes encounter confusion in unveiling the points of law and rendering accounts," he noted, insisting that they were "poorer paid, harder cursed, and harder worked than any other people in America." Some of the men he hired simply did not have the education and sophistication to properly make out accounts, Longstreet revealed. When asked whether it would help the "integrity of the service" to have a "judicious system of public schools" in the South, Longstreet replied, "By all means; it would be a blessing that we would hardly know how to appreciate. We would be so delighted with a thing of that kind that you would see the tears of joy rolling down our cheeks." Another necessary reform was clearer rules and regulation "such as those of the army," Longstreet suggested—establishing standard contracts with transportation companies, for example, so that deputies would not get gouged when buying tickets.[17]

This defense at least partially thwarted the attempts to portray Longstreet as a political failure and liability to the Republican Party. The extensive newspaper coverage of the marshal controversy tended to acknowledge both competing interpretations of Longstreet's removal—that he had badly administered the marshal's office on the one hand, and that Arthur was repaying a political debt to Bryant's clique on the other. Bryant and his allies succeeded in pushing Longstreet out of office, but not in pushing him out of Georgia politics. Feeling betrayed by Arthur, Longstreet became a Georgia elector-at-large for Arthur's rival for the Republican nomination, James G. Blaine (to whom Longstreet had reported while minister to Turkey, as Blaine had been secretary of state). Blaine won the nomination, but went down to a narrow defeat, with the Democrat Grover Cleveland sweeping the Solid South.[18]

III

With Cleveland's 1884 victory and his second term in 1892 (after losing to Republican Benjamin Harrison in 1888), Georgia Republicans were largely on the outs and in disarray from 1884 until William McKinley's election in 1896. Some "half-hearted, spasmodic sort of cooperation" with the state's Populist movement yielded few results in the meantime, "even on a short-term basis," as historian Olive Hall Shadgett has argued. Although the Democratic ascendancy obviated Longstreet's assuming a new federal post, he remained active in state political intrigues.[19]

Scholars have cast Longstreet as an inept politician in his Georgia years, fundamentally unsympathetic to Black Republicans and unpopular among them. His true interests, so this argument goes, were revealed in 1884, when he joined an ill-conceived movement to form a "white man's party" in Georgia, akin to the old Whig Party. Like his brief flirtation with the breakaway Liberal Republican movement in 1872, this episode is revealing of Longstreet's lasting racism, his political ambition, and, ultimately, his resilient Republicanism.

The idea of a "white man's party" was first proposed in 1880 by businessman Jonathan Norcross, a New Englander who had moved South before the war and served a term as mayor of Atlanta. An "old-time Whig" turned postwar Republican, Norcross was embittered when he lost a Georgia gubernatorial bid in 1876. He was nostalgic, as some other white Southern Republicans were, for the prewar days when the Whig Party, with its message of economic modernization, had served as a viable alternative to the Democrats in the Deep South. Norcross's 1880 proposal to segregate the Georgia Republican Party, with whites and Blacks holding separate conventions, was intended to draw conservative former Whigs to the Republican banner and to hoard the party's patronage spoils for whites. The proposal went nowhere in 1880, but in the spring of 1884, it gained some traction, as Norcross met together with Longstreet and a small cadre of other disaffected Republicans to launch the Whig Republican movement. They suggested that whites and Blacks should seek the "common end" of Republican electoral victories on separate tracks, with Blacks relegated to a separate, subordinate wing of the party.[20]

Longstreet's motives and his agenda were complex. His support for the Whig Republican gambit came at a time when he harbored maximum bitterness against the Buck-Bryant carpetbagger leaders of his own Republican faction, who had sought to push him out of the marshal's office, and keen frustration with Black voters; in his eyes, they'd been ill-served by carpetbagger leadership and lured into casting misguided votes for Democrats. Longstreet continued to loathe the Southern Democratic Party and to see it as a bad-faith actor pushing retrograde ideas. And he knew perfectly well that the Republican Party's viability depended on Black support: even as he lamented their perceived lack of party loyalty, Longstreet described Georgia's Black voters as a "very intelligent class" who were trying to show whites that "neither party of the South can claim a monopoly of the colored vote." The gambit of forming a white man's party in the spring of 1884 was a ploy to achieve two ends: to outmaneuver the Buck-Bryant clique, by insisting that Longstreet and his backers represented the most "respectable" elements of the party in Georgia, and to neutralize the Democrats' long-standing tactic of equating Republicanism with "negro rule."[21]

The Whig Republican bid soon fizzled, principally because it was flatly rejected by Black leaders, who saw it as a contemptibly racist effort by ungrateful whites to seize "all the spoils" of party patronage for themselves. The Black press, which had long lamented the reliance of Black Georgia politicians on Longstreet's patronage coattails, called the Whig Republican movement the "depths of deviltry" and Longstreet a "whitewashed relic of the confederacy." "Old dogs cannot be learned new tricks," the *Christian Recorder* editorialized, lamenting that Longstreet had abandoned the Radical Republican cause. When Norcross's proposal for separate conventions was summarily turned down by delegates at the Georgia Republicans' state convention in May 1884—forcing Norcross to concede publicly that Republicans "could do nothing without the colored vote"—the Black press rejoiced that the "white Republican Party of Georgia" had "died aborning."[22]

Significantly, conservative Democrats also rejoiced at the failure of the Whig Republicans to posture as a white man's party. "Any proposed split in the Republican ranks South is but temporary snarling over some bone, that will eventually end in a social equality wallow in the old Republican mud-hole," as an Athens paper put it. In the eyes of Georgia's dominant Democrats, both factions of the Georgia's Republicans were "Radicals." The conservative press saw the 1884 white Republican movement as "nothing more than the discontented growling of a minority wing of the radical party." Longstreet's nemesis Jubal Early got in on the act, telling an interviewer that Longstreet's "new party" was a "shrewd attempt on his part to draw away from the Democratic party enough old-time whigs to make a party that would once more make the negro vote a power in Georgia."[23]

Despite bitter partisan infighting and some egregious missteps in the 1880s, Longstreet maintained, on balance, a strong, positive reputation among African Americans. While the Black press and leadership was under no illusion that Longstreet was a racial egalitarian, they also shared with him common enemies, and some common goals. Longstreet was a figure with national stature whose story could be mobilized, rhetorically, for many purposes: to herald progress, or to condemn retrenchment, or to call out the hypocrisy of whites. His consistent support for Black voting resonated at the national level: none other than Frederick Douglass, in an 1879 speech in New York decrying white Southerners' violent resistance to change, proclaimed: "I wish they were all like Key and Longstreet." (David Key was the former Confederate general appointed US postmaster general by Rutherford B. Hayes.) Other Black commentators lamented Longstreet's ostracism and the fact that his example did not do more to kindle white Southern allegiance to the Republican Party. As the USCT veteran and pioneering Black historian George Washington Williams wrote in his 1883 *History of the Negro Race in America*, commenting on Hayes's appointing Longstreet minister to Turkey, the president's "heart was right" in seeking to heal sectional wounds, but his reasoning was faulty: he "put too much confidence in Southern statesmen" like Longstreet, who "had no following, and were, therefore, valueless to his cause."[24]

Crucially, Longstreet had a knack for making course corrections after he fell out of favor with Black Republicans. His decision in the 1884 election cycle to abandon Chester A. Arthur and side instead with the party nominee James Blaine was such a correction. Arthur had earned the deep distrust of Black leaders such as T. Thomas Fortune, editor of the leading Black newspaper in the country, the *New York Age*, for snubbing his Black constituents and for coddling white Southern Independents and even some Democrats in the name of sectional comity. When the Republican National Convention passed over the ailing Arthur (who was suffering from kidney disease) and chose Blaine, a champion of big business and the tariff, as their standard-bearer, Black voters rallied to support the Republican ticket, largely out of enthusiasm for Blaine's running mate, John A. Logan, a Radical Republican with real credentials as a defender of civil rights. Longstreet's endorsement of the Blaine-Logan ticket was motivated primarily by patronage calculations, but it had the effect of realigning him with the Black electorate and garnering him renewed credibility among Black voters.[25]

Ultimately, Longstreet's various shifting alliances with Black political leaders formed and reformed out of their mutual dependence, and their surprising willingness—born of necessity—not to hold grudges. Longstreet was willing to work with former party rivals, and they in turn abided him. For example, the influential lawyer-editor William A. Pledger, a critic of the syndicate who eventually joined its ranks, described Longstreet in an 1889 interview as the "[peer] in character and ability of any of our Northern Republicans." Fortune, for his part, condemned the "southern pig-headedness" that pitted whites in the region against progress, and he held up Longstreet as a martyr, noting that "the whites of the South treated with brutal severity any white person who undertook to accept federal office, to give the blacks political advice, or to teach them. Poor Longstreet!

How he suffered for his courage." Longstreet would soon retool, and burnish, his image as a martyr—for the cause of reunion.[26]

IV

As Longstreet's tenure as US marshal ended, his defense of his wartime record escalated. He offered the public a sustained history lesson in a series of five articles he published, from 1885 to 1887, in *Century* magazine. On the face of it, this assignment had much in common with his *Philadelphia Times* one—like Alexander McClure, the *Century* editorial team, led by Robert Underwood Johnson and Clarence C. Buel, commissioned a series of veterans' reminiscences as a "depoliticized vehicle of sectional reconciliation," using "point-counterpoint battle narratives," as David Blight explains, to dramatize the martial valor of all Civil War soldiers. With its massive circulation and anthologizing of articles in the four-volume *Battles and Leaders of the Civil War*, the *Century* project exemplified the commodification of Civil War memory. But much had transpired since Longstreet's *Times* articles appeared. The national cult of reunion, which took shape during the centennial year of 1876, gained momentum as white Americans retreated from Reconstruction and avidly consumed accounts of the war era that emphasized the shared values, and heroism, of combatants on both sides. "Reconciliationists often pointed to Appomattox," the historian Gary W. Gallagher has noted, "as the beginning of a healing process that reminded all Americans of their shared history and traditions." While the Reconciliation Cause movement was intended as an antidote to sectionalism, it involved, Gallagher adds, "a measure of Northern capitulation to the white South and the Lost Cause tradition," as it posited the moral equivalency of the Union and Confederacy.[27]

Against this backdrop, a new set of interlocutors insinuated themselves into the Longstreet-Gettysburg controversy: the editorial team of the ambitious newspaper the *Atlanta Constitution*. Two members of the

Constitution staff, Josiah Carter and Joel Chandler Harris (the author of the popular *Uncle Remus* stories), were selected to help Longstreet with writing and editing the *Century* pieces. Another staffer, Pascal J. Moran, would eventually help Longstreet with his memoir. And the man who had aided him with the *Philadelphia Times* articles back in 1877, Henry W. Grady, had in the meantime risen up the journalistic ranks from reporter to celebrated editor-publisher, purchasing a one-fourth interest in the *Constitution* in 1880 and building it into one of the South's leading newspapers.[28]

These men brought their own distinct political spin to the project of sectional reconciliation. By the mid-1880s, Grady was the premier national spokesman of the New South movement, which wedded the themes of "intersectional white racial brotherhood" and Southern commercial and industrial development. As self-styled Southern "liberals," they distanced themselves rhetorically from the "bitter-end extremists," as the historian Daniel Singal has put it, who thought the "very social fabric of the South stood in mortal danger as a result of emancipation and its aftermath." Liberals offered instead an "updated version of paternalism" in which whites would support industrial education and some material improvements for Blacks in exchange for their "continued subservience." Grady and his ilk, in boosterism aimed at attracting Northern investors, painted a rosy picture of Southern social and material progress, denying that Blacks were oppressed—even as they also sought to deny Blacks the right to vote and hold office, and developed new tools of oppression such as the convict-lease system. The *Constitution* clique, as the mouthpiece of Georgia's Bourbon Democrats, blended elements of the Lost Cause creed with elements of the cult of reconciliation: Grady professed to be glad that slavery was "swept forever from American soil," while also insisting that "the South has nothing for which to apologize . . . nothing to take back." He was fully committed to the Lost Cause narrative in which white Southerners were vindicated by their victory over Republican Reconstruction.[29]

Grady's Atlanta ring took a keen interest in Longstreet, seeing in him—as a native Georgian, hero of the greatest Confederate victory on

Georgia soil at Chickamauga, and popular figure in the North—a potential asset to the New South movement. As the historian Sarah E. Gardner has explained, some Southerners in this era sought to "strength[en] the weak links in their defense of the Confederacy" by making room in the Lost Cause mythology for those, like Longstreet, on its margins: they could thereby present the North "with a united front." But before Longstreet could be useful as a New South symbol, he needed to be neutralized as a political threat.[30]

Given Longstreet's evident determination to exercise political clout, the question for Georgia Democrats was what they could do to deter, distract, and divert him. The *Constitution* and Grady's team tried a carrot-and-stick approach to luring Longstreet away from Republican politics. In the rare moments (such as the 1881–82 Fusion bid) when the beleaguered state Republicans seemed poised to gain some ground in Georgia, the *Constitution* wielded a rhetorical stick, portraying Longstreet in an unfavorable light as a party hack selling his soul for the rewards of patronage. But in the long stretches of time when the Georgia Republicans were in disarray or retreat, Grady and his circle enticed Longstreet with praise, defending his war record to incentivize his return to the fold. Grady previewed this approach in the 1879 interview he conducted with Longstreet at the general's Gainesville home for the *Philadelphia Times*.

Despite his South Carolina birth, "General Longstreet is a Georgian," Grady began. He praised the Longstreet family as "people of intelligence and authority," and called Longstreet the "most accomplished soldier on the Southern side of the late war." Even as Longstreet offered up a good many pointed opinions in the interview—deeming Joseph Johnston the Confederacy's best general, for example—Grady depicted Longstreet as a man "so thoroughly military in his habits that the soldier always rose above the partisan." Grady editorialized that the rancor against Longstreet for his Reconstruction-era politics had faded, as his advice to Southerners to "accept the situation" was now seen as pure of motive. Quietly tending to his farm and hotel and postmastership, Longstreet "has a charming family, a fair competency, a peaceful home," Grady observed in closing, "and will probably end a life stormy, potent and terrible in the highest degree in a placid and grateful contentment." This was less a prediction than a form of advice: Grady was suggesting implicitly that a disavowal of politics was Longstreet's path back into the affections of white Georgians. This 1879 piece became the template for many a journalist's visit to interview the old general. Grady depicted Gainesville as a quaint mountain hamlet ennobled by the unlikely presence of the dignified, imposing war hero. Grady's treatment also signaled that the reconciliationist press was happy to publicize Longstreet's tendentious views on the war—they made good copy and sold papers—provided that Longstreet stuck to military affairs.[31]

Once Grady assumed its leadership, the *Atlanta Constitution* took a similar tack. When the Hayes administration appointed Longstreet US minister to the Ottoman Empire in 1880, the paper approved of the appointment, declaring bluntly that since the South had defeated the forces of Radical Reconstruction, the paper was willing "to be rather tolerant of other people's opinions, particularly since such opinions can work no harm." "We believe that General Longstreet is thoroughly devoted to the best interests of the South as he understands them; and we are willing to admit that his motives have been misconstrued, but him and not the South, is to blame for that," the *Constitution* reckoned. It helped that Longstreet himself was willing enough to signal his commitment to the New South movement's economic agenda. "We have put aside politics in Georgia," he told the *New York World* rather disingenuously in 1883, singing from Grady's hymnal. "What we are bending all our energies to is to attract Northern capital and to develop our great industrial and mineral resources."[32]

Grady and the *Constitution* encountered significant resistance within Georgia, from conservative Democrats who opposed the appointment of Blacks to federal offices and who persisted in depicting Longstreet as a tool of Radical Republicans, "always ready to prove his sorrow for his rebellious acts and, at the same time, to rub salt in the wounds of his fellow white citizens," as the *Savannah Morning News* opined. Determined to further rehabilitate Longstreet and promote Confederate reconciliation, Grady made his most brazen move in 1886, when he orchestrated Longstreet's appearance at the unveiling of a new monument to the late senator Benjamin H. Hill in Atlanta. Jefferson Davis was to be the guest of honor. Davis and Longstreet had long been estranged, as Davis joined in the chorus of those scapegoating the general for Gettysburg, and Longstreet in return critiqued Davis's wartime leadership. Somehow Grady, master of ceremonies for the event, persuaded Longstreet not only to attend the unveiling but also to ride in on horseback bedecked in his old dress uniform, in a grand, dramatic gesture. In what the *Constitution* described as the "greatest occasion Atlanta ever saw," Longstreet strode to the podium, and he and Davis embraced, to the roar of the crowd numbering in the tens of thousands. "The very clouds quivered with the shouts that went up," as the *Constitution* put it. Here was a tableau of Southern solidarity and of sectional reconciliation that won praise among reunion-minded Southerners and Northerners alike. As one Northern paper put it, noting Longstreet's prominence as a Republican Party leader, the embrace between him and Davis was "particularly touching," for "as they stood on the stage clasped in each other's arms, all the animosities of political strife were forgotten."[33]

Read in this context, Longstreet's *Century* articles of 1885 through 1887, prepared with Carter's and Harris's editorial help, seem fully consistent with Grady's agenda of sectional reconciliation and New South boosterism. The articles covered a series of major battles and campaigns (Seven Days, Second Manassas, Antietam, Fredericksburg, and Gettysburg), offering up a multitude of military opinions, while steering clear of politics. Focusing on tactical details, Longstreet called attention to the failings of Union and Confederate generals alike, criticizing Northern general John Pope, for example, for underestimating the Confederates at Second Manassas, and taking Stonewall Jackson to task for his lateness at the Seven Days, and Lee to task for dividing his army during the Antietam campaign. While Longstreet's account of Gettysburg repeated the charge that Lee had asked his men to do the impossible, and lashed out against the

Early clique ("the Virginians") for scapegoating him, the article ended on an unreservedly reconciliationist note: "I thought before the war, and during its continuation, that the people would eventually get together again in stronger bonds of friendship than those of their first love," Longstreet claimed, fashioning himself a prophet of national reunion.[34]

V

During the 1885–87 window in which he published the *Century* essays, the theme of sectional reconciliation became markedly more prominent in Longstreet's public musings about the war. The tragic death of Ulysses S. Grant in July 1885, after his agonizing battle with throat cancer, was heartbreaking for Longstreet, but also inspirational. Using interviews and speeches as a vehicle, Longstreet pressed the case that Appomattox was the defining moment of his postwar career—that he took part in Reconstruction out of gratitude to Grant and to uphold the terms of his Appomattox parole. Longstreet also reiterated his claim that "nobody but the politicians wanted the war to continue": soldiers such as he and Grant had yearned for and sought peace well before hard-liners—Jefferson Davis in particular—were willing to end the conflict. These were not new themes for Longstreet, but after Grant's death, they had a greater public resonance. As Grant's biographer Joan Waugh has explained, "By the time of his funeral, Grant had become as much a symbol of national reconciliation as he was earlier a symbol of uncompromising Union victory." During his prolonged, painful demise, Grant had "bask[ed] in an unanticipated but welcomed wave of tributes from former enemies," gestures that "tipped Grant's inclination toward embracing sectional harmony." National reunion became the keynote of the national mourning and commemoration of Grant's passing. While some Lost Causers—Jubal Early, for one—remained resistant to this trend, others, such as Fitzhugh Lee and P. G. T. Beauregard, "saluted the Christian compassion" of Grant's lenient terms at Appomattox.[35]

Feeling the loss of Grant's friendship keenly, Longstreet became more and more committed to the image of Grant as a peacemaker. On July 23, 1885, the day the former president died, a grief-stricken Longstreet was visited in Gainesville by a *New York Times* reporter. After noting that they had been "on terms of the closest intimacy," Longstreet described Grant as "the truest as well as the bravest man that ever lived," and "the highest type of manhood America has produced." Longstreet contrasted Grant's commitment to reconciliation with Jefferson Davis's stubborn defiance, saying, "Mr. Davis never did give up 'the cause' as entirely lost. He expects to be President yet." Fighting back against the charges that he was himself an unscrupulous place seeker, Longstreet emphasized that he had not sought out political office, but instead had accepted his first postwar appointment, as surveyor of the port of New Orleans, at President Grant's behest. Grant had forwarded Longstreet's name to the Senate; Longstreet had demurred, for fear of causing controversy; Grant had urged him to take the post; and Longstreet accepted, in order to be consistent with his Appomattox pledge to accept "reconstruction and reconciliation."[36]

This was a promising tack. But once again, as in the case of the *Philadelphia Times* essays a decade earlier, Longstreet's articles and interviews failed to silence his harshest critics, who were simply unwilling to detach his military judgments from his political record—or to see him as an avatar of peace. As the *Charleston News and Courier* put it, taking umbrage at Longstreet's criticism of Jackson and Lee in the *Century* article on the Seven Days:

> It is unfortunate for General Longstreet that he survived the war. Had it been his lot to die in the Wilderness from the wound which he received in the moment of victory, what a halo of glory would have surrounded his name! Neither "Gettysburg" nor "New Orleans" would have been written against his record, and he would have been honored as Lee and Jackson are honored. It avails him nothing to endeavor now to draw Jackson down to his own plane.

The effort is futile, and worse than futile. Jackson's reputation and place in history are beyond the reach of his old comrade's envious tongue and hostile arm.[37]

Stung by such coverage but not deterred, Longstreet turned to rebooting his political career and to writing his memoir.

VI

In his quest for a new office, occasioned by the election of Republican Benjamin Harrison as president in 1888, Longstreet fell short. Harrison was a Union Civil War veteran and senator from Indiana who ran on a platform of high-tariff protection for industry, expanded benefits for veterans, and civil service reform. His 1888 victory, on the strength of his support in the North and Midwest, was a Republican interlude in the two-term presidency of Democrat Grover Cleveland. Longstreet served as a Harrison elector for the state of Georgia and lobbied assiduously for a patronage post in the new administration—ideally, he hoped, a Cabinet office or a diplomatic assignment in Latin America or Europe. Longstreet called on Harrison in Indianapolis in December 1888, telling the president-elect, as a kind of self-appointed spokesman for the region, that Southerners "simply want to be treated kindly and considerately."[38]

Longstreet had some reason for optimism about his patronage prospects, as his public profile as a reconciliationist was further burnished when he was received warmly at the July 1888 commemoration of the twenty-fifth anniversary of Gettysburg. The event was a gathering of blue and gray veterans staged to prove that "old foes are friends now," as newspaper coverage proclaimed; in a symbolic gesture typical of the era's veterans' reunions, former enemies literally clasped hands in peace. Longstreet attended the dedication of a monument to a regiment from New York and was thronged and cheered heartily by Union veterans eager to shake his hand.

Longstreet balanced such appearances with equally crowd-pleasing performances at Republican Party functions. In February 1889, for example, he made a memorable speech on national unity at the annual Washington's Birthday banquet of the Michigan Club, a venerable Republican organization, in Detroit. Although Longstreet did not make the trip in person, he appreciated the importance of the occasion and provided comments through his proxy, Atlanta politico Alton Angier. Longstreet's speech offered up red-meat themes to his audience of Northern Republicans. He disavowed as sophistry the Calhounian theory of states' rights; embraced the Federalist theory of a strong perpetual Union as articulated by George Washington and Daniel Webster; declared the results of the Civil War "irreversible and final"; and called for "freedom of the press, freedom of speech, a free ballot, and a fair count" and the "industrial emancipation and reconstruction of the South." Republican policies, he proclaimed, would unite Michigan and Georgia within the "grand sisterhood of States."[39]

This playing to multiple constituencies paid some dividends. The numerous letters of endorsement that were sent to president-elect Harrison and his secretary, urging an appointment, reveal that Longstreet had succeeded, over the course of the 1880s, in cultivating a far-flung network of supporters representing a range of political views. Those boosters included staunch Southern Republicans such as journalist J. W. Fairfax and lawyer W. B. Merchant, who had served under Longstreet during the war and followed him into the Louisiana Republican Party thereafter. These men wrote to Harrison testifying that Longstreet's appointment to a high-level position would "give courage to thousands in every Southern State to at once openly, boldly enlist under the Republican banner," in Fairfax's words. Only Longstreet, among all other hopefuls, could "bring about a change of sentiment, and policy on the part of the Southern people on the question of a free ballot, and fair count at elections," Merchant added. Stephen W. Parker, a lawyer representing Cherokee clients in Georgia, wrote the president-elect his own appeal on behalf of *true* Southern Republicans, which he defined as those who had "stood with the South until Slavery became extinct on the memorable 9th day of April at Appomattox, and since that time have been true to the Union and Reconstruction. Genl James Longstreet is the noblest 'Roman of them all,'" Parker told Harrison.

The party faithful in the Northern states wrote Harrison, too, vouching that Longstreet was "thoroughly reconstructed" and that his leadership at the national level "would ruin the democratic party and destroy the last hope of the advocates of Peonage for the negroes of the Cotton States." (Peonage referred to the form of debt servitude in which employees pay off debts to their employers with work.)[40]

Even as some supporters emphasized Longstreet's abiding commitment to the Reconstruction of the South, others cast him as a conservative figure ideally suited to return the region to the antebellum status quo. Invoking Benjamin Harrison's lineage as the grandson of antebellum Whig president William Henry Harrison, these supporters argued that Longstreet was the Southerner best positioned to win over to the Republican Party the South's "old line Whigs"—men who favored political compromise, economic development, and nationalism over sectionalism. Only Longstreet, wrote the journalist M. B. Hewson, could restore the "old-time Union" by reviving two-party competition in the South: he could attract Whigs who served in the Confederacy, and thus break the Democrats' sway over the Solid South. As if to illustrate this argument, old-line Whig William Miller Owen of New Orleans, Longstreet's former artillery officer and postwar business partner, recalled the glories of William Henry Harrison's 1840 "Log Cabin" campaign in his own letters to the president-elect, urging Longstreet's appointment.[41]

More surprisingly, some Georgia Democrats reached out to Harrison on Longstreet's behalf. Confederate veteran and Atlanta publisher Joseph Van Holt Nash spearheaded an impressive petition, signed by dozens of Georgia dignitaries and dated December 26, 1888, arguing that Longstreet could, if he represented the South in the new administration, promote "genuine reconciliation" and the "final extinguishment of the dying embers of sectional strife." The signatories included prominent legislators, judges, merchants, lawyers, and journalists, including Pascal J. Moran and Joel Chandler Harris of the *Atlanta Constitution*. They did not deny that Longstreet was an "outspoken and consistent Republican," but they believed that his party identity was counterbalanced by his reputation as an "upright and unsullied gentleman, [and] heroic soldier and patriot." It is likely that the petition was motivated by a series of pragmatic calculations: that Longstreet was preferable, as an appointee, to a carpetbagger or Radical Republican choice; that he may be less a threat in a national position than in a local one; and that he could be persuaded to dispense patronage to some Georgia Democrats, especially if he felt himself to be in the debt of his conservative backers.[42]

The more Longstreet emphasized national reunion rather than Republican Reconstruction, the more he could act as a political screen onto whom the many stakeholders of reconciliation could project their various agendas. But Longstreet's self-reinvention did not, at this moment, translate into political preferment. Harrison favored the Buck faction of the Georgia party over Longstreet's and was not enthusiastic about advancing the fortunes of a prominent ex-Confederate. A December 1888 letter by William Tecumseh Sherman on the subject of Harrison appointments hints at lingering unease among some Union veterans about bestowing prominent national offices on ex-rebels. Sherman professed respect and friendship for Longstreet but felt that Cabinet and diplomatic posts should be withheld from former Confederates, as "no nation on earth can afford to put a premium on treason." Another critical tack was taken by some commentators in the Black press, who argued, as did a correspondent to the *Star of Zion* newspaper (the official organ of the AME Zion Church), that it was naïve to believe that white Southern Republicans, however "eminent," could bring their fellow "erring brothers" into the party fold. "The South recognizes nothing but force. It governs by force and always bows its head to force and nothing else," the correspondent insisted, asking for a return to Reconstruction policies in which the military provided civil rights protections.[43]

Harrison decided against Longstreet. Bitter about being snubbed, Longstreet publicly railed against the "carpetbagger and negro combination," led by Alfred Buck, that had outmaneuvered him. Longstreet knew perfectly well that such racist language echoed the Democrats' attacks on Reconstruction and demands for "home rule" of the South. But even after the white man's party idea was thoroughly discredited, Longstreet still at times pandered cynically to conservative voters in the hope that "respectable" Southern Republicans could build a base within the white electorate.[44]

Revealingly, Harrison snubbed not only Longstreet but also the second most prominent ex-rebel aspirant for a patronage appointment: William Mahone of Virginia. Mahone, whom Longstreet recommended to Harrison as worthy of a Cabinet post, was a railroad magnate and former Confederate general who left Virginia's Conservative Party in the late 1870s to found a new party, the Readjusters. (The name referred to its platform of "readjusting" or repudiating some of Virginia's state debt, thereby freeing up funds for programs such as public education and tax relief.) Attracting support from poor whites and African Americans with a message of economic fairness, Mahone served in the US Senate from 1881 to 1887, and caucused there with the Republicans. His Readjusters briefly governed Virginia and promoted Black voting and officeholding, only to meet with a fierce, violent white supremacist backlash that divided the party and drove it from power.[45]

Longstreet saw Mahone both as a political ally and as a particularly reliable source of historical information. The two men corresponded extensively, sharing recollections of the war and a desire to defend their own roles in it. "You are in a similar position to mine," Longstreet confided to Mahone in a blunt 1894 letter. "Your politics don't please the other side, and they won't hesitate to stab you in the back when you least expect it, as they have me." Indeed, Longstreet's critics often lumped him together with Mahone and with a few other controversial rebels-turned-Republicans such as John Singleton Mosby of Virginia and James R. Chalmers of Mississippi. These men, so Southern Democrats charged, were attempting to trade on their military reputations for political advancement, and making promises—to deliver Southern votes to the Republicans—that they could not keep. "The fact that Mahone and Longstreet were Confederate generals does not carry the slightest weight here, and their appointment by Mr. Harrison will not placate or gratify a single ex-Confederate except the lucky appointees themselves," the *New Orleans Times-Democrat* insisted in 1889. Although Mahone's racial politics drew the wrath of Lost Causers such as Jubal Early (who called him a "contemptible coward"), Mahone never received the kind of sustained abuse, as a scapegoat for Confederate defeat, that Longstreet did. There were many reasons for this: Mahone was not nearly as prominent a Confederate figure as Longstreet during the war; Mahone did not commit himself fully to the Republican Party; he refrained from criticizing Robert E. Lee; and he never led Black militiamen against former Confederates. Longstreet remained, despite political setbacks that limited his power, traitor number one in the eyes of those determined to drive the Republicans out of the South.[46]

VII

The year 1889 brought Longstreet personal tragedy as well as professional disappointment. In April his residence in Gainesville was destroyed by fire, leaving it a "smouldering heap of ruins," as the press reported. Longstreet, who was sick at the time, was convalescing at his Piedmont Hotel; his family generally spent the winter months there, transferring to the country house for the summers. He helplessly watched the destruction of his house from nearly two miles away. The fire did thousands of dollars of damage, consuming his own wartime relics, such as his old uniforms, and much of his furniture and library and files; it thus set back his project of writing his memoir of the war. The blaze seems to have originated in a defective flue in the kitchen chimney, where some African American hired servants were working, perhaps preparing the house for the family's summer arrival.

Georgia newspapers speculated that the Longstreet home was another casualty of a wave of destructive fires that had swept the countryside as the result of a spell of unusually dry weather. After the fire, the family moved into a three-room cottage on the property that Longstreet had built for a tenant.[47]

The family rebounded, only to be pitched into grief by the death, on December 30, 1889, of Louise Longstreet, after a monthslong battle with cancer. Obituaries described her as a "woman of remarkable strength and character." These qualities had been on display the previous year, when she made two forays into the public sphere to defend her husband's reputation. Back in January 1888 the *Atlanta Constitution* had published a letter from a Confederate veteran claiming that Longstreet was languishing in "poverty, neglect, and distress," and asking fellow veterans to contribute to a fund for the relief of the old "war-horse." Louise Longstreet immediately sent a pointed reply to the *Constitution*, denying that Longstreet was in financial straits, and insisting on the return to sender of any funds gathered under that pretext. The general was no "object of charity," Louise wrote, correcting the record—he was able, with what he owned, to "live in comparative comfort." Louise's letter drew the praise of the Georgia press as evidence of "the proud Southern spirit." In a further display of her pride, and of the family's means, Louise offered the use of the Piedmont Hotel for the annual meeting of the Georgia Press Association in July 1888. She presided as hostess with panache, and political savvy, telling the Democratic guests, in a spirit of reconciliation, "We are all democrats now," and saying to an ex-Union solider in attendance, "We were on different sides during the war, but we are all in the Union now."[48]

Longstreet was devasted by the loss of his wife. "The old general himself looks as if he could not stand many more wintry blasts," the *Macon Telegraph* observed, in its notice of Louise's death. But Longstreet would again confound expectations, rolling out an extensive memoir that he intended to silence his critics once and for all.[49]

Chapter 10

WAR ON THE PAGE

I

"I am not sorry that I write of the war thirty years after its close, instead of ten or twenty," James Longstreet proclaimed in 1896, in the preface to his book, *From Manassas to Appomattox: Memoirs of the Civil War in America.* "I believe that now, more fully than then, the public is ready to receive, in the spirit in which it is written, the story which I present."[1]

In choosing these words to frame his 690-page account of the Civil War, Longstreet sought final vindication in the protracted conflict over his wartime record. Longstreet's reference to the passing of the decades was no mere literary boilerplate, but a guide to how that war of words had unfolded: the mid-1870s and mid-1880s had been flash points in the contest over Longstreet's reputation, moments at which his own public pronouncements, in the forms of articles, letters, speeches, and interviews, had drawn a swift backlash, leaving him determined to tell the full story of his wartime experiences and to set the record straight.

Longstreet's memoir is the key to understanding his "paradoxical popularity in the late nineteenth century," to use biographer William Garrett Piston's phrase. Scholarly treatments of Longstreet have painted him as his own literary worst enemy—as a man so engulfed in bitterness against his various detractors, and so in over his head, that his public accounts of his own war

295

record and of his political purposes were mired in self-defeating mistakes and misrepresentation, making him an easy mark for those who sought to scapegoat him. They have also noted that Longstreet's reputation improved considerably in his last years, so much so that at the time of his death in 1904, he was widely mourned as a great hero of the Civil War. Unable to square their negative assessment of Longstreet's literary output with evidence of his improving reputation, scholars such as Piston have ventured that his popularity "came despite, not because of, his prolific writings in self-defense": Longstreet benefitted in his late years from the general public fascination with the Civil War generation and the growing traction of the Lost Cause memory tradition.[2]

A close look at Longstreet's memoir—and at his prolonged process of writing it—reveals a very different story. Longstreet was not blinded by bitterness but instead relished the process of writing the memoir, building it from careful research and prolific short-form writings and interviews, and then preparing the public, through savvy use of the press, to receive the memoir "in the spirit in which it [was] written." And he was no easy mark: his critics kept coming at him, in waves of vituperation, precisely because he was a formidable literary and political foe who posed a clear and present threat to Lost Cause orthodoxies.

Longstreet succeeded, with the memoir, in positioning himself as a prophet of sectional reconciliation between the North and South. But the book's reception reveals, too, how and why Longstreet fell short of a full rehabilitation among Southern whites: reconciliation *among* Confederates, who persisted in fighting one another over the meaning and legacy of the war, proved elusive, with race relations and the memory of Reconstruction as the key points of contention.

II

Between 1887, when the last of the *Century* magazine articles appeared, and 1896, when the J. B. Lippincott Company rolled out *From Manassas to Appomattox*, Longstreet often gave interviews meant to create anticipation for his forthcoming tome. A July 1887 article entitled "Longstreet in Peace" by the *Atlanta Constitution*'s Josiah Carter circulated through the press promising that the memoir would "be made up mainly of accounts of adventures in the wars in which Gen. Longstreet has taken part" and that it would "contain some very startling statements about the late war." Subsequent interviews by the *St. Louis Globe-Democrat* and other newspapers repeated the promise of "startling" revelations.[3]

During these years, Longstreet continued to build up his image as a herald of reunion. He played up a popular story for which the Northern press had an insatiable appetite: the tale of how Grant and Longstreet, after the failed Hampton Roads Peace Conference of February 1865, had discussed having their respective wives reach out to each other to open an "unofficial" channel of communications between Grant and Lee, through which they could discuss moving toward peace. In Longstreet's telling of the tale, Lee unwittingly sabotaged the overture by making a "direct request" through official channels for a peace conference with Grant; Grant duly declined that request, as formally treating for peace was beyond the bounds of his authority and jurisdiction. The two sides continued fighting until April 9, 1865. The story served to foreshadow the reunion of Grant and Longstreet at Appomattox, at which Grant had greeted Longstreet warmly as a friend and reminisced about the old days. In Longstreet's view, Grant's dispending of clemency and of patronage to him was an "olive branch," extended, out of the goodness of his "big, generous heart, not to the individual but to the South."[4]

Many in the Southern press proved surprisingly receptive to such symbolism. Indeed, Longstreet found an enthusiastic collaborator in the person of Pascal J. Moran of the *Atlanta Constitution*'s editorial staff. (Although Henry Grady died of pneumonia in 1889 at just thirty-nine years of age, the paper's leadership, under Clark Howell, remained committed to the New South agenda.) Moran was a Canadian who had immigrated to the United States in 1866 and gradually earned a reputation as one of the

South's most respected journalists. He seized on the idea that Longstreet and Grant had "sought a revival of the fraternal relations which should never have been broken." In a widely reprinted 1890 article by Moran, Longstreet recalled how he felt when Grant extended him the hand of mercy at Appomattox: "Great God, I thought to myself, how my heart swells out to such a magnanimous touch of humanity. Why do men fight who were born to be brothers?" Insisting that this sense of brotherhood with Grant was the key to Longstreet's postwar course of action, Moran editorialized, "If it were given all men to know the motives which influenced Longstreet in the year which followed the war, sympathy, if not approval, would at least be extended to him." Evidently appreciative of this relatively even-handed portrayal, Longstreet contracted with Moran in 1892 to help him edit, fact-check, and revise his memoir manuscript before it went to press.[5]

But Longstreet's detractors pushed back at such attempts to make him into a symbol of the fraternal bonds between blue and gray veterans, and instead insisted that "his military opinions have become biased by his political opinions." A newspaper in Summerville, Georgia, opined: "An effort is being made to dispel the cloud which has hung over Longstreet since the day he led a company of colored troops at New Orleans against his own race. But the memory of that deed cannot be forgot."

When Longstreet attended a blue-gray reunion in Knoxville in October 1890, he gave an address in which he mused regretfully on his decision to call for a Confederate retreat at the November 1863 Battle of Fort Sanders. "How far the moral conviction of a hopeless cause may have operated in creating my indecision," he noted, referring to the prospects of a successful attack on that day, it was useless "now to conjecture." It is clear from the context of this comment that Longstreet felt in retrospect the Fort Sanders battle may have been winnable, but also that victory at that juncture would not have changed the ultimate outcome of the war. Southern critics jumped on the speech as an admission by Longstreet that "his heart was not in it" and that he "was in very much the same mood at

Gettysburg." Longstreet's "avowed lack of interest and faith in the cause," the *Charleston News and Courier* charged, "contributed to its final defeat." "Far better for him if he had died on the field of battle," it added cruelly.[6]

The reaction to a June 1893 interview Longstreet gave to the *Washington Post* further exemplifies the tactics of his critics. The interview, in which Longstreet "talked . . . unreservedly on every conceivable phase of the war," and blamed the late Jefferson Davis (who died in 1889) for mismanaging the Confederate war effort, aroused the wrath of former Confederate general Dabney H. Maury of Richmond. Maury was a founder of the Southern Historical Society and part of the Virginia clique of Longstreet's persecutors; he was a vocal critic of the Grant administration, calling it a "sad spectacle of States overthrown and . . . laws set aside." Leveling a series of accusations at Longstreet reaching back to Reconstruction, Maury insisted that Longstreet tried to "sell out the South to the 'Grant party of the North,'" and noted contemptuously that he presided as a "vice president of a negro meeting in Lafayette Square!" and later "went over body and bones to the radical party, marchin[g] in procession with the negroes and baser whites." Maury was referring to two actual events: the May 1867 visit by the abolitionist statesman Henry Wilson to a Republican rally in New Orleans, which Longstreet attended but did not preside over, and the April 30, 1870, public celebration of the ratification of the Fifteenth Amendment in New Orleans, at which Longstreet did preside. Maury's ilk regarded both events as unimpeachable evidence of Longstreet's radicalism and treachery.[7]

Longstreet published a pointed reply in the *Washington Post*. He confirmed that he had indeed ridden "in a carriage in a procession to mark the adoption of the Fifteenth Amendment to the Constitution." Reminding readers that Maury had supported the Liberal Republican faction that challenged Grant in 1872, and that supported both the Fifteenth Amendment and blanket amnesty for former Confederates, Longstreet then skewered Maury for hypocrisy, saying, "He probably thinks the back door more honorable than the front." The attack from Maury was followed in short order by another salvo, this one from the *New Orleans Times-Democrat*, which charged that Longstreet had "prostituted his knowledge of the art military to the training and drilling of a negro constabulary" in New Orleans, and "attempted to put white necks under black heels." In this instance, the Republican Chicago *Inter Ocean* rushed to Longstreet's defense, countering, "Longstreet did good service to the South in war, and he has also done good service to that section in peace, trying to show that the South accepts the settlement of the sword as final." Longstreet himself reiterated this defense in subsequent interviews, such as a *Washington Post* piece in the spring of 1894 subtitled "He Asks Only a Fair Hearing." He emphasized that Confederates "accepted paroles of honor at the capitulation at Appomattox Court House under pledges to obey and respect the laws of Congress."[8]

To further shore up his credentials as a herald of blue-gray reunion, Longstreet participated in two major reconciliation-themed events in 1895: the dedication of the Chickamauga and Chattanooga National Military Park on September 18–20, and the famous Cotton States and International Exposition in Atlanta, which lasted from September to December and attracted a million spectators. Longstreet began his speech at Chickamauga by quoting Lincoln's Gettysburg Address, picking up Lincoln's phrase about dedication to the "great task remaining before us," and then identifying that task as sectional reunion and modernizing the US Army and Navy. "I believe there is an abounding patriotism, broad and deep in all Americans," Longstreet declaimed, that "throbs the heart and pulses the being as ardently of the South Carolinian as the Massachusetts Puritan." With such sentiments, Longstreet stuck to the script more than many other speakers, whom, as the historian Caroline Janney has noted, strayed from the designated agenda of reunion to instead defend the righteousness of either the Union or the Confederate cause.[9]

The 1895 Atlanta exposition, best known as the occasion for Booker T. Washington's famous "Five Fingers" speech advocating that Blacks prioritize economic progress over social and political equality, was, as the historian William Link has explained, "a visual symbol for Grady's New South." Although Henry Grady did not live to see the event, he had masterminded two earlier such Atlanta gatherings. On September 21, 1895, the exposition honored Civil War soldiers in its Blue and Gray Day festivities, which drew thousands of veterans, including Longstreet. According to the *Constitution*, his reception was the highlight of the day, as "there was such a demonstration from both blue and gray that it made the old man's heart beat with the impulsiveness of youth." Longstreet's speech fondly recalled his Mexican War service, when "northerners and southerners shoulder to shoulder fought for the flag."[10]

Longstreet fared less well in commemorative events focused on the Confederacy. As William Garrett Piston explains, such events were "almost completely controlled by his avowed enemies," and by one of them in particular: his fellow Georgian and former Army of Northern Virginia Second Corps commander, general John Brown Gordon. After Reconstruction, Gordon, with the help of Grady and the *Atlanta Constitution*, had become the dominant force in state politics, serving two terms as a US senator (1873–80 and 1891–97) and one as governor of Georgia (1886–90). The animosity between Brown, Georgia's leading Democrat, and Longstreet, its most famous Republican, illustrated the obstacles to Grady's vision of a united New South. Seeing Longstreet not only as a political opponent but also as a rival for military laurels, Gordon began in the mid-1880s to ally himself publicly with Jubal Early's anti-Longstreet faction. In 1889, Gordon became the founding president of the United Confederate Veterans organization, which came to include one-third of all living Confederate veterans, and committed itself to "the worship of Lee and the use of Longstreet as scapegoat for Gettysburg and by extension for the loss of the war," to quote Piston. Longstreet regarded the UCV as an unabashedly political organization that did the bidding of Solid South Democrats like Gordon; ever the loyal Republican, Longstreet regarded it "as a high compliment to be excluded" from UCV membership. On occasions when Longstreet did venture to participate in Confederate memorialization—such as the 1890 unveiling in Richmond of the Lee statue, or the 1892 third annual meeting of the UCV, in New Orleans—he did so warily, and only at the special request of some of his own former troops, who insisted on his receiving an invitation even though the events managers would have preferred that Longstreet stayed away. As Longstreet divulged to Thomas Goree in 1894, it was unpleasant for the UCV's managers to have Longstreet in their midst, and "especially unpleasant to General Gordon." The rank and file invariably gave "Old Pete" a warm reception: "The old soldiers, when they see me, forget their new leader in peace, and it tries his patience."[11]

In private correspondence, such as his exchanges with Goree, Longstreet did not pull any punches, writing, for example, that "contemptible as was the career of Early, it was better as a soldier than that of Gordon." But in his public utterances, Longstreet was eager to cultivate a reputation as a man of fair judgments. And so he hammered home one last theme in order to prepare the way for his memoir: namely, that his account would be scrupulously researched. He did not claim to be a historian, but he did aim to provide the raw material for future historians—a detailed account based on his own firsthand experience, informed by his deep understanding of the "art" and "science" of war, and supported by the documentary record. In an 1890 interview, Longstreet pointed up the shortcomings of the *Century* series of articles by veterans, noting that "they are no good as historical matter . . . because they have no official backing. The trouble is that one man writes a war story as he saw it, and some other fellow comes along and writes it another way." The only way to produce a useful account was to "compile it from the official records."[12]

He found a key ally in the person of War Department clerk Leslie J. Perry, a Union veteran who rose up the bureaucratic ranks after the Civil War to become, in 1889, one of the civilian experts compiling the massive, 128-volume comprehensive documentary reference work *The War of the Rebellion: A Compilation of the Official Records of the Union and Confederate Armies*. In the ten years he worked on collecting and editing material for the *Official Records* (as the series came to be called), Perry stepped forward in public to defend Longstreet's account of Gettysburg and generally to burnish Longstreet's military reputation. At first, Perry shared with the press his notes from "copious conversations" with Longstreet on Gettysburg and other matters, and then waded directly into the controversy himself. Perry made the case, "excluding evidence not in accord with the official records," that Lee and not Longstreet bore primary responsibility for the Southern defeat and that Lee "was a victim of his own self-confidence." As the historian Yael Sternhell has explained, the compiling of the *Official Records* was itself an engine of sectional reconciliation, as it became a joint project between Northerners and Southerners, and as the volumes themselves avoided "explicit engagement with politics or ideology" and were packaged as "an impartial body of records published by a seemingly reliable source."[13]

By the fall of 1895, with his long process of researching and writing the memoir finally coming to its conclusion, Longstreet took a victory lap of sorts, visiting the publisher J. B. Lippincott in Philadelphia to attend to the last details of publication. The prestigious Union League Club held a reception and banquet in his honor, at which "ex-Union soldiers and commanders ... grasped General Longstreet's hand all the heartier in bearing testimony to his valor on the field." So keen was the interest in Longstreet's travails as an author that the *Washington Star* would observe, in October 1895, that as "every one knows, he has for the past eight years been engaged in writing his memoirs," and that "next to his family and the famous old white horse, that book is nearer and dearer to the warrior's heart than anything he ever possessed during life." The memoir had been "such a constant source of pleasure to him," Longstreet's son Lee (as Robert Lee was known) told the *Star*, "that I don't know how he will get along now it is completed and in the hands of publishers."

In a last prepublication salvo, Longstreet, at Lippincott's behest, published an open letter on October 26, 1895, in which he claimed, "My narrative is a plain statement of facts as recorded in the reports of events as they passed. . . . I have faith that the time has arrived when people are not averse to reading of facts." As advance copies and excerpts started to become available in the late fall of 1895, and as Lippincott recruited agents to hawk the book on subscription, promising "unprecedented" sales, the time had come to find out: Would James Longstreet finally get his fair hearing?[14]

III

"Honor to all!" This would be his theme, Longstreet announced in his preface. Insisting, as he had done for years, that "political passions and prejudices" had led to the "misrepresentation" of his war record, Longstreet pledged to readers that he would offer them "the materials of history" in a spirit of sectional reconciliation; he repeated, too, the line from his September 1895 speech at Chickamauga, about the patriotism throbbing in American breasts from South Carolina to Massachusetts.[15] What followed was a chronological march through Longstreet's career, moving quickly through his prewar life and Mexican War adventures, and arriving at First Bull Run by page 35. Early on, Longstreet established his friendship with Grant as a defining motif, observing on page 17, in a section on his West Point education, that Grant, "a lovable character, a valued friend," was the "man who was to eclipse all."[16]

The pace of the memoir then slowed down as Longstreet offered an intricate account of the Seven Days battles and Second Manassas, arriving at the Antietam campaign by page 200. Longstreet considered this first third of the book a "plain narrative of occurrences," emphasizing Confederate strategy and tactics, and reprising details from his *Century* articles. While he got in some passing swipes at Early and Fitzhugh Lee and Stonewall Jackson, criticizing aspects of their military performance, his tone was mostly rather dry and detached. But in chapter 20, entitled "Review of the Maryland Campaign," Longstreet dropped his reserve and signaled that his cumulative details were adding up to an argument: he was demonstrating that Confederates lost the war not because of the Union's overwhelming numbers and resources, but instead because of their own failings. The principal failing, one that afflicted both armies at times but proved more costly to Confederates, was hubris. As he put it, referring to Lee's decision to divide his army during the Antietam campaign:

> Providence helps those who can avail themselves of His tender care, but permits those who will to turn from Him to their own arrogance. That His gracious hand was with the Confederates in their struggles on the Chickahominy, and even through the errors of the Bull Run campaign, cannot be questioned. When, however, in self-confidence, they lost sight of His helping hand, and in contempt of the enemy dispersed the army, they were to give up the reward to vainglory.

Indulging in some counterfactual fantasies, Longstreet imagined that if Confederates had concentrated their power at Antietam, they would have not only won the day but also forestalled "one of the decisive political events of the war": namely, Lincoln's issuance of his preliminary Emancipation Proclamation.[17]

Longstreet not only called out Confederate overconfidence—the belief that McClellan was an unworthy foe "seemed to pervade our army," he lamented—but also traced it to its source: the leadership of Lee. Longstreet's portrayal of Lee in the first third of the memoir was paradoxical. He emphasized the two men's intimacy, proudly quoting Lee's "Here is my old war-horse at last!" line to encapsulate their mutual trust and respect. But he also foreshadowed the troubles to come, saying on page 159, "Our personal relations remained as sincere after the war until politics came between us in 1867." Trying to stake a claim as a fair and balanced arbiter not blinded by political passions or prejudices, Longstreet concluded his review of the Maryland campaign by observing of Lee and McClellan, "Both were masters of the science but not the art of war. Lee was successful in Virginia, McClellan in Maryland." He had used such phraseology, in interviews, before, to make the point that while Lee and McClellan, as trained engineers, were possessed of great military learning and skill, they lacked some qualities of character—self-control, calmness, adaptability, generosity of spirit—that Longstreet attributed to men he considered superior generals: namely, Joe Johnston and Grant. Jomini's influence on Longstreet is plain to see: decades of military experience had borne out, for Longstreet, Jomini's teachings about the importance of concentrating force; the dangers of fighting on the tactical offensive; and the role of "moral courage" in military leadership. In Jomini's view, one of the key tests of a leader's character was whether he could resist having "too great a contempt for the enemy."[18]

Longstreet's evident aim in his treatment of Lee, and of the other Confederate "marble man," Stonewall Jackson, was to demythologize them. In his description of Second Bull Run, for example, Longstreet offered humanizing details about both, noting of Jackson that he had the habit of raising his right hand not "as an invocation of Divine aid," as some of his followers liked to think, but instead because a wound from First Bull Run had left his hand partially paralyzed and impeded its blood circulation. A few lines later, Longstreet described how Lee was thrown from his horse and "pulled . . . violently to the ground," severely spraining his wrist and breaking some of the bones in his hand. Such anecdotes were meant to bring these men off their pedestals and down to earth.[19]

Covering the Chancellorsville and Gettysburg campaigns, Longstreet's next ten chapters developed additional elements of his explanation for Confederate defeat: that Confederate leaders were often at cross-purposes with one another and often lured into fighting battles that yielded needlessly costly, "fruitless" victories. Longstreet provocatively second-guessed Lee's decision-making at Chancellorsville—a battle widely considered Lee's tactical masterpiece—by suggesting that if Lee had waited a few days to concentrate more troops to attack Joseph Hooker, the battle could have been a Fredericksburg-style rout. Instead, "Lee was actually so crippled by his victory that he was a full month restoring his army to condition to take the field." This, of course, foreshowed Gettysburg: "When the hunt was up," Longstreet observed, Lee's "combativeness was overruling." In Longstreet's view, Lee was too entranced by what military historian Cathal Nolan has recently called "the allure of battle": the view, with roots that stretched back to ancient warfare, that heroic genius—"sheer will and brilliance" on the part of generals—could produce hinge moments in which grand-scale, decisive, iconic battles turn the tide of history. Lee would have been better served, Longstreet maintained, by the realization that the Civil War was a war of grinding exhaustion and attrition.[20]

The memoir's account of Gettysburg largely reprised his *Philadelphia Times* and *Century* articles: Lee reneged on their agreement for an offensive strategy but defensive tactics; there had been no sunrise order on the second day; Longstreet had proposed an alternate, more practical plan; Longstreet's First Corps had given the battle its all and performed heroically, despite lacking proper support from Lee's other two corps; Lee had assumed the responsibility for the battle's outcome and conceded later that Longstreet's plan would have been better. Longstreet continued to maintain that "Lee had lost his balance" at Gettysburg. He had used this formulation in earlier writings, observing in his 1877 *Philadelphia Times* account that Lee "lost the matchless equipoise that usually characterized him" and was "thrown from his balance" both by overconfidence and by the failings of Stuart, A. P. Hill, Ewell, and others; in his 1885 *Century* piece on the Seven Days, Longstreet added that Lee was "remarkably well balanced—always so, except on one or two occasions of severe trial when he failed to maintain his exact equipoise."

In choosing the image of balance (or its synonym *equipoise*) to conjure Lee's state of mind, Longstreet was drawing on a popular vocabulary, in his era, for describing the characteristics of military leaders. Soldiers and civilians alike saw equipoise as a key attribute of successful commanders. For example, William Tecumseh Sherman, in an 1887 *Century* article, lauded the "magnificent equipoise of Gen. Grant." Military biographers such as Alfred Thayer Mahan and Theodore Ayrault Dodge praised the equipoise—the balance of character and intellect, and of boldness and caution—of military idols such as Napoleon I and Admiral Lord Nelson. Longstreet himself deployed the term in an 1895 interview to compare Grant and Napoleon, observing, "Napoleon was undoubtedly brighter and quicker, but he did not have the equipoise of Grant."[21]

Longstreet's righteous indignation at the Lee-worship of Early's crew flashed hotter in *From Manassas to Appomattox* than in his earlier publications. Longstreet's original claim that Lee atypically lost his equipoise at Gettysburg became an altogether more stinging indictment. "[Lee] was excited and off his balance," Longstreet charged in the memoir, and "labored under that oppression until enough blood was shed to appease him." In this rendering of their Gettysburg disagreement, Longstreet seemed to attribute to Lee not overconfidence and overexcitement—an excess of qualities that in their proper measure were good and benign—but instead a willful, hubristic, and even sinister desire to impose his will and exact his tribute, no matter what the cost to his own men. In his 1877 account, Longstreet had ventured criticism of Lee while also fulsomely professing "the greatest affection" for him and the "greatest reverence for his memory"; in his memoir, Longstreet again alluded to their friendship, but in a more rueful, clipped way. Reasserting that he had the "kindest relations" with Lee until "interrupted by politics in 1867," Longstreet, on page 401, got to the heart of the issue: that it was Early and his ilk who had done the real damage to Lee's reputation. In dredging up Lee's alleged criticisms of Longstreet and suggesting that Lee himself sought to "shift the disaster" to Longstreet's shoulders, Early had *either* lied about Lee's postwar intentions (if Lee in truth did not seek to cast blame) *or* exposed some very unbecoming truths about Lee's own pettiness (if Lee was pretending to be Longstreet's friend while treacherously undermining him). "It does not look like generalship to lose a battle and a cause and then lay the responsibility upon others," Longstreet declared bluntly in the memoir, revealing that Early's relentless campaign had worn away at Longstreet's *own* faith in his friendship with Lee.[22]

After covering the Southern army's retreat back into Virginia in a chapter wistfully entitled "The Wave Rolls Back," Longstreet turned his attention, in nine chapters numbering 118 pages, to his stint in the western theater, where he was transferred in September 1863 to join Braxton Bragg's army in its face-off with Union general William Rosecrans. Theoretically, this move had suited Longstreet; he had, after all, urged since the spring of 1863 a grand concentration of Confederate forces in the West. But in personal terms, his contempt for Bragg augured poorly. Longstreet folded his accounts of the Confederate victory at Chickamauga (which many consider his finest hour as a commander) and the disastrous Knoxville campaign (by all accounts a low point) into his overarching narrative of Confederate cross-purposes, fruitless victories, and missed opportunities. Longstreet's deft generalship of the Confederate left wing on September 20, 1863, at Chickamauga had been decisive in what he called "the first pronounced victory in the West." But in his view, it was too little, too late: this western strategy should have been effected much earlier. Recounting his October 10 meeting with Jefferson Davis (who visited the army) and his offer to Davis that he resign amid bitter Confederate infighting, Longstreet reflected, "In my judgment, our last opportunity was lost when we failed to follow the success at Chickamauga, and capture or disperse the Union army."[23]

Longstreet would again ask to be relieved of command, and again have that offer declined, after the "tragic debacle" at Knoxville: his futile attempt to dislodge the Federal forces under General Ambrose Burnside in East Tennessee, featuring the ill-conceived and uncharacteristic frontal assault on the Union defenses at Fort Sanders. In Longstreet's telling, the failed campaign was doomed by the poor leadership of his superiors, who left his detached units poorly supplied and provisioned, outnumbered and cut off from reinforcements. Under Davis's leadership, the Confederacy was mired in a "settled policy of meeting the enemy where he was prepared for us."[24]

Longstreet's remaining chapters on the war, covering his return to Lee's side in Virginia and the epic yearlong clash between Grant and Lee that culminated at Appomattox, gave him the chance to hammer home his main contention: that Confederate failings lost them the war. Recognizing that the war was attritional in nature, Longstreet maintained nonetheless that "the power of battle is in generalship more than in the number of soldiers." The Confederates might have outgeneraled the Yankees but did not—and while infighting, ego battles, logistical failures, tactical errors, and other factors all added up, in the end it came down to Lee versus Grant. "They were equally pugnacious and plucky," Longstreet averred, but Grant had a key edge, as he was "the more deliberate." Grant not only possessed superior numbers and resources, but also he knew how to use them. Paraphrasing French Revolutionary leader Georges Jacques Danton's famous epigram on the effectiveness of audacity in wartime, "L'audace, L'audace, toujours l'audace!," Longstreet countered that "an Americanism which seems an appropriate substitute is *A level head, a level head, always a level head.*"

"President Lincoln's good judgment told him that Grant was the man for the times," and Grant proved it, in the Overland campaign, trench warfare outside Petersburg and Richmond, and most especially with his lenient terms at Appomattox. "As the world continues to look at and study the grand combinations and strategy of General Grant, the higher will be his award as a great soldier," Longstreet concluded. Confederates should be "foremost in crediting him with all that his admirers so justly claim."[25]

This portrait of Grant stood in sharp contrast to Longstreet's treatment of his postwar critics. Recounting how he was severely wounded by friendly fire at the Wilderness on May 6, 1864, Longstreet wrote, in one of the most biting passages in his memoir, "Bad as was being shot by some of our own troops in the battle of the Wilderness,—that was an honest mistake, one of the accidents of war,—being shot at, since the war, by many officers, was worse." Refuting Fitzhugh Lee's 1878 charge that Longstreet had "lost his way and reached the Wilderness twenty-four hours behind time," Longstreet reviled him for bearing false witness. In his Appomattox chapter, Longstreet took Pendleton to task for calling a "mutinous" meeting, on April 7, 1865, of officers who wanted to suggest to Lee that he should surrender. These "knights of later days," as Longstreet called the postwar Virginia cabal, claimed that they sought to relieve Lee of the humiliation of proposing peace, but their actions, Longstreet fumed, "would not stand the test of the military tribunal."[26]

Longstreet portrayed himself in these last pages of the memoir as someone who was weary of war and open to a negotiated peace (he again retailed his story of his peace overtures with Ord in February 1865), but also utterly determined to do his soldierly duty, and to fight the enemy and seek victory vigorously until no choice was left but to surrender. This was a more honest self-portrait than the one Longstreet had offered in suggesting that he knew the cause was lost after Chickamauga. His account of the surrender set up the memorable rhetorical flourish of Longstreet's final chapter, on the postwar years: the proposition that "those who are forgiven most love the most." Longstreet had uttered this catchphrase of reconciliation in earlier speeches, to sum up his gratitude for Grant's leniency at Appomattox and for Grant's subsequent role in helping secure him amnesty under President Andrew Johnson's restoration policy. Here Longstreet pivoted to a brief but pointed defense of his Reconstruction stance, reprising his familiar arguments that he had sought a practical path toward reconciliation, and that he felt that respect for the laws of Congress—including its Reconstruction Acts enfranchising Black men—counted among the obligations attaching to the Confederates' paroles at Appomattox. Longstreet repeated his earlier formulation: that his appointment as customs surveyor in 1869 came from "the bigness of [Grant's] generous heart."[27]

In the final paragraph of Longstreet's memoir, he called to mind a former slave, his "old nurse," Daniel, who resided, along with other freedmen and women who had once been owned by the Longstreet family, in Macon, Mississippi, and who "called on" Longstreet whenever the old general visited there. During Longstreet's last visit, Daniel had seemed more concerned about the general's well-being than ever and had asked Longstreet if he belonged to a church. Longstreet replied, "I try to be a good

Christian." Daniel "laughed loud and long, and said—'Something must have scared you mighty bad, to change you so from what you was when I had to care for you.'" The last two lines of the memoir read: "In a recent letter [Daniel], sent me a message to say that he is getting to be a little feeble. Blessings on his brave heart!"[28]

The anecdote about Daniel seems at first glance the kind of paternalistic sentimental cant so often trafficked in by Lost Cause defenders of slavery, waxing nostalgic about the days before emancipation and about the devotion and loyalty of their "servants." But when read in context, following as it does Longstreet's contrast between the bitter "animus" of his "latter-day" Confederate critics and the openhearted generosity of Grant, another layer of meaning to the Daniel story becomes visible. Longstreet ascribed to Daniel, who after emancipation had become an exhorter in a Black church, some of the "moral courage" he ascribed to Grant: the impulse to forgiveness.[29]

Longstreet's reference in the memoir to his family's ex-slaves in Macon, Mississippi, speaks to an important subtext of his own political transformations. Among the many unusual features of his conversion to Republicanism was that it served to align him politically, for a time, with those ex-slaves and their descendants. In the mid-1870s, while Longstreet was building a new political base in Georgia, a former slave of the Longstreet family, J. W. Longstreet (born in 1857), was making his name, at great risk, as an operative in Mississippi's Republican Party. J. W. Longstreet testified in 1875 congressional hearings on white supremacist violence in Mississippi, describing the lynching of a coworker and adding "I have well grounded fears of my life." He corresponded with prominent Black leaders such as Mississippi senator Blanche K. Bruce; served as a delegate from Noxubee County to state and national Republican conventions; and secured a federal job as railway clerk, rewarded as the "highest salaried colored mail clerk in the service" for never having "averaged less than ninety-eight percent in his [civil service] examination." Whether James Longstreet knew of J.W.'s career, or ever met with him in Macon, is unclear. But that silence is itself revealing. Longstreet chose in his memoir to highlight Daniel's story because it, by evoking the purported affection between former masters and slaves, suited Longstreet's retreat from radicalism and turn toward reconciliationism.[30]

IV

Longstreet's campaign to fashion himself as a fair-minded arbiter paid off in critical acclaim. Northern reviewers heaped praise on him for offering an account "so well supported by argument and evidence," as the *Milwaukee Journal* put it. The paper noted: "Gen. Longstreet criticizes his own associates even more freely than the leaders of the opposite side, probably because he knew them better and also had a better knowledge of the facts upon which his conclusions are based." The Midwestern journalist Murat Halstead commented that "the value of Longstreet's journal is greatly enhanced by the value of impartiality": Longstreet had told the truth about the likes of Davis and Lee "not with petty animosity, but the solemnity of competent judgment." The *St. Louis Globe-Democrat* called *From Manassas to Appomattox* a "manifestly honest book," while the *Cincinnati Commercial Gazette* wrote of Longstreet, "he writes conscientiously and impartially . . . [he] is not dogmatic, nor personal in his assaults on others, but defends himself by the testimony of others." Generally, Northern reviewers did not see the book as hostile to Lee but instead as evidence of Longstreet's "real admiration for Lee as a man and as a General." Though he had found fault with some of Lee's decisions, Longstreet "spoke from a purely military point of view, at the same time expressing the highest opinion of the character and manhood of Lee," the *New York Sun* maintained, while the review in the liberal political magazine the *Nation* found that Longstreet had given "evidence of Lee's confidence in him as a soldier and his trust in him as a faithful comrade." Northern reviewers delighted in Longstreet's portrayal of Grant and accepted Longstreet's argument that the two men's friendship, rather than partisanship or ambition, provided the impetus for Longstreet's political career: "The modest office of Surveyor of Customs was bestowed upon him by Gen. Grant unasked, moved by his personal generosity," the *Nation* review noted.[31]

In short, Northern reviews generally reflected back to Longstreet the reconciliationist image he tried to project, and confirmed his sense that the time was right for his literary offering. Writing of his memoir that "it will tend to hasten the era of good fellowship," the *Morning Democrat* of Davenport, Iowa, quoted Longstreet's opening paean to the "patriotism in all Americans" as representative of the "fine fraternal spirit" in which the book was written. The *Brooklyn Daily Eagle*'s review noted that "time has proved the wisdom of General Longstreet's prompt acceptance of the results of the war and has softened the political asperities which his conduct evoked." "Of the old sectional bitterness there is not a trace in this book," claimed a review in the *Buffalo Evening News*. "It was indeed fortunate, as the author himself thinks, that he abandoned a design of former years and waited till that bitterness was a thing of the past before he told his story." The *Philadelphia Times*, for its part, which had done so much to launch Longstreet's defense back in 1877, commented that since his memoir was "written at a later period than any of the other important works from the leading generals of both sides, it [was] evidently more free from passion, prejudice, and insensibly conceived errors than any of them."[32]

Some reviewers seemed disappointed that Longstreet's memoir was not more caustic. The *Baltimore Sun* noted that while there was "occasional bitterness" in Longstreet's account, it was "largely, however[,] impersonal"—simply a military history of the campaigns in which Longstreet took part. The *New York Tribune* was clearly chagrined by Longstreet's choice to offer a detailed campaign history rather than an extended polemic, commenting, "It would have been vastly more effective if those portions which are general had been strictly subordinated to the personal narrative. Then every point on which General Longstreet differs from his literary adversaries, most of whom were his companions in arms, would have been plain to the reader. As it is, many of them must escape attention until renewed criticism brings them into prominence."[33]

The Black press had its own take, predicting, during the lead-up to publication, that the memoir would have "the authority of accuracy which is lacking in most popular war histories" and that it would evoke strong reactions from "old soldiers whose feelings may be rasped" by Longstreet's views. Black reviewers regarded Longstreet's penchant for controversy as the key to his book's success. Rather than foregrounding the theme of reunion, they chose to emphasize Longstreet's "unsparing criticism" of the "most famous Confederate leaders, men whose names are held as almost sacred by the rebels," as the *Washington Bee* reported. Noting that the memoir's first edition was "exhausted almost as soon as it left the press," the weekly Utah newspaper the *Broad Ax* added that the book "evoked enough comment, favorable, and antagonistic, to keep the general's pen busy with answers."[34]

Predictably, Longstreet's ex-Confederate literary antagonists mobilized swiftly to make sure no point of controversy escaped attention. They simply would not accept that the memoir had any veracity or merit. Fitzhugh Lee, Walter H. Taylor, and J. William Jones led the way, with a host of others following, in articles with titles such as "Longstreet a Traitor," "Longstreet's Book of Malice," and "Setting Longstreet Straight." Their aim was to condemn Longstreet for slandering Lee, and to suggest that Longstreet had been treasonously insubordinate at Gettysburg, with a "deliberate intention" to "defeat his own general." Fitzhugh Lee mused that "advancing years have made [Longstreet's] memory vague" on Lee's record and that "proven facts" contradicted the memoir's claims. Taylor accused the author of depicting Lee "to the world as an insatiate, cruel, and bloodthirsty monster," and threatened that such a charge "will but recoil with crushing force on him who made it or approved it." Jones, for his part, commented that Lee's only fault was "that he allowed his tender feelings for his 'old warhorse' to prevent him from putting Longstreet under arrest and cashiering him for disobedience of orders." Seeking to dispel the image of Longstreet as a "meek martyr whom his critics have persecuted and goaded into saying some ugly things," Jones charged that Longstreet himself had kept the controversy alive, claiming that "ever since Longstreet became a Republican, a partisan Republican press has labored to make him the great general on the Confederate side, and to exalt him at Lee's expense." Jones and his cabal started unfounded rumors that Longstreet's editorial helper Pascal J. Moran had a major hand in writing the memoir and that he was an untrustworthy Yankee who served as "an officer in a negro regiment." And they took aim, too, at War Department historian Leslie J. Perry, who had assisted Longstreet in his research and publicly supported his findings; they accused Perry of "garbl[ing] the official record and adroitly manipulate[ing] the facts" with his "prejudices and unsound theories."[35]

Even as they pilloried Longstreet in public, Lee's Virginia acolytes also slandered him in their private correspondence, suggesting to one another that he had forfeited any right whatsoever to their respect. In an 1896 letter to former Confederate cartographer Jedediah Hotchkiss, Walter H. Taylor claimed to have "always entertained a strong affection" for Longstreet—until, that is, the publication of the memoir. That work demonstrated "the impairment of [Longstreet's] mental faculties," as Taylor put it. Such critiques illustrate how inimical Longstreet's theme of forgiveness was to the Lost Cause creed. Its adherents were not disposed either to offer repentance for the Confederacy's sins or to extend forgiveness to their political enemies. Even those prominent Confederate veterans who were relatively forthright in their appraisals of Longstreet's military record and of Lee's—such as Edward Porter Alexander—were unwilling to forgive Longstreet for what they considered the worst of his excesses. As Alexander wrote, reflecting on the memoir, Longstreet's "*great* mistake was not in the *war* but in some of his awkward & apparently bitter criticism of Gen Lee in his own book. One instance you will find on page 384, where he says that Lee was off his balance 'until enough blood was shed to appease him.' Many an old soldier will *never forgive* Longstreet such a sentiment."[36]

Many other Southern critics reminded readers of Longstreet's political apostasy during Reconstruction. A paper in Wilmington, North Carolina, professed pity for Longstreet, as "he behaved badly after the war and alienated hundreds of thousands of the strong and faithful men of the South." It added: "Every time he writes he makes it harder to forget the past and withhold censure." A few Southern newspapers picked up on Longstreet's closing anecdote featuring his former slave Daniel, recounting it under the headline "Privileged Darky Makes Caustic Remark to Gen. Longstreet."[37]

These critics, however, as much as they postured as champions of the region, did not speak for all white Southerners. The publisher, Lippincott, advertised and sold the memoir in the South, and found willing agents and promoters for it, including among Confederate veterans.

Colonel A. W. Moore, for example, the "special agent" in charge of selling the book in Virginia and the Carolinas, offered buyers testimonials from three former Confederate generals—John D. Kennedy, John Hagood, and John Bratton—vouching that Longstreet's memoir was a valuable firsthand account that "should be in the library of every Southerner." A few positive reviews from Southern periodicals ran counter to the stream of negative reviews. Richmond lawyer and scholar S. S. P. Patteson, for example, published a praiseworthy commentary in the literary magazine the *Sewanee Review*, calling Longstreet's memoir a "serious military history" that "every Southern man who loves fair play will hail with delight." Patteson attributed the unkind reviews Longstreet had received in the South to the still-prevalent belief that his "change of politics . . . tended to endanger white supremacy." But Patteson urged readers to value the book for its revealing perspective on military events.[38]

Fittingly, the *Atlanta Constitution* took the lead in promoting the book among white Southerners. In two lengthy reviews—one by Joel Chandler Harris's son Julian Harris, an up-and-coming editor, and the other by Pascal Moran—the *Constitution* praised both the historical value and literary merit of *From Manassas to Appomattox*. Harris took a somewhat critical line, saying that the memoir was marred in places by "apparent bitterness." But he concluded that "there is very little that demands a sweeping condemnation when the history is viewed without prejudice." In emphasizing that Lee had assumed responsibility for Gettysburg, Longstreet had "brought out the grandeur of Lee's character." Lee, in his generous acceptance of blame, had testified to humanity's fallibility: "Who could not love a man like that?" Harris asked. In the final analysis, the young reviewer found the memoir "well worth reading" and "written in a fine style."[39]

Moran, for his part, in a March 29, 1896, *Constitution* article that both reviewed the memoir and gave Longstreet the chance to answer his critics, emphasized its reconciliationist elements. The book, Moran editorialized, "discards the political interests which led to the war and deals with its military features almost exclusively." Longstreet obligingly seconded that interpretation, telling Moran, "In writing this book of the war, I was dealing with a congenial subject and one which should be a matter of pride to every American heart. While it portrays the struggle of two contending armies, both of American birth and lineage, it holds them up as the highest ideals to be found in military history, and no matter to what side the reader may belong, he cannot but feel a pride that these high-minded and brave men were his countrymen."[40]

In the interest of promoting Confederate reconciliation, this review/interview had Longstreet again emphasizing his strong bond with Lee—the way that Lee had continued to repose trust in him after Gettysburg, and the fact that Lee had refrained from any critique of Longstreet's war record. This was the *Constitution*'s story, and Moran and Longstreet's other New South defenders stuck to it. In an article subtitled "The Old Warhorse Who Stood by General Lee," Moran wrote that Longstreet's memoir had paid the "highest possible military tribute" to Lee not by "slobbering over him" but instead by "giving his true measurement with military exactness and historic accuracy." Trying to give his fellow Southerners a window into his own motivations, Longstreet told Moran that the memoir was "a book about the future. My thought always was that the south should try to build up and recover somewhat of that she lost."[41]

V

In the fall of 1897 Longstreet made the news for social rather than political reasons: at the ripe old age of seventy-six, he courted and married the journalist Helen Dortch, who was forty-two years his junior. Dortch had been the roommate of Longstreet's daughter, Maria Louisa, at Georgia Baptist Female Seminary in Gainesville; the future couple's paths crossed again at Lithia Springs, a popular resort, and at the Georgia state library, where Longstreet was researching his memoir and Dortch was assistant state librarian.[42]

Dortch, who switched her name from Ellen to Helen around the time of the marriage, had already achieved some public visibility in Georgia politics as editor of the *Carnesville Tribune* in northeast Georgia (taking over for her father in that role), and then as editor of the more prominent *Milledgeville Chronicle* in 1893. In her early journalism career, Dortch's favorite causes were opposition to the Southern Farmers' Alliance (the precursor to the Populist movement); support for the Democratic Party, and particularly its gubernatorial candidate William Yates Atkinson; and the promotion of higher education and career opportunities for women. Dortch positioned herself as a spokeswoman for farmers in her native Upper Piedmont region of Georgia, but she disagreed with the tactics of the Southern Farmers' Alliance, which entered politics in this era to challenge the Democratic Bourbon leadership, and to push reforms such as tariff and income tax reductions and government control of the railroads. Dortch, who felt that private enterprise was the best way to bring economic relief to debt-ridden farmers, denounced the Alliance, arguing that its policies would raise the government's debt and lead to higher taxes. As the historian William F. Holmes has observed, Dortch's opposition to the

Alliance had a personal edge: she blamed the local Alliance leadership for forcing her father, James, who was ailing at the time, from his position on the Franklin County School Board; when he died of a stroke during a difficult appeal process for reinstatement, Helen blamed the Alliance for his death. Holmes suggests that Dortch's Catholicism also kept her at odds with the Alliance, as its Protestant evangelical leadership and base sometimes trafficked in anti-Catholic rhetoric.[43]

Dortch's main worry was that "the Alliance's entry into politics . . . might lead to a new party which would threaten Democratic solidarity in the South." And when the People's Party (or Populists) emerged in Georgia in 1892, she warned Georgians to stay away, decrying the party's demagoguing, its divisiveness, and the willingness of some of its leaders to recruit Black voters. In 1894 Dortch threw herself into the election of Atkinson as governor. Atkinson represented a new breed of reform-minded Georgia Democrats, eager to displace the old Confederate generation and to steal some of the thunder of the rising Populist movement. He promoted law and order and fiscal responsibility to attract investment in the state, and, like Dortch, championed public education. Dortch avidly backed his campaign, and when he was elected in 1894, he reciprocated, naming her to the post of assistant state librarian (making her the first woman to hold a salaried position in a Georgia executive department). The Georgia press generally hailed Dortch's journalistic career and her appointment to state office, bestowing titles on her such as "the invincible Joan D'Arc of Georgia journalism and Georgia democracy."[44]

Reveling in her image as a model career woman, Dortch eventually supported the women's suffrage movement. Like many white Southern suffragists of this era, she believed that women's higher education and voting and work outside the home were fully compatible with the cult of "separate spheres." That set of gender conventions stipulated that, as the more pious, tender, emotional, virtuous sex, women should emanate morality within their designated "sphere": the private, domestic realm of home and family.

Dortch, along with many mainstream suffrage leaders, upheld the view that women and men were fundamentally different, and argued that women should bring their moral superiority to bear on social problems outside the household. She lobbied for women's admittance to state universities and for the founding of a Normal Industrial Training School for Georgia girls. After being appointed assistant state librarian, she moved quickly to leverage her new authority by lobbying to have a law passed that would make women eligible to hold the top state librarian position. She succeeded in persuading the legislature to enact the measure but not in convincing Atkinson to appoint her to the post. One Georgia paper applauded this rebuff with the comment "We don't think it well to have petticoats too much in evidence."[45]

Her campaign for higher office was in full gear when, in August 1897, Dortch's engagement to Longstreet became public knowledge. The pair wed at the Executive Mansion in Atlanta on September 8, with Governor Atkinson presiding; the date was the anniversary of the famous Mexican War battle at Molino del Rey, in which Longstreet had participated. The match became a cause célèbre in the national press, with Helen (or Ellen, as she was sometimes called) receiving much positive coverage as "one of the most progressive young women in the South" and "a favorite all over the State."

Public attitudes toward Longstreet himself were much more mixed. Some defended the May-December wedding by arguing that Dortch had a seriousness and maturity beyond her years and that Longstreet was rejuvenated by this romance. "His love affair seems to have renewed his youth," the *Chicago Daily Tribune* opined, in a typical formulation. The marriage was also seen as evidence of "the sturdiness of the old confederate," who had outlasted so many of the war's other storied generals: Grant, Sherman, Sheridan, Lee, Beauregard, and so on. And it filled the absence in Longstreet's household left by Louise's death. After he became widowed, Longstreet turned for a time to his daughter to manage his house for him.

After Louisa's own marriage, he relied on the help of a Black tenant family living on the corner of his farm—according to newspaper reports, "The man looks after [Longstreet's] farming operations, while the wife cooks the General's meals at their cabin and carries them to him at his cottage, and does such little odd jobs in the way of housekeeping as his simple surroundings require." Now Helen would take on the challenge of keeping house in Longstreet's "straitened circumstances," as a New York paper put it; the paper praised her "will and ambition" and predicted her success.[46]

But the age differential between bride and groom struck many as unseemly. The *North Georgia Citizen* called the marriage "a mistake for which there is no excuse," attributing it to Longstreet's "senile vanity." Newspaper coverage often played up the age gap by describing Helen as in her early twenties rather than midthirties, and Longstreet as an octogenarian rather than in his seventies. Rumors circulated of friction between the bride and Longstreet's adult children, and of Helen having her own doubts—looking "very weak and pale" and even fainting on her wedding day. Predictably, newspapers that objected to Longstreet's politics were generally the harshest in their condemnations of the marriage, fuming that "no congratulations" were in order to a man so "bitterly antagonistic to everything Southern and to all Southern interest."[47]

Longstreet initially stumbled in his efforts to defend the marriage. On the eve of the wedding, he quipped in an interview that "Old men get lonely . . . and must have company." This "sort of apology for his remarrying" was accompanied by a "hearty laugh," the interviewer noted. But on his wedding day, Longstreet offered a more thoughtful and less callous account of his union with Dortch. In response to a request from the *New York World*, Longstreet telegraphed the newspaper a long reflection on his motivations and state of mind.

"Youth is a relative term and is not correctly expressed by years," he mused. "There are glorious years ahead of me which I can appreciate because I have at last learned their value." Longstreet offered to Dortch, he continued, "the dignity of partnership," writing:

My wife has an understanding of business, she has been the editor of a paper and has literary talent. It will be a pleasure to her to enter into all my business enterprises, and together we can plan and consult and perfect, thus passing days of happy anticipation as well as of realization. She understands my situation thoroughly and I understand hers, and so our minds are as one, based upon knowledge and not upon hap-hazard.[48]

Printed in the *World*, the *Atlanta Constitution*, and scores of other newspapers, Longstreet's candid explanation further stoked public curiosity, and the *New York Journal*, in a "lively rivalry over the publication of news relating to the marriage," reached out to Helen for her side of the story. She obliged, furnishing the reading public her own elaborate justification for the marriage. Dortch criticized conventional marriages in which young women married "undeveloped men, who afterwards prove to be nothing but the veriest clods of clay." She emphasized not Longstreet's young-at-heart vitality but instead his established character: "The man who is advanced in years has his record made up, and the woman can decide for herself whether he be such a one as would develop all that was best in herself." Echoing Longstreet's paean to partnership, Helen, who resigned her post as assistant librarian shortly after the wedding, expressed her hope that she would be a companion to her husband and not a "mere housekeeper."[49]

Conservative papers objected that the newlyweds, in these public professions, had overstepped the boundaries of "true delicacy of sentiment." "The way the Longstreets are parading their views on marriage is absolutely disgusting," the *Dalton Argus* editorialized. It speculated that with James seeking a Republican patronage appointment and Helen a Democratic one, the marriage was no more than an "office-seeking combination"—a win-win arrangement for the couple, no matter which party was in power. Swirling through such press coverage was the most obvious charge against the young wives of older men: the accusation of gold-digging. Dortch's real motivation, as one Alabama paper put it, was to find "an early opportunity to wear becoming widow's weeds."[50]

But Longstreet's defenders interwove his memoir and his marriage into a narrative of his continued political vitality—a case bolstered by President William McKinley's appointment of Longstreet to the federal patronage position of US railroad commissioner (replacing the popular Confederate veteran and Democratic appointee Wade Hampton). As he had with Benjamin Harrison, Longstreet lobbied McKinley for a foreign posting, in this case as consul general to Paris.[51] But although a diplomatic appointment did not materialize, Longstreet would seize the opportunities presented by the railroad commissioner job to travel the United States and extend his popularity.

VI

William McKinley, newly elected as a Republican big business candidate, whose policies such as tariff protection promised to foster industrial development and cure unemployment in the throes of an economic depression that had begun in 1893, was the last Civil War veteran to serve as president. His 1896 campaign "wrapped McKinley in a conservative class appeal against William Jennings Bryan's Populist insurgency within the Democratic Party," the historian David Blight has explained, with Republicans making an "economic and emotional appeal for reconciliation as protection against the 'mob.'" Longstreet was chosen by the Georgia Republican Party as an elector-at-large for the state, with the strong backing of Black leaders, including William A. Pledger. As state party chairman Alfred Buck explained to Longstreet in an August 1896 letter of congratulations, it was the "colored men" who made the elector nomination and a "half dozen or more spoke for you." Longstreet was then honored at "the largest Republican meeting since the Reconstruction period" in Augusta in October, and he delivered, by proxy, a "sound money" speech on behalf of the gold standard and against "incendiary demagogues" such as Bryant, who stoked class and sectional strife.[52]

For the Northern press, Longstreet, as a prospective officeholder, continued to serve as a singularly powerful symbol of reunion: as the *Washington Post* noted in an article entitled "Foes in War, Friends in Peace," Longstreet was appointed to office by a series of chief executives—Grant, Hayes, Garfield, and now McKinley—who had literally faced his rebel legions on the battlefield, in the 1862 Maryland campaign (Hayes and McKinley), at Chickamauga (Garfield), and at the Wilderness (Grant). That these "stubborn fighters" had become "dearest friends" proved the nation was building a "firm bedrock of universal peace," the *Post* editorialized wishfully. There continued to be some Longstreet detractors among Union veterans, such as the Texas Unionist John W. Parks, who wrote imploringly to McKinley that Longstreet should not be appointed commissioner. Such a vaunted post should go to a Union veteran, Parks noted pointedly, so as to reward those who "offered up *their lives* that this nation and government *might not be destroyed*."[53]

Such objections were drowned out. Longstreet secured the commissionership with the help of an influential delegation of Georgia Republicans, including Walter Johnson (who succeeded Buck as chair of the State Central Committee), and attorney Judson W. Lyons, businessman Henry Rucker, and editor John H. Deveaux—all leading Black Republicans in the state party. Southern press coverage was divided, but not along strictly party lines. The *Atlanta Constitution* endorsed the appointment as altogether appropriate given Longstreet's staunch loyalty to the Republican Party, and as "gratifying to the many friends of that superb old soldier." Noting that the patronage plum followed on the heels of his marriage to Helen Dortch, the *Constitution* "most heartily" extended Longstreet a "double measure of congratulation." Some Southern Democrats took a different tack and strenuously objected to McKinley's elevation of Longstreet. The objections, as the Senate confirmation debates revealed, focused both on Longstreet's record as an "oppressor of his people" in New Orleans (especially at Canal

Street in 1874), and "his criticism of General Lee in his book on the war" as Virginia senator John W. Daniel specified. But to a surprising degree, Southern newspaper coverage echoed the *Constitution*. "Gen. Longstreet, in the troublesome erstwhile, had a good many ups and downs, but everything seems to come his own way now," the *Houston Post* noted. The Senate finally confirmed Longstreet in January 1898 by a vote of 33 to 15, with Georgia's Democratic senator Augustus Bacon voting in favor on the grounds that Longstreet "had been a gallant Confederate officer" and that "disagreements which succeeded the war and the friction which resulted therefrom should be forgotten." Capturing the optimism of the reconciliation movement, the Brooklyn *Standard Union* saw something in the appointment for everyone: "Republicans should remember that statesmanship that beamed in Longstreet's New Orleans letter on reconstruction, and Confederates should be proud of his military history." Longstreet would insist more fervently than ever, in the final act of his political career, that his Republican and Confederate identities were compatible.[54]

Chapter 11

A NEW CENTURY

I

In the fall of 1897 Longstreet accompanied Andrew Montgomery of Atlanta, a formerly enslaved 103-year-old preacher, to Washington, DC, to introduce him to President McKinley. The audience at the White House was part of a tour Montgomery was embarking on in the North, to raise funds for constructing an old-age home for African Americans in Atlanta. Longstreet and Montgomery had more in common than their Georgia roots: both men fascinated the public because of their longevity, and both had highly variable public images. For Atlanta Blacks, Montgomery was "Father Montgomery," a community leader revered for founding the city's first independent Black church, Old Bethel. Having "lived during the dark days of slavery, and bor[ne] the cruel treatment characteristic of those days," Montgomery was, the minister-historian E. R. Carter wrote in 1894, a vital interpreter, for the younger generation, of Atlanta's early history. For white Southerners, Montgomery was "Uncle Andy," an Uncle Remus–like figure dispensing folk wisdom in dialect. In his youth, Montgomery had been a "very unruly negro," the *Atlanta Constitution* noted, "always desiring to be free." But in his very advanced old age, "Uncle Andy" no longer seemed threatening—for whites in the New South, he had come to symbolize piety and homespun "old-timey" values.[1]

Longstreet did not leave any firsthand impressions of Montgomery, but an 1898 newspaper interview (which Montgomery gave to the *Brooklyn Daily Eagle* while visiting the city) conveys something of the tenor of their interactions. In recounting his visit to the White House, Montgomery explained that he was pushed to the margins of the visiting chamber as a crowd thronged President McKinley—and that Longstreet intervened, announcing in a loud voice, "Mr. Andrew Montgomery, the President of the United States." McKinley responded, "I'm honored by your acquaintance, Mr. Montgomery." Effecting a humble posture and cagily playing on white paternalism, Montgomery proceeded to tell the president that as the "father" of the country, McKinley should remember to treat all of his children alike. After his audience with the president, Montgomery visited DC church congregations and called on Cabinet members. "Gen. Longstreet has been most kind to him and aided him in any project he might have in hand," the press reported as Montgomery headed north to visit cities and luminaries there. White Southern papers expressed support for the fundraising mission, implying that ex-slaves were indigent and in need of charity because they no longer had masters to care for them. But in his public utterances Montgomery made it clear, subtly but unmistakably, that he was fundraising in the North because such a goodwill tour was impossible in the hostile Jim Crow South.[2]

His sponsorship of Montgomery illustrates Longstreet's political balancing act, in which he offered gestures of fellowship to progressives, moderates, and conservatives alike. Increasingly, Longstreet's appeals were tied to his selective appropriation of elements from four distinct Civil War memory traditions. The Lost Cause tradition, with its claims of Confederate righteousness, was promulgated in the new century by descendants' organizations like the United Daughters of the Confederacy. It proved quite compatible with the Reconciliation tradition, embraced by political leaders such as McKinley and Theodore Roosevelt, which emphasized the need for Americans to put aside sectional animosities and focus on achieving national prosperity and international power. This message of comity was dramatized at veterans' reunions, where elderly former soldiers in blue and gray continued to "clasp hands across the bloody chasm" to symbolize reunion. Together the Reconciliation and Lost Cause traditions fostered the idea that Union and Confederacy could share the moral high ground in American memory of the war.[3]

These two traditions sought to displace and suppress a pair of rival memory traditions, each with its own long history and champions: a "Won Cause" tradition, advanced by Union veterans and their descendants, emphasizing the superior righteousness of the cause of Union and the superior valor of the Federal army; and an Emancipation tradition, championed by Black leaders such as Frederick Douglass, who held up the abolition of slavery as the noble purpose and great achievement of the war. As a rich modern scholarship on Civil War memory has revealed, the Lost Cause and reconciliation traditions held sway over American culture for much of the twentieth century. Longstreet's willingness to invoke elements of each tradition augmented his popularity, but failed to reconcile the competing viewpoints on the war's meaning.[4]

In his last years, Longstreet was ever more determined to intervene in how he himself would be remembered. But his legacy would prove to be a battlefield of its own.

II

During the McKinley administration, Longstreet continued to relish the role of influencing patronage decisions. In the spring of 1897 he and his longtime party rival, state party chairman A. E. Buck, effected a full rapprochement, to maximize the patronage prospects of both: Longstreet supported Buck's bid for a foreign posting (McKinley named Buck minister to Japan) and Buck in turn supported Longstreet's railroad commissioner appointment.[5]

Moreover, Longstreet promoted the political aspirations of the most influential and ambitious trio of Black Georgia Republicans—Judson W. Lyons, Henry Rucker, and John H. Deveaux—in exchange for their support of his own bid for federal office. As the historian John Dittmer has noted, "Georgia led the South in the number of blacks holding federal jobs" during the McKinley years, with the best offices going to Deveaux (as customs collector in Savannah), Rucker (as internal revenue collector in Atlanta), and Lyons, appointed as register of the US Treasury—the "highest appointive federal office" held by an African American.[6]

These men, no less than the Louisiana activists Longstreet had worked with in the early 1870s, were visionary leaders who spoke out fearlessly against anti-Black proscription and violence—and also elaborated the emancipationist tradition of Civil War memory. Lyons, for example, was often a featured speaker at Emancipation Day celebrations (marking the January 1 anniversary of Lincoln's proclamation) around the country, sharing the podium with other Black leaders such as P. B. S. Pinchback. Lyons used these occasions not only to celebrate Black patriotism and progress but also to urge vigilance. At a 1901 emancipation celebration in Baltimore, Lyons invoked the "wave of disfranchisement that is sweeping over the country" and urged resistance, intoning "we must fight the danger and wipe it from the face of the earth."[7]

As Lyons knew too well, Blacks' gains as civil servants came in the face of vicious opposition by recalcitrant white Southerners, who tried to undermine and preempt Black officeholding through violence and intimidation. In the fall of 1897, for example, the Black postmaster of Hogansville, Georgia, Isaac H. Loftin, was shot and nearly killed by white terrorists; the assassination attempt was a flash point in a long campaign by white Democrats in Georgia to argue that "republican victory means negro-officeholders and negro domination," as the *Atlanta Constitution* put it, editorializing on "that Hogansville affair." It had taken immense courage for Loftin to accept the postmastership, as his brother Augustus, a federal appointee (as deputy revenue collector) under the Harrison administration, had been murdered by whites to send the message that Black officeholding would not be tolerated. When Isaac Loftin recovered enough to resume work as postmaster, whites boycotted and vandalized his post office. The McKinley administration professed its horror at this backlash and its determination to protect Black officeholders, but it also yielded to the grim realities on the ground. Loftin was eventually persuaded to leave Hogansville for a federal appointment in Washington, DC. Meanwhile, Judson Lyons, initially slated by McKinley for the Augusta, Georgia, postmastership, was himself given a Washington posting instead after white Georgians leveled protests and threats against his taking office in Augusta. Black civil servants in Washington, DC, found some strength in numbers, as they made up 10 percent of the federal workforce there by 1891.[8]

Longstreet conspicuously allied himself with Georgia's Black politicians in Washington, frequently joining them in the small "delegations" that called on senators and administration officials to influence patronage. He also maneuvered behind the scenes, attempting, sometimes awkwardly, to call in favors from Black leaders. Hoping that Buck's posting in Japan augmented his own relative power within the Georgia Republican leadership, Longstreet brazenly tested the limits of his influence. In the winter of 1897–98, in an ill-considered attempt at nepotism, Longstreet angled to secure a postmastership in LaGrange, Georgia, for his son-in-law Jasper E. Whelchel (Whelchel had wed Longstreet's daughter Louisa in 1895). The move was controversial, as Whelchel did not reside in LaGrange: he was a schoolteacher in Hogansville, and rumored to be a Democrat, with no Republican credentials to speak of. E. A. Angier of Atlanta, US attorney for North Georgia and a longtime Longstreet ally and confidant, urged him to get an endorsement for Whelchel from Judson Lyons, by reassuring Lyons that Whelchel was not one of those hostile Democrats boycotting Postmaster Loftin at Hogansville; Longstreet should also promise that Whelchel would hire Black activist Curtis Beall, a former LaGrange postmaster, whom Longstreet had favored and who had proven an excellent appointee. The postmaster bid fell short, but Whelchel soon landed, with Longstreet's help, a job in Washington, DC, working for the Census Bureau. Longstreet and Lyons remained cordial and willing to do each other good turns, when it suited them both: in 1900, for example, Longstreet obtained Lyons a free railroad pass (one of the perks the railroad commissioner could bestow); Lyons wrote him, "This is a real favor and I assure you I appreciate it fully."[9]

Longstreet used the railroad commissioner post to go on his own goodwill tours of the country, mixing work and pleasure and burnishing his popularity. Helen loved the social scene and access to power in DC: she would "stroll over to the White House almost any morning, without invitation," she recalled, and be "ushered up to Mrs. McKinley's private quarters for a little intimate chat." But Longstreet himself professed to dislike the weather in the capital and looked for chances to "escape from it." Thus he and Helen, along with an entourage including his personal secretary, Lewis W. Haskell, departed Washington at the end of July in 1898 to undertake an ambitious inspection tour of all the "bond-aided and land grant railroads in the west," and thereby to ensure that the railroads were "keeping in good faith the contracts they had with the government." He visited Midwest stops including Chicago and Omaha; West Coast stops such as San Francisco and Seattle; and even crossed the border to visit Mexico City—and reminisce about his days as a soldier there—during his tour through the Southwest. He and his traveling party received warm welcomes and gushing press coverage wherever they went. "In our judgment Longstreet had the soundest and strongest military mind in the Confederate army," a Portland, Oregon, paper opined, adding, "His mind was like that of Grant, solid rather than showy." Upon his return to Washington, DC, Longstreet publicly issued a detailed annual report on the state of the railroad that garnered him still more positive press coverage, as he declared the railroads to be in good condition, while also calling for the government construction and operation of a transcontinental route linking Missouri and California, as a way to both "draw the people nearer together in interests" and promote trade relations with Pacific seaports.[10]

III

These recommendations reflected seismic developments in American foreign relations. Longstreet's appointment and tour as commissioner coincided with the Spanish-American War: the imperial conflict, lasting from April to December 1898, that ended Spain's overseas empire in the Western Hemisphere; established Cuba's independence; ceded Puerto Rico and Guam to the United States; and set the stage for the longer and bloodier US-Philippine War. Longstreet had taken an interest in the fate of Cuba since the 1870s, and closely followed American debates over intervening in the island's war of liberation. Those debates roiled the Republican Party and pitted pro-war "jingos" such as Theodore Roosevelt, eager for the United States to establish an overseas empire, against the cautious McKinley, a Civil War veteran who was loathe to lead the nation into another bloodbath. Longstreet initially sympathized with McKinley's caution, writing the president in May 1897 that he should broker a peace between Spain and Cuba through the "slow process of diplomacy." But once the sinking of the battleship *Maine* in Havana Harbor in February 1898 forced McKinley's hand, Longstreet rallied to the administration and to the cause. Even before the United States formally declared war on Spain in April 1898, Longstreet symbolically, for newspaper consumption, volunteered to don the uniform, declaring "my services and sword are at my country's call." He also volunteered the literal services of his son James Longstreet Jr., who duly enlisted, as would Robert "Lee" Longstreet, too; both young men proved able and popular as officers and further enhanced their father's military reputation. Robert, born during the Civil War and named after Robert E. Lee, grew up to be a staunch Republican. James Jr. was born in Virginia right after the war and was thus referred to by Longstreet as his "Union son"—and he turned out to be a Democrat. The two sons served as symbols, for Longstreet, that "political alignment should be based on conviction alone."[11]

Politically, the Spanish-American War was harnessed to the theme of sectional reconciliation, with countless commentators celebrating the ways Northern and Southern men were reunited, to fight together under the American flag against a foreign foe. Notably, four former Confederate generals—Fitzhugh Lee, Thomas Rosser, Joseph Wheeler, and Matthew G. Butler—served in the US Army. Longstreet embraced the reunion narrative—to a point. He rejoiced that the war did "much to obliterate the last vestiges of sectional feeling," as he put it in a widely publicized interview in August 1898. But in his characteristic way, Longstreet also struck contrarian notes in his commentary on the war, criticizing General William Shafter's siege of Santiago, Cuba. Although Shafter's infantry operations resulted in the capture of the city and featured the heroics of Teddy Roosevelt's "Rough Riders" on the San Juan heights, Longstreet believed "only luck averted great disaster" in the siege, as a provocative headline ran. Shafter had made himself vulnerable with a lack of reinforcements, Longstreet observed, and it was only the "lack of food and confidence among the Spaniards" that prevented them from repulsing the Americans.[12]

In the same August interview, Longstreet also staked out a position on American imperial ambitions, revealing that he remained, as he had been during his ministerial tour in Turkey in the 1880s, enthusiastic about market expansion and commercial diplomacy, but not about "a policy of conquest" that would gobble up overseas possessions. Aggressive imperialism of the jingoistic variety, he insisted, "was un-American and unwise." In his view, peace with Spain would ideally yield "freedom for Cuba, a reasonable war indemnity, and half a dozen coaling stations throughout the East and West Indies" for the United States. Longstreet looked forward to augmented trade in "tropical products" and urged more continental railroad construction to move such commerce.[13]

Behind the scenes, Longstreet also engaged with one of the most controversial issues of the Spanish-American War: whether African Americans, approximately 10,000 of whom enlisted, should be permitted to serve as commissioned line officers above the rank of lieutenant. Black leaders, including P. B. S. Pinchback, James Lewis, and Judson Lyons, pushed McKinley to designate regiments for Black enlistees, as most states had refused to accept Black volunteers; they noted that Southern Blacks could fill the ranks of "immunes," or those who had already been exposed to malarial climates and were "used to conditions similar to those confronted in Cuba." These leaders also insisted that such enlistees should be permitted to serve as company commanders. McKinley acceded to the first demand, designating four "immune" regiments, the 7th through 10th US Volunteer Infantry, for Black recruits and lieutenants. But the War Department capped the number of African American officers, commissioning only one hundred. That meant Black regiments were mostly led by white officers—including none other than Longstreet's son James Jr., who served as regimental adjutant in the 9th USVI. That regiment was raised primarily in New Orleans—which meant James Jr. was leading Black New Orleans troops as his father had done during Reconstruction. Revealingly, Longstreet himself lobbied McKinley (in vain) to appoint African American men to regimental command positions, personally vouching for Treasury Department clerk Thomas S. Kelly, who had served as a sergeant in the USCT and then, during Reconstruction, as an officer in Longstreet's Louisiana militia.[14]

As the scholar David Blight has noted, "the subtext of virtually all black response to the Spanish-American and Philippine wars was violence toward blacks at home." Longstreet addressed such violence in a July 1899 polemical piece in the New York weekly journal the *Independent*, known for its liberal leanings and abolitionist roots. Entitled "The Loyal South To-Day," the article began by praising Southern contributions to the war effort in the Spanish-American conflict, but then pivoted to race relations. "We need more Booker T. Washingtons at the South. . . . If we had more such influences our race troubles would be of short duration," Longstreet declared. He continued,

> The lynchings in Georgia and elsewhere throughout the South
> are much to be deplored, but, as indicated in the case of your

strikes, disorders that even lead to considerable loss of life are not by any means confined to the South. In these lynchings the same crime is always charged. It is a crime against our womankind at the thought of which men are driven crazy, and they, when in that condition, commit lawless acts. I notice that two men charged with this crime were lately quietly brought to trial. One was found guilty and sentenced to be hanged in thirty days, and the other was acquitted, as the evidence against him failed. The people had been ready to lynch him, and if they had done so would have taken the life of an innocent man. It is certainly not pleasant to contemplate the possibility that such mistakes have been made.

The solution, in Longstreet's view, was for whites to cooperate with Booker T. Washington in discouraging crime, as "the community which commits lawlessness, of course, must always suffer from its own deeds."[15]

Here was the ultimate expression of the political balancing act Longstreet had been performing since 1867. Although he generally steered clear, in the 1890s, of overt commentary on lynching, he had offered broad condemnations of "mob law," such as an 1894 letter, quoted by the *New York Times*, in which Longstreet had written that "organized lawlessness should be made to clearly understand that law and order will and must be sustained and the civil government upheld." The Black newspaper the *Cleveland Gazette* seized on that statement as oblique warning that "lynching will surely undermine the foundations of this government if it is not checked and stopped." In casting lynching as a punishment for rape, in his 1899 essay, Longstreet clearly trafficked in racist propaganda; in comparing lynching to labor strikes in the North, he set up a false equivalency that was meant to mitigate white Southern guilt. But at the same time, Longstreet condemned lynching as deplorable; acknowledged the role of fraud in accusations against Black men; incorporated white misbehavior into his condemnation of lawlessness; recognized Booker T. Washington's role as a political leader whom Southerners, white and Black, should heed;

and folded Blacks like Washington into the category of patriots consti-
tuting "the loyal South." Which of these themes was paramount was in
the eye of the beholder. The *Milwaukee Sentinel*, for example, summarized
Longstreet's piece under the heading "Southern Tribute to a Negro," and
credited him with trying to secure for Washington the kind of Southern
support that the "Wizard of Tuskegee" already enjoyed in the North.[16]

The timing of Longstreet's endorsement of Washington is significant.
Washington, who had endeared himself to New South advocates with his
1895 "Five Fingers" speech, had, in 1898 and 1899, "gone way over the
line of the white South's tolerance," the scholar Robert J. Norrell notes.
The waves of white supremacist violence in Georgia peaked in 1899, with
dozens of documented lynchings. These acts of terrorism included the hor-
rifying torture, mutilation, burning, and lynching of Sam Hose in Coweta
County, Georgia, in April 1899, before a crowd of 2,000 spectators—an
act that Georgia white supremacists such as Rebecca Latimer Felton brazenly and chillingly defended. As the historian W. Fitzhugh Brundage has
explained, "Between 1895 and 1910, a decisive shift occurred in the tone
and substance of race relations in Georgia," as white supremacist violence
crested, reflecting a host of factors, including "the rise of a new generation
of racial extremists, bitterness borne of the collapse of Populism, the un-
easiness of whites prompted by the training and stationing of black troops
in the state during the Spanish-American War, and the anger of southern
whites aroused by the racial policies of the Republican administrations of
William McKinley and Theodore Roosevelt." In his rousing "Peace Jubilee"
speech in Chicago in 1898, and in a June 1899 open letter on lynching,
Washington decried racism and demanded justice—and thereby alienated old allies, including Clark Howell, editor of the *Constitution*; that fall
Washington went on to campaign against disfranchisement in Georgia.[17]

Longstreet's 1899 piece in the *Independent* posed a challenge to his
image as the contented old soldier whose priority was reconciliation. But
the *Atlanta Constitution*, in its own review (by Atlanta journalist/histo-
rian Wallace Putnam Reed) of Longstreet's essay, finessed the situation. It

began by emphasizing that "the general has regained much of his former popularity in the south" because people had come to realize that "many good soldiers . . . have shown themselves to be blundering politicians, getting on the wrong side of politics." "Nobody at the present time care a rap about Longstreet's politics," the article continued. "He is regarded as a historic figure, a great general who proved himself a hero in his long fight for the confederacy." Lest anyone be tempted to draw the wrong conclusions from Longstreet's political commentary, the *Constitution* then interpreted Longstreet's essay for readers, claiming that his purpose was to display the "slow but steady advance in the direction of prosperity and law and order" in the South, and his "confidence in the loyalty and patriotism of both sections." The *Constitution* article closed on a didactic note, by instructing readers that "Such a man may go wrong in politics, but he will not be harshly judged. At heart Longstreet is just as true a southerner as he was when he fought the battles of the confederacy."[18]

Here was the ultimate expression of the *Constitution*'s own balancing act: sending the public the message that Longstreet's politics should be dismissed or ignored, while sending Longstreet himself the message that the rehabilitation of his military reputation depended on his exercising caution in his political pursuits.

IV

Longstreet was received with acclaim during his second annual railroad inspection tour of western railways in 1899, dining with U. S. Grant Jr. in San Diego, reviewing regiments in San Francisco, and generally being feted wherever he went. Longstreet continued in the new century to attend blue-gray reunions and to wield his patronage power. With Judson Lyons's help, for example, Longstreet secured the Milledgeville postmastership for his nephew James Longstreet Sibley.[19]

Meanwhile Longstreet began to maneuver for a new federal position

for himself. William McKinley's reelection in 1900, on a campaign platform of continued economic prosperity, secured Longstreet a second term
as federal railroad commissioner. He and Helen rejoiced at McKinley's triumph and were among the first to call on the president to extend their congratulations. But the triumph was short-lived: the shocking assassination
of President McKinley at the Pan-American Exposition in Buffalo in September 1901 by anarchist Leon Czolgosz plunged the nation into sorrow.
In a scene that seemed torn from the pages of the Civil War, McKinley was
shot in the stomach and lingered in eight days of agony as he developed
gangrene. Longstreet attended McKinley's funeral services at the Capitol
as a "representative citizen," on behalf of the South.[20]

With a new president, Spanish-American war hero Theodore Roosevelt, assuming power, Longstreet's own political future was unclear.
Congress's failure to make proper appropriations for the railroad commissioner's office (on the grounds that it had become obsolete) raised Longstreet's concern, and he eyed a potential transfer to the National Military
Parks, as the head of a Civil War battlefield site such as Chickamauga.
Longstreet's allies wrote Roosevelt asking for both an extension in the
commissionership funding and a new post in the National Parks; those
allies included another maverick Republican, the progressive Catholic
Archbishop John Ireland, who was a confidant of Roosevelt's and a vocal
supporter of Black civil rights. Against this backdrop, Robert L. Longstreet urged his father to attend the funeral services of Union war hero
(and Longstreet West Point classmate and fellow Catholic) General William Rosecrans in May 1902. "The President will be the chief guest and it
appears to me an appropriate time to show your . . . associations & history
with the Union soldiers and fix your appropriateness for appointment to
a Military Park Commissionership," Robert wrote. He added, alluding to
the ways Helen Dortch was a political asset: "Get your wife to make all
inquiries & arrangements for you and *take her too.*"[21]

Longstreet followed his son's counsel and attended the Rosecrans
burial at Arlington National Cemetery on May 17, 1902. "Towering above

all" with his "commanding form," Longstreet, along with some Union veterans, flanked Roosevelt onstage as the president offered a stirring tribute to the righteousness of Rosecrans and his men, and the "gallantry and self-devotion of those who wore the gray." That fall, Longstreet wrote a widely published letter to Union general Dan Sickles, his former foe at Gettysburg, saying of the Confederate loss there, "It was the sorest and saddest reflection of my life for many years; but today I can say, with the sincerest emotion, that it was and is the best that could have come to us all—north and south; and I hope that the nation, reunited, may always enjoy the honor and glory brought to it by that grand work." In what had become a familiar pattern, Northerners saw Longstreet's sentiments as evidence that the wounds of war had finally healed—while some white Southerners arraigned him for rejoicing in the South's failure.[22]

For all of the popularity of the cult of reconciliation, Longstreet gave voice, in private writings, to frustration at the continued power of sectionalism to blind white Southerners to their own best interests. In a 1901 letter to his son Randolph, about the family finances and property-holding, Longstreet lamented the lack of economic innovation in the South and the region's inability to attract enough Northern capital. "I had thought when I located in Gainesville the people would give up their sectional ideas and begin to see where their interests lay," he reflected, "but they are just now beginning to see." Even if Southerners had more capital, he noted discouragingly, it would amount to little as they did not know how to use it wisely. This theme—the price the South paid for its recalcitrance—linked the phases of Longstreet's political career in Gainesville and in New Orleans, and his economic and political critiques of the region. Writing from Gainesville to his former business partner William Miller Owen in New Orleans, Longstreet had, back in 1890, urged Owen to support a moderate Republican candidate for Congress, the incumbent Hamilton D. Coleman. Coleman, a Confederate veteran, would "strengthen the south in the eyes of the world" and among the "conservative elements" in the North, Longstreet explained, adding, "He represents your political interests to greater advantage" than the Democratic Party. Longstreet confided to Owen that he retained a keen interest in the welfare of the people of Louisiana. But such appeals were in vain—Coleman lost his reelection bid and was the last Republican to represent Louisiana in Congress until 1973.[23]

V

In the literary sphere as well as the political one, Longstreet continued, into his eighties, to show vitality and ambition. In 1898 he contributed an introductory essay to a volume, *Pickett and His Men*, written by Confederate widow LaSalle Corbell Pickett. Her late husband, George E. Pickett, had been a great friend of Longstreet's since the two men's service in the Mexican War. As commander of one of Longstreet's three divisions at Gettysburg, Pickett had given his name to the Confederate assault of the third day and was indelibly associated with its failure. Devastated by the loss at Gettysburg, Pickett declined after the war and passed away in 1875. His widow, LaSalle, determined to rehabilitate his reputation, churned out writings portraying Pickett in a romantic light, as a chivalric symbol of the "gallant South." Longstreet's introduction to *Pickett and His Men* cannily melded the two men's stories. Longstreet praised Pickett for having gracefully "accepted the situation" after the war and for his loyalty and stoicism: for uttering "no word of blame, or censure even, of his superior officers" (Longstreet included) after the war. With Louise Longstreet and Helen Dortch, as well as LaSalle, in mind, Longstreet paid homage to Confederate widows, noting that "in the silent passages of the heart many severer battles are waged than were ever fought at Gettysburg."[24]

Longstreet also kept up a lively correspondence with the editors of magazines including *McClure's* and *Century*. *McClure's* invited him in 1898 to pen an essay on "The History of Our Country as It Might Have Been Written If the Southern Confederacy Had Been Successfully Established." But he was more interested in pitching papers on the Mexican War, and a project near and dear to his heart. Provisionally titled "Since the Days of Lincoln," this essay, Longstreet explained to the *Century*, would "embrace interesting reminiscences of the republican administrations since the war, with every one of which I have been officially connected, with the single exception of that of Harrison." Longstreet also contemplated making updates to his memoir, writing the publisher J. B. Lippincott in 1899 that he was willing to forego collecting royalties on the book, in order for the copyright to be restored to him so that he would have "the privilege of revision when I may desire it." Helen remained his partner in these literary pursuits, offering the *Century*, on his behalf in 1903, "some racy and picturesque magazine papers . . . from his unpublished memoir of the Mexican war." "He was in every battle of the conflict which gave to us our great western empire," she noted in her pitch, "and is one of about six West Point officers of that war now living."[25]

Although no more of his essays would see the light of day, Longstreet achieved new levels of visibility in the last years of his life not only as a writer and politico, but also as symbol of the rampant consumerism of the "Gilded Age." At a time when patent medicines multiplied to offer home remedies for a range of ailments, including those of disabled veterans, Longstreet was featured in countless newspaper ads for the pharmaceutical "blood and nerve" remedies Nervura and Peruna, which, he vouched, helped alleviate his chronic catarrh, or throat congestion. After Longstreet's son Robert contracted malaria in the army in Cuba, he joined his father in shilling Peruna as "the soldier's friend." No less than his 1885 essays in *Century* magazine, Longstreet's medical endorsements were part of a process by which entrepreneurs and advertisers capitalized on the "lingering effects" of the war for veterans and civilians alike, and tapped the rising militarism in American culture, and the ubiquitous view that soldierly virtues and exertions would revitalize the nation. The commercialization of Civil War memory took a dazzling array of forms, with wartime heroes and reconciliationist messages adorning cigarettes, trading cards, stereo views and cycloramas, children's books, and other such products.[26]

The rosy picture of Longstreet's vitality painted by advertisements was belied by mounting evidence of his physical decline. Longstreet's health worsened in 1902, as he suffered from hearing loss, attacks of "rheumatism" (arthritic joint pain), the lingering effects of his old wartime throat wound, and the onset of cancer. In the summer of 1903 Helen accompanied him to Chicago for "x-ray treatment" on his cancerous right eye. He convalesced at home in Georgia, relying on his bookkeeper Herman Schreiner and clerk Katharine M. Schmidt in Washington, DC, to manage the railroad commissioner office. "[He] is suffering so with his eyes," Schmidt revealed in August 1903, "that he is unable to read, and I know that Mrs. Longstreet writes all his letters." When Longstreet turned eighty-two in the fall of 1903, the press marveled at his durability—long after the Civil War's other great soldiers had passed, "General Longstreet stands in the white light of a wonder-working new century," as the *St. Louis Republic* put it poetically.[27]

But Longstreet would not see another birthday, succumbing to acute pneumonia in January 1904. Thousands of mourners and well-wishers marched in his funeral procession in Gainesville, Georgia; church bells tolled, battle flags waved, and Longstreet was given full military honors, lying in state at the county courthouse, his casket bedecked in the American and Confederate flags. Over his grave in Alta Vista Cemetery, the sons of men who had served under him during the Civil War fired a salute. A Catholic prelate, Bishop Benjamin J. Keiley of Savannah, offered his blessing and shed light on Longstreet's conversion. "Deep down in the heart and breast of every man … there is a longing for some means of communicating with loved ones who have been taken from us by death," he observed, invoking Longstreet's own family tragedies. Catholicism had provided "a golden chain which links and binds together the children of God here and above."[28]

Tributes poured forth from the press and from veterans in the North and the South. In Northern eyes Longstreet was a prophetic patriot who "put himself at once where all now stand,—on the broad, high ground of American citizenship," as the *New York Journal* put it. Archbishop John

Ireland, the liberal priest and Longstreet ally, wrote to Helen Dortch, "Truly a great man has passed away. The whole country mourns. . . . He was a pious servant of the Lord always ready to hearken to the voice of conscience." Anti-Confederate Southerners, too, praised Longstreet as beyond reproach: the *Southwestern Christian Advocate*, an organ of Black Methodists, observed in its notice of Longstreet's passing that "he has been accused of disobeying Gen. Lee's orders at the Battle of Gettysburg, but the charge was so emphatically and successfully refuted that it would seem none but the most prejudiced believe it."[29]

Those ex-Confederates who wanted to claim Longstreet could at last do so without having to blunt his continued prominence in Republican politics. Predictably, the *Constitution* led the way in eulogizing him, recalling his wartime heroism and his 1886 reunion in Atlanta with Jefferson Davis. And to an unprecedented degree, other Southern whites followed. Helen Dortch received a flood of condolences from Confederate veterans' camps and from individual soldiers. "If after Appomattox, Longstreet made mistakes, or we imagined he did, the mantle of death covers them all," one United Confederate Veterans camp resolved, adding, "If Jackson was Lee's right hand, Longstreet was his left from Manassas to Appomattox." In the same spirit, most Southern papers chose to explain away, set aside, or forgive Longstreet's political choices. "Now that the stout warrior is dead and gone to eternal judgment," the *Vicksburg Herald* intoned in a typical formulation, "all should speak of his virtues, his glorious deeds of arms, without thought or reference to that sad error of judgment that, no smaller in its intent and inception than 'a man's hand,' grew to a dark cloud between Longstreet and his people." "Let the Dead Lion sleep in peace," the *Birmingham Ledger* of Alabama proclaimed. "The heroic Longstreet needs no higher eulogy than the single phrase, He was the friend of Grant and Lee."[30]

But amid this chorus of acclaim there were discordant notes that sounded the limits of national and of Confederate reconciliation. Public funerals in this era were, the historian Sarah J. Purcell has argued, "durable forms of political expression" that wove together Union and Confederate memories in "some unpredictable ways." To a striking degree, Lost Cause themes and iconography predominated over the message of reconciliation at Longstreet's funeral, in part because of the prominent role municipal and state authorities played in claiming Longstreet as Georgia's own (the governor of Georgia and mayor of Atlanta were pallbearers), and in part because of the centrality of Confederate veterans and their descendants in the ceremony. Bishop Keiley, himself a veteran of Longstreet's corps, and a fervent Democrat, used his eulogy as the occasion for a caustic and partisan defense of states' rights—a defense of the kind Longstreet had rejected after the war. Keiley was echoed in local tributes across the South that chose, instead of sidestepping Longstreet's Republican politics, to subsume them into Lost Cause messaging. In that spirit, Confederate veterans in Houston County, Georgia, honored Longstreet for having fought for "a principle which did not, and thank God, could not die."[31]

At the same time, the very scope of Longstreet's funeral conveyed a mixed message. It was the largest ever such gathering in Gainesville, as the newspapers noted, but it remained a local not a national event. The 1898 burial of Jefferson Davis's daughter Winnie, by contrast, was a national spectacle. Winnie was a popular socialite who had become an iconic symbol of white Southern womanhood, and her public funeral rites were extensive, replete with a funeral train, bearing her remains, that was thronged by thousands of mourners, it made its way from New England to Virginia. The Spanish-American War had "hastened a culture of martial reconciliation," and Winnie Davis could represent sectional reunion for white Northerners and sectional pride for Southern whites. Davis's elaborate funeral thus illustrates how "reconciliation simultaneously meant different things to different people, even as they engaged in the reunification process together," as Purcell has explained.[32]

Lamenting Longstreet's "partially neglected burial," James R. Randall, a Confederate poet and Catholic who had penned the secessionist anthem "Maryland, My Maryland," mused that Longstreet's religion as well as his politics muted the ceremony. If Longstreet had been a Methodist or Baptist, and thus in the mainstream of Southern culture, Randall speculated, "he would have had a larger funeral." Randall's view may have some merit, but no sources have come to light directly corroborating it. Political objections, however, were clearly a factor in circumscribing the public mourning for Longstreet. The Savannah chapter of the United Daughters of the Confederacy, for example, pointedly refused to send a laurel wreath to Longstreet's graveside (to the eternal disgust of Helen Dortch Longstreet); this refusal accorded with the UDC's campaign to tell the "true" history of the Confederacy, focused on Lee's infallibility and the failures of his subordinates.[33]

While Helen Longstreet was as keen as any other UDC member to defend the honor and bravery of Confederate soldiers, her version of reconciliation made room for themes that had been emphasized by James himself: the courage and skill of Union soldiers; the dynamism of Northern society; the central role Grant played in reunification; and Longstreet's own pride in his role as a peacemaker. She found invariably that Northerners were more receptive to this understanding of reconciliation than white Southerners. Thus she valued the many appreciations she received from Union veterans and Northern civilians, such as an August 1904 letter from O. O. Howard, a Union general known for his evangelical piety, abolitionism, and leadership of the Freedmen's Bureau during Reconstruction. Howard wrote on behalf of the Grand Army of the Republic encampment at Boston, to convey its admiration of Longstreet "for his noble qualities as citizen of the reunited nation" and "commendable service to his country when the war was over." Helen responded, in a spirit of reciprocity, that Howard's words had deeply touched her heart, and that she would "hold in proud appreciation any token the Grand Army encampment might send to me evincing the esteem in which Gen Longstreet was held by his brave and victorious opponents." She cherished, too, a June 1904 letter from the White House, in which President Theodore Roosevelt praised the "high-souled patriotism" that made

Longstreet "as staunchly loyal to the Union as he had been loyal to the cause for which he fought during the war itself."[34]

VI

"For years he lived as a stranger in a strange land," the Chicago Black newspaper the *Broad Ax* editorialized in January 1904, remarking on how Longstreet "became a republican" and "remained a republican until the end." "Now that he is dead perhaps his reward may come, but the tragedy of his life cannot be obliterated." The *Broad Ax* was rare among African American papers in editorializing on Longstreet's death. Generally, the response of the Black press was muted—it covered his demise in a minimal fashion, drawing from white papers without additional commentary. If Blacks participated in any of the funeral ceremony in Gainesville, no record of that participation has come to light. This silence and absence are not surprising. Once Longstreet could no longer wield influence in the national Republican Party and in Georgia patronage, there was no longer a need to abide his peculiar politics. He had at times been a valuable ally to the freedom struggle, but not a fully committed one. After relocating from New Orleans to Gainesville, Longstreet refrained from using his bully pulpit to offer a sustained public defense of Black civil rights, or a critique of Jim Crow proscription and violence. Reconciliation-themed commemorative culture, especially at settings like Longstreet's funeral, where Lost Cause iconography predominated, was openly hostile to Blacks, and sought to crowd out their emancipationist interpretation of the war.[35]

The *Broad Ax* nonetheless captured the pathos of Longstreet's life and the turbulence of his afterlife. Controversy would continue to swirl around him, as he and other prominent veterans who had competed for military laurels and political influence during their lifetimes were brandished, in their afterlives, as symbols and icons in partisan combat and in memory wars. A considerable number of holdouts rejected or resisted reconciliation-tinged efforts to lionize Longstreet. Opposition persisted in Richmond, where, as William Garrett Piston has noted, "the *Southern Historical Society Papers* continued to print bitterly anti-Longstreet articles up to the eve of the First World War." It persisted, too, in Louisiana. A monument (a thirty-five-foot stone obelisk) was erected in downtown New Orleans in 1891, to memorialize the White League's attempted coup on September 14, 1874. Annual commemoration of the battle of Canal Street, or "Liberty Place," as white conservatives called it, brought forth waves of invective against Longstreet as one of the "henchmen" of the Radicals, trying to fasten the "despotism of negro supremacy" on Louisiana whites. A 1906 editorial in the *Southern Sentinel* called for the Liberty Place anniversary to be celebrated "with the same éclat in Louisiana as the Fourth of July," as the day Longstreet and his integrated militia went down to "utter rout."[36]

Confederate memorial culture continued to marginalize Longstreet. Revealingly, when John Brown Gordon died, within a week after Longstreet's death, in January 1904, Confederate veterans' organizations and publications lavished much more praise on him than they had on his political rival Longstreet. Gordon, in his 1903 *Reminiscences of the Civil War* and in an article on Gettysburg drawn from the book, had renewed the attacks on Longstreet's wartime record, blaming him for losing the battle that might have won the war. Coinciding as they did, the two men's deaths invited a new round of assessments and comparisons. "Thousands and thousands more people of the South will grieve because of the death of Gen. Gordon than for Gen. Longstreet," a letter to the editor of the *Macon Telegraph* pronounced on January 13, 1904, for when during Reconstruction "it became a question of [the] negro or white man," Longstreet had chosen the "negro side of the fence," while Gordon "knew the current of thought in the masses" and "chose the popular way," and was thus able to do "more as a national harmonizer than Gen. Longstreet."[37]

Fearing that it would prove easier than ever to scapegoat a man who could no longer defend himself, Helen Dortch Longstreet stepped forward to do literary battle with his adversaries, writing and self-publishing her own account of his life. Her 1904 tome, *Lee and Longstreet at High Tide*, built on Longstreet's 1896 memoir, foregrounding his intimacy, and the respect he shared, with both Lee and Grant. Its introduction, by former Union general Dan Sickles, described Longstreet as the "rainbow of reconciliation that foreshadowed real peace between the North and South."[38]

Helen's defense of her husband reflected her own racial politics. Socialized in the virulent racism of the Southern Democrats, she adopted a paternalist posture after marrying Longstreet, holding that Black progress could come only under white stewardship and domination. Unlike her husband, she had as yet expressed no public support for Black officeholding or voting or sought out alliances with Black leaders. Instead, she sought to align herself with Confederate memorialists, joining the United Daughters of the Confederacy chapter organized in Gainesville in 1896; it dubbed itself the "Longstreet chapter" in "marked appreciation" of Longstreet's "valued service in defense of the South during the war." The Longstreet UDC chapter threw itself into typical Confederate commemorative activities, including unveiling a "standing soldier" Confederate monument in Gainesville; celebrating Robert E. Lee's birthday; and decorating Confederate soldiers' graves on Memorial Day. At the time of her husband's death, Helen's primary interest was in cultivating the good favor of whites, and to that end her account in *Lee and Longstreet at High Tide* made no mention of Longstreet's interracial alliances, in Louisiana or Georgia. Indeed she emphasized Longstreet's support for a "white man's party" to challenge the Southern Democrats.[39]

Helen's rhetorical strategy in *Lee and Longstreet at High Tide* was to cast James as the victor in his decades-long battles with his detractors. In her view he *had*, as the outpouring of funeral tributes proved, vindicated himself—and it was churlish and graceless of his critics, against the grain of national sentiment, to deny him that vindication, and to "revive" the "cruel aspersion[s]" on her husband's character. "The outrageous charges against Longstreet have been wholly disproved," she noted, and "many of the more intelligent Southerners" now saw Longstreet as "the victim of a great wrong." Helen tried, in other words, to ostracize James's ostracizers, picking apart the military accounts of critics like Pendleton, and accusing them of having willfully conspired to distort the historical record.[40]

While she refrained from overtly defending Republican policies, Helen did selectively take aim at certain key aspects of Lost Cause ideology and at the Southern Democrats. She insisted that the anti-Longstreet crusade was illegitimate precisely because it was politically motivated. And she described Longstreet's stance during Reconstruction as "heroic." To see Reconstruction as a time of Republican heroism flew in the face of the Southern Democratic view of it as a "tragic era" of Northern misrule. If James were still alive, she wrote, "I would tell him that his unmatched courage to meet the enemies of the peace time outshines the valor of the fields whereon his blood was shed so copiously in the cause of his country. I would tell him that his detractors are not the South; they are not the Democratic party; they represent nobody and nothing but the blindness of passion that desires not light." No clasping of hands would seal the breach that Helen referred to, and the memory wars over Longstreet's image would rage on.[41]

Epilogue

OF MONUMENTS AND MEMORY

I

Helen Dortch Longstreet would wage a decades-long campaign, deep into the twentieth century, to memorialize her husband. Playing out against the backdrop of her own political awakening, that campaign dramatized how fractured James Longstreet's image remained—and remains.

As William Garrett Piston has explained, the early twentieth century brought forth a new "spate of works by key members of the anti-Longstreet faction" such as memoirs by Jubal Early and Charles Marshall, as well as various reminiscences by other Confederate veterans casting Longstreet's military record in a negative light. School textbooks, including ones published in the North, Piston reveals, either scapegoated Longstreet for Southern defeat or overlooked his role as Lee's "war-horse," even as a new generation of historians, including Lee biographer Douglas Southall Freeman, and Longstreet biographers Hamilton J. Eckenrode and Bryan Conrad, derided Longstreet as "tardy and insubordinate" during the war. Their views reflected the surging "national veneration of the Lost Cause" in the 1930s, as typified by the popularity of Margaret Mitchell's 1936 novel, *Gone with the Wind*.[1]

Helen Dortch Longstreet's defense of her husband would gradually shift during this era, as her own views on race relations underwent a protracted transformation. In the decade after her husband's death, Helen remained mired in Lost Cause racial assumptions and showed none of James's willingness to challenge them. For example, in 1906, after being appointed postmaster of the Gainesville office by Theodore Roosevelt, she strenuously denied rumors that she would hire Blacks to work as mail couriers or in other such roles, as such hiring was considered "unacceptable" by whites. Six years after James's death, in an ill-conceived and ill-fated stunt, she attempted to start a movement to erect a statue in Atlanta to the "loyal" slaves of the Old South. She hoped the statue would close "a chasm which ought never to have existed between the races"—but she was perpetuating a pernicious Lost Cause trope of the "loving service" of slaves to their masters. In 1912 she succeeded in having a "Lincoln memorial fountain" erected in Gainesville, to represent Lincoln's nationalism, and the hope that "north and south would clasp hands in a brotherhood which knows no sectionalism and admits no hate"—but the memorial design enforced racial segregation, with drinking fountains on "one side for white people, the other for colored."[2]

Helen's efforts to ingratiate herself with Gainesville's whites paid off, as the local Longstreet Chapter of the UDC proved willing to honor James Longstreet, in the 1930s, with a highway marker along the "Longstreet Bridge" spanning the Chattahoochee River on US 129; an "imposing bench" in town; and a marker stone at the site of his home. Like his headstone at Alta Vista Cemetery, these markers celebrated his Confederate service, to the exclusion of all else: the plaque at his home site reads simply "General James Longstreet—Lee's 'Old War-Horse.'" Whatever they thought of Longstreet's postwar politics, Gainesville's boosters and business community could revel in the fact that Longstreet's residence there had put the town on the map—they hoped that their markers to him would "give Gainesville a national identification."[3]

But Helen was starting to sow the seeds of her own rebellion. Embittered by her ouster from the postmastership when the Democrat Woodrow Wilson became president; exposed to new perspectives during stints living in Los Angeles and the Virgin Islands; energized by her activism as a conservationist (she lobbied in vain against the building of the Tallulah Falls Dam) and by her patriotic war work (with the Veterans Bureau) to support US troops during World War I, Dortch was emerging from Longstreet's— and Gainesville's—shadow. She had aspirations to be a national voice, not merely a regional one. The resurgence of the Ku Klux Klan and explosion of anti-Black violence in the wake of World War I disrupted her fantasies of peaceful reunion and paternalistic harmony, and Helen began to speak out. In 1922, she briefly made headlines for asserting that "slavery caused the Civil War." She was objecting to the fact that Confederate veterans at a Richmond reunion had recently passed resolutions blaming Lincoln for starting the war. Deploring this "slur" on the former president, Helen cast her late husband as a truth-teller: General Longstreet had always told her, she wrote, that "impartial history would have to rest the blame for the war between the states upon the crime of slavery," and that all other differences "could have been adjusted without the shedding of blood." Tellingly, Helen had never attributed to her husband such sharp language (calling slavery a crime) before—but as her own eyes opened she saw his career in a new light. She also explicitly endorsed his view that Lincoln was a "knightly friend to the South" whose assassination was "her cruelest blow in the reconstruction period." The Richmonders who criticized Lincoln, she charged, were trying to "open the bloody rift that has been bridged for more than fifty years."[4]

With this stance, Helen was intervening in a bitter public battle over curriculum and school textbooks in the South. In 1919, the UDC and its "historian," Margaret Lewis Rutherford, together with other Confederate heritage organizations, had launched a coordinated campaign to demand the teaching of Lost Cause themes—the defense of slavery, secession, Confederacy, and white supremacy—in Southern schools. They targeted for censorship books such as the Northern history professor David Muzzey's 1911 survey *An American History*, on the grounds that Muzzey, by praising Abraham Lincoln and criticizing Jefferson Davis and the Confederacy, had violated the UDC's "standards" for approved curriculum. Helen lashed out against the "schoolbook trust" that was willing to deride Lincoln, a man "born in our own southern mountains, whose name will forever lead the list of those who loved their fellow men." Dortch pivoted from the history wars to the anti-Black violence engulfing the South. With Rutherford and her ilk in mind, Helen chided the "female historians of the Confederacy" for relitigating the past rather than addressing the "ignoble history now in the making." Invoking the "crimes of our twentieth century civilization," and echoing James's 1899 essay, Helen denounced lynching. "America is the only country in the world that burns a human being at the stake," she intoned. "Lawlessness, like a prairie fire, may be started by any maniac, but it takes an army to put it out."

In 1938 Helen used the seventy-fifth anniversary gathering at Gettysburg to form the Longstreet Memorial Association. Its purpose was to raise money to erect a statue to her late husband within Gettysburg National Military Park, and it attracted support from Confederate veterans and their descendants with messaging that echoed the UDC's: namely, that Longstreet was a military hero, who "obeyed every order he received from Lee." But Helen, in a move reminiscent of James's own appeals to multiple audiences, also articulated for the LMA a broad, ambitious mission suited to the moment. Citing the "worldwide menace of totalitarianism," she cast her memorialization efforts as a bid to foster "increased devotion to the greatest democracy men have founded and the purest left in a war-torn world—our United States." The LMA commissioned an equestrian statue from a noted sculptor and secured a site (where Longstreet's right wing was positioned on July 2) from the National Park Service. The July 1941 dedication of the site abounded with Lost Cause and reconciliationist themes and iconography, but also (unlike the Gainesville Longstreet memorial unveilings) included "Won Cause" imagery and highlighted Longstreet's postwar career. For example, the cover of the printed program for the event juxtaposed the Confederate flag with a 1904 poem from the *Chicago Tribune*, praising Longstreet's "loyal soul" and declaring that "in the fields of peace [he] more glories won / Than in the battles his gray warriors fought!"[5]

With American society mobilizing for a new war, the planned July 1944 Longstreet statue unveiling never transpired. World War II would have a profound effect on Helen's politics. At age eighty, to the public's delight, she worked as a riveter in the Bell Aircraft Corporation plant, building B-29 bombers, in Marietta, Georgia. "I couldn't stay out of this war," she told the press. "The thought of American sons dying on the battlefields made me realize that I had to do my part in achieving victory." The realization that African Americans were doing "excellent work in war plants" across the country and that Black soldiers "fought as bravely and died as gallantly as white men fought and died" had an epiphanic effect on Helen, and stoked her growing progressivism on issues of race. In the war's aftermath, in 1947, she took a bold public stance against the "white primary" bill proposed by Georgia Democrats (restricting participation in party races to whites only), condemning it as retrograde. In explaining her new embrace of civil rights, Helen invoked Black patriotism in both world wars. "Foreign fields sodden with Negros' life blood, foreign skies in which he fought, and foreign seas on which he died to give peoples of other lands rights denied him in his own country, cry aloud in protest" against any restriction on Black suffrage, she testified before the Georgia Senate in hearings on the legality of such measures. Her outspoken defense of Black voting rights garnered her extensive praise in the Black press; a "flood of letters" in support; and an award from civil rights activists in the interracial "Institute on Race Relations," based in Washington, DC. In accepting the award, she wrote to Tomlinson D. Todd, president of the Institute, a remarkable letter in which she again invoked Black patriotism, and offered a scathing critique of white bigotry:

> Small caliber politicians, who, for the purpose of holding power and office for themselves, glibly prate of white supremacy, should be told that long before Columbus sailed the seas … "Darkest Africa" was holding aloft the torch of culture, while the boastful Nordic race was struggling in the jungles. Celebrated historians

have reached the conclusion that civilization was handed down from Negroland to Egypt.[6]

In 1950, at the age of eighty-seven, she announced that she would like to run for governor in Georgia and promised that if elected she would "annihilate the Ku Klux Klan." (She garnered a total of ninety-one votes as a write-in candidate.) The *Atlanta Daily World*, the oldest Black newspaper in the state, praised her for "still following in the footsteps of the general turned Republican," and cast her civil rights activism as an extension of her efforts to fight the political persecution of "her dashing husband."[7]

Those efforts were ongoing. Like James had, Helen stubbornly clung to the idea that she could harmonize her integrationist politics with her continued glorification of the Confederacy. Tailoring her messages to her audiences, she likened Longstreet to Abraham Lincoln, as a martyr to the goal of "fraternal unity," in a speech before the Illinois State Historical Society; Longstreet was "crucified on a cross of falsehood by the people whose battles he had fought!" she exclaimed, in florid language chastising ex-Confederates. But when addressing a United Daughters of the Confederacy chapter in Cincinnati in May 1946, she sang a different tune, waxing nostalgic about the loyalty of her "old black Mammy"; claiming that Southerners fought the Civil War to defend states' rights; and calling the Confederate army the "most gallant Army the world has known." What linked these dissonant messages was Helen's insistence that the Civil War should furnish patriotic lessons, in the era of the world wars, about shared valor—that "Americans surrender only to Americans," as she put it.[8]

Like her husband had, Helen strove to foster national reunion, but in so doing exposed persistent enmities between white Southerners. She felt snubbed when she was not among the invitees to the National Park Service's dedication of the McLean House at Appomattox in 1950, noting that it "would have given [her] a patriotic thrill" to be there, given Longstreet's central role as the South's senior commissioner arranging the terms of surrender. She bemoaned the outsized influence of Lee biographer Douglas Southall Freeman, who was featured as the keynote speaker at the Appomattox dedication despite his "circulating diatribes against General Longstreet's military renown which are false," as she lamented in a letter to a Virginia journalist. In 1949 Helen revived the Longstreet Memorial Association, and pledged the remaining years of her life to erecting a monument to her husband on the Gettysburg battlefield. Her final appeals on behalf of that project cagily glorified Longstreet's "military genius" and his accomplishments as a statesman in equal measure. While she would not live to see a Gettysburg statue unveiled, Helen could take satisfaction from the placement, by the Georgia Historical Commission, of a historical marker in Gainesville's courthouse square in 1954—in keeping with her own understanding of his legacy, the marker referenced Longstreet's string of Federal civil service appointments as well as his military career.[9]

Despite Helen's half century of agitation, James remained a target of controversy and critique. The publication in 1952 of a fair-minded biography—Donald Bridgman Sanger and Thomas Robson Hay's *James Longstreet: I. Soldier; II. Politician, Officeholder, and Writer*—did little to move the needle of public opinion, as the tome was scholarly and dry. And it remained the case that scholars favorably disposed toward Longstreet were vastly outnumbered by unsympathetic ones. This was evident in Indiana University Press's 1960 edition of Longstreet's memoir, *From Manassas to Appomattox*, which featured an introduction by James I. Robertson Jr., then one of the leading Civil War historians. Robertson purported, in his framing of the memoir, to find a middle ground between the "slanderous" critiques offered by Eckenrode and Conrad in their 1936 Longstreet biography and the "eulogistic" take of Sanger and Hay. But Robertson nonetheless depicted Longstreet as an embittered and pathetic figure, observing that in the postwar controversies over his military record, "Longstreet proved his own worst enemy. The more he wrote, the more bitter he became." The elaborate Civil War Centennial ceremonies of 1961 through 1965, of which Robertson was executive director, only further diminished

Longstreet. Virginian interpretations of the Lost Cause dominated the scene, with the sanctification of Lee casting Longstreet, more than ever, in the role of scapegoat.[10]

When Helen Dortch Longstreet died at age ninety-nine in 1962, in the second year of the centennial commemorations, her obituaries made little effort to connect her career as a political maverick with her husband's. They emphasized instead that she had been one of the very last living Confederate widows, and a reminder of "how close—from the standpoint of history—was the Civil War in which her husband was a famous commander," as one newspaper put it sentimentally.[11]

II

The public interest in Longstreet was recalibrated by the publication of Michael Shaara's wildly popular novel *The Killer Angels* in 1974. A finely grained fictional account of the Gettysburg campaign, the book conjured the strained relationship of Longstreet and Lee, casting Longstreet as a prescient pragmatist oriented toward the future, who symbolized modern warfare, and Lee as the prideful romantic, backward-looking and resigned to fate. "Shaara implies that if Longstreet had directed the Southern warfare, American history would have taken a different course," one reviewer noted, capturing the appeal of the book. Ron Maxwell's screen adaptation of *Killer Angels*, the 1993 movie *Gettysburg*, further countered the Lost Cause critiques of Longstreet as insubordinate. "Most viewers would likely conclude that Longstreet is the better general and Lee a noble anachronism with little understanding of how to fight an enemy whose weaponry renders frontal assaults suicidal," the historian Gary W. Gallagher has observed of the film.[12]

In the past half century, modern scholars have continued to debate Longstreet's military performance and the efficacy of his self-defense against his postwar critics. The historian Robert Krick has taken the harshest line, critiquing Longstreet's battlefield conduct and his "mean-spirited" and "small minded" efforts to justify that conduct. Krick and other such critics have been challenged by Longstreet defenders such as Cory M. Pfarr, who accuse these modern detractors of perpetuating an older tradition of Lee worship. In between these interpretive extremes, modern biographers such as William Garrett Piston and Jeffry Wert have aimed at a historiographical "rebalancing": they have tried to move beyond Lost Cause myths and the blame game to use Longstreet as a window into Confederate defeat and its legacies. In the spirit of rebalancing, Christian Keller, in his introduction to a 2020 edition of Longstreet's memoir, acknowledges Longstreet's "penchant for self-justification," but emphasizes that Longstreet was "far from alone in evaluating his experiences in the war through a personal lens." Keller praises Longstreet's "ability to see the big picture."[13]

The realm of historical memory, too, has continued to be a site of contestation. In 1991 the North Carolina Division of the Sons of Confederate Veterans began a seven-year campaign to erect a Longstreet monument at Gettysburg. Their new Longstreet Memorial Fund shared a core assumption with Helen Dortch Longstreet's earlier LMA: that Longstreet had been fully vindicated of any *"alleged* disobedience" to Lee, as the Fund's chairman, Robert C. Thomas, put it in a letter to North Carolina senator Jesse Helms. But unlike Dortch Longstreet, the LMF went out of its way to specify that it was "not honoring the General for his postwar activities"—only memorializing him for "his war service." The interpretive tablets the LMF designed made no mention of Longstreet's political about-face or the attendant controversies. The LMF's public appeals for donations, featuring the slogan "It's About Time," glorified Longstreet's devotion to the Lost Cause. To raise funds, the LMF sold T-shirts with defiant messages—one featured the likenesses of Longstreet and Stonewall Jackson with the caption "The Undefeated," and another the "Stars and

Bars" flag with the caption "'Not Yet': Longstreet to Lee." "We consider ALL soldiers who served the Confederacy as HEROES who deserve to be respected and memorialized," as Thomas put it.[14]

Some of those who supported the LMF favored a broader, more inclusive framing of its mission—for example, the historian Gabor Boritt, director of Gettysburg College's Civil War Institute, hoped that the monument would help make Gettysburg "the home to the memory of Federals and Confederates, blacks and whites, soldiers and civilians, men and women, young and old," while Longstreet's granddaughter Jamie Longstreet Patterson was eager to preserve "Longstreet's important, though often overlooked, individual and public contributions toward reconciliation following the war." But Thomas held his ground, reiterating that the LMF was founded to honor Longstreet's Confederate career, not his postwar politics. The equestrian statue that the LMF commissioned from the artist Gary Casteel was inaugurated with great fanfare at Gettysburg on July 3, 1998, in a ceremony redolent with Lost Cause imagery. "Southerners in attendance broke into cheers and authentic Rebel yells" as a fife-and-drum corps played "Dixie," and the statue was unveiled from behind a giant Confederate flag.[15]

In essence, the event dramatized the difficulty of memorializing Longstreet. As Thomas and the LMF recognized, it would have been discordant to honor both Longstreet's Confederate record and his Republican record, as the two were at odds. But it also proved impossible to separate the phases of Longstreet's life. The LMF's slogan, "It's About Time," alluded to Longstreet's fall from grace among Confederates, and the press's keen interest in that part of the story meant Thomas and his fellow memorializers had, in the coverage of the event, to address it. "Southern Democrats after the war were banned from holding public office," and thus Longstreet had sided with Republicans so that Southerners "could change things from the inside instead of sitting on the outside throwing rocks," Thomas claimed, misleadingly, in a July 1998 press interview. This was a muddling of history: it had been the resurgence and recalcitrance of Southern Democrats during Andrew Johnson's presidency that occasioned the 1867 Reconstruction Acts and sparked Longstreet's conversion. Thomas's take defused the image of Longstreet as a traitor by repurposing the Lost Cause narrative of white Southern victimization at the hands of Yankee conquerors. Ironically, the Gettysburg Longstreet statue quickly gained a reputation as being decidedly unheroic: cast in bronze, Longstreet rides an undersized horse, positioned on the grass rather than atop a pedestal, on the edge of the battlefield park, blocked from view by trees.[16]

III

America's overdue reckoning with Confederate memorialization, catalyzed by white supremacist violence in Charleston and Charlottesville, has reframed Longstreet's life and legacy. Remarking on the absence, outside of Gettysburg, of any statue in his honor, a spate of published opinion pieces has asked, rhetorically, "Where are the monuments to Confederate Gen. James Longstreet?" The answer, highlighting his postwar life, is that Longstreet's embrace of Republicanism and Reconstruction rendered him unfit as a symbol of the Lost Cause. He is thus the exception that proves the rule: Confederate statues were not simply "tributes to military heroism," but instead "totems of white supremacy," as the historian Kevin Waite has put it.[17]

One such totem—an explicitly anti-Longstreet memorial—was among the first to come down, leading a wave of removals. Long a divisive and controversial symbol, the towering "Battle of Liberty Place" monument in downtown New Orleans was modified in 1974 (a plaque was added noting that the monument no longer reflected modern attitudes), and finally taken down in 2017, with the support of Mayor Mitch Landrieu. Reflecting on the shadow cast by Confederate statuary in the city, Landrieu observed,

To literally put the Confederacy on a pedestal in our most prominent places of honor is an inaccurate recitation of our full past. It
is an affront to our present, and it is a bad prescription for our future. History cannot be changed. It cannot be moved like a statue.
What is done is done. The Civil War is over, and the Confederacy
lost and we are better for it. Surely we are far enough removed
from this dark time to acknowledge that the cause of the Confederacy was wrong.[18]

The January 6, 2021, insurrection at the US Capitol following incumbent Donald J. Trump's defeat in the 2020 presidential election brought
forth more allusions to Longstreet's role at "Liberty Place," as commentators drew out the parallels between the 1874 attempted coup and current
events. Sounding a warning about the need to hold the modern rioters to
account, *New York Times* columnist Jamelle Bouie explained that "impunity
in the face of mob violence" would lead to more violence. He noted that
because the 1874 Canal Street coup went unpunished, "the White League
became a model for others in the South who sought an end to 'Negro rule'
in their states."[19]

As statues of Robert E. Lee and Stonewall Jackson and Jefferson
Davis and other Confederate leaders have come down, some commentators have explicitly called for the erection of new statues to Longstreet, in
recognition of his postwar political stance. Former governor of Georgia
Roy Barnes, for example, argued in 2021 that a statue of Longstreet should
replace the statue of John Brown Gordon at the state capitol—Gordon's
role in the Klan made him unworthy, while Longstreet's support for Black
freedom made him worthy, Barnes argued.[20]

But Longstreet has never fit the profile of a marble man, whose life
story could be set in stone. His political evolution and public image were
too complex and contradictory for that. Longstreet fought the Civil War
to win it. If he had succeeded, slavery would have persisted—and his own

remarkable reinvention, and the reforms he promoted after Appomattox, would have never come to pass.

"To me, the surrender of my sword was my reconstruction. I looked upon the 'Lost Cause' as a cause totally, irrevocably lost." So Longstreet mused in 1880, capturing why he has been the most embattled military figure from America's Civil War. We like to bestow praise on historical figures who had the courage of their convictions. Longstreet's story is a reminder that the arc of history is sometimes bent by those who had the courage to change their convictions. He accepted defeat with a measure of grace and tried to learn, and then to teach, the past's lessons. And for that, he commands our attention as one of the most enduringly relevant voices in American history.[21]

ACKNOWLEDGMENTS

Historians always have debts of gratitude to libraries and archives, but in this case, my debt is especially steep. The COVID shutdowns of 2020–21 would have forestalled this project were it not for the extensive digitization of historical documents by repositories such as the Library of Congress and National Archives, and for the willingness of librarians and archivists across the country to make unpublished manuscript sources available remotely, as scans, xeroxes, and microfilms. I am grateful to all of the institutions listed in my bibliography, and especially to the special collections staffs at Emory University; the University of North Carolina, Chapel Hill; and Duke University, for making key Longstreet papers accessible to me during COVID.

I treasure, as always, my connection to UVA's John L. Nau III Center for Civil War History and thank Carrie Janney and Brian Neumann for their stellar leadership of the Center and of UVA's community of Civil War scholars. We are all deeply appreciative of John Nau's support for the Center and his generous gift of Civil War primary sources to the UVA library system. The Nau Center's founding director, Gary W. Gallagher, read my entire manuscript and improved it immeasurably with his sage suggestions.

My research assistant for this project, UVA undergraduate Paul H. Adams, did a superb job of culling newspaper collections for commentary by and about James and Helen Dortch Longstreet; he showed impeccable judgment in sifting out salient articles.

Michael A. Ross at the University of Maryland generously shared with me his expertise on nineteenth-century New Orleans and his own pathbreaking research on Longstreet's involvement in education reform.

ACKNOWLEDGMENTS

Elizabeth D. Leonard at Colby College discovered some revealing correspondence between Longstreet and Ben Butler and provided me with a transcription of it. These and other such dialogues and exchanges enhanced my research and writing. I benefitted especially from discussing New Orleans politics and culture with current and former students such as Jake Calhoun and Clayton Butler, who have research specialties in Louisiana history.

Portions of chapter 8 appeared as an article in the *Journal of the Civil War Era*, and I thank editors Greg Downs and Kate Masur for their input; portions of chapter 10 appeared as an essay in the book *Civil War Witnesses and Their Books* (Louisiana State University Press, 2021), edited by Gary W. Gallagher and Stephen Cushman, and am grateful to them, too, for helping to launch this project. My greatest intellectual debt is, once again, to my husband and fellow historian, Will Hitchcock. His encouragement and edits and example all energized this book; he inspired me to try my hand at narrative history and connected me to his editor, Bob Bender, at Simon & Schuster. It has been a pleasure to work with Bob and with Johanna Li at S&S and I thank them for their confidence in me. My literary agent, Anthony Arnove, has been a wonderful guide to the publishing world, and I look forward to further collaborations.

My children, Ben and Emma (now adults charting their own journeys), continue to fill me with joy and wonder and admiration. We treasure them as the center of our universe.

This book is dedicated to my late father, Bension Varon, and to Will's late father, David Hitchcock—and particularly to the life-affirming friendship between these two men. We lost them both in the space of the past three years, and feel blessed by their memories and humbled by the love and support they ceaselessly gave to us. That they found each other—as lunch buddies, Washingtonian politicos, men of the world, lovers of classical music, devoted husbands and fathers, and epitomes of elegance and grace—is a source of enduring comfort to our extended family. Everything they did was for us, and they live on in our hearts.

NOTES

Abbreviations Used

ABL   Augustus Baldwin Longstreet

FMTA   James Longstreet, *From Manassas to Appomattox: Memoirs of the Civil War in America* (1896; reprint, New York: Da Capo Press, 1992)

GLI   Gilder Lehrman Collection, Gilder Lehrman Institute of American History, New York, accessed online at https://www.gilderlehrman.org/collection /american-history-1493-1945

HDL   Helen Dortch Longstreet

LC   Library of Congress, Washington, DC

LVA   Library of Virginia, Richmond

OR   US War Department, *The War of the Rebellion: A Compilation of the Official Records of the Union and Confederate Armies*, 128 vols. (Washington, DC: Government Printing Office, 1880–1901)

NA   National Archives and Records Administration, Washington, DC

NYHS   New-York Historical Society, New York

PUSG   *Papers of Ulysses S. Grant*, vols. 14–24, edited by John Y. Simon (Carbondale and Edwardsville: Southern Illinois University Press, 1985–2000)

RLD   Duke University, David M. Rubenstein Rare Book & Manuscript Library, Durham, NC

RLE   Emory University, Stuart A. Rose Manuscript, Archives, and Rare Book Library, Atlanta

SCL   University of South Carolina, South Caroliniana Library, Columbia

SHSP   *Southern Historical Society Papers*, 1876–1910, Virginia Historical Society, Richmond

UNC   University of North Carolina, Wilson Special Collections Library, Chapel Hill

UVA   University of Virginia, Albert and Shirley Small Special Collections Library, Charlottesville

VMHC Virginia Museum of History and Culture, Richmond

Prologue: Confederate Judas

1. *New Orleans Republican*, Oct. 25, 1870.

2. Ibid.

3. Hogue, *Uncivil War*, 68–70.

4. *New Orleans Republican*, Oct. 25, 1870.

5. Longstreet scholars have paid far greater attention to his Civil War military record and the postwar litigation of it than they have to his political career or views. They have generally been dismissive of Longstreet the politician, casting him as naïve and ineffectual. See, for example, Piston, *Lee's Tarnished Lieutenant*, 166–69; Wert, 412–13, 418–19, 423–27; Sanger and Hay, 400, 433–36; Pfarr, 180–83.

6. *Le Carillon* (New Orleans), Oct. 18, 1874; *Newnan Herald* (GA), Oct. 9, 1874; *Galveston Daily News* (TX), Oct. 29, 1874; *Rome Tri-Weekly Courier* (GA), Dec. 29, 1874; *Savannah Morning News*, Sept. 16, 1874.

7. *New Orleans Times*, March 19, 1867.

8. On political conflict and violence in New Orleans in these years, see Hogue, *Uncivil War*.

9. James Longstreet to Henry B. Dawson, March 27, 1876, Civil War Letters Collection, New-York Historical Society.

10. For op-eds on the absence of Longstreet memorials, see, for example, Holmes, "Where Are the Monuments to Confederate Gen. James Longstreet?"; Lane, "The Forgotten Confederate General Who Deserves a Monument"; Waite, "The Missing Statues That Expose the Truth About Confederate Monuments."

Chapter 1: The Making of a Rebel

1. *OR*, 11, pt. 3, 605–6; this speech was published in the *Richmond Daily Dispatch* on June 23, 1862, and reprinted in other Confederate papers thereafter, including the *Charleston Tri-Weekly Courier* (SC), June 26, 1862.

2. Wert, 21; Burton, *In My Father's House Are Many Mansions*, 4–6, 35–37.

3. *Augusta Herald* (GA), March 7, 1816; Longstreet Purchase of Nance, December 19, 1822, Edgefield, South Carolina, Slave Records, 1774–1866, box 12, pkg. 403, 144, accessed at Ancestry.com, ancestry.com/imageviewer/collections/60512. US Census records show that twenty-four enslaved persons lived at James Longstreet Sr.'s Edgefield, South Carolina, property in 1820 and that sixteen lived at his property near Augusta in 1830. James Longstreet entries, 1820 and 1830 US Federal Census, NA, accessed at Ancestry.com.

4. Wert, 24–25. Augustus B. Longstreet is best known today as the author of *Georgia Scenes, Characters, Incidents, etc. in the First Half Century of the Republic* (1835), which helped give rise to the literary genres of Southwestern humor and "local color" stories featuring the customs and dialect of rural folk and thus creating an antecedent for Mark Twain. As the intellectual historian Michael O'Brien explains in *Conjectures of Order: Intellectual Life and the American South, 1810–1860*, 755, in this genre "the civilized narrator looks out on an unsafe and uncontrollable world disfigured by passionate license. . . . The chaos never quite reaches him, but he knows about it." On the racial and gender politics of Longstreet's *Georgia Scenes*, see Wegman, 1–13.

5. A. B. Longstreet, quoted in Oscar Penn Fitzgerald, *Judge Longstreet*, 45–46. On Augustus Longstreet's transfer of slaves to James, see Auslander, 302, 322–23. On Augustus's slaveholding, see the 1840 census, which shows that he owned fifteen slaves in Mississippi, and the 1850 census, which shows that he owned ten slaves. A. B. Longstreet entry, 1850 US Federal Census, Slave Schedules.

6. Wert, 26; Millett et al., 120 (quotation).

7. JL, *FMTA*, 15; Jomini, 38, 51, 56–65. On the influence of Jomini at West Point, see Millett et al., 118–19, and Reardon, *With a Sword in One Hand and Jomini in the Other*.

8. Wert, 28 (quotation), 31; JL, *FMTA*, 17.

9. Wert, 34.

10. JL, *FMTA*, 18–19.

11. ABL, *Letters on the Epistle of Paul to Philemon*, 6, 8, and *A Voice from the South*, 18–22.

12. *Courier-Journal* (Louisville, KY), July 25, 1885. On the ideological underpinnings of the Mexican War, see Varon, *Disunion!*, 183.

13. Mendoza, 2–5.

14. Millett et al., 138–41.

15. Guardino, 248–49; *Charleston Mercury* (SC), quoted in *Edgefield Advertiser* (SC), Nov. 10, 1847.

16. *Charleston Mercury* (SC), quoted in *Edgefield Advertiser* (SC), Nov. 10, 1847; Guardino, 264–68; Winders, 127.

17. Wert, 45.

18. *Charleston Mercury* (SC), quoted in *Edgefield Advertiser* (SC), Nov. 10, 1847; Wert, 45; *Daily Chronicle & Sentinel* (Augusta, GA), Feb. 24, 1848; *Daily Constitutionalist* (Augusta, GA), Feb. 20, 1848.

19. Mendoza, 5; Howe, 791.

20. *Arkansas State Gazette* (Little Rock), June 16, 1848; Howe, 791; Hughes and Stonesifer, 362–64. On Longstreet's testimony, see, for example, *Baltimore Sun*, June 10, 1848, *Trenton State Gazette* (NJ), June 28, 1848.

21. *Brooklyn Citizen*, Jan. 23, 1890; JL, *FMTA*, 20, 24, 26, 28.

22. *Brooklyn Citizen*, Jan. 23, 1890; Piston, "Petticoats, Promotions, and Military Assignments," 55–58.

23. Hämäläinen, 167–68, 181–82, 186, 201 (quotation), 233 (quotation), 292 (quotation), 305–7; Wooster, 123–26.

24. Haas, "Fort Lincoln"; *Texas State Gazette* (Austin), Jan. 26, 1850.

25. Piston, "Petticoats, Promotions, and Military Assignments," 59; Alwyn Burr, *Black Texans*, 24; James Longstreet entry, 1850 US Federal Census, Slave Schedules.

26. Wynes, ed., 267. On the Parker H. French incident, see, for example, *Baltimore Sun*, Oct. 7, 1850; *Daily Alta California* (San Francisco), Feb. 20, 1850; *Sacramento Daily Union*, Sept. 9, 1858.

27. Coker and Humphrey, 394, 401–3 (quotations).

28. Newcombe Jr., 166–72.

29. *Daily Alta California* (San Francisco), November 20, 1858; Clary, 38–39.

30. Wert, 50; JL to ABL, Nov. 19, 1859, Augustus Baldwin Longstreet Papers, 1841–1859, RLD.

31. Piston, "Petticoats, Promotions, and Military Assignments," 66; JL to William Porcher Miles, Feb. 27, 1860, William Porcher Miles Papers, UNC.

32. May, 857, 859, 866, 871, 874–75, 877.

33. Baker, 108–10.

34. On secession, see Dew, *Apostles of Disunion.*

35. Sacks, 109–14; *Saint Paul Weekly Pioneer and Democrat* (Minnesota Territory), June 21, 1861.

36. Gallagher, *Becoming Confederates,* 14.

37. *Philadelphia Times,* July 27, 1879.

38. Wert, 52; J. L. M. Curry to Governor Moore, February 1861, Longstreet Compiled Service Record, NA.

39. JL to George W. Crawford, Feb. 21, 1850, GLI; Edmunds Holloway to Eliza Holloway, Feb. 10, 1861; JL to Eliza Holloway, October 26, 1895, July 15, 1896, in Edmunds Holloway Family Letters, DeGolyer Library, Southern Methodist University, Dallas, TX.

40. JL to R. B. Reynolds, April 17, 1861, UVA; Wert, 52–53; William Dent Longstreet to Jefferson Davis, Feb. 22, 1861, Longstreet Compiled Service Record, NA.

41. Wert, 53–54.

42. On the story of Daniel, see Longstreet's letter of Nov. 8, 1895, reprinted in Cockrum, 302–4. On the role of body servants, see Woodward, 82–83.

43. *National Era* (Washington, DC), Feb. 26, 1857; *Yorkville Enquirer* (SC), March 31, 1859; *Weekly Champion and Press* (Atchison, KS), April 23, 1859; *Charleston Tri-Weekly Courier* (SC), Dec. 15, 1859.

44. For newspaper coverage of the Statistical Congress incident, see, for example, *Baltimore Sun,* Aug. 13, 1860, and *Weekly Mississippian* (Jackson, MS), Aug. 22, 1860; for the "Appeal to the South," published originally in the *Southern Guardian* (Columbia, SC), see *Constitution* (Washington, DC), Dec. 21, 1860.

45. JL to ABL, March 17, 1861, James Longstreet Papers, SCL.

46. *Oxford Intelligencer* (MS), quoted in *Charleston Daily Courier* (SC), June 27, 1861.

Chapter 2: Enemies Without and Within

1. McCurry, 13–17, 31, 219, 251. See also Glymph, *Out of the House of Bondage*.

2. Mendoza, 8; Longacre, 82, 143.

3. Mendoza, 9; Longacre, 201, 251, 267; *OR*, 2, 461–62; *Richmond Daily Dispatch*, July 31, 1861; JL to ABL, Aug. 13, 1861, bound vol. 136, Fredericksburg and Spotsylvania National Military Park, VA.

4. Varon, *Armies of Deliverance*, 25–26.

5. Piston, *Lee's Tarnished Lieutenant*, 14; JL, *FMTA*, 54; *Daily Alta California* (San Francisco), Aug. 30, 1861.

6. JL to Col. Thomas Jordan, Aug. 22, 27, 28, 29, Sept. 1, 6, 17, 18, 23, 26, 27, 1861, Longstreet Compiled Service Record, NA; *Richmond Daily Dispatch*, Sept. 19, 1861.

7. Karlton Smith, "The Best Staff Officers in the Army"; Cutrer, ed., *Longstreet's Aide*, 24, 30, 40, 45, 60, 68; *OR*, 2, 543.

8. Longacre, 440–41; Mendoza, 10–12.

9. *Richmond Daily Dispatch*, Dec. 13, 1861.

10. Wert, 96–97; Cutrer, ed., *Longstreet's Aide*, 72.

11. *Charleston Mercury* (SC), quoted in *Daily Sun* (Columbus, GA), Feb. 1, 1862; Sorrel, 37–38.

12. *Richmond Daily Dispatch*, Feb. 14, 1862.

13. Piston, *Lee's Tarnished Lieutenant*, 18; *OR*, 11, pt. 1, 275 (Johnston quotation); Hubbell, 29–31; Mendoza, 12–14; Wert, 6–7; Varon, *Armies of Deliverance*, 79–80.

14. *OR*, 11, pt. 3, 580.

15. Varon, *Armies of Deliverance*, 79–80; Wert, 117–24; Mendoza, 13–14; *OR*, 11, pt. 1, 934, 941; JL to Joseph Eggleston Johnston, June 7, 1862, Joseph E. Johnston Papers, Huntington Library, San Marino, CA.

16. *Richmond Daily Dispatch*, June 23, 1862.

17. Ibid.; Brasher, 86–90, 105, 142–45.

18. Glatthaar, 20; Sheehan-Dean, 35.

19. *Richmond Daily Dispatch*, June 23, 1862; on meanings of courage in the Civil War era, see Linderman, *Embattled Courage*.

20. *Charleston Tri-Weekly Courier* (SC), June 26, 1862; *Macon Telegraph* (GA), June 24, 1862; *Houston Tri-Weekly Telegraph*, July 11, 1862; *New York Times*, June 26, 1862. For ad-

ditional Northern coverage of the speech, see *Daily Missouri Republican* (St. Louis), June 30, 1862; *Norwich Morning Bulletin* (CT), June 27, 1862; *Evening Courier and Republic* (Buffalo), July 5, 1862.

21. JL, *FMTA*, 127; Varon, *Armies of Deliverance*, 90–91.

22. JL, "The Seven Days' Fighting About Richmond," 426.

23. Varon, *Armies of Deliverance*, 92.

24. Cutrer, ed., *Longstreet's Aide*, 91, 98; Wert, 150–52; Mendoza, 15; Guelzo, *Robert E. Lee*, 245; Gallagher, "Scapegoat in Victory," 302.

25. Wert, 154–55; *Charleston Tri-Weekly Courier* (SC), July 31, 1862.

26. Harsh, 108–18; Varon, *Armies of Deliverance*, 129–30.

27. Hennessy, 93; Harsh, 134–58.

28. Gallagher, "Scapegoat in Victory," 298 (Longstreet quotation), 305; Mendoza, 15; *OR*, 12, pt. 2, 565.

29. Sorrel, 98; Wert, 172–73, 178; Gallagher, "Scapegoat in Victory," 298 (Longstreet quotation).

30. Harsh, 158–63; JL, "Our March Against Pope," 602, 610; Piston, *Lee's Tarnished Lieutenant*, 32.

31. "The Second Confiscation Act," Freedmen and Southern Society Project online, http://www.freedmen.umd.edu/conact2.htm.

32. *Boston Traveller*, July 26, 1862; *Burlington Daily Times* (VT), July 28, 1862.

33. Harsh, 8–9, 18–19; Varon, *Armies of Deliverance*, 135–37.

34. Weigley, 144–47.

35. JL, "The Invasion of Maryland," 309–10.

36. Weigley, 148–49; JL, "The Invasion of Maryland," 312.

37. Weigley, 151–52.

38. Varon, *Armies of Deliverance*, 140.

39. Wert, 196–99.

40. Varon, *Armies of Deliverance*, 142; *OR*, 19, pt. 1, 840–41 (Longstreet quotations).

41. Osmun Latrobe, diary entry, Sept. 17, 1862, VMHC; Wert, 200, 205–6; Piston, *Lee's Tarnished Lieutenant*, 25.

42. JL to Joseph Johnston, Oct. 6, 1862, James Longstreet Papers, RLD; Mendoza, 17–19; Wert, 206–7, 227; Piston, *Lee's Tarnished Lieutenant*, 27.

43. JL to Joseph Johnston, Oct. 6, 1862, RLD; JL, *FMTA*, 200, 220.

44. Sorrel, 130–31; Rable, *Fredericksburg!*, 32; Knudsen, 63–64.

45. Rable, *Fredericksburg!*, 83–87.

46. Wert, 216; Sorrel, 140.

47. Rable, *Fredericksburg!*, 226–33; *OR*, 21, 570.

48. Latrobe, diary, Dec. 12, 16, 1863, VMHC; *Richmond Daily Dispatch*, December 19, 1862; *Charleston Mercury* (SC), December 27, 1862; Rable, *Fredericksburg!*, 343–53; General Orders No. 53, Dec. 18, 1862, James Longstreet Collection, NYHS; Cooke, 184.

49. The *Inquirer* article was reprinted in papers such as the *Buffalo Commercial*, Nov. 15, 1862, and *New Albany Ledger* (IN), Nov. 19, 1862. For examples of refugee reports see *OR*, 19, pt. 2, 534; *Vermont Phoenix* (Brattleboro), Jan. 1, 1863; on the Walkers, see Crotty, "Confederate Dirty Laundry."

50. JL, *FMTA*, 289; Wyckoff, ed., 230; Moseley, ed., 109. On the enslaving of captured Blacks at Harpers Ferry, see *Macon Telegraph* (GA), Sept. 23, 1862; *New Orleans Times-Picayune*, Sept. 25, 1862; and Gallagher, "The Net Result of the Campaign Was in Our Favor," 14. On Longstreet's visit to the Confederate Congress, see *Raleigh Register* (NC), Feb. 25, 1863; for the final text of the Retaliatory Act, see https:/hd.housedivided .dickinson.edu/node/39620.

51. Wert, 229–34; Piston, *Lee's Tarnished Lieutenant*, 36–37.

52. *OR*, 18, 918.

53. Ibid., 18, 926–27.

54. Wert, 235.

55. *American Citizen* (Canton, MS), May 8, 1863; on Uniontown, see Taylor, 73, 94, and Cormier, 217–18.

56. On Longstreet's preoccupation with securing impressed slave labor, see, for example, *OR*, 42, pt. 3, 1324; for Peck's accounts, see *OR*, 18, 281–82, and Moore, ed., 123–26.

57. *OR*, 18, 954, 966; *New York Herald*, May 12, 1863; *Daily Sun* (Columbus, GA), April 30, 1863. The Eli Johnson story comes to light in the Union Provost Marshal File on Daniel H. Boyd [Byrd], who was wrongly accused of murdering Johnson and demonstrated in his defense that Johnson was executed on Longstreet's orders: see John A. Baker and C. B. Duffreed testimony, Boyd case, 1866, Union Provost Marshal Files of Papers

Relating to Individual Citizens, Union Citizens File, M345, RG 109, NA, accessed through Fold3. On use of the term "negro runners," see Emory Thomas, *The Confederate State of Richmond*, 155.

58. John Bentford File, 1867 (No. B568), Records of the Adjutant General's Office: Letters Received, RG 94, NA.

59. Wert, 239; *OR*, 18, 1049; *Richmond Dispatch*, May 12, 1863.

60. For a critique of Longstreet, see *Richmond Whig*, April 23, 1863; for positive coverage of the Suffolk campaign, see *Camden Confederate* (SC), May 1, 1863 (first and last quotations); *Staunton Spectator* (VA), April 28, 1863 (second quotation); *Macon Telegraph* (GA), May 12, 1863; *Fayetteville Observer* (NC), May 18, 1863; and *Richmond Enquirer*, quoted in *Alexandria Gazette* (VA), May 13, 1863.

Chapter 3: Crossroads at Gettysburg

1. HDL, *Lee and Longstreet at High Tide*, 249–50.

2. Varon, *Armies of Deliverance*, 242.

3. Sears, 13–14; Fremantle, 237, 249; Varon, *Armies of Deliverance*, 242.

4. JL to Louis T. Wigfall, May 13, 1863, Wigfall Papers, LC; Wert, 244–45; Varon, *Armies of Deliverance*, 243–44.

5. Sears, 107–8; David G. Smith, "Race and Retaliation," 147.

6. *Janesville Daily Gazette* (WI), June 25, 1863; Creighton, 127; *Philadelphia Inquirer*, June 19, 1863; *New York Herald*, June 20, 1863.

7. *Franklin Repository* (PA), July 8, 1863; *New York Herald*, July 12, 1863; *OR*, 51, pt. 2, 732–33; David G. Smith, "Race and Retaliation," 137–44; Creighton, 130; *Savannah Republican*, July 6, 1863; David G. Smith, *On the Edge of Freedom*, 190 (quotation).

8. *Savannah Republican*, July 13, 1863; *Richmond Daily Dispatch*, Aug. 8, 1863; *Richmond Enquirer*, Aug. 8, 1863, reprinted in *New York Herald*, Aug. 31, 1863.

9. Sears, 84; Varon, *Armies of Deliverance*, 246.

10. Sears, 115, 150–52; JL, *FMTA*, 324, 332–33; Sorrel, 164.

11. Varon, *Armies of Deliverance*, 246–47.

12. Ibid., 246–47, 249.

13. Pfarr, 22–23; JL, "General Longstreet's Second Paper on Gettysburg," 257–69; JL,

"Lee in Pennsylvania," 421–22; Gallagher, "'If the Enemy Is There, We Must Attack Him,'" 21–22; Fremantle, 256.

14. Allan, 13–14. For overviews of these postwar debates, see especially Gallagher, "'If the Enemy Is There We Must Attack Him,'" 20–22, and Pfarr, 17–27, 39–45 (Lee quotation on 22).

15. Pfarr, 17–27, 39–45; JL, *FMTA*, 331, 358.

16. Pfanz, 26–27.

17. For an example of a strident modern critique of Longstreet, see Krick, 58, 85.

18. Sorrel, 167; Wert, 268; Pfarr, 93–94.

19. JL, *FMTA*, 362–63; Fremantle, 257–58; Alexander, 242.

20. Wert, 262–65 (quotation on 265); Gallagher, "'If the Enemy Is There We Must Attack Him,'" 25.

21. Gragg, ed., 203–4 (first quotation); JL, "Lee in Pennsylvania," 424–25; Sears, 260–63.

22. Lafayette McLaws, quoted in Pfanz, 153–54, 328; Krick, 70–71; Wert, 272; Pfarr, 94.

23. Alexander, 236–37, 240, 242–43, 278.

24. Pfarr, 94; *OR*, 27, pt. 2, 358–59; JL, *FMTA*, 370–74. Pfarr is echoed by Knudsen, *James Longstreet*, 136, whose recent study finds that "all the time spent in getting the troops positioned and in the planning is accounted for and reasonable," and that Lee, "present on Longstreet's side of the field much of the afternoon," was "fully aware of the work going on."

25. JL, *FMTA*, 367; Pfarr, 88–89; Pfanz, 166–67; Gragg, ed., 169 (Hood quotation).

26. JL, *FMTA*, 368.

27. Krick, 70–72; Pfanz, 5.

28. JL, *FMTA*, 370–74, and "Lee in Pennsylvania," 424.

29. JL, "Lee in Pennsylvania," 428–29, and *FMTA*, 387.

30. James B. Walton to JL, Nov. 6, 1877, and JL to James B. Walton, Nov. 23, 1877, Walton-Glenny Family Papers, Historic New Orleans Collection, New Orleans, LA.

31. Hess, *Pickett's Charge*, xv, 9, 23–29; JL, "Lee in Pennsylvania," 430.

32. JL, "Lee in Pennsylvania," 430–31, and *FMTA*, 392; Hess, *Pickett's Charge*, 27, 160–61; Alexander, 254.

33. JL, "Lee in Pennsylvania," 431; Sears, 441.

34. Weigley, 254; Stiles, 219–20; Alexander, 267; Raymer, 88.

35. Fremantle, 269; Allan, 15.

36. Hess, *Pickett's Charge*, 28–29, 32–33, 389; Alexander, 266; Weigley, 255–56; Varon, *Armies of Deliverance*, 271.

37. Guelzo, *Gettysburg*, 381.

38. Pfarr, 150–55; Fremantle, 266.

39. Piston, "Cross Purposes," 46.

40. Pfarr, 22–23; JL, "General Longstreet's Second Paper on Gettysburg," 257–69; JL, *FMTA*, 388.

41. Reardon, *Pickett's Charge*, 31–34, 52–56; Gallagher, "Lee's Army Has Not Lost Any of Its Prestige," 4–6.

42. *OR*, 27, pt. 2, 357–63.

43. Styple, ed., 161–76; Styple's *Writing & Fighting the Confederate War* reprints Alexander's *Savannah Republican* articles from July 20, 21, 27, 30, 1863. On Alexander's influence, see Reardon, *Pickett's Charge*, 57.

44. Styple, ed., 161–76.

45. See, for example, *Richmond Enquirer*, July 24, 1863, and *Richmond Dispatch*, April 15, 1864; Reardon, *Pickett's Charge*, 55–57.

46. Wert, 298–302 (Longstreet quotation on 301); *Richmond Enquirer*, Sept. 18, 1863.

Chapter 4: Toward Appomattox

1. *OR*, 29, pt. 2, 699.

2. *OR*, 29, pt. 2, 699; Mendoza, 22–23.

3. Wert, 303; Varon, *Armies of Deliverance*, 286–87.

4. Wert, 300; Mendoza, 23, 25–26; *OR*, 29, pt. 2, 713–14.

5. Mendoza, 33–35; Varon, *Armies of Deliverance*, 286–87.

6. Cozzens, 310; Varon, *Armies of Deliverance*, 286–87.

7. Cozzens, 315–16, 368 (quotation on 315); Wert, 310–21 (quotations on 311, 321); Mendoza, 41–49.

8. *OR*, 29, pt. 2, 749; *OR*, 30, pt. 4, 705–6; *Richmond Daily Dispatch*, Oct. 5, 1863. Longstreet would later describe the battle, in his memoirs, as the "first pronounced victory in the West and one of the most stubbornly contested battles of the war." JL, *FMTA*, 456.

9. *Richmond Daily Dispatch*, Nov. 12, 1863; *OR*, 30, pt. 4, 705–6; JL to D. H. Hill, Oct. 18, 1863, GLI.

10. *OR*, 30, pt. 2, 289–90; Varon, *Armies of Deliverance*, 287.

11. Mendoza, 63; Wert, 326–28; Sorrel, 200; JL, *FMTA*, 466–68.

12. *OR*, 31, pt. 3, 634.

13. *OR*, 31, pt. 3, 635; *OR*, 52, pt. 2, 559–60; Hess, *The Knoxville Campaign*, 31; Mendoza, 118.

14. Hess, *The Knoxville Campaign*, 95, 105–110.

15. *OR*, 31, pt. 3, 719.

16. Wert, 359–60; *OR*, 31, pt. 1, 455–66. On Longstreet's dismissal of Major General Lafayette McLaws and the bitter trial and testimony that ensued, see Wert, 360–65.

17. Varon, *Armies of Deliverance*, 291.

18. *OR*, 31, pt. 1, 467–68; Wert, 360.

19. JL to Col. W. Preston Johnston, Dec. 6, 1863, and JL to Gen. S. Cooper, Dec. 8, 1863, Letters and Telegrams Sent, Gen. James Longstreet's Command, Oct. 1863–March 1865, chap. 2, vol. 277, Record Books of Executive, Legislative, and Judicial Offices of the Confederate Government, 1874–1879, Record Group 109: War Department Collection of Confederate Records, NA, referred to hereafter as vol. 277, RG 109; JL to Cooper, Jan. 2, 1864, Confidential Letters and Telegrams Sent, Gen. James Longstreet's Command, Feb. 1863–Feb. 1865, chap. 2, vol. 269, pt. 1, Record Books of Executive, Legislative, and Judicial Offices of the Confederate Government, 1874–1879, Record Group 109, NA, referred to hereafter as vol. 269/1, RG 109; JL to Cooper, Jan. 19, 1864, Letters Sent, Gen. James Longstreet's Command, Jan. 1864–Feb. 1865, chap. 2, vol. 276, Record Books of Executive, Legislative, and Judicial Offices of the Confederate Government, 1874–1879, Record Group 109, NA, referred to hereafter as vol. 276, RG 109; Wert, 367.

20. Wert, 371; JL, *FMTA*, 328, 466, 481–82; *OR*, 31, pt. 3, 680.

21. JL, *FMTA*, 466.

22. Mendoza, xix–xx; JL, General Orders No. 11, Dec. 16, 1863, Civil War Military Records Digital Collection, Tennessee State Library and Archives.

23. Varon, *Armies of Deliverance*, 307–8.

24. JL to Maj. Gen. John G. Foster, January 3, 1864, vol. 269/1, RG 109; Wert, 367.

25. JL to Foster, Jan. 11, 1864, vol. 276, RG 109; *Richmond Daily Dispatch*, Jan. 30, 1864; Varon, *Armies of Deliverance*, 307–8.

26. *Richmond Daily Dispatch*, March 2, 1864; Cutrer, ed., *Longstreet's Aide*, 116–17.

27. JL to James Seddon, Feb. 22, 1864; JL to Robert E. Lee, Feb. 27, March 4, 1864; JL to P. G. T. Beauregard, March 7, 1864, all in vol. 269/2, RG 109; Gallagher, *Becoming Confederates*, 21, 24; Wert, 369.

28. *OR*, 32, pt. 3, 637–42; JL to A. R. Lawton, March 5, 1864, and JL to Cooper, March 19, 1864, vol. 269/2, RG 109.

29. JL to Brig. Gen. T. Jordan, March 27, 1864, vol. 269/2, RG 109; Varon, *Armies of Deliverance*, 352–53, 370–71.

30. Wert, 370–72; JL to Lee, April 1, 1864, vol. 269/1, RG 109; Alexander, 345–46; Glatthaar, 363.

31. JL to ABL, May 2, 1864, Nau Collection, UVA.

32. Porter, 47 (Longstreet quotation); Dunkerly et al., 10–12; Wert, 380–84.

33. Wert, 385; *Richmond Daily Dispatch*, May 7, 1864; James Longstreet Confederate Pension Application, Georgia Archives Virtual Vault, University of Georgia System, https:// vault.georgiaarchives.org/; Steckler and Blachley, 357; Dawson, 116.

34. Wert, 389–92; JL to M. L. Bonham, July 16, 1864, GLI; Sorrel, 274; Blackford and Blackford, 261–62.

35. Sorrel, 257–58.

36. Powers, 75, 181–87; Varon, *Armies of Deliverance*, 331–38.

37. Wert, 392; Varon, *Armies of Deliverance*, 345–47, 385–90.

38. Powers, 192, 210–11; Sorrel, 274; JL, *FMTA*, 574.

39. *Sumter Republican* (Americus, GA), Oct. 29, 1864.

40. Wert, 394–96; Latrobe, diary, typescript, 4, VMHC; JL to Colonel Charles Marshall, Oct. 31, 1864, and JL to Lee, Feb. 14, 1865, vol. 269/1, RG 109; *OR*, 46, pt. 2, 1250, 1258.

41. JL to Marshall, Oct. 31, 1864, and JL to Lee, Feb. 14, 1865, vol. 269/1, RG 109; *OR*, 46, pt. 2, 1250, 1258; General Orders No. 21, Nov. 20, 1864, issued by command of James Longstreet, Nau Collection, UVA.

42. Levine, 27–30 (Cleburne quotation on 27); Varon, *Armies of Deliverance*, 390–91. Longstreet's views were conveyed to his fellow Confederate generals through Osmun Latrobe, *OR*, 46, pt. 2, 1236.

43. Levine, 51, 95, 101, 125; *OR*, 46, pt. 2, 1237.

44. Varon, *Armies of Deliverance*, 390–91; Levine, 119–21; JL, *FMTA*, 653.

45. Washington A. Roebling to Emily, March 30, 1864, Washington A. Roebling Family Letters, Brooklyn Public Library, NY; Jeter, 84; *Richmond Daily Dispatch*, March 29, 1865.

46. JL, *FMTA*, 646 (Lee quotation).

47. JL, *FMTA*, 583–84; Schulte, "A 'Visionary' Plan?, Part 2."

48. Schulte, "A 'Visionary' Plan?, Part 3" and "A 'Visionary' Plan?, Part 4"; JL, *FMTA*, 584–87; Ulysses S. Grant to E. O. C. Ord, Feb. 24, 27, 1865, *PUSG*, vol. 14, Feb. 21–April 30, 1865, 34–35, 63–64. On Longstreet's desire to meet Grant, see *OR*, ser. 2, 8, 315.

49. JL, *FMTA*, 585–88; *OR*, 46, pt. 2, 825, 1275–76; Grant to Edwin M. Stanton, March 3, 4, 1865, and Grant to Lee, March 4, 1865, *PUSG*, vol. 14, 90–91, 98–100.

50. *Richmond Daily Dispatch*, March 15, 1865; *Evening Star* (Washington, DC), March 20, 21, 1865; *State Journal* (Alexandria, VA), March 21, 1865; *New Orleans Picayune*, April 2, 1865; *Philadelphia Inquirer*, March 22, 23, 1865; Varon, *Appomattox*, 25–28; JL, *FMTA*, 586–87, 647–48.

51. Stanton's March 3, 1865, letter on the Ord-Longstreet meeting, containing Lincoln's instructions—explaining to Grant that the president and not military leaders would resolve political issues—was a template for the Appomattox surrender terms. Varon, *Appomattox*, 30–33.

52. Carmichael, "A Whole Lot of Blame to Go Around," 92–93, 99.

53. Varon, "The Fall of Petersburg and Appomattox," 606–9.

54. Ibid., 608–9; JL, *FMTA*, 618.

55. JL, *FMTA*, 619; Varon, *Armies of Deliverance*, 400–404.

56. Varon, *Appomattox*, 25; JL, *FMTA*, 618–21.

57. Ulysses S. Grant, *Personal Memoirs of U. S. Grant*, 595; *OR*, 46, pt. 3, 619; JL, *FMTA*, 619; Varon, *Appomattox*, 28–29.

58. John Brown Gordon, *Reminiscences of the Civil War*, 435–35; Fitzhugh Lee to R. E. Lee, April 22, 1865, Papers of Fitzhugh Lee, UVA; Varon, *Appomattox*, 37–38.

59. JL, *FMTA*, 626–27; Cutrer, ed., *Longstreet's Aide*, 166–67; Varon, *Appomattox*, 45–46.

60. JL, *FMTA*, 624, 627–28; Varon, *Appomattox*, 51–52.

61. Varon, *Appomattox*, 53–60; Grant, *Personal Memoirs*, 596–608.

62. Varon, *Appomattox*, 61–71; Janney, *Ends of War*, 27.

63. Grant, *Personal Memoirs*, 101, 114–119, 601; *OR*, 46, pt. 1, 1267; Lee, *Memoirs*, 414; Varon, "Fall of Petersburg and Appomattox," 613.

64. Varon, *Appomattox*, 68–73, 112.

65. Varon, "Fall of Petersburg and Appomattox," 614–15; Bergeron, ed., *The Papers of Andrew Johnson*, 22.

66. *New York Times*, July 24, 1885; *Philadelphia Times*, May 15, 1892; Wert, 403–4; Varon, "*From Manassas to Appomattox*," 23. On the agreement reached by the commissioners that day—most notably the provision that after stacking their arms and flags Confederates were to march home under charge of their officers—see Janney, *Ends of War*, 32, 52–53.

67. Cutrer, ed., *Longstreet's Aide*, 160; Varon, *Appomattox*, 169–74.

68. *Richmond Daily Dispatch*, March 29, 1865.

69. *Baltimore Sun*, April 15, 1865; JL and Lee to Latrobe, April 11, 1865, appended to Latrobe, diary, VMHC.

Chapter 5: Burying the Past

1. JL, *FMTA*, 636–37; Varon, *Appomattox*, 239–41.

2. Janney, *Ends of War*, 32, 52–53; *Weekly Inter Ocean* (Chicago), Feb. 26, 1880.

3. Wert, 407–8; Cutrer, ed., *Longstreet's Aide*, 145–47.

4. Janney, *Ends of War*, 215.

5. Ibid.; calendar entries, May 28, 1865, *PUSG*, vol. 15, 494–95; *OR*, 46, pt. 3, 1218; *Daily Constitutional Union* (Washington, DC), June 3, 1865; *Cleveland Daily Leader*, June 9, 1865; *Brooklyn Union*, June 3, 1865; *Hartford Courant*, June 6, 1865; *Weekly Republican* (Plymouth, IN), June 15, 1865.

6. Cutrer, ed., *Longstreet's Aide*, 143–48; on Hairston, see, for example, "The Richest Man in Virginia," *De Bow's Review* 18 (Jan. 1855), 53.

7. Cutrer, ed., *Longstreet's Aide*, 149–52. James Longstreet Sr.'s 1830 will had divided his property equally among his children and named his wife, Mary Ann, brother Augustus, and eldest son, William, as executors. Smedes and Marshall, 467–68. The 1850 census shows Longstreet's widowed mother owning fourteen slaves in Noxubee County, Mississippi, where she had settled, and the 1860 Noxubee census shows her son William D. Longstreet owning thirty-nine slaves. Mary A. Longstreet entry, 1850 US Federal Census, Slave Schedule; Wm. D. Longstreet, 1860 US Federal Census Slave Schedule— both for Noxubee County, Mississippi, NA.

8. JL, *FMTA*, 638; Cockrum, 302–4; R. Ruff, Wm. D. Longstreet, E. Dismukes, and C. B. Ames entries, 1860 US Federal Census Slave Schedule for Noxubee County; Dan Longstreet entry, 1880 Federal Census for Noxubee County, NA. On Black Longstreets and Dismukeses, see, for example, Joseph Longstreet entry, 1870 US Federal Census, and Nancy Longstreet entry, 1880. On Noxubee County during Reconstruction, see *National Anti-Slavery Standard* (New York), May 13, 1871. On J. W. Longstreet, see, for example, *Weekly Mississippi Pilot* (Jackson), Sept. 18, 1875; *Clarion-Ledger* (Jackson, MS), May 12, 1880; and J. W. Longstreet to Blanche K. Bruce, Dec. 30, 1877, Jan. 2, 1878, April 10, 1880, Blanche K. Bruce Papers, Moorland-Spingarn Research Center, Howard University, Washington, DC.

9. Wert, 408–9; *South-Western* (Shreveport, LA), Jan. 24, 1866.

10. Bergeron, *Andrew Johnson's Civil War*, 75.

11. Varon, *Appomattox*, 200–202; JL to Grant, June 8, 1865, and Aug. 30, 1865, *PUSG*, vol. 15, 523, 594; Janney, *Ends of War*, 221, 225.

12. JL to Andrew Johnson, Nov. 7, 1865, and Grant to Johnson, Nov. 7, 1865, James Longstreet Pardon Application, Confederate Amnesty Papers, 1865–1867, RG 94: Records of the Adjutant General's Office, 1762–1984, NA; *Chicago Tribune*, Sept. 24, 1865; *New Orleans Picayune*, Nov. 26, 1865.

13. *Vermont Record* (Brandon), Sept. 30, 1865; *Baltimore Sun*, Nov. 3, 1865; *Little Rock Gazette* (AR), Nov. 14, 1865; *New Orleans Picayune*, Nov. 26, 1865; *Cleveland Daily Herald*, Nov. 18, 1865.

14. Sanger and Hay, 322; *New Orleans Times*, Nov. 14, 1865.

15. Wert, 409–10; Janney, *Ends of War*, 251; Maria Louisa Longstreet to Andrew Johnson, Sept. 20, 1865, in Maria Louisa Longstreet Pardon Application, RG 94, NA; Grant to Adam Badeau, Dec. 26, 1865, in *PUSG*, vol. 15, 402.

16. Varon, *Appomattox*, 192–95.

17. Foner, *A Short History of Reconstruction*, 94–95.

18. *New Orleans Times*, Dec. 29, 1865; *Milwaukee Daily Sentinel*, Dec. 19, 1865.

19. *Daily Richmond Examiner*, Feb. 6, 1866; *Evening Telegraph* (Philadelphia), June 19, 1866; *New Orleans Picayune*, Nov. 3, 1866.

20. *New Orleans Crescent*, June 1, 1866; *New Orleans Picayune*, Oct. 28, 1866.

21. Nystrom, "Reconstruction"; on the Afro-Creole population, see also Ross, 5–6, 27–29, 31 (quotations on 27 and 31); Daggett, xiii.

22. Varon, *Armies of Deliverance*, 340.

23. Ibid.; Tunnell, 76.

24. On Louisiana's Black Union officers, see Hollandsworth, 110–11, and Weaver, ed., xvi.

25. Tunnell, 103–6, 113 (quotation); Egerton, 208–9 (quotation on 209).

26. Tunnell, 107–13.

27. Rable, *But There Was No Peace*, 60, 68; Early as quoted in Gallagher, *Becoming Confederates*, 79.

28. *New Orleans Times*, March 19, 1867; Wert, 410–11; Richter, 216–17.

29. *New Orleans Times*, March 19, April 7, 1867.

30. *Richmond Daily Dispatch*, March 27, 1867; *Columbia Daily Phoenix* (SC), March 28, 1867; *Macon Weekly Telegraph* (GA), June 21, 1867 (Semmes quotation).

31. *Augusta Constitutionalist* (GA), quoted in *Macon Weekly Telegraph* (GA), April 5, 1867; *Memphis Public Ledger*, March 22, 1867.

32. *New Orleans Republican*, May 17, 1867; *New Orleans Times*, June 8, 1867.

33. *New Orleans Times*, June 8, 1867. (The June 3 and 7 letters appear in the June 8 issue.)

34. Ibid., June 8, 1867.

35. *Macon Weekly Telegraph* (GA), June 21, 1867.

36. *Louisiana Democrat* (Alexandria, LA), June 19, 1867; *Wheeling Daily Intelligencer* (WV), July 19, 1867; *Wheeling Daily Register* (WV), July 23, 1867.

37. *Charleston Mercury* (SC), quoted in *Macon Weekly Telegraph* (GA), June 28, 1867; *Mobile Daily Tribune* (AL), quoted in *Bossier Banner* (Bellevue, LA), July 6, 1867.

38. Varon, *Appomattox*, 69–71.

39. Wetta, 16, 51–52, 140–41, 183–86.

40. Ibid., 164–66.

41. *New York Times*, April 5, 1867; *San Francisco Daily Evening Bulletin*, April 25, 1867; *North American and United States Gazette* (Philadelphia), June 13, 1867; *Milwaukee Daily Sentinel*, April 17, 1867.

42. JL to Benjamin F. Butler, June 27, 1867, Benjamin F. Butler Papers, LC; Leonard, 121.

43. *New Orleans Republican*, June 11, 16, 1867; *Union Flag* (Jonesborough, TN), June 21, 1867.

44. *New Hampshire Patriot and Gazette* (Concord), June 19, 1867; Chauncey Burr, "The South and Her Faltering Men" and "Editor's Table," *Old Guard*, Aug. 1867, 615–25, and Nov. 1868, 878–80, respectively.

45. Wert, 412–13; Piston, *Lee's Tarnished Lieutenant*, 106–8 (Longstreet quotation on 106); *New Orleans Tribune*, quoted in *Lowell Daily Citizen and News* (MA), June 13, 1867; Richter, 229.

46. *New Orleans Times*, April 7, 1867.

47. JL to John G. Walker, May 25, 1866, GLI.

48. Sanger and Hay, 334–35 (quotations), 336–37.

49. Ibid.; JL to Robert E. Lee, June 8, 1867, James Longstreet Papers, RDL.

50. *Advance* (Chicago), June 3, 1869; Keckley, 243–44.

51. Sanger and Hay, 341.

52. Grant to JL, April 16, 1867, *PUSG*, vol. 17, 116–17; Grant to Thaddeus Stevens, April 30, 1868, *PUSG*, vol. 18, 241; Sanger and Hay, 341–42.

53. *Troy Times* (NY) interview, reprinted in *Daily Evening Express* (Lancaster, PA), Feb. 10, 1869; *New Orleans Advocate*, March 13, 1869; JL to William J. Fowler, June 7, 1894, GLI.

54. Waugh, 109; Wert, 413; Varon, *Appomattox*, 245–46; *New York Tribune*, Aug. 24, 1868.

55. Caryn Cossé Bell, 154; Tunnell, *Crucible of Reconstruction*, 116–19.

56. Rodrigue, xvi–xl; Vincent, "Oscar Dunn"; Nystrom, "P. B. S. Pinchback."

57. *New York Tribune*, Aug. 24, 1868.

58. Ibid. On Johnson's use of the "Black rule" trope, see Varon, "Andrew Johnson."

59. ABL, "From Out the Fires," *XIX Century* (Dec. 1869), 543–49, and "Review of Perry's Sketch of J. C. Calhoun," *XIX Century* (Jan. 1870), 623.

60. *Mobile Daily Tribune* (AL) in *Ripley Bee* (OH), Sept. 16, 1868; JL, Nov. 1868 letter in *Boston Daily Advertiser*, Dec. 29, 1868; *Daily Cleveland Herald*, Dec. 30, 1868.

61. *New Orleans Republican*, Dec. 8, 1868; *New Orleans Tribune*, Feb. 10, 24, 1869; Sanger and Hay, 335.

62. *Mobile Tribune* (AL), quoted in *Ripley Bee* (OH), Sept. 16, 1868; *New Orleans Republican*, Dec. 8, 1868; *New Orleans Advocate*, Dec. 19, 1868.

63. Tunnell, 153–57 (quotation on 153).

64. For a roundup of the press coverage, see *New Orleans Advocate*, March 27, 1869; for examples of both the nepotism and olive branch arguments, see *Cincinnati Commercial*, March 20, 29, 1869.

65. *Boston Daily Advertiser*, March 13, 1869; *New Orleans Advocate*, March 27, 1869; *Buffalo Commercial*, March 15, 1869; *Philadelphia Post*, quoted in *Milwaukee Daily Sentinel*, March 18, 1869; *Wyoming Democrat* (Tunkhannock, PA), March 17, 1869; *Quincy Whig* (MA), April 10, 1869.

66. JL to Grant, March 31, 1868, *PUSG*, vol. 19, 405; *New York Herald*, April 1, 3, 1869; *Harrisburg Telegraph* (PA), April 5, 1869.

67. *New York Times*, April 20, 1869; *Christian Recorder* (Philadelphia), May 1, 1869; *Boston Daily Advertiser*, May 15, 1869.

68. Rankin, 422, 436; *New Orleans Times*, April 15, 1869; *New Orleans Crescent*, March 14, 16, April 15, 1869; *Atlanta Constitution*, April 11, 1869; Ross, 17.

69. Sanger and Hay, 341; Orleans Parish (La.) Seventh District Court. *State of Virginia v. James Longstreet*, 1872, New Orleans Public Library, New Orleans, LA.

70. Orleans Parish (LA) Seventh District Court. *State of Virginia v. James Longstreet*, 1872; United States, *Register of Civil, Military, and Naval Service*, 102.

71. Nystrom, *New Orleans After the Civil War*, 83–87 (quotations on 83).

72. Brook, 180–81; Ross, 38–39, 47; Nystrom, *New Orleans After the Civil War*, 36–37, 75–89; Hogue, *Uncivil War*, 66–67. While New Orleans led the way, both chronologically and numerically, in the integration of its police force, by the 1870s, Blacks were serving as police officers under Republican administrations in cities such as Montgomery, Alabama; Vicksburg, Mississippi; Charleston, South Carolina; and Houston, Texas. Dulaney, 12–13.

73. Tunnell, 117, 167; *New Orleans Tribune*, Jan. 30, 1869.

74. *Charleston Tri-Weekly Courier* (SC), Sept. 7, 1869.

75. *Wisconsin State Journal* (Madison), July 30, 1869; *New Orleans Picayune*, Aug. 4, 1869; *Pittsburgh Weekly Gazette*, Aug. 30, 1869; *Burlington Free Press* (VT), Sept. 1, 1869; Michael W. Fitzgerald, *Urban Emancipation*, 170–74, 180–84 (quotation on 184).

76. Rawick, ed., 483–85; United States, *Register of Civil, Military, and Naval Service*, 103.

77. *Times-Argus* (Selma, AL), Aug. 4, 1869; *Weston Democrat* (WV), Sept. 27, 1869; *New*

Orleans Picayune, Aug. 26, 1861; *Independent Monitor* (Tuscaloosa, AL), Oct. 5, 1869; Rosen, 140; *Eagle* (Fayetteville, NC), Sept. 30, 1869.

78. *New Orleans Picayune*, Jan. 29, 1870; *New Orleans Republican*, March 25, 1870.

79. *New Orleans Republican*, April 16, 19, 30, 1870.

80. Ibid., April 30, May 1, 4, 1870.

81. Ibid., May 1, 1870; *South-Western* (Shreveport, LA), May 11, 1870; *Daily Standard* (Raleigh, NC), May 18, 1870.

82. *South-Western* (Shreveport, LA), May 11, 1870; *New Orleans Picayune*, May 1, 1870; *Daily Standard* (Raleigh, NC), May 18, 1870; *Lowell Daily Citizen* (MA), May 16, 1870; *Fall River Daily Evening News* (MA), May 14, 1870.

Chapter 6: Radical Republican

1. Hogue, *Uncivil War*, 68–69; Tunnell, 161. Longstreet's appointment not only represented an opportunity to play a more central role in Republican politics but also augmented his federal surveyor salary, promising a measure of financial security. Sawyer, 68.

2. Nystrom, *New Orleans After the Civil War*, 89.

3. Emberton, 617–21; Rable, *But There Was No Peace*, 103.

4. Hogue, *Uncivil War*, 68–69; Nystrom, *New Orleans After the Civil War*, 89; Tunnell, 161; Hogue, "The Strange Career of Jim Longstreet," 159.

5. Hogue, *Uncivil War*, 70–74; Louisiana Adjutant General's Office, *Annual Report for 1870*, 6–10.

6. Hogue, *Uncivil War*, 70–74 (quote on 74); Louisiana Adjutant General's Office, *Annual Report for 1870*, 6–10.

7. Louisiana Adjutant General's Office, *Annual Report for 1870*, 6–10; Hogue, *Uncivil War*, 70, 73; Nystrom, *New Orleans After the Civil War*, 89, 96–98, 101; Rankin, 436–40; A. E. Perkins, 523–28.

8. For additional biographical details on Barber, see *Weekly Louisianian* (New Orleans), Oct. 30, 1875; *New Orleans Republican*, April 30, 1870; Vincent, *Black Legislators*, 32, 42, 121–22 (first quotation on 121), 126–27, 160–64; Hogue, *Uncivil War*, 70–74 (second quotation on 70), 73; Louisiana Adjutant General's Office, *Annual Report for 1872*, 48; Rankin, 417–40.

9. *New Orleans Picayune*, May 15, June 16, 19, July 12, 19, 1870; *Charleston Tri-Weekly Courier* (SC), May 24, 1870; *Fayetteville Observer* (TN), July 21, 1870.

10. Louisiana Adjutant General's Office, *Annual Report for 1870*, 39–40; *New Orleans Republican*, Oct. 22, 1870.

11. *New Orleans Republican*, Oct. 23, 25, Nov. 5, 1870; Hogue, *Uncivil War*, 122.

12. Louisiana Adjutant General's Office, *Annual Report for 1870*, 3–4, 5, 39–40.

13. Tunnell, 164; *New Orleans Republican*, Nov. 22, 1870.

14. Devore, 39–50; *Weekly Louisianian* (New Orleans), March 12, 1871; Brook, 134–45.

15. *Weekly Louisianian* (New Orleans), March 30, 1871; *New Orleans Republican*, March 7, Oct. 10, 1872, Jan. 10, July 3, 1873; *New Orleans Picayune*, Dec. 11, 1873.

16. *Weekly Louisianian* (New Orleans), April 27, 1871; Devore, 40.

17. *Daily Phoenix* (Columbia, SC), Nov. 6, 1870; JL to Lawrence M. Duncan, Nov. 30, 1870 (misdated 1890), Special Collections, Tulane University, New Orleans; *New Orleans Picayune*, Dec. 17, 1870.

18. *Philadelphia Inquirer*, Jan. 21, 1871; *American Missionary* (New York), Feb. 2, 1871; *Daily Telegraph* (Monroe, LA), Feb. 20, 1871.

19. JL to Grant, Nov. 18, 1870; JL to Warmoth, Jan. 19, 1871, Warmoth Papers, UNC; Vincent, *Black Legislators in Louisiana*, 8–10, 58, 79, 115.

20. JL to Grant, Nov. 18, 1870; JL to Warmoth, Jan. 19, 1871, Warmoth Papers, UNC; Nystrom, *New Orleans After the Civil War*, 103–4.

21. JL to Warmoth, July 8, 1871, Warmoth Papers, UNC.

22. Tunnell, 169–70; Nystrom, *New Orleans After the Civil War*, 107; *Weekly Louisianian* (New Orleans), Aug. 20, 1871; *Cincinnati Commercial* interview reprinted in *New Orleans Republican*, Sept. 2, 1871.

23. Hogue, *Uncivil War*, 80–82.

24. Nystrom, *New Orleans After the Civil War*, 108; Hogue, *Uncivil War*, 83; Sanger and Hay, 356 (quotation).

25. Hogue, *Uncivil War*, 84–85; Wetta, 140–46 (quotations on 140 and 142).

26. Tunnell, 170; Nystrom, *New Orleans After the Civil War*, 109–11; JL to William H. Emory, Jan. 8, 1872, in US House, *Testimony Taken by Select Committee*, House Misc. Doc. 211, 81–82; *New Orleans Republican*, Jan. 9, 1872.

27. *New Orleans Republican*, Jan. 9, 1872; Emberton, 622–23.

28. Tunnell, 170–71; Hogue, *Uncivil War*, 91–95; Nystrom, "P. B. S. Pinchback"; Pinchback to Warmoth, Sept. 11, 1872, Warmoth Papers, UNC.

29. Tunnell, 170–71; Hogue, *Uncivil War*, 91–95; Nystrom, *New Orleans After the Civil War*, 131–33; "P. B. S. Pinchback"; and "Battle of Liberty Place" (quotations).

30. JL to Warmoth and Warmoth to JL, April 19, 1872, Warmoth Papers, UNC.

31. *New Orleans Republican*, May 28, 1872; Nystrom, *New Orleans After the Civil War*, 128; JL to Warmoth, April 19, 1872, Warmoth Papers, UNC; Sanger and Hay, 359; *New York Times*, Oct. 20, 1872.

32. *Weekly Louisianian* (New Orleans), Nov. 2, 1872; JL quotation from *New York Herald* in *New Orleans Picayune*, July 31, 1872; James Lewis to P. B. S. Pinchback, Aug. 27, 1872, Pinckney Benton Stewart Pinchback Papers, Moorland-Spingarn Research Center, Howard University, Washington, DC.

33. JL to Governor Warmoth, Nov. 16, 1872, Warmoth Papers, UNC; JL Deposition, Jan. 27, 1873; and Durrell Court Order Dec. 6, 1872, in US Senate, *Louisiana Investigation, Pt. 2*, Senate Doc. 457, 251-54, 442.

34. William P. Kellogg to George H. Williams, Nov. 27, 1872; US Commissioner Jewett to George H. Williams, Nov. 11, 1872; James F. Casey to U. S. Grant, Dec. 11, 1872; S. B. Packard to George H. Williams, Dec. 15, 1872; "Address to the President and People of the United States, from the Republicans of Louisiana," Jan. 6, 1873, in US House, *Condition of Affairs in Louisiana*, House Exec. Doc. 91, 1–6, 19 (Casey quotation), 51–59, 103–23.

35. *New Orleans Times*, Dec. 8, July 12, 29, 1872; Casey to U. S. Grant, Dec. 11, 1872, and "Address to the President and People of the United States," in US House, *Condition of Affairs in Louisiana*, House Exec. Doc. 91, 19, 108, 121.

36. Hogue, *Uncivil War*, 96–100 (quotation on 98); *New York Times*, Dec. 14, 1872; *New Orleans Republican*, Dec. 14, 1872. On the Washington Artillery, see J. B. Walton et al., 210–17.

37. "Address to the President and People of the United States," in US House, *Condition of Affairs in Louisiana*, House Exec. Doc. 91, 105, 109; *Shreveport Times* (LA), Nov. 14, 16, 1872; *New York Herald*, Jan. 11, 1873; *Carlisle American Volunteer* (PA), Jan. 16, 1873; John Lynch Testimony, Jan. 29, 1873, in US Senate, *Louisiana Investigation, Pt. 2*, Senate Doc. 457, 444–45.

38. *New York Times*, Jan. 24, 1873; Hogue, *Uncivil War*, 100–103 (quotation 101).

39. Nystrom, *New Orleans After the Civil War*, 136, numbers the Ogden militia forces at 500–600, and Hogue, *Uncivil War*, 105, at 200; Nystrom, "Battle of Liberty Place"; William P. Kellogg to U. S. Grant, March 5, 1873, quotation in *PUSG*, vol. 24, 54.

40. *New Orleans Republican*, March 7, 1873; *Harper's Weekly*, March 22, 1873; *New York Daily Herald*, March 7, 1873.

41. Kellogg, *Annual Message of His Excellency Governor Wm. Pitt Kellogg to the General Assembly of Louisiana*, 21–22; Louisiana Adjutant General's Office, *Annual Report for 1873*, 1–7, 19, 43–45, 75.

42. Hogue, *Uncivil War*, 109–12; Tunnell, 192; Lemann, 14–23; Keith, *The Colfax Massacre*, 95–98.

43. US House, *Condition of Affairs in the South*, House Report 261, pt. 3, 16, 475 (R. R. Marr testimony); 263–64 (Kellogg testimony); *New Orleans Picayune*, May 8, 1873.

44. "History of the Riot at Colfax," in US House, *Condition of Affairs in Louisiana*, House Report 261, 891–99; Lane, *The Day Freedom Died*, 59–62 (quotation on 58); *New Orleans Picayune*, May 8, 1873.

45. Tunnell, 193; Hogue, *Uncivil War*, 124. The Cruikshank ruling reinforced the message sent by the Supreme Court in the *Slaughter-House Cases*—an earlier decision that had come down on April 14, 1874, just one day after the Colfax massacre. In these property rights cases, the court had ruled that a group of Louisiana butchers could not use the Fourteenth Amendment's citizenship protections to break the monopoly the Louisiana legislature had granted to one favored slaughterhouse; the decision, upholding Louisiana state law, weakened the scope of the Fourteenth Amendment by holding that states retained jurisdiction over their citizens and the enforcing of civil rights.

46. Hogue, *Uncivil War*, 124–26 (quotation on 124); Tunnell, 197–202; Lane, 216–19.

47. *New Orleans Picayune*, Jan. 17, 1874; *New Orleans Republican*, Feb. 24, March 21, 1874.

48. Kamen, 315–18.

49. Shinn Jr., 177–78; *San Francisco Daily Evening Bulletin*, Nov. 6, 1873; *New Orleans Republican*, Nov. 11, 1873; *Boston Daily Advertiser*, Dec. 27, 1873.

50. *New Orleans Republican*, Nov. 20, 23, Dec. 9, 1873; *Weekly Louisianian* (New Orleans), March 21, 1874.

Chapter 7: The Canal Street Coup, 1874

1. *New Orleans Bulletin*, July 2, 1874.

2. Douglass also praised one of Barber's officers, Captain A. L. Boree, "the grandson of General Dessaline [*sic*]," one of the leaders of the Haitian Revolution, for still bearing "the lineaments of the great General from whom he is descended." *Weekly Louisianian* (New Orleans), April 21, 1872; *New Orleans Republican*, Nov. 14, 1873, Jan. 15, Feb. 5, 22, May 31, 1874; *New Orleans Bulletin*, July 2, 1874; Itkin, 62–64; Vincent, *Black Legislators in Louisiana*, 126–27, 160–64. On Chester, see Blackett, ed., pp. 74–79. On the white press's portrayal of Barber and Chester, see, for example, *New Orleans Picayune*, Jan. 9, 15, 17, 24, March 26, May 31, 1874; *New Orleans Bulletin*, May 1, June 2, 1874.

3. *New Orleans Picayune*, May 31, 1874; *New Orleans Bulletin*, June 2, 1874.

4. *New Orleans Republican*, July 1, 1874; *New Orleans Bulletin*, July 1, 1874; *New Orleans Picayune*, July 1, 1874; Nystrom, *New Orleans After the Civil War*, 163–64; Blackett, ed., 77.

5. *New Orleans Republican*, July 1, 2, 1874; *New Orleans Bulletin*, July 1, 1874; *New Orleans Picayune*, July 1, 5, 1874; *Shreveport Times* (LA), July 8, 1874; Nystrom, *New Orleans After the Civil War*, 163–64.

6. Nystrom, *New Orleans After the Civil War*, 165, 168; Badger testimony in US House, *Conditions of Affairs in the South*, House Report 261, pt. 3, 399; on Walton, see James B. Walton to JL, Nov. 23, 1877, Walton-Glenny Family Papers, Historic New Orleans Collection; *New Orleans Crescent*, May 9, 1861; *New Orleans Picayune*, Oct. 2, 1874.

7. Nystrom, *New Orleans After the Civil War*, 165, 168; Badger testimony in US House, *Conditions of Affairs in the South*, House Report 261, pt. 3, 399; *New Orleans Republican*, Sept. 11, 1874.

8. *Inter Ocean* (Chicago), Sept. 14, 1874; *New Orleans Bulletin*, Sept. 13, 1874; Nystrom, *New Orleans After the Civil War*, 169.

9. Hogue, *Uncivil War*, 134–35; Nystrom, *New Orleans After the Civil War*, 172–73; *New Orleans Picayune*, Sept. 15, 1874.

10. Hogue, *Uncivil War*, 134–35; Nystrom, *New Orleans After the Civil War*, 172–73; S. B. Packard telegrams to Attorney General Williams, Sept. 14, 1874, in US Senate, *Message of the President, Communicating Information on Alleged Interference in Organiza-*

tion of General Assembly of Louisiana. Senate Exec. Doc. 13, 13–14; Kellogg testimony, Jan. 6, 1875, US House, *Condition of Affairs in Louisiana*, House Report 101, 199.

11. *New Orleans Republican*, Sept. 20, 1874; Nystrom, "Battle of Liberty Place."

12. For Longstreet's firsthand accounts of the action, see *New Orleans Republican*, Sept. 20, 1874, and *New Orleans Picayune*, July 29, 1885; for Badger's, see US House, *Condition of Affairs in the South*, House Report 261, pt. 3, 399–400.

13. *New Orleans Republican*, Sept. 20, 1874; *New Orleans Picayune*, July 29, 1885; US House, *Condition of Affairs in the South*, House Report 261, pt. 3, 399–400; *New Orleans Weekly Times-Democrat*, July 25, 1885; Nystrom, "Battle of Liberty Place."

14. *New Orleans Republican*, Sept. 20, 1874; *New Orleans Picayune*, July 29, 1885; US House, *Condition of Affairs in the South*, House Report 261, pt. 3, 399–400; *New Orleans Weekly Times-Democrat*, July 25, 1885.

15. For accounts of Longstreet ordering people to disperse, see, for example, *Memphis Daily Appeal*, Sept. 15, 1874, and *Cleveland Daily Herald*, Sept. 15, 1874; on Fairfax conveying his messages to Badger, see *Chicago Tribune*, Sept. 16, 1874; on Longstreet retreating with his reinforcements as Metropolitans fled, see *New Orleans Picayune*, Sept. 15, 1874, and *Caucasian* (Alexandria, LA), Sept. 19, 1874. Historians' accounts reflect the confusion in the primary sources. Wert has Longstreet hit by a spent bullet and taken to the rear as a prisoner: *General James Longstreet*, 416; Hogue, *Uncivil War*, 136, has him thrown from his horse and taken to the Custom House.

16. Nystrom, "Battle of Liberty Place"; Nystrom, *New Orleans After the Civil War*, 176–77.

17. Nystrom, *New Orleans After the Civil War*, 176–77.

18. *Vicksburg Herald* (MS), Sept. 15, 1874; *Memphis Daily Appeal*, Sept. 16, 1874; *New Orleans Bulletin*, Sept. 22, 1874; *Augusta Constitutionalist* (GA), Oct. 4, 1874. As had been the case throughout Reconstruction, conservative Democrats in the North joined in the chorus of criticism against Longstreet. The *New York World* compared his conduct on September 14 to that of the British in Boston on the eve of the American Revolution, using armed bodies to break up lawful popular assemblies in a "deliberate assault upon the fundamental principles of freedom." *New York World*, quoted in *Cumberland Alleganian* (MD), Sept. 23, 1874.

19. *New Orleans Bulletin*, Oct. 4, 1874; *Weekly Louisianian* (New Orleans), May 16, 1874.

20. Rousey, 225, 231; *New Orleans Picayune*, Sept. 18, 1874; Hogue, *Uncivil War*, 66.

21. Rousey, 231, 235, 240; Nystrom, "African Americans in the Civil War"; Itkin, 53–55, 59; *New Orleans Republican*, May 24, 1874; *Weekly Louisianian* (New Orleans), Jan. 4, May 16, 1873; Rankin, 439; Desdunes, 114–20.

22. It was widely reported in Southern and Northern papers, based on the first dispatches to leave the city, that the Black Metropolitans had broken and run; see, for example, *Vicksburg Herald* (MS), *Baltimore Sun*, *New York Times*, and *Chicago Daily Tribune*, Sept. 15, 1874; Rousey, 232; *New Orleans Bulletin*, Sept. 26, 1874; *Le Carillon* (New Orleans), Sept. 20, 1874.

23. *Weekly Louisianian* (New Orleans), Sept. 19, 26, 1874; *New Orleans Bulletin*, Sept. 26, 1874; *New Orleans Picayune*, July 1, 1874; Nystrom, *New Orleans After the Civil War*, 163–64; Blackett, ed., 77–78; *Harrisburg Patriot* (PA), interview in *New Orleans Picayune*, Sept. 22, 1874; *Harrisburg Telegraph* (PA), Sept. 17, 1874; Jno F Clarmont entry, 1870 US Federal Census, NA; *New York Times*, Sept. 16, 1874; Sept. 15 Inquests, Coroner's Office. Records of Inquests and Views. Vol. 23–24, 1872–1874; and Board of Metropolitan Pension Fund Ledger, 1870–1876, 156–96, both at New Orleans Public Library, New Orleans, LA.

24. *New Orleans Bulletin*, Sept. 26, 1874; Blackett, ed., 77–78; *Harrisburg Patriot* (PA) interview, in *New Orleans Picayune*, Sept. 22, 1874; James Lewis testimony, Dec. 31, 1874, US House, *Condition of Affairs in Louisiana*, House Report 101, pt. 2, 41–42; Louisiana Adjutant General's Office, *Annual Report for 1874*, 1.

25. T. B. Stamps testimony, Jan. 1, 1875, US House, *Condition of Affairs in Louisiana*, House Report 101, pt. 2, 87.

26. Daggett, 95–96, 115–16, 121 (quotation).

27. Kellogg Testimony, Jan. 6, 1875, US House, *Condition of Affairs in Louisiana*, House Report 101, pt. 2, 193–99.

28. *New Orleans Picayune*, Sept. 16, 1874; Kellogg Testimony, Jan. 6, 1875, US House, *Condition of Affairs in Louisiana*, House Report 101, pt. 2, 199.

29. *New Orleans Republican*, Sept. 20, 1874.

30. *Indianapolis Journal*, Sept. 24, 1874.

31. Ibid.

32. *Independent Statesman* (Concord, NH), Nov. 5, 1874; *Inter Ocean* (Chicago), Sept. 17, 1874; *Le Carillon* (New Orleans), Oct. 18, 1874; *Newnan Herald* (GA), Oct. 9, 1874;

Galveston Daily News (TX), Oct. 29, 1874; *Rome Tri-Weekly Courier* (GA), Dec. 29, 1874; *Savannah Morning News*, Sept. 16, 1874.

33. A. S. Badger to John B. Badger, Dec. 22, 1874, Algernon Badger Family Papers, Tulane University Special Collections Library, New Orleans.

34. *Macon Telegraph and Messenger* (GA), July 23, 1885; *New Orleans Picayune*, July 29, 1885.

35. Sanger and Hay, 372–74; Hogue, *Uncivil War*, 143–47; US Senate, *Message of the President*, Senate Exec. Doc. 13, 8; Wetta, 166, 189.

36. Nash, 3667–69.

37. Piston, *Lee's Tarnished Lieutenant*, 137 (quotation); Wert, 417. On Longstreet's Louisianan activities and furloughs, see, for example, *Rome Tri-Weekly Courier* (GA), Dec. 29, 1874; *New Orleans Picayune*, Jan. 1, Aug. 5, Nov. 1, 1875; *New Orleans Times*, Aug. 7, 1875; *New Orleans Republican*, Sept. 12, 1875; *New Orleans Bulletin*, Sept. 28, Oct. 2, 1875. On his welcome in Georgia, see *Savannah Advertiser* in *Southern Watchman* (Athens, GA), Feb. 24, 1875, and *Daily Constitutionalist* (Augusta, GA), June 17, 1875.

38. On Gainesville, see, for example, *Augusta Constitutionalist* (GA), Sept. 11, 1875; *Sun* (Hartwell, GA), May 15, 1878; *Union and Recorder* (Milledgeville, GA), March 9, 1880; *Southern World* (Atlanta), Oct. 14, 1884; *Bainbridge Democrat* (GA), May 7, 1885; *Gainesville Eagle* (GA), Aug. 9, 1888; *New York Times*, Dec. 16, 1888.

39. Charles Calhoun, *Conceiving a New Republic*, 147–58; Piston, *Lee's Tarnished Lieutenant*, 138; *Daily Times* (Columbus, GA), Aug. 17, 1875; *North Georgia Citizen* (Dalton), Oct. 14, 1875; *Weekly Chronicle & Sentinel* (Augusta, GA), April 5, 1876; *Columbus Daily Enquirer* (GA), June 14, 1876.

40. Hogue, *Uncivil War*, 164–76.

41. US Senate, *Report and Testimony of the Select Committee of the United States Senate to Investigate the Causes of the Removal of the Negroes from the Southern States to the Northern States, Pts. 2–3*, 512–21 (quotations on 521). On Murrell, see also *New Orleans Republican*, Feb. 24, March 4, 1874.

42. *New Orleans Picayune*, Jan. 8, 10, 1877; *New Orleans Republican*, Aug. 2, 1876; Nystrom, *New Orleans After the Civil War*, 180–81; Piston, *Lee's Tarnished Lieutenant*, 138.

43. HDL, *Lee and Longstreet at High Tide*, 118–19.

44. *Baltimore Sun*, May 4, 1877; *Savannah Morning News*, April 26, 1877; *New Orleans Daily Democrat*, Sept. 8, 1877.

45. Wert, 422–23; Piston, *Lee's Tarnished Lieutenant*, 118–123.

46. *The Southern Home* (Charlotte, NC), March 24, 1873; *Rutland Weekly Herald* (VT), May 1, 1873.

47. *Chicago Tribune*, Jan. 29, 1871; Wert, 422; Gary W. Gallagher, "Introduction," in Jubal A. Early, *A Memoir of the Last Year of the War of Independence*, xv.

48. *Richmond Dispatch*, June 18, 1873; *New York Times*, Sept. 7, 1873; *St. Louis Globe*, quoted in *New Orleans Republican*, May 22, 1874; Hood, ed., 206-7.

49. *Dallas Herald*, quoted in *Lake Charles Echo* (LA), Oct. 10, 1874; *New Orleans Bulletin*, Dec. 25, 1874; JL to Charles S. Venable, May 30, 1875, Minor-Venable Papers, UVA; William Nelson Pendleton to JL, April 14, 1875, William Nelson Pendleton Papers, LVA.

50. Cutrer, ed., *Longstreet's Aide*, 158; Alexander, 96, 110, 245, 252; Hesseltine and Gara, 9.

51. Cutrer, ed., *Longstreet's Aide*, 160.

52. Ibid.

53. *Morning Republican* (Little Rock, AR), May 14, 1873; *Daily Evening Bulletin* (San Francisco), Aug. 2, 1873.

54. Charles Marshall to JL, May 7, 1875, and A. L. Long to JL, May 31, 1875, James Longstreet Papers, RLE; HDL, *Lee and Longstreet at High Tide*, 58 (Taylor letter).

55. *Inter Ocean* (Chicago), July 16, 1875.

Chapter 8: Return of the Prodigal

1. *New Orleans Republican*, Jan. 25, 1876.

2. Hess, *Pickett's Charge*, 373; Erasmus Taylor to JL, Sept. 10, 1889, Longstreet Papers, RLE.

3. *New Orleans Democrat*, March 16, 1876; *Norfolk Virginian*, Feb. 12, 1876.

4. *Alexandria Gazette* (VA) in *Valley Virginian* (Staunton), Feb. 17, 1896; *Baltimore Sun*, March 3, 1876; *Knoxville Daily Tribune* (TN), March 25, 1876 (reprint of Fitzhugh Lee to *Alexandria Gazette* [VA], March 17, 1876); Erasmus Taylor to JL, March 12, 1876, James Longstreet Papers, RLD; *New Orleans Republican*, March 26, 1876.

5. Blight, 164; Piston, *Lee's Tarnished Lieutenant*, 131; McClure, 399–400.

6. JL to Henry B. Dawson, March 27, 1876, Civil War Letters Collection, New-York Historical Society, NY; McClure, 399–400.

7. Blight, 158–60; Jubal A. Early, "Letter from Gen. J. A. Early," 50–68.

8. *Philadelphia Weekly Times*, Nov. 3, 1877, reprinted as JL, "General James Longstreet's Account of the Campaign and Battle," 54–86.

9. Pfarr, 22–23; JL, "General Longstreet's Second Paper on Gettysburg," 257–69.

10. John Walter Fairfax to JL, Nov. 12, 1877, John Walter Fairfax Papers, VMHC. On Merchant and Fairfax during Reconstruction, see *New Orleans Republican*, Aug. 1, 1871, Jan. 14, 1872, Feb. 24, 1874; on Ochiltree, see Hall, 347–76. For another ex-Confederate who gave JL a sympathetic hearing, see JL to Henry Thweatt Owen, March 24, April 21, 1878, Henry Thweatt Owen Papers, LVA.

11. Early, "Leading Confederates on the Battle of Gettysburg: A Review by General Early," 241–302, and "Reply to General Longstreet's Second Paper," 270–87; *Galveston Daily News* (TX), Dec. 23, 1877; *Montgomery Advertiser* (AL), Nov. 18, 1877; *Daily American* (Nashville), Dec. 14, 1877; *Intelligencer* (Anderson, SC), Jan. 31, 1878; *Columbus Daily Enquirer-Sun* (GA), Nov. 6, 1877.

12. Marvel, 86, 93, 108–9, 183, 225, 265, 273, 297 (quotation).

13. Ibid., 309, 310, 330; Wert, 172; *New York Daily Herald*, Jan. 12, 1879.

14. *Philadelphia Times*, July 27, 1879.

15. D. H. Hill to JL, Aug. 5, 1879, Feb. 11, May 14, 21, 1885, Feb. 5, 1887, in James Longstreet Papers, RLD.

16. *Savannah Advertiser* quoted in *Atlanta Constitution*, Feb. 11, 1875; Sarah E. Gardner, *Blood & Irony*, 140.

17. For the most comprehensive account, see Shadgett, 1–49 (quotation on 30).

18. JL to Benjamin Alvord, March 17, 1877, Rutherford B. Hayes Papers, Rutherford B. Hayes Presidential Library & Museums, Fremont, OH; Sanger and Hay, 380–81; *Atlanta Constitution*, Nov. 13, 1877; *Rome Tri-Weekly Courier* (GA), Jan. 9, 1879; *Brenham Weekly Banner* (TX), Jan. 24, 1879. For evidence that Longstreet coveted the US marshal job, see Benjamin H. Hill to JL, July 30, 1877, Department of Literary and Historical Manuscripts, Morgan Library & Museum, New York.

19. *News and Herald* (Winnsboro, SC), Feb. 1, 1879; *Weekly Inter Ocean* (Chicago), Feb. 26, 1880. On Longstreet's Republican Party identity in these years, see also JL interview with *New York World* reprinted in *Columbus Daily Enquirer* (GA), May 25, 1883; *Chicago Tribune*, Sept. 18, 1883; *Atlanta Constitution*, Nov. 14, 1883.

20. Sanger and Hay, 384; Priest, 120–21, 151.

21. *Baltimore Sun*, June 2, 1880 (JL quotation); *Macon Telegraph and Messenger* (GA), Sept. 14, 1877, Nov. 19, 1877, Aug. 27, 1880; Wert, 412–13.

22. For the terms in office of these ex-Confederate diplomats, see "People," US Department of State Office of the Historian online, https://history.state.gov /department history /people/. For the Hoar speech, see *Boston Daily Advertiser*, July 1, 1885; for positive press coverage, see *Baltimore Sun*, May 19, 1880; *Fitchburg Sentinel* (MA), May 20, 1880; *Weekly Louisianian* (New Orleans), May 22, 1880; *Frank Leslie's Illustrated Newspaper* (New York), July 3, 1880.

23. Grant Army of the Republic Ford Post, No. 14, June 17, 1880, Rutherford B. Hayes Presidential Library & Museums, Fremont, OH. For Southern critiques of the appointment, see, for example, *Shreveport Daily Standard* (LA), May 21, 1880; *Gainesville Eagle* (GA), May 28, 1880; *Norfolk Virginian* (VA), May 22, 1880. On Southern ambivalence, see *Atlanta Constitution*, May 23, 1880; *Daily Arkansas Gazette* (Little Rock), May 21, 1880; *Troy Messenger* (AL), May 27, 1880; *Observer* (Raleigh, NC), May 25, 1880.

24. Charles Calhoun, *Conceiving a New Republic*, 168–79; Arrington, 140–46.

25. *Wichita Weekly Beacon*, May 26, 1880; *Intelligencer Journal* (Lancaster, PA), July 7, 1880; *Topeka Post* (KS), July 30, 1880; *Huntington Democrat* (IN), May 27, 1880; *Weekly Register* (Point Pleasant, WV), Oct. 6, 1880.

26. *London Telegraph*, quoted in *Macon Telegraph and Messenger* (GA), Nov. 19, 1880.

27. For the argument that, outside of the US West, "the nature of national power realized during the Civil War proved self-limiting during Reconstruction," see Sexton, 15–33.

28. *Baltimore Sun*, Sept. 7, 1880; *Raleigh News and Observer* (NC), Oct. 27, 1880.

29. Roberts, 7, 28–30, 133; Finkel, 460, 466–67, 478; Hanioglu, 142.

30. Walther, 1–6; Conroy-Krutz, 225–27; Sahin, 7; Makdisi, 4, 11.

31. Walther, 58–59, 80–86, 90–91; Prior, 861–62, 872; Makdisi, 3.

32. *Christian Union* (New York), Nov. 3, 1880; Boyar and Fleet, pp. 38, 46, 89, 154, 320–21, 330; Roberts, 48, 138; Finkel, 484–86, 488, 491, 496.

33. *New York Times*, Dec. 15, 1880; *Omaha Daily Herald*, Dec. 21, 1880.

34. *Nashville American*, Jan. 15, 1881; *Public Ledger* (Memphis), Jan. 18, 1881; *Philadelphia Telegraph*, quoted in the *New Orleans Picayune*, Jan. 15, 1881.

35. Roberts, 99; Archaeological Institute of America, 30, 34; JL to William M. Evarts, Feb. 14, 1881, Despatches from US Ministers to Turkey, 1818–1906, Record Group 59: General Records of the Department of State, 1763–2002, NA, (referred to hereafter as Despatches, RG 59, NA).

36. Archaeological Institute, 30, 34; JL to Evarts, Jan. 19, Feb. 14, 1881; Despatches, RG 59, NA; Prior, 864.

37. Yiğit, 528; Archaeological Institute, 30, 34; JL to Blaine, April 11 (quotations), 23, 1881, Despatches, RG 59, NA; *Buffalo Morning Express*, April 30, 1881.

38. JL to Blaine, April 7, 1881, Despatches, RG 59, NA; *Lloyd's Weekly Newspaper* (London), April 10, 1881; *La Turquie* (Istanbul), April 11, 1881.

39. Eutychides to JL, Feb. 4, 1881; JL to Evarts, Feb. 14, 1881; JL to Assim Pasha, Jan. 11, 1881, Despatches, RG 59, NA. (*Pasha*, the title of Turkish officers and dignitaries, is sometimes rendered *Pacha* by American correspondents; I use the more common *Pasha* throughout, for consistency.) On extraterritoriality, see Phelps, 137.

40. *St. Louis Globe-Democrat*, June 12, 1881 (JL interview and quotation).

41. Sahin, 43–44; JL to Assim, Feb. 11, 1881; Assim to JL, Feb. 24, 1881; JL to Blaine, April 29, 1881; Despatches, RG 59, NA.

42. JL to Assim, Feb. 11, March 21, April 29, 1881; Assim to JL, April 16, 1881, Despatches, RG 59, NA.

43. Assim to JL, April 16, 1881; JL to Assim, April 29, 1881, Despatches, RG 59, NA.

44. Sahin, 5–6, 9–11, 14, 25, 66, 100, 119, 121.

45. Beisner, 28–31; *Advance* (Chicago), Jan. 20, 1881; *Baltimore Sun*, Sept. 7, 1880; for coverage of Longstreet's meeting with the sultan, see *Levant Herald* (Constantinople), quoted in *Army and Navy Journal* (New York), Jan. 15, 1881; *Examiner* (London), Dec. 25, 1880.

46. Beisner, 26, 60; *St. Louis Globe-Democrat*, June 12, 1881 (Paris interview); *Cincinnati Enquirer*, June 17, 1881 (New York interview).

47. For Longstreet's admiration of the North, see *Cincinnati Enquirer*, June 17, 1881; *Columbus Daily Enquirer* (GA), May 25, 1883; *Atlanta Constitution*, April 28, 1896;

Omaha World-Herald, Oct. 31, 1903; *Philadelphia Times*, July 27, 1896; Beisner, 30–33, 87–89.

48. JL to Tom Ochiltree, Dec. 11, 1880, and Ochiltree to James A. Garfield, Jan. 12, 1881, James A. Garfield Papers, ser. 4, General Correspondence, LC.

49. JL to Ochiltree, Dec. 11, 1880, and Ochiltree to Garfield, Jan. 12, 1881, Garfield Papers, LC; JL to E. M. Marsh, April 9, 1884, Rutherford B. Hayes Presidential Library & Museums, Fremont, OH.

50. For objections to Longstreet's appointment as US marshal, see, for example, *Burlington Free Press* (VT), March 29, 1881; *Omaha Daily Herald*, April 20, 1881; *Wheeling Register* (WV), April 21, 1881. For examples of positive coverage, see *Vicksburg Herald* (MS), April 20, 1881; *Republic* (Columbus, IN), April 20, 1881; *Washington Post*, June 28, 1881. For the "home mission" quotation, see *New Orleans Picayune*, April 11, 1881; for the Speer quotation, *Macon Telegraph and Messenger* (GA), May 8, 1881.

51. *Chicago Daily Tribune*, June 20, 1881; *Burlington Free Press* (VT), June 23, 1881; *Daily Memphis Avalanche*, June 23, 1881; *Nashville Banner*, July 14, 1881; *New York Times*, July 24, 1881.

52. *Burlington Free Press* (VT), June 23, 1881; *New York Times*, July 27, 1881; *Georgia Weekly Telegraph and Messenger* (Macon), Dec. 16, 1881.

Chapter 9: Keeping the Peace

1. On the Republicans' difficulties projecting power at home and overseas, see Sexton, 15–33. On the party's shifting ideologies, see Richardson, 66, 91–99, 117, 120, 124.

2. *Weekly News and Advertiser* (Albany, GA), June 23, 1881 (Longstreet quotation). The marshalship gets only brief mention in Piston, *Lee's Tarnished Lieutenant*, 139, Wert, 420, and Sanger and Hay, 390–91.

3. Shadgett, 70–75, 94–101; *Atlanta Constitution*, Jan. 2 (quotation), Feb. 18, March 29, Aug. 3, 1882.

4. On divisions in the Republican ranks, see Donald L. Grant, *The Way It Was in the South*, 132–35; Matthews, 360–62; *Atlanta Constitution*, Aug. 3, 1882. On Longstreet's support for Black officeholders, see, for example, *Weekly News and Advertiser* (Albany, GA), Feb. 18, 1880; *Columbus Daily Enquirer-Sun* (GA), Nov. 1, 1881; *Weekly Sumter Republi-*

can (Americus, GA), Jan. 13, 1882; and *Savannah Morning News*, Aug. 4, Nov. 24, 1882. On their support for him, see, for example, *Atlanta Constitution*, Aug. 5, and Nov. 15, 1882; *Savannah Morning News*, Nov. 16, 1882; and Sanger and Hay, 386 (Lonon quotation). For an appeal to Longstreet as US marshal, see the J. C. Cook letter in the *Atlanta Constitution*, Nov. 14, 1883. On factional divisions among African Americans elsewhere in the South, see Michael W. Fitzgerald, *Urban Emancipation*, 5, 182, 186, 266.

5. Frederick S. Calhoun, *The Lawmen*, 132 (first quotation), 138 (second quotation), 139 (third quotation), 140–41.

6. Ibid., 110–28.

7. Huebner, 42–44.

8. *Atlanta Constitution*, Oct. 14, 23, 24, 1883; *Savannah Morning News*, Oct. 27, 1883; *Jackson Herald* (GA), Sept. 14, 1883, *Bloomington Daily Leader* (IL), Oct. 16, 1883; *New York Times*, Aug. 2, Oct. 15, Dec. 31, 1883 (Yarbrough quotation).

9. *Ex parte Yarbrough*, 110 US 651; 28 L. Ed. 274; 4 S. Ct. 152; *Savannah Morning News*, Oct. 27, 1883; *Chicago Daily Tribune*, Dec. 22, 1883; *Atlanta Weekly Constitution*, Dec. 25, 1883.

10. Huebner, 45; Aucoin, 4; Claude, 122; Foner, *The Second Founding*, 148–49.

11. *Atlanta Constitution*, Oct. 18, 24, 26, 28, 1883, Nov. 10, 1883, Jan. 15, 1884; *Savannah Morning News*, Oct. 26, 1883; *Jackson Herald* (GA), Sept. 14, 1883; *True Citizen* (Waynesboro, GA), Dec. 21, 1883. For coverage of Longstreet's requisition, see, for example, *Union and Recorder* (Milledgeville, GA), Nov. 20, 1883, and *New York Times*, Nov. 10, 1883.

12. *Ex parte Yarbrough*, 110 US 651; 28 L. Ed. 274; 4 S. Ct. 152; *Banner-Watchman* (Athens, GA), Jan. 29, 1884; *Atlanta Weekly Constitution*, Dec. 25, 1883; US Supreme Court, *Transcript of Record, US Supreme Court 1883*, 15, Original, 110 US 651. 4 S. Ct. 152, 28 L. Ed. 274, 1-22-1884, 24.

13. *Cincinnati Commercial Gazette*, reprinted in *St. Louis Globe-Democrat*, Dec. 22, 1883; *Cleveland Herald*, Dec. 31, 1883; *New York Times*, Dec. 31, 1883.

14. *Atlanta Constitution*, Nov. 20, 1883; *Banner Watchman* (Athens, GA), Dec. 25, 1883, Jan. 8, 1884.

15. Piston, *Lee's Tarnished Lieutenant*, 140; Wert, 420–21; *Philadelphia Times*, Feb. 8, 1884.

16. US House, *Testimony Taken by the Committee on Expenditures in the Department of Jus-*

tice, 354–55 (Wallace testimony), 357 (Longstreet quotation), 376 (Martin testimony), 576–77 (Speer charges and Longstreet rebuttal), 916 (vaporings quotation).

17. US House, *Testimony Taken by the Committee on Expenditures*, 358–59, 572.

18. Wert, 419; Piston, *Lee's Tarnished Lieutenant*, 140; *St. Louis Post-Dispatch*, July 21, 1884; *New York Times*, July 2, 1884; Sanger and Hay, 395.

19. Shadgett, 94–101 (quotation on 101).

20. Ibid., 57–60, 87–89; Piston, *Lee's Tarnished Lieutenant*, 138–40; Wert, 419; *New York Times*, April 9, 1884.

21. Shadgett, 94; *Columbus Daily Enquirer* (GA) (reprint of *New York World* interview), May 25, 1883; *Atlanta Constitution*, March 26, 1884; JL to Chester A. Arthur, June 28, 1882, Chester A. Arthur Papers, LC; JL to E. M. Marsh, April 9, 1884, Hayes Papers.

22. *New York Globe*, August 18, 1883, April 12, 1884; *State Journal* (Harrisburg, PA), April 12, 1884; *Washington Bee* (DC), May 3, 1884; *Huntsville Gazette* (AL), May 10, 1884; *Pittsburgh Post-Gazette*, May 2, 1884; *Christian Recorder* (Philadelphia), April 24, 1881.

23. Shadgett, 73–77; *Weekly News and Advertiser* (Albany, GA), Sept. 30, 1882; *Banner-Watchman* (Athens, GA), April 15, 1884; *Weekly Telegraph and Messenger* (Macon, GA), May 30, 1884 (Early quotation).

24. Frederick Douglass, "Alonzo B. Cornell and the Republican Party," Address delivered in Utica, New York, Oct. 30, 1879, in Frederick Douglass Papers Digital Edition; Williams, 523.

25. De Santis, 148–59; *Savannah Morning News*, July 29, 1884; *New York Globe*, Oct. 4, 1884; *Washington Bee* (DC), Aug. 2, 1884.

26. *Freeman* (New York), Aug. 22, 1885; *Daily Inter Ocean* (Chicago), Oct. 19, 1889.

27. Gallagher, *Causes, Won, Lost, and Forgotten*, 33.

28. Blight, 158–60; Piston, *Lee's Tarnished Lieutenant*, 144–45.

29. Singal, 47; Ayers, 21; Link, 150–53; Blight, 200 (Grady quotation); Davis, 1–38.

30. *Savannah Advertiser*, quoted in *Atlanta Constitution*, Feb. 11, 1875; Gardner, *Blood & Irony*, 140.

31. *Atlanta Constitution*, Nov. 3, 1877; *Philadelphia Times*, July 27, 1879.

32. *Wheeling Register* (WV), May 27, 1880; *Atlanta Constitution*, May 25, 1880; *Columbus Daily Enquirer-Sun* (GA), May 25, 1883.

33. *Atlanta Constitution*, Jan. 15, 1888; *Saint Paul Globe* (MN), May 7, 1886. On images of

Longstreet as a Radical tool, see, for example, *Savannah Morning News*, Oct. 27, 1881; *Bainbridge Democrat*, Aug. 24, 1882; and *Banner-Watchman* (Athens, GA), April 1, 1884; Donald L. Grant, *The Way It Was*, 135.

34. JL (all five of the following articles), "The Seven Days' Fighting About Richmond," *Century* 30 (July 1885), 469–77; "Our March Against Pope," *Century* 31 (Feb. 1886), 601–14; "The Invasion of Maryland," *Century* 32 (June 1886), 309–15; "The Battle of Fredericksburg," *Century* 32 (Aug. 1886), 609–26; "Lee's Invasion of Pennsylvania," *Century* 33 (Feb. 1887), 622–36.

35. Longstreet had recounted the Ord episode in the July 6, 1881, edition of the *Washington Post*, lamenting that "a little diplomacy at that time would have ended the war and been of unquestionable advantage to both sections of the country." See also *Chicago Tribune*, Sept. 14, 1883, and *Daily Inter Ocean* (Chicago), July 10, 1893 ("nobody but the politicians" quotation); Waugh, 237, 239, 240.

36. *New York Times*, July 24, 1885; *St. Louis Globe-Democrat*, Sept. 8, 1887; *New York Times*, Dec. 16, 1888.

37. *Charleston Courier and News* (SC), quoted in *Alexandria Gazette* (VA), July 13, 1885.

38. Sanger and Hay, 400–401; *Philadelphia Inquirer*, Dec. 4, 1888; *Philadelphia Times*, Dec. 4, 1888.

39. *National Tribune* (Washington, DC), July 12, 1888; *The World* (New York), *Philadelphia Inquirer*, Dec. 4, 1888; *Philadelphia Times*, Dec. 4, 1888; Farnsworth, 37–40; *Daily Inter Ocean* (Chicago), Oct. 19, 1889.

40. J. W. Fairfax to Benjamin Harrison, Feb. 6, 1889; W. B. Merchant to Benjamin Harrison, Feb. 13, 1889; James B. Galloway to E. W. Halford, Jan. 5, 1889; and James Peck to Benjamin Harrison, Jan. 10, 1889. All in James Longstreet, Applications and Recommendations for Public Office, boxes 64 and 72, State Department Records, RG 59, NA. Some of these letters are reproduced here: Langbart, https://text-message.blogs.archives.gov /2016/11/01/james-longstreet-after-the-civil-war/.

41. M. B. Hewson to Benjamin Harrison, Nov. 16, 28, Dec. 31, 1888; Halbert B. Case to E. W. Halford, Jan. 22, 1889; William Miller Owen to Benjamin Harrison, Feb. 1, 1889, in Longstreet Applications, RG 59, NA.

42. Van Holt Nash to Benjamin Harrison, Oct. 11, 1889, and petition, Dec. 26, 1888, in Longstreet Applications, RG 59, NA.

43. Sanger and Hay, 400–401; *Milwaukee Sentinel*, March 18, 1891 (Sherman 1888 letter); *Star of Zion* (Charlotte, NC), Feb. 28, 1889.

44. *New Orleans Daily Picayune*, March 30, 1890.

45. *Daily American* (Nashville), Jan. 29, 1889, *Chicago Tribune*, Feb. 4, 1889; JL to Benjamin Harrison, Nov. 19, 1888, Benjamin Harrison Papers, LC; on Mahone and the Readjusters, see Dailey, 39–67.

46. *New Orleans Times-Democrat*, Feb. 10, 21, 1889; JL to William Mahone, Feb. 21, 1894, William Mahone Papers, LVA; Early, quoted in Gallagher, Introduction to Early, *Autobiographical Sketch*, xx.

47. *Atlanta Constitution*, April 10, 1889; *Gwinnett Herald* (Lawrenceville, GA), April 16, 1889; *Macon Telegraph* (GA), April 10, 1889; *Charleston Weekly News and Courier* (SC), Sept. 15, 1897.

48. *Atlanta Constitution*, Jan. 15, 24, July 10, 1888; *Lincolnton News* (GA), Jan. 27, 1888.

49. *Macon Telegraph* (GA), Dec. 31, 1889.

Chapter 10: War on the Page

1. JL, *FMTA*, xv.

2. Piston, *Lee's Tarnished Lieutenant*, 166–69; Wert, 412–13, 418–19, 423–27; Sanger and Hay, 400, 433–36; Pfarr, 180–83.

3. *Burlington Free Press* (VT), July 21, 1887; *Montgomery Advertiser* (AL), July 21, 1887; *Los Angeles Times*, July 30, 1887; *St. Louis Globe-Democrat*, Sept. 8, 1887.

4. *Philadelphia Times*, May 15, 1892; *Inter Ocean* (Chicago), May 20, 1894.

5. *Atlanta Constitution*, July 6, 1888; *New York Times*, Jan. 12, 1890; *New Orleans Daily Picayune*, July 13, 1892. On Moran's reputation, see, for example, *Macon Telegraph* (GA), March 12, 1892.

6. *Chattooga News* (Summerville, GA), July 13, 1888; *Knoxville Daily Tribune* (TN), Oct. 8, 12, 1890.

7. *Washington Post*, June 11, 1893, Aug. 2, 1893; *Carroll Free Press* (Carrollton, GA), Aug. 4, 1893 (reprint of Maury letter); Janney, *Remembering the Civil War*, 150.

8. *Washington Post*, Aug. 2, 1893, May 21, 1894; *New Orleans Times-Democrat*, June 15, 1893; *Inter Ocean* (Chicago), June 20, 1893.

9. *Milwaukee Sentinel*, Sept. 20, 1895; Janney, "'I Yield to No Man an Iota of My Convictions,'" 394–420.

10. Link, 164; *Atlanta Constitution*, Sept. 22, 1895.

11. Piston, *Lee's Tarnished Lieutenant*, 141, 157, 163–65; Cutrer, ed., *Longstreet's Aide*, 176–77.

12. JL interview with St. Louis *Globe-Democrat*, reprinted in *Atlanta Constitution*, June 11, 1890.

13. On Perry, see, for example, *Daily Charlotte Observer* (NC), June 18, 1893, and *Philadelphia Inquirer*, Nov. 13, 1895. On the *Official Records* (commonly referred to as the *OR*), see Sternhell, 10, 26–27.

14. *Washington Star* (DC), Oct. 12, 1895; *Atlanta Constitution*, Oct. 15, 1895. Longstreet's memoir carries a copyright date of 1895 and a publication date of 1896. As Wert explains in *General James Longstreet*, 423, "Longstreet expected publication by Christmas 1895, but it was delayed at the printers until early in 1896." On Longstreet at the Union League, see *North American* (Philadelphia), Sept. 30, 1895. On sale of the book by subscription, see, for example, *Boston Globe*, Oct. 13, 1895, and *Harrisburg Telegraph* (PA), Dec. 24, 1895.

15. JL, *FMTA*, xvi–xvii.

16. Ibid., 17.

17. Ibid., 39, 54, 152, 196, 283–84 (quotation), 288–89. Taking issue with the "overwhelming numbers" interpretation of Confederate defeat, Longstreet indicated in an October 26, 1895, public letter on his book's purposes that "To claim that the people went apart from the Union to embark in a hopeless cause will be to put them in a false light in order to conceal individual indiscretions, for events have illustrated reasonable hope of success." *Galveston Daily News* (TX), Nov. 9, 1895.

18. JL, *FMTA*, 159 (second quotation), 220 (first quotation), 288 (third quotation); Jomini, 38, 51, 56–65. For Longstreet's previous references to the "art of war," see, for example, *Morning Oregonian* (Portland), July 5, 1893.

19. JL, *FMTA*, 92.

20. Ibid., 330; Nolan, 4–13 (quotation on 13).

21. JL, *FMTA*, 362, 384; *Philadelphia Weekly Times*, Nov. 3, 1877 ("matchless equipoise" quotation); JL, "Seven Days' Fighting," 477; *National Tribune* (Washington, DC), Oct. 3, 1895. In Longstreet's view, another time that Lee lost his balance was in the Wilderness

on May 6, 1864, when Lee, in the excitement of battle, began moving into the line of fire with an advancing brigade, only to be summoned back to relative safety by Longstreet and others. *Philadelphia Times*, July 27, 1879. On equipoise, see *St. Louis Globe-Democrat*, July 1, 1887 (Sherman quotation); Mahan, 680; Dodge, 684.

22. *Philadelphia Weekly Times*, Nov. 3, 1877; JL, *FMTA*, 384, 401, 405.

23. JL, *FMTA*, 456 (first quotation), 466 (second quotation), 468 (third quotation). See also Wert, 300, 311, 321, 323, 329 (fourth quotation), 486.

24. JL, *FMTA*, 486, 541 (quotation).

25. Ibid., 534 (third quotation), 551 (first quotation), 566 (second quotation).

26. Ibid., 568–69 (quotation on 568), 583–85, 620–21.

27. Ibid., 625–28, 634 (first quotation), 637 (second quotation). The biblical verse Longstreet alluded to is from Luke 7:47, KJV.

28. Ibid., 638. Longstreet also related the story of Daniel in an 1895 letter reprinted in Cockrum, 302–4.

29. Daniel, born in Georgia, had moved with Longstreet's widowed mother to Macon after her husband died; he appears as Daniel Johnson, age fifty, in the 1870 census records for Noxubee County, Mississippi, where he worked as a farm laborer, and as Dan Longstreet ten years later in the 1880 census. Federal Census Records, 1870 and 1880, NA.

30. US Senate, *Mississippi in 1875*, 44th Cong., 1st Sess., Rpt. 527, Pt. 2, 43–44; J. W. Longstreet to Blanche K. Bruce, Dec. 30, 1877, Jan. 2, 1878, Blanche K. Bruce Papers, Howard; *Clarion-Ledger* (Jackson, MS), May 12, 1880; *Vicksburg Herald* (MS), April 23, 1884; *Colored American* (Washington, DC), Dec. 1, 1900.

31. Piston, *Lee's Tarnished Lieutenant*, 166; *Milwaukee Journal*, March 28, 1896; *Daily Leader* (Lexington, KY), March 3, 1896 (Halstead quotation); *St. Louis Globe-Democrat*, Jan. 10, 1896; *Cincinnati Commercial Gazette*, Jan. 19, 1896; *Buffalo Evening News*, Jan. 22, 1896; *New York Sun*, April 9, 1897; *Nation*, Feb. 13, 1896, 146.

32. *Morning Democrat* (Davenport, IA), Feb. 2, 1896; *Buffalo Evening News*, Jan. 22, 1896; *Philadelphia Times*, Jan. 12, 1896.

33. *New York Tribune*, March 18, 1896.

34. *Afro-American Advocate* (Coffeyville, KS), Aug. 12, Oct. 13, 1892; *Washington Bee* (DC), Nov. 16, 1895; *Broad Ax* (Salt Lake City, UT), July 11, 1896.

35. *Commercial Appeal* (Memphis), Oct. 29, Dec. 22, 1895 (Jones quotation); *Wilmington*

Messenger (NC), Jan. 24, 1896; *Weekly News and Courier* (Charleston, SC), March 11 (Lee and Taylor quotations), June 24, 1896; *Richmond Dispatch*, Feb. 16, 1896 (second Jones quotation). On Moran, see Hassler, 24–25. On criticism of Perry by Jones and others, see *Commercial Appeal* (Memphis), Dec. 22, 1896, and *Daily Commercial Herald* (Vicksburg, MS), Aug. 13, 1895. As he acknowledges in its preface, Longstreet also received editorial assistance in his manuscript revisions from Alfred Matthews, a Philadelphia-based freelance writer and editor who published essays in the popular journals of the era on subjects such as the settlement of the Midwest and railroad construction. JL, *FMTA*, xvii; *Philadelphia Times*, Jan. 11, 1902.

36. W. H. Taylor to Jedediah Hotchkiss, June 23, 1896, Hunter Holmes McGuire Papers, VMHC; E. P. Alexander to Mr. Bancroft, Oct. 30, 1904, James Longstreet Papers, RLE. On Northern arguments that peace should be grounded in forgiveness and charity and the Lost Cause creed's inversion of those arguments, see Janney, *Remembering the Civil War*, 173, 234, 259.

37. *Wilmington Messenger* (NC), Jan. 24, 1896. On the Daniel anecdote, see *Jennings Daily Times-Record* (LA), Oct. 28, 1903.

38. *Daily Charlotte Observer* (NC), April 29, 1896; *Wilmington Morning Star* (NC), May 8, 1896; Patteson, 326, 328, 333.

39. *Atlanta Constitution*, Jan. 26, 1896.

40. Ibid., March 29, 1896.

41. Ibid.

42. Gardner, "Helen Dortch Longstreet (1863–1962)"; *Chicago Daily Tribune*, Aug. 18, 1897.

43. Holmes, 149–72.

44. Ibid., 162–64; Hulett, "William Y. Atkinson (1854–1899)"; *Weekly News and Advertiser* (Albany, GA), July 23, 1892.

45. Holmes, 153; *Macon Telegraph* (GA), Dec. 14, 1896; *Jackson Herald* (GA), Jan. 22, 1897; *New Orleans Daily Picayune*, Sept. 9, 1897.

46. *Milwaukee Journal*, Sept. 8, 1897; *Chicago Daily Tribune*, Aug. 18, 1897; *St. Joseph Weekly News* (MO), Jan. 7, 1898; *Daily Morning Journal and Courier* (New Haven, CT), Sept. 10, 1897; *New York Sun*, quoted in *Charleston Weekly News and Courier* (SC), Sept. 15, 1897.

47. *North Georgia Citizen* (Dalton), Sept. 9, 16, 1897; *Rome Tribune* (GA), Sept. 11, 1897;

Daily Morning Journal and Courier (New Haven, CT), Sept. 10, 1897; *New Orleans Daily Picayune*, Sept. 9, 1872; *Hustler of Rome* (GA), Sept. 13, 1897.

48. *Weekly News and Courier* (Charleston, SC), Sept. 15, 1897; *Evening Star* (Washington, DC), Sept. 7, 1897; *Atlanta Constitution*, Sept. 12, 1897.

49. *Knoxville Sentinel* (TN), Sept. 14, 1897; *Vienna Progress* (GA), Nov. 4, 1897; *Weekly News and Courier* (Charleston, SC), Sept. 22, 1897.

50. *Wilmington Messenger* (NC), Oct. 10, 1897; *Dalton Argus* (GA), Sept. 18, 1897; *Age-Herald* (Birmingham, AL), Sept. 16, 1897.

51. JL to Mark A. Hanna, Nov. 10, 1896, Longstreet file, State Department Applications and Recommendations for Public Office, RG 59, NA.

52. *Savannah Morning News*, July 27, 1896; A. E. Buck to JL, Aug. 3, 1896, Longstreet Papers, RLE; *Indianapolis Journal*, Oct. 10, 1896.

53. Blight, 346; *Washington Post*, June 23, 1897; John W. Parks to William McKinley, May 10, 1897, James Longstreet, Charges and Protests File, Appointments Division, RG 48: Records of the Office of the Secretary of the Interior, NA.

54. *Savannah Tribune*, March 27, 1897; *Evening Times* (Washington, DC), May 5, 1897; *Atlanta Constitution*, May 12, Oct. 30, 1897, July 20, 1898; *Weekly Advertiser* (Montgomery, AL), April 9, 1897; *News & Observer* (Raleigh, NC), Jan. 23, 1898; *New Orleans Daily Picayune*, Jan. 24, 1898; *Salt Lake Tribune* (UT), Nov. 5, 1897 (which contained a rundown of press coverage of the appointment); *Standard Union* (Brooklyn), Nov. 4, 1897; *State* (Columbia, SC), Jan. 23, 1898. On Longstreet in the West, see, for example, *Salt Lake Semi-Weekly Tribune* (UT), Aug. 23, 1898, and *Portland Oregonian* (OR), Sept. 6, 1898.

Chapter 11: A New Century

1. *New York Times*, Nov. 16, 1897; *Leavenworth Herald* (KS), Nov. 27, 1897; *New York World*, Nov. 27, 1897; Carter, 12–14; *Atlanta Constitution*, Oct. 25, 1897, Sept. 2, 1903.

2. *Brooklyn Daily Eagle*, Jan. 9, 1898; *Macon Telegraph* (GA), Nov. 26, 1897; *New York Sun*, Jan. 9, 1898.

3. Gallagher, *Causes Won, Lost, and Forgotten*, 15–40.

4. Gannon, 145–77; Blight, *Race and Reunion*, 65–139; Janney, *Remembering the Civil War*, 103–96.

5. *Brunswick Times* (GA), March 11, 1897; *Savannah Morning News*, March 11, 1897; *Evening Times* (Washington, DC), May 5, 1897; A. E. Buck to JL, May 20, 1897, James Longstreet Papers, RLE.

6. On this alliance, see, for example, *Savannah Morning News*, March 11 and July 27, 1896; *Americus Times-Recorder* (GA), May 7, 1897; *Atlanta Constitution*, May 12, 1897; and Dittmer, 91–92.

7. *Evening Star* (Washington, DC), April 17, 1899; *Colored American* (Washington, DC), Jan. 12, 1901, Aug. 20, 1904; *Baltimore Sun*, Jan. 2, 1901.

8. *Evening Star* (Washington, DC), Sept. 16, 1897; *Atlanta Constitution*, Sept. 18, 1897; *Chicago Daily Tribune*, Sept. 20, 26, 1897; Bacote, 223–25; Yellin, 22–47.

9. *Savannah Morning News*, March 31, 1897; *Georgia Cracker* (Gainesville), Dec. 25, 1897; *Macon Telegraph* (GA), Jan. 4, 1898; *Chicago Daily Tribune*, Jan. 8, 1898; E. A. Angier to JL, Jan. 14, 1898, James Longstreet Papers, RLE; *Summerville News* (GA), Aug. 7, 1902; Judson W. Lyons to JL, March 16, 1900, James Longstreet Papers, RLE; JL to Judson Lyons, Sept. 20, 1900, and Herman Schreiner to JL, April 1, 1899, Letters Sent by General James Longstreet, 1897–1903, Records of the Commissioner of Railroads, RG 193, NA.

10. JL to James Longstreet Jr., Jan. 27, 1903, James Longstreet Papers, RLE; Helen Longstreet to Frances Perkins, Jan. 11, 1934, Helen Dortch Longstreet Papers, Georgia Historical Society; *Salt Lake Semi-Weekly Tribune* (UT), Aug. 23, 1898; *Portland Oregonian*, Sept. 7, 1898; *Age-Herald* (Birmingham, AL), Oct. 4, 1898; *New York Times*, Nov. 22, 1898.

11. JL to McKinley, May 24, 1987, William McKinley Papers, ser. 1: General Correspondence, 1847–1902, LC; *Denver Evening Post*, March 28, 1898; *Baltimore Sun*, March 28, June 10, 1898; *Morning News* (Savannah), May 24, 1898.

12. *Cincinnati Enquirer*, Aug. 2, 1898; *Rome Hustler-Commercial* (GA), Aug. 4, 1898; on the theme of reconciliation, see also *Age-Herald* (Birmingham, AL), Oct. 4, 1898; HDL, *Lee and Longstreet at High Tide*, 109–10.

13. *Cincinnati Enquirer*, Aug. 2, 1898; *Rome Hustler-Commercial* (GA), Aug. 4, 1898; *St. Joseph Weekly* Gazette (MO), Aug. 5, 1898; *New York Times*, Nov. 22, 1898.

14. *Asheville Citizen-Times* (NC), May 17, 1898; *Morning News* (Savannah, GA), May 24, 1898; Cunningham, "The Black 'Immune' Regiments in the Spanish-American War";

Powell, "Roster of the 9th United States Volunteer Infantry, 1898 to 1899." On Longstreet's support for Kelly, see Cunningham, "'His Influence with the Colored People Is Marked,'" 23, 27.

15. Blight, 349; JL, "The Loyal South of To-Day," *Independent,* July 6, 1899.

16. *New York Times,* July 24, 1894; *Cleveland Gazette,* June 16, 1894; *Milwaukee Sentinel,* July 8, 1899.

17. Norrell, 164–65 (quotation on 165), 172–79, 187; Karen Cook Bell, *Claiming Freedom,* 70–71; Brundage, 197.

18. *Atlanta Constitution,* July 10, 1899.

19. *Los Angeles Times,* Aug. 7, 10, 1899; *Baltimore Sun,* May 31, 1900; Lyons to JL, Jan. 16, 1901, and Sibley to JL, Jan. 26, 28, 1901, James Longstreet Papers, RLE; *Savannah Morning News,* March 2, 1901.

20. *Philadelphia Inquirer,* Nov. 11, 1900; *Aberdeen Daily News* (SD), Sept. 18, 1901.

21. John Ireland to Theodore Roosevelt, April 16, 1902; "Memorandum on James Longstreet" c. 1902, Theodore Roosevelt Digital Library, https://www .theodoreroosevelt center.org; Robert L. Longstreet to JL, May 15, 1902, James Longstreet Papers, Virginia Tech, Blacksburg, VA.

22. *Philadelphia Times,* May 18, 1902; *Evening Star* (Washington, DC), May 17, Sept. 30, Oct. 10, 1902; *Daily New Era* (Lancaster, PA), Sept. 30, 1902; *Virginian-Pilot* (Norfolk), Nov. 6, 1902.

23. JL to Randolph Longstreet, June 29, 1901, South Caroliniana Library, University of South Carolina, Columbia; JL to William Miller Owen, Nov. 1, 1890, https://alincoln bookshop.com/product/james-longstreet-autograph-letter-signature-2/. Longstreet did not forsake New Orleans after resettling in Georgia, but remained "always endeared to the old city," as he put in as in 1892, when returning there for a Confederate veterans' gathering. *New Orleans Times-Democrat,* April 7, 1892.

24. Pickett, xi–xiii; Lesley J. Gordon, "George E. Pickett (1825–1875)" and *General George E. Pickett in Life and Legend,* 52, 75, 86, 97; Gallagher, "A Widow and Her Soldier," 344.

25. JL to the *Century,* Feb. 1, March 11, 1898, and HDL to the *Century,* Dec. 3, 1903, *Century* Collection, New York Public Library, NY; JL to J. B. Lippincott, Jan. 17, Feb. 1, 1899, Records of the Commissioner of Railroads, RG 193, NA.

26. *Bangor Daily Whig & Courier* (ME), March 9, 1898; *Omaha Daily Bee,* April 23, 1901; *Los Angeles Times,* April 14, 1901; *Daily Times* (Richmond), June 24, 1900; Jones, 31–47.

27. *New York Times,* Aug. 22, 1903; *Americus Times-Recorder* (GA), May 16, 1903; *St. Louis Republic,* Oct. 4, 1903; Katharine M. Schmidt to A. W. Weddell, Aug. 4, 1903, Records of the Commissioner of Railroads, RG 193, NA.

28. HDL, *Lee and Longstreet at High Tide,* 217–21; on Longstreet's funeral, see also Alvarez, 70–77.

29. HDL, *Lee and Longstreet at High Tide,* 242, 332a–332d; *Southwestern Christian Advocate* (New Orleans), Jan. 14, 1904.

30. HDL, *Lee and Longstreet at High Tide,* 231, 238, 240, 242, 282, 316, 342; *Savannah Morning News,* Jan. 6, 1904.

31. *Home Journal* (Perry, GA), Feb. 4, 1904; Purcell, 211; *Columbus Ledger* (GA), Jan. 28, 1904; *Macon Telegraph* (GA), Jan. 7, 1904.

32. Purcell, 212, 218.

33. *Columbus Ledger* (GA), Jan. 28, 1904.

34. HDL, *Lee and Longstreet at High Tide,* 331, 354–55; *Boston Globe,* Aug. 17, 1904.

35. *Broad Ax* (Chicago), Jan. 16, 1904; *Richmond Planet,* Jan. 9, 1904.

36. Piston, *Lee's Tarnished Lieutenant,* 168–69, 172. On coverage of the Liberty Place anniversary, see, for example, *Daily Picayune,* Sept. 14, 1899, and *Southern Sentinel* (Winnfield, LA), Sept. 14, 1906. Mitch Landrieu, "New Orleans Mayor: Why I'm Taking Down My City's Confederate Monuments."

37. Alvarez, 74; Piston, *Lee's Tarnished Lieutenant,* 168–69, 172; *Macon Telegraph* (GA), Jan. 13, 1904.

38. HDL, *Lee and Longstreet at High Tide,* 228, 235, 238–40, 310, 316, 317 (Sickles quotation).

39. Ibid., 113; *Columbus Enquirer-Sun* (GA), Oct. 16, 1902; *New York Age,* Dec. 1, 1910; *Savannah Tribune,* Dec. 10, 1910; *Atlanta Constitution,* Nov. 13, 1910. On the Longstreet chapter of the UDC, see *Gainesville Eagle* (GA), April 16, 1896; *Gainesville News* (GA), Nov. 1, Dec. 6, 1905; Jan. 25, 1907; April 28, June 9, 1909.

40. HDL, *Lee and Longstreet at High Tide,* 31, 34, 56–63.

41. Ibid., 33, 85, 90, 112.

Epilogue: Of Monuments and Memory

1. Piston, *Lee's Tarnished Lieutenant*, 171–180 (quotations on 171, 176, 178). As the historian Nina Silber explains in *This War Ain't Over: Fighting the Civil War in New Deal America*, during the 1930s, a wide range of Americans turned to the Civil War for "valuable lessons" about "survival and resiliency" in midst of the Great Depression and this impulse "lent added force to a long-standing Lost Cause narrative."

2. *Gainesville News* (GA), Sept. 20, 1906; *Macon Daily Telegraph* (GA), Nov. 29, 1912.

3. *Atlanta Constitution*, Jan. 3, 1932, April 27, 1933; *Greenville News* (SC), Jan. 9, 1932.

4. *Washington Herald* (DC), June 26, 1922; *Washington Evening Star* (DC), June 27, 1922; *New York Tribune*, July 3, 1922.

5. *Buffalo Evening News*, July 2, 1938; *Savannah Evening Press*, March 30, 1940; "Ceremonies of Dedicating the Site on the Gettysburg Battlefield for the Equestrian Statue of General James Longstreet, July 2, 1941," in folder 7, Brochures and Broadsides, Longstreet Memorial Fund Records, 1991–1999 [hereafter LMF Records], UNC.

6. HDL to Tomlinson D. Todd, March 31, 1947, Anacostia Community Museum Archives, Washington, DC. *Evening Star* (Washington, DC), Oct. 13, 1943, Feb. 7, 1947, April 1, 1947; *People's Voice* (New York), Feb. 15, 1947; *Hartford Chronicle*, Feb. 22, 1947; *Pittsburgh Courier*, Feb. 15, 1947; *Baltimore Afro-American*, Feb. 15, 1947.

7. *Atlanta Daily World*, April 4, 1947, April 16, 1950.

8. HDL, "Longstreet: Soldier and Citizen," Oct. 5, 1938, and "Liberty Born of a Patriot's Dream," May 1946, in Helen Dortch Longstreet Papers, Speeches and Statements, 1938–1955, Kenan Research Center, Atlanta History Center, Atlanta; HDL, "Fadeless Glory," n.d., in Helen Dortch Longstreet Papers, Speeches, Civil War, Georgia Historical Society, Savannah, GA.

9. *Gettysburg Times* (PA), Jan. 11, 1949; HDL, "The Great American," 5–10; *Atlanta Constitution*, July 1, 1954; Helen Dortch Longstreet to Kenneth E. Crouch, April 17, 1951, Nau Collection, UVA.

10. For Robertson's introduction and Keller's foreword, see the 2020 Indiana University Press edition of James Longstreet, *From Manassas to Appomattox*, xxii–xxiv, xxxii. See also Krick, 184.

11. *Pensacola News* (FL), May 4, 1862; *Times* (Muster, IN), May 8, 1962.

12. *Orlando Sentinel* (FL), Dec. 1, 1974; Gallagher, *Causes Won, Lost, and Forgotten*, 57. In the slipstream of *The Killer Angels*, another favorable account of Longstreet's military record appeared, with the publication of Wilbur D. Thomas's 1979 biography, *General James "Pete" Longstreet, Lee's "Old War Horse": Scapegoat for Gettysburg*. Building on Sanger and Hay's work, the book sought to "neutralize the charge of culpability against Longstreet," but garnered little public notice (page x).

13. Keller, xxxii–xxxiii.

14. Robert C. Thomas to Jesse Helms, Nov. 22, 1991; Robert C. Thomas to Michael Hill, Feb. 9, 1993; Bill Johnson to Kathy Harrison, July 28, 1995; Robert Thomas to "Patrons of General Longstreet," Winter/Spring 1998, and Robert C. Thomas, "Voices from the Past: An Appeal for Support," LMF Records, UNC; Longstreet Memorial Fund T-Shirt Flyer, lent to the author by Gary W. Gallagher from his file of documents on the LMF.

15. Gabor Boritt to Robert C. Thomas, April 23, 1996, and Jamie Longstreet Paterson to "Whom It May Concern," May 2, 1996, LMF Records; *Daily News* (Lebanon, PA), July 4, 1998; *Intelligencer Journal* (Lancaster, PA), July 4, 1998.

16. *Greenville News* (SC), July 4, 1998; Gallagher, *Causes Won, Lost, and Forgotten*, 140.

17. For op-eds noting the absence of Longstreet memorials, see, for example, Holmes, "Where Are the Monuments to Confederate Gen. James Longstreet?"; Waite, "The Missing Statues That Expose the Truth About Confederate Monuments"; Foner, "Confederate Statues and 'Our' History"; Sinha, "What Those Monuments Stand For"; Serwer, "The Myth of the Kindly General Lee." It is not just the absence of statues that signifies Longstreet's marginalization. As the historians Mark E. Neely Jr., Harold Holzer, and Gabor S. Boritt have noted in their book on Confederate iconography, *The Confederate Image: Prints of the Lost Cause*, white Southerners turned to Northern printmakers to churn out the lithographs and engravings of Confederate heroes (such as Lee and Jackson) that were ubiquitous in Southern homes in the late nineteenth century. But "ardent reconciliationists" like Mosby and Longstreet were not featured in such prints.

18. Landrieu, "New Orleans Mayor: Why I'm Taking Down My City's Confederate Monuments." The Liberty Place monument was temporarily removed during a road construction project on Canal Street in 1989 and then reinstalled one block north four years later. Schafer, "The Battle of Liberty Place."

19. For opinion pieces connecting the 1874 Canal Street coup and January 6, 2021, see, for example, Bouie, "Running Out the Clock on Trump Is Cowardly and Dangerous"; Landrieu, "Only Accountability Will Allow the US to Move Forward."

20. On Barnes, see Richards, "Ex-Governor: Replace Confederate Statue"; see also Lane, "The Forgotten Confederate." The naming of army bases and other US military assets further bespeaks the controversies over Longstreet's politics. US military bases were named after Confederate leaders, including some of Longstreet's principal nemeses—such as Braxton Bragg and John Brown Gordon—and a World War II tank was named after J. E. B. Stuart. But Longstreet's only such honor proved a pyrrhic victory. A naval vessel (a steel steam freighter) christened the SS *James Longstreet* was built during World War II as a dry cargo carrier, only to be blown aground and dry-docked, and then destined to continue its career into the Korean and Vietnam wars as a target ship that US Navy ships and military planes used for testing bombs. More revealing still, to this day, the West Point website does not list Longstreet among its notable graduates—although it does list other Confederates, including Lee, Davis, Stuart, Pickett, Jackson, and A. P. Hill. See Beyle, *The Target Ship in Cape Cod Bay* and "Notable Graduates," United States Military Academy at West Point online, https://www .westpoint.edu /about/history-of-west-point/notable-graduates.

21. *Weekly Inter Ocean* (Chicago), Feb. 26, 1880.

BIBLIOGRAPHY

Unpublished Sources

Anacostia Community Museum Archives, Washington, DC
  Helen Dortch Longstreet to Tomlinson D. Todd, March 31, 1947
Atlanta History Center, Kenan Research Center
  Helen Dortch Longstreet Papers
Brooklyn Public Library, New York
  Washington A. Roebling Family Letters
Duke University, Rubenstein Library, Durham, NC
  Augustus Baldwin Longstreet Papers
  James Longstreet Papers
Emory University, Stuart A. Rose Manuscript, Archives, and Rare Book Library, Atlanta, GA
  James Longstreet Papers
Fredericksburg and Spotsylvania National Military Park, VA
  James Longstreet to Augustus Baldwin Longstreet, August 13, 1861
Georgia Archives Virtual Vault, University of Georgia System
  James Longstreet Confederate Pension Application
Georgia Historical Society, Savannah, GA
  Helen Dortch Longstreet Papers
Gilder Lehrman Collection, Gilder Lehrman Institute of American History, New York
  Longstreet Letters (assorted letters covering 1850–1894)
Rutherford B. Hayes Presidential Library & Museums, Fremont, OH
  Rutherford B. Hayes Papers
Historic New Orleans Collection, New Orleans, LA
  Walton-Glenny Family Papers

BIBLIOGRAPHY

Howard University, Moorland-Spingarn Research Center, Washington, DC

Blanche K. Bruce Papers

P. B. S. Pinchback Papers

Huntington Library, San Marino, CA

Joseph E. Johnston Papers

Library of Congress, Washington, DC

Chester A. Arthur Papers

Benjamin F. Butler Papers

James A. Garfield Papers

Benjamin Harrison Papers

William McKinley Papers

Louis T. Wigfall Papers

Morgan Library & Museum, Department of Literary and Historical Manuscripts, New York, NY

Benjamin H. Hill to James Longstreet, July 30, 1877

National Archives and Records Administration, Washington, DC

Record Group 29: Records of the Bureau of the Census

- US Federal Census Records (1820–1900) and Slave Schedules (1820–1860)

Record Group 48: Records of the Office of the Secretary of the Interior

- Charges and Protests File, Appointments Division

Record Group 59: General Records of the Department of State, 1763–2002

- Despatches from US Ministers to Turkey

- Applications and Recommendations for Public Office

Record Group 193: Records of the Commissioner of Railroads

- Letters Sent by General James Longstreet

Record Group 94: Records of the Adjutant General's Office

- Confederate Amnesty Papers

Record Group 109: War Department Collection of Confederate Records

- James Longstreet, Compiled Service Record

New Orleans Public Library, New Orleans, LA

Coroner's Office. Records of Inquests and Views, vols. 23–24, 1872–74.

Board of Metropolitan Police Pension Fund Ledger, 1870–1876

Orleans Parish (LA) Seventh District Court, *State of Virginia v. James Longstreet*,
    1872

New-York Historical Society, New York

    Civil War Letters Collection

    James Longstreet Collection

New York Public Library, New York

    Century Collection

Southern Methodist University, DeGolyer Library

    Edmunds Holloway Family Letters

Tennessee State Library and Archives, Nashville

    Civil War Military Records Digital Collection

Theodore Roosevelt Digital Library

    John Ireland to Theodore Roosevelt, April 16, 1902, and "Memorandum on James
        Longstreet," c. 1902

Tulane University, Special Collections, New Orleans

    Algernon Badger Family Papers

    Longstreet to Lawrence M. Duncan, November 30, 1870

University of North Carolina, Wilson Special Collections Library, Chapel Hill, NC

    James Longstreet Papers

    Longstreet Memorial Fund Records

    William Porcher Miles Papers

    Henry Clay Warmoth Papers

University of South Carolina, South Caroliniana Library, Columbia, SC

    James Longstreet Papers

Library of Virginia, Richmond

    Samuel G. Estes to W. A. Estes, May 10, 1863

    Mahone Family Papers

    Henry Thweatt Owens Papers

    William Nelson Pendleton Papers

University of Virginia, Albert and Shirley Small Special Collections Library,
    Charlottesville, VA

    John L. Nau III Civil War History Collection

BIBLIOGRAPHY

Papers of Fitzhugh Lee

James Longstreet to Daniel E. Sickles, September 19, 1902

Longstreet Memorial Association Broadside

Minor-Venable Papers

Papers of Thomas Lafayette Rosser Jr.

Virginia Museum of History and Culture, Richmond

John Walter Fairfax Papers

Osmun Latrobe Diary

Hunter Holmes McGuire Papers

Virginia Tech, Blacksburg, VA

James Longstreet Papers

Published Primary Sources

Alexander, Edward Porter. *Fighting for the Confederacy: The Personal Recollections of General Edward Porter Alexander*, edited by Gary W. Gallagher. Chapel Hill: University of North Carolina Press, 1989.

Allan, William. "Memorandum of Conversations with General Robert E. Lee." In *Lee, The Soldier*, edited by Gary W. Gallagher. Lincoln: University of Nebraska Press, 1996.

Archaeological Institute of America. *Second Annual Report of the Executive Committee, 1880–81*. Boston: John Wilson and Son, 1881.

Bergeron, Paul H., ed. *The Papers of Andrew Johnson*, Vol. 8, *May–August, 1865*. Knoxville: University of Tennessee Press, 1989.

Blackett, R. J. M., edited by *Thomas Morris Chester: Black Civil War Correspondent: His Dispatches from the Virginia Front*. Baton Rouge: Louisiana State University Press, 1989.

Blackford, Susan Leigh, and Charles Minor Blackford. *Letters from Lee's Army, or Memoirs of Life in and out of the Army in Virginia During the War Between the States*. New York: Scribner, 1947.

Burr, Charles Chauncey. "Editor's Table." *Old Guard*, November 1868.

———. "The South and Her Faltering Men." *Old Guard*, August 1867.

BIBLIOGRAPHY

Carter, Rev. E. R. *The Black Side: A Partial History of the Business, Religious and Educational Side of the Negro in Atlanta, Ga.* Atlanta: n.p., 1894.

Cockrum, William M. *History of the Underground Railroad as It Was Conducted by the Anti-Slavery League.* Oakland City, IN: J. W. Cockrum Printing, c. 1915.

Cooke, John Esten. *A Life of Gen. Robert E. Lee.* New York: D. Appleton, 1871.

Cutrer, Thomas W., ed. *Longstreet's Aide: The Civil War Letters of Major Thomas J. Goree.* Charlottesville: University Press of Virginia, 1995.

Dawson, Francis W. *Reminiscences of Confederate Service, 1861–1865.* Charleston, SC: News and Courier Book Press, 1882.

Dodge, Theodore Ayrault. *Napoleon: A History of the Art of War.* Vol 4. Boston: Houghton Mifflin, 1907.

Douglass, Frederick. "Alonzo B. Cornell and the Republican Party." Address delivered in Utica, New York, October 30, 1879, in Speeches, Debates and Interviews. Vol. 4: 1864–1880, Frederick Douglass Papers Digital Edition.

Early, Jubal. "Leading Confederates on the Battle of Gettysburg: A Review by General Early." *Southern Historical Society Papers* 4 (Dec. 1877).

———. "Letter from Gen. J.A. Early." *Southern Historical Society Papers* 4 (Aug. 1877).

———. "Reply to General Longstreet's Second Paper." *Southern Historical Society Papers* 5 (June 1878).

Farnsworth, Fred. E. *Proceedings of the Fourth Annual Meeting of the Michigan Club.* Detroit: Winn & Hammond, 1890.

Fitzgerald, Oscar Penn. *Judge Longstreet: A Life Sketch.* Nashville: Methodist Episcopal Church South, 1891.

Fremantle, Arthur J. L. *Three Months in the Southern States: April–June, 1863.* 1864. Reprint, Lincoln: University of Nebraska Press, 1991.

Gordon, John Brown. *Reminiscences of the Civil War.* 1903. Reprint, Baton Rouge: Louisiana State University Press, 1993.

Grant, Ulysses S. *Papers of Ulysses S. Grant,* edited by John Y. Simon. Vols. 14–24. Carbondale and Edwardsville: Southern Illinois University Press, 1985–2000.

———. *Personal Memoirs of U. S. Grant.* 1885. Reprint, New York: Penguin, 1999.

Hood, John Bell, *The Lost Papers of Confederate General John Bell Hood.* Edited by Stephen M. Hood. El Dorado Hills, CA: Savas Beatie, 2015.

Jeter, Henry N. *Pastor Henry N. Jeter's Twenty-Five Years Experience with the Shiloh Baptist Church and Her History*. Providence: Remington, 1901.

Jomini, Baron Henri de. *The Art of War*. Philadelphia: Lippincott, 1862.

Keckley, Elizabeth. *Behind the Scenes. Or, Thirty Years a Slave, and Four Years in the White House*. New York: G. W. Carleton, 1868.

Kellogg, William Pitt. *Annual Message of His Excellency Governor Wm. Pitt Kellogg to the General Assembly of Louisiana*. New Orleans: Republican Office, 1874.

Lee, Susan P. *Memoirs of William Nelson Pendleton*. Philadelphia: Lippincott, 1893.

Longstreet, Augustus B. *A Voice from the South*. Baltimore: Samuel E. Smith, 1847.

———. "From Out the Fires." *XIX Century* (December 1869).

———. *Letters on the Epistle of Paul to Philhemon, or the Connection of Apostolical Christianity with Slavery*. Charleston, SC: B. Jenkins, 1845.

———. "Review of Perry's Sketch of J. C. Calhoun," *XIX Century* (January 1870).

Longstreet, Helen D. "The Great American: General James Longstreet." *Mark Twain Quarterly* 9 (Winter 1953).

———. *Lee and Longstreet at High Tide: Gettysburg in the Light of the Official Records*. Self-published, Gainesville, GA, 1904.

Longstreet, James. "The Battle of Fredericksburg." *Century* 32 (August 1886).

———. *From Manassas to Appomattox: Memoirs of the Civil War in America*. 1896. Reprint, New York: Da Capo Press, 1992.

———. "General James Longstreet's Account of the Campaign and Battle." *Southern Historical Society Papers* 5 (Jan. 1878).

———. "General Longstreet's Second Paper on Gettysburg." *Southern Historical Society Papers* 5 (June 1878).

———. "The Invasion of Maryland." *Century* 32 (June 1886).

———. "Lee in Pennsylvania." In *The Annals of the Civil War: Written by Leading Participants North and South*. 1878. Reprint, New York: Da Capo Press, 1994.

———. "Lee's Invasion of Pennsylvania." *Century* 33 (Feb. 1887).

———. "The Loyal South of To-Day." *Independent*, July 6, 1899.

———. "Our March Against Pope." *Century* 31 (Feb. 1886).

———. "The Seven Days' Fighting About Richmond." *Century* 30 (July 1885).

Louisiana Adjutant General's Office. *Annual Report of the Adjutant General of the State of Louisiana, for the Year Ending December 31, 1870.* New Orleans: A. L. Lee, State Printer, 1871.

———. *Annual Report of the Adjutant General of the State of Louisiana for the Year Ending December 31, 1872.* New Orleans: Republican Office, 1873.

———. *Annual Report of the Adjutant General of the State of Louisiana for the Year Ending December 31, 1873.* New Orleans: Republican Office, 1874.

———. *Annual Report of the Adjutant General of the State of Louisiana, for the Year Ending December 31, 1874.* New Orleans: Republican Office, 1875.

Mahan, Alfred Thayer. *The Life of Nelson: The Embodiment of the Sea Power of Great Britain.* Vol. 1. London: Sampson Low, Martston, 1897.

McClure, Alexander. *Colonel Alexander K. McClure's Recollections of Half a Century.* Salem, MA: Salem Press, 1902.

Moore, Frank, ed. *Rebellion Record: A Diary of American Events.* Vol. 11. New York: D. Van Nostrand, 1868.

Moseley, Ronald, ed. *The Stillwell Letters: A Georgian in Longstreet's Corps, Army of Northern Virginia.* Macon, GA: Mercer University Press, 2002.

Nash, Charles E. "Political Condition of the South." *Congressional Record,* 44th Cong., 1st Sess., June 7, 1876, 3667–69.

Patteson, S. S. P. "Longstreet and the War Between the States." *Sewanee Review* 4 (May 1896).

Pickett, LaSalle Corbell. *Pickett and His Men.* Atlanta: Foote and Davies, 1900.

Porter, Horace. *Campaigning with Grant.* 1897. Reprint, New York: Da Capo Press, 1986.

Raymer, Jacob Nathaniel. *Confederate Correspondent: The Civil War Reports of Jacob Nathaniel Raymer, Fourth North Carolina.* Edited by E. B. Munson. Jefferson, NC: McFarland, 2009.

Smedes, W. C., and T. A. Marshall. *Reports of Cases Argued and Determined in the High Court of Errors and Appeals for the State of Mississippi.* Boston: Charles C. Little and James Brown, 1848.

Sorrel, G. Moxley. *At the Right Hand of Longstreet: Reflections of a Confederate Staff Officer.* 1905. Reprint, Lincoln: University of Nebraska Press, 1999.

Stiles, Robert. *Four Years Under Marse Robert.* New York: Neale, 1903.

Styple, William B., ed. *Writing & Fighting the Confederate War: The Letters of Peter Wellington Alexander, Confederate War Correspondent.* Kearny, NJ: Belle Grove, 2002.

US House. *Condition of Affairs in Louisiana.* House Executive Document 91. 42nd Cong., 3rd Session. Washington, DC: Government Printing Office, 1873.

————. *Condition of Affairs in Louisiana.* House Report 101, Pt. 2, 43rd Cong., 2nd Session. Washington, DC: Government Printing Office, 1875.

————. *Condition of Affairs in the South.* House Report 261, Pts. 1–3, 43rd Cong., 2nd Session. Washington, DC: Government Printing Office, 1875.

————. *Testimony Taken by the Committee on Expenditures in the Department of Justice.* Washington, DC: Government Printing Office, 1884.

————. *Testimony Taken by Select Committee to Investigate Condition of Affairs in Louisiana.* House Misc. Doc. 211, 42nd Cong., 2nd Session. Washington, DC: Government Printing Office, 1872.

US, *Register of Civil, Military, and Naval Service.* Washington: Government Printing Office, 1871.

US Senate. *Louisiana Investigation, Pt. 2: State Constitution, Election Laws, Testimony, Returns, and Exhibits*, Senate Doc. 457, 42nd Cong., 3rd Session and Special Session. Washington, DC: Government Printing Office, 1872.

————. *Message of the President, Communicating Information on Alleged Interference in Organization of General Assembly of Louisiana.* Senate Exec. Doc. 13, 43rd Cong., 2nd Session. Washington, DC: Government Printing Office, 1875.

————. *Report and Testimony of the Select Committee of the United States Senate to Investigate the Causes of the Removal of the Negroes from the Southern States to the Northern States, Pts. 2–3.* Washington: Government Printing Office, 1880, 512–21.

US Supreme Court. *Ex parte Yarbrough*, 110 US 651; 28 L. Ed. 274; 4 S. Ct. 152.

————. *Transcript of Record, US Supreme Court 1883*, 15, Original, 110 US 651. 4 S. Ct. 152, 28 L. Ed. 274, 1-22-1884.

US War Department. *The War of the Rebellion: A Compilation of the Official Records of the Union and Confederate Armies.* 128 vols. Washington, DC: Government Printing Office, 1880–1901.

Walton, J. B., J. A. Chalaron, B. F. Eschelman, and W. M. Owen. "Sketches of the

History of the Washington Artillery." *Southern Historical Society Papers* 11 (Jan. to Dec., 1883).

Weaver, C. P., ed. *Thank God My Regiment Is an African One: The Civil War Diary of Colonel Nathan W. Daniels.* Baton Rouge: Louisiana State University Press, 1998.

Williams, George W. *History of the Negro Race in America from 1619 to 1880.* Vol. 2. New York: G. P. Putnam's Sons, 1883.

Wyckoff, Mac, ed. *The Civil War Letters of Alexander McNeill, 2nd South Carolina Infantry Regiment.* Columbia: University of South Carolina Press, 2016.

Selected Newspapers

Atlanta Constitution

Augusta Constitutionalist (GA)

Baltimore Sun

Banner Watchman (Athens, GA)

Broad Ax (Salt Lake City and Chicago)

Cincinnati Enquirer

Charleston Tri-Weekly Courier (SC)

Chicago Tribune

Christian Recorder (Philadelphia)

Cleveland Daily Herald

Columbus Daily Enquirer-Sun (GA)

Constitution (Washington, DC)

Daily Chronicle & Sentinel (Augusta, GA)

Evening Star (Washington, DC)

Frank Leslie's Illustrated Newspaper (NY)

Freeman (NY)

Gainesville Eagle (GA)

Gainesville News (GA)

Inter Ocean (Chicago)

Le Carillon (New Orleans)

Macon Telegraph (GA)

BIBLIOGRAPHY

National Era (Washington, DC)

New Orleans Picayune

New Orleans Republican

New Orleans Times

New York Age

New York Globe

New York Herald

New York Times

New York Tribune

Philadelphia Inquirer

Philadelphia Times

Richmond Daily Dispatch

Richmond Examiner

Richmond Planet

St. Louis Globe-Democrat

Savannah Morning News

Savannah Republican

Savannah Tribune

South-Western (Shreveport, LA)

Southwestern Christian Advocate (New Orleans)

Star of Zion (Charlotte, NC)

Troy Times (NY)

Washington Bee (DC)

Washington Post

Weekly Louisianian (New Orleans)

Weekly News and Courier (Charleston, SC)

Secondary Sources

Alvarez, Eugene. "'The Death of the 'Old War Horse' Longstreet." *Georgia Historical Quarterly* 52 (March 1968).

BIBLIOGRAPHY

Arrington, Benjamin T. *The Last Lincoln Republican: The Presidential Election of 1880*. Lawrence: University Press of Kansas, 2020.

Aucoin, Brent J. *A Rift in the Clouds: Race and the Southern Federal Judiciary, 1900–1910*. Fayetteville: University of Arkansas Press, 2007.

Auslander, Mark. *The Accidental Slaveowner: Revisiting a Myth of Race and Finding an American Family*. Athens: University of Georgia Press, 2011.

Ayers, Edward. *The Promise of the New South: Life After Reconstruction*. New York: Oxford University Press, 1992.

Bacote, Clarence A. "Negro Officeholders in Georgia Under President McKinley." *Journal of Negro History* 44 (July 1959).

Baker, Jean H. *James Buchanan*. New York: Henry Holt, 2004.

Beisner, Robert L. *From the Old Diplomacy to the New, 1865–1900*. Wheeling, IL: Harlan Davidson, 1986.

Bell, Caryn Cossé. "'Une Chimere': The Freedmen's Bureau in Creole New Orleans." In *The Freedmen's Bureau and Reconstruction: Reconsiderations*, edited by Paul A. Cimbala and Randall M. Miller. New York: Fordham University Press, 1999.

Bell, Karen Cook. *Claiming Freedom: Race, Kinship, and Land in Nineteenth-Century Georgia*. Columbia: University of South Carolina Press, 2018.

Bergeron, Paul H. *Andrew Johnson's Civil War and Reconstruction*. Knoxville: University of Tennessee Press, 2011.

Beyle, Noel W. *The Target Ship in Cape Cod Bay*. Orleans, MA: First Encounter Press, 1992.

Blight, David. *Race and Reunion: The Civil War in American Memory*. Cambridge, MA: Harvard University Press, 2001.

Boyar, Ebru, and Kate Fleet. *A Social History of Ottoman Istanbul*. Cambridge: Cambridge University Press, 2010.

Brasher, Glenn David. *The Peninsula Campaign and the Necessity of Emancipation: African Americans and the Fight for Freedom*. Chapel Hill: University of North Carolina Press, 2014.

Brook, Daniel. *The Accident of Color: A Story of Race in Reconstruction*. New York: Norton, 2019.

Brundage, W. Fitzhugh. *Lynching in the New South: Georgia and Virginia, 1880–1930*. Urbana: University of Illinois Press, 1993.

BIBLIOGRAPHY

Burr, Alwyn. *Black Texans: A History of the African Americans in Texas, 1528–1995.*
Norman: University of Oklahoma Press, 1996.

Burton, Orville Vernon. *In My Father's House Are Many Mansions: Family and
Community in Edgefield, South Carolina.* Chapel Hill: University of North Carolina
Press, 1985.

Busey, John W., and Travis W. Busey. *Confederate Casualties at Gettysburg: A Comprehensive
Record.* Jefferson, NC: McFarland, 2016.

Busey, John W., and David G. Martin. *Regimental Strengths and Losses at Gettysburg.*
East Windsor, NJ: Longstreet House, 2005.

Calhoun, Charles. *Conceiving a New Republic: The Republican Party and the Southern
Question, 1869–1900.* Lawrence: University Press of Kansas, 2006.

Calhoun, Frederick S. *The Lawmen: United States Marshals and Their Deputies,
1789–1989.* New York: Penguin Books, 1991.

Carmichael, Peter S. "A Whole Lot of Blame to Go Around: The Confederate Collapse
at Five Forks." In *Petersburg to Appomattox: The End of the War in Virginia,* edited by
Caroline E. Janney. Chapel Hill: University of North Carolina Press, 2018.

Clary, David A. " 'I Am Already a Texan': Albert J. Myer's Letters from Texas,
1854–1856." *Southwestern Historical Quarterly* 82 (July 1978).

Claude, Richard. "Constitutional Voting Rights and Early US Supreme Court
Doctrine." *Journal of Negro History* 51 (April 1966).

Coker, Caleb, and Janet G. Humphrey. "The Texas Frontier in 1850: Dr. Ebenezer Swift
and the View from Fort Martin Scott." *Southwestern Historical Quarterly* 96 (January
1993).

Conroy-Krutz, Emily. "The Vast Kingdom of God." *William & Mary Quarterly* 78
(April 2021).

Cormier, Steven A. *The Siege of Suffolk: The Forgotten Campaign, April 11–May 4, 1863.*
Lynchburg, VA: H. E. Howard, 1989.

Cozzens, Peter. *This Terrible Sound: The Battle of Chickamauga.* Urbana: University of
Illinois Press, 1994.

Creighton, Margaret S. *The Colors of Courage: Gettysburg's Forgotten History* (New York:
Basic Books, 2005).

Crotty, Rob. "Confederate Dirty Laundry: Spies and Slaves." *Pieces of History* (blog).

BIBLIOGRAPHY

National Archives online, https://prologue.blogs.archives.gov/2011/02/11/confederate-dirty-laundry-spies-and-slaves/.

Cunningham, Roger D. "The Black 'Immune' Regiments in the Spanish-American War." Army Historical Foundation online, https://armyhistory.org/the-black-immune-regiments-in-the-spanish-american-war/.

———. "'His Influence with the Colored People Is Marked': Christian Fleetwood's Quest for Command in the War with Spain and Its Aftermath." *Army History* 51 (Winter 2001).

Daggett, Melissa. *Spiritualism in Nineteenth-Century New Orleans: The Life and Times of Henry Louis Rey*. Jackson: University Press of Mississippi, 2017.

Dailey, Jane. *Before Jim Crow: The Politics of Race in Postemancipation Virginia*. Chapel Hill: University of North Carolina Press, 2000.

Davis, Harold E. "Henry W. Grady, Master of the Atlanta Ring, 1880–1886." *Georgia Historical Quarterly* 69 (Spring 1985).

De Santis, Vincent P. "Negro Dissatisfaction with the Republican Policy in the South, 1882–1884." *Journal of Negro History* (April 1951).

Desdunes, Rodolphe Lucien. *Our People and Our History: Fifty Creole Portraits*. Baton Rouge: Louisiana State University Press, 1973.

Devore, Donald E. "Race Relations and Community Development: The Education of Blacks in New Orleans, 1862–1960." PhD diss., Louisiana State University, 1989.

Dew, Charles B. *Apostles of Disunion: Southern Secession Commissioners and the Causes of the Civil War*. Charlottesville: University of Virginia Press, 2001.

Dittmer, John. *Black Georgians in the Progressive Era, 1900–1920*. Urbana: University of Illinois Press, 1977.

Dulaney, W. Marvin. *Black Police in America*. Bloomington: Indiana University Press, 1996.

Dunkerly, Robert M., Donald C. Pfanz, and David R. Ruth. *No Turning Back: A Guide to the 1864 Overland Campaign, from the Wilderness to Cold Harbor, May 4–June 13, 1864*. El Dorado Hills, CA: Savas Beatie, 2014.

Egerton, Douglas R. *The Wars of Reconstruction: The Brief, Violent History of America's Most Progressive Era*. New York: Bloomsbury Press, 2014.

Emberton, Carole. "The Limits of Incorporation: Violence, Gun Rights, and Gun Regulation in the Reconstruction South." *Stanford Law Review* 17 (2006).

Finkel, Caroline. *Osman's Dream: The Story of the Ottoman Empire*. New York: Perseus Books, 2005.

Fitzgerald, Michael W. *Urban Emancipation: Popular Politics in Reconstruction Mobile, 1860–1890*. Baton Rouge: Louisiana State University Press, 2002.

Foner, Eric. *Freedom's Lawmakers: A Directory of Black Office Holders During Reconstruction*. Baton Rouge: Louisiana State University Press, 1996.

———. *The Second Founding: How the Civil War and Reconstruction Remade the Constitution*. New York: Norton, 2019.

———. *A Short History of Reconstruction*. New York: Harper Perennial, 1990.

Gallagher, Gary W. "A Widow and Her Soldier: Lasalle Corbell Pickett as Author of the George E. Pickett Letters." *Virginia Magazine of History and Biography* (July 1986).

———. *Becoming Confederates: Paths to a New National Loyalty*. Athens: University of Georgia Press, 2013.

———. *Causes Won, Lost, and Forgotten: How Hollywood and Popular Art Shape What We Know About the Civil War*. Chapel Hill: University of North Carolina Press, 2008.

———. "'If the Enemy Is There, We Must Attack Him': R. E. Lee and the Second Day at Gettysburg." In *The Second Day at Gettysburg: Essays on Confederate and Union Leadership*, edited by Gary W. Gallagher. Kent, OH: Kent State University Press, 1993.

———. Introduction to *Autobiographical Sketch and Narrative of the War Between the States*, by Jubal Early. 1912. Reprint, Wilmington, NC: Broadfoot, 1989.

———. Introduction to *A Memoir of the Last Year of the War of Independence, in the Confederate States of America*, by Jubal A. Early. 1866. Reprint, Columbia: University of South Carolina Press, 2001.

———. "Lee's Army Has Not Lost Any of Its Prestige: The Impact of Gettysburg on the Army of Northern Virginia and the Confederate Home Front." In *The Third Day at Gettysburg and Beyond*, edited by Gary W. Gallagher. Chapel Hill: University of North Carolina Press, 1994.

———. "The Net Result of the Campaign Was in Our Favor: Confederate Reactions to the Maryland Campaign." In *The Antietam Campaign*, edited by Gary W. Gallagher. Chapel Hill: University of North Carolina Press, 1999.

———. "Scapegoat in Victory: James Longstreet and the Battle of Second Manassas." *Civil War History* (December 1988).

Gannon, Barbara. *The Won Cause: Black and White Comradeship in the Grand Army of the Republic*. Chapel Hill: University of North Carolina Press, 2011.

Gardner, Sarah E. *Blood & Irony: Southern White Women's Narratives of the Civil War, 1861–1937*. Chapel Hill: University of North Carolina Press, 2004.

———. "Helen Dortch Longstreet (1863–1962)." New Georgia Encyclopedia, https://www.georgiaencyclopedia.org/articles/history-archaeology/helen-dortch-longstreet-1863-1962.

Glatthaar, Joseph T. *General Lee's Army: From Victory to Collapse*. New York: Free Press, 2008.

Gordon, Lesley J. *General George E. Pickett in Life and Legend*. Chapel Hill: University of North Carolina Press, 2000.

———. "George E. Pickett (1825–1875)." https://encyclopediavirginia.org/entries/pickett-george-e-1825-1875/.

Gragg, Rod, ed. *Eyewitness Gettysburg: The Civil War's Greatest Battle*. Washington, DC: Regnery History, 2013.

Grant, Donald L. *The Way It Was in the South: The Black Experience in Georgia*. Athens: University of Georgia Press, 1993.

Glymph, Thavolia. *Out of the House of Bondage: The Transformation of the Plantation Household*. Cambridge: Cambridge University Press, 2008.

Guardino, Peter. *The Dead March: A History of the Mexican-American War*. Cambridge, MA: Harvard University Press, 2017.

Guelzo, Allen C. *Gettysburg: The Last Invasion*. New York: Knopf, 2013.

———. *Robert E. Lee: A Life*. New York: Knopf, 2021.

Haas, H. E. "Fort Lincoln." Texas State Historical Association online, https://www.tshaonline.org/handbook/entries/fort-lincoln.

Hall, Claude D. "The Fabulous Tom Ochiltree: Promoter, Politician, and Raconteur." *Southwestern Historical Quarterly* 71 (January 1968).

Hämäläinen, Pekka. *The Comanche Empire*. New Haven, CT: Yale University Press, 2008.

Hanioglu, M. Sukru. *A Brief History of the Late Ottoman Empire*. Princeton, NJ: Princeton University Press, 2008.

Harsh, Joseph L. *Confederate Tide Rising: Robert E. Lee and the Making of Southern Strategy, 1861–1862*. Kent, OH: Kent State University Press, 1998.

Hassler, William W. "The 'Ghost' of General Longstreet." *Georgia Historical Quarterly* 65 (Spring 1981).

Hennessy, John J. *Return to Bull Run: The Campaign and Battle of Second Manassas.* Norman: University of Oklahoma Press, 1993.

Hess, Earl J. *The Knoxville Campaign: Burnside and Longstreet in East Tennessee.* Knoxville: University of Tennessee Press, 2012.

———. *Pickett's Charge: The Last Attack at Gettysburg.* Chapel Hill: University of North Carolina Press, 2001.

Hesseltine, William B., and Larry Gara. "Georgia's Confederate Leaders After Appomattox." *Georgia Historical Quarterly* 35 (March 1951).

Hogue, James K. "The Strange Career of Jim Longstreet: History and Contingency in the Civil War Era." In *The Struggle for Equality: Essays on Sectional Conflict, the Civil War, and the Long Reconstruction,* edited by Orville Vernon Burton, Jerald Podair, and Jennifer L. Weber. Charlottesville: University of Virginia Press, 2011.

———. *Uncivil War: Five New Orleans Street Battles and the Rise and Fall of Radical Reconstruction.* Baton Rouge: Louisiana State University Press, 2006.

Hollandsworth, James G. *The Louisiana Native Guards: The Black Military Experience During the Civil War.* Baton Rouge: Louisiana State University Press, 1998.

Holmes, William F. "Ellen Dortch and the Farmers' Alliance." *Georgia Historical Quarterly* 69 (Summer 1985).

Howe, Daniel Walker. *What Hath God Wrought: The Transformation of America, 1815–1848.* New York: Oxford University Press, 2007.

Hubbell, John T, "The Seven Days of George Brinton McClellan." In *The Richmond Campaign of 1862,* edited by Gary W. Gallagher. Chapel Hill: University of North Carolina Press, 2000.

Huebner, Timothy S. "Emory Speer and Federal Enforcement of the Rights of African Americans, 1880–1910." *American Journal of Legal History* 34 (2015).

Huffman, Greg. "Twisted Sources: How Confederate Propaganda Ended Up in the South's Schoolbooks." *Facing South* online, April 10, 2019, https://www.facingsouth.org/2019/04/twisted-sources-how-confederate-propaganda-ended-souths-school-books.

Hughes, Nathaniel Cheairs, and Roy P. Stonesifer. *The Life and Wars of Gideon J. Pillow.* Chapel Hill: University of North Carolina Press, 2011.

Hulett, Keith. "William Y. Atkinson (1854–1899)." New Georgia Encyclopedia, https://www
.georgiaencyclopedia.org/articles/government-politics/william-y-atkinson-1854-1899/.

Itkin, Beth Kressel. "'What Might Have Been a Fuss': The Many Faces of Equal Public
Rights in Reconstruction-Era Louisiana." *Louisiana History* 56 (Winter 2015).

Janney, Caroline E. *Ends of War: The Unfinished Fight of Lee's Army After Appomattox.*
Chapel Hill: University of North Carolina Press, 2021.

———. "'I Yield to No Man an Iota of My Convictions': Chickamauga and Chattanooga National Military Park and the Limits of Reconciliation." *Journal of the Civil
War Era* 2 (September 2012).

———. *Remembering the Civil War: Reunion and the Limits of Reconciliation.* Chapel
Hill: University of North Carolina Press, 2013.

Jones, Jonathan S. "Buying and Selling Health and Manhood: Civil War Veterans
and Opiate Addiction 'Cures.'" In *Buying & Selling Civil War Memory in Gilded Age
America,* edited by James Marten and Caroline E. Janney. Chapel Hill: University of
North Carolina Press, 2021.

Kamen, Henry A. "Remember the Virginius: New Orleans and Cuba in 1873." *Journal
of the Louisiana Historical Association* 11 (Autumn 1970).

Keith, LeeAnna. *The Colfax Massacre: The Untold Story of Black Power, White Terror, and
the Death of Reconstruction.* New York: Oxford University Press, 2009.

Keller, Christian. Foreword to *From Manassas to Appomattox*, by James Longstreet.
Edited by James I. Robertson Jr. Bloomington: Indiana University Press, 2020.

Knudsen, Harold M. *James Longstreet and the American Civil War: The Confederate
General Who Fought the Next War.* El Dorado Hills, CA: Savas Beatie, 2022.

Krick, Robert K. "'If Longstreet . . . Says So, It Is Most Likely Not True': James Long-
street and the Second Day at Gettysburg." In *The Second Day at Gettysburg: Essays on
Confederate and Union Leadership,* edited by Gary W. Gallagher. Kent, OH: Kent State
University Press, 1993.

Lane, Charles. *The Day Freedom Died: The Colfax Massacre, the Supreme Court, and the
Betrayal of Reconstruction.* New York: Henry Holt, 2008.

Langbart, David. "James Longstreet: After the Civil War." *The Text Message* (blog).
National Archives online, https://text-message.blogs.archives.gov/2016/11/01/james
-longstreet-after-the-civil-war/.

Lemann, Nicholas. *Redemption: The Last Battle of the Civil War*. New York: Farrar, Straus and Giroux, 2006.

Leonard, Elizabeth D. *Benjamin Franklin Butler: A Noisy, Fearless Life*. Chapel Hill: University of North Carolina Press, 2022.

Levine, Bruce. *Confederate Emancipation: Southern Plans to Free and Arm Slaves During the Civil War*. New York: Oxford University Press, 2005.

Linderman, Gerald. *Embattled Courage: The Experience of Combat in the American Civil War*. New York: Simon & Schuster, 1987.

Link, William A. *Atlanta, Cradle of the New South: Race and Remembering in the Civil War's Aftermath*. Chapel Hill: University of North Carolina Press, 2013.

Longacre, Edward G. *The Early Morning of War: Bull Run, 1861*. Norman: University of Oklahoma Press, 2014.

Makdisi, Ussama. *Artillery of Heaven: American Missionaries and the Failed Conversion of the Middle East*. Ithaca, NY: Cornell University Press, 2009.

Marvel, William. *Radical Sacrifice: The Rise and Ruin of Fitz John Porter*. Chapel Hill: University of North Carolina Press, 2021.

Matthews, John M. "Black Newspapermen and the Black Community in Georgia, 1890–1930," *Georgia Historical Quarterly* 68 (Fall 1984).

May, Robert E. "Young American Males and Filibustering in the Age of Manifest Destiny: The United States Army as a Cultural Mirror." *Journal of American History* 78 (December 1991).

McCurry, Stephanie. *Confederate Reckoning: Power and Politics in the Civil War South*. Cambridge, MA: Harvard University Press, 2020.

Mendoza, Alexander. *Confederate Struggle for Command: General James Longstreet and the First Corps in the West*. College Station: Texas A&M University Press, 2008.

Millett, Allan, Peter Maslowski, and William B. Feis. *For the Common Defense: A Military History of the United States from 1607 to 2012*. New York: Free Press, 2012.

Neely, Mark E., Harold Holzer, and Gabor S. Boritt. *The Confederate Image: Prints of the Lost Cause*. Chapel Hill: University of North Carolina Press, 1987.

Newcombe, Jr., William W. "German Artist on the Pedernales." *Southwestern Historical Quarterly* 82 (October 1978).

Nolan, Cathal J. *The Allure of Battle: A History of How Wars Have Been Won and Lost.* New York: Oxford University Press, 2017.

Norrell, Robert J. *Up from History: The Life of Booker T. Washington.* Cambridge, MA: Harvard University Press, 2009.

Nystrom, Justin. "African Americans in the Civil War." *64 Parishes* online, https://64parishes.org/entry/african-americans-in-the-civil-war.

———. "Battle of Liberty Place." *64 Parishes* online, https://64parishes.org/entry/the-battle-of-liberty-place.

———. *New Orleans After the Civil War: Race, Politics, and a New Birth of Freedom.* Baltimore: Johns Hopkins University Press, 2010.

———. "P. B. S. Pinchback." *64 Parishes* online, https://64parishes.org/entry/p-b-s-pinchback.

———. "Reconstruction." *64 Parishes* online, https://64parishes.org/entry/reconstruction.

O'Brien, Michael. *Conjectures of Order: Intellectual Life and the American South, 1810–1860.* Vol. 2. Chapel Hill: University of North Carolina Press, 2004.

Perkins, A. E. "Some Negro Officers and Legislators in Louisiana." *Journal of Negro History* 14 (October 1929).

Pfanz, Harry W. *Gettysburg: The Second Day.* Chapel Hill: University of North Carolina Press, 1987.

Pfarr, Corey M. *Longstreet at Gettysburg: A Critical Reassessment.* Jefferson, NC: McFarland, 2019.

Phelps, Nicole M. "One Service, Three Systems, Many Empires: The US Consular Service and the Growth of US Global Power, 1789–1924." In *Crossing Empires: Taking US History into Transimperial Terrain*, edited by Kristin L. Hoganson and Jay Sexton. Durham, NC: Duke University Press, 2020.

Piston, William Garrett. "Cross Purposes: Longstreet, Lee, and Confederate Attack Plans for July 3 at Gettysburg." In *The Third Day at Gettysburg and Beyond*, edited by Gary W. Gallagher. Chapel Hill: University of North Carolina Press, 1994.

———. "Lee's Tarnished Lieutenant: James Longstreet and His Image in American Society." University of South Carolina. ProQuest Dissertations, 1982.

———. *Lee's Tarnished Lieutenant: James Longstreet and His Place in Southern History.* Athens: University of Georgia Press, 1987.

————. "Petticoats, Promotions, and Military Assignments: Favoritism and the Antebellum Career of James Longstreet." In *James Longstreet: The Man, the Soldier, the Controversy*, edited by R. L. DiNardo and Albert A. Nofi. Conshohocken, PA: Combined, 1998.

Powell, Anthony L. "Roster of the 9th United States Volunteer Infantry, 1898 to 1899." The Spanish American War Centennial Website, https://www.spanamwar.com/9thus .htm.

Powers, J. Tracy. *Lee's Miserables: Life in the Army of Northern Virginia from the Wilderness to Appomattox*. Chapel Hill: University of North Carolina Press, 1998.

Priest, Andrew. *Designs on Empire: America's Rise to Power in the Age of European Imperialism*. New York: Columbia University Press, 2021.

Prior, David. "'Crete the Opening Wedge': Nationalism and International Affairs in Postbellum America." *Journal of Social History* 42 (Summer 2009).

Purcell, Sarah J. *Spectacle of Grief: Public Funerals and Memory in the Civil War Era*. Chapel Hill: University of North Carolina Press, 2022.

Rable, George C. *But There Was No Peace: The Role of Violence in the Politics of Reconstruction*. Athens: University of Georgia Press, 1984.

————. *Fredericksburg! Fredericksburg!* Chapel Hill: University of North Carolina Press, 2002.

Rankin, David C. "The Origins of Black Leadership in New Orleans During Reconstruction." *Journal of Southern History* 40 (August 1974).

Rawick, George P., ed. *The American Slave: A Composite Autobiography*. Supplement, Ser. 1, Vol. 7, *Mississippi Narratives, Part 2*. Westport, CT: Greenwood Press, 1977.

Reardon, Carol. *Pickett's Charge in History & Memory*. Chapel Hill: University of North Carolina Press, 1997.

————. *With a Sword in One Hand and Jomini in the Other: The Problem of Military Thought in the Civil War North*. Chapel Hill: University of North Carolina Press, 2012.

Richardson, Heather Cox. *To Make Men Free: A History of the Republican Party*. New York: Basic Books, 2014.

Richter, William L. "James Longstreet: From Rebel to Scalawag." *Louisiana History* 11 (Summer 1970).

Roberts, Mary. *Istanbul Exchanges: Ottomans, Orientalists, and Nineteenth-Century Visual Culture.* Oakland: University of California Press, 2015.

Rodrigue, John C. Introduction to *War, Politics, and Reconstruction: Stormy Days in Louisiana,* by Henry Clay Warmoth. 1930. Reprint, Columbia: University of South Carolina Press, 2006.

Rosen, Hannah. *Terror in the Heart of Freedom: Citizenship, Sexual Violence, and the Meaning of Race in the Postemancipation South.* Chapel Hill: University of North Carolina Press, 2009.

Ross, Michael A. *The Great New Orleans Kidnapping Case: Race, Law, and Justice in the Reconstruction Era.* New York: Oxford University Press, 2015.

Rousey, Dennis C. "Black Policemen in New Orleans." *Historian* (February 1987).

Sacks, B. "The Creation of the Territory of Arizona." *Arizona and the West* 5 (Summer 1963).

Sahin, Emrah. *Faithful Encounters: Authorities and American Missionaries in the Ottoman Empire.* Montreal: McGill-Queen's University Press, 2018.

Sanger, Donald Bridgman, and Thomas Robson Hay. *James Longstreet: I. Soldier; II. Politician, Officeholder, and Writer.* Baton Rouge: Louisiana State University Press, 1952.

Sawyer, Gordon. *James Longstreet: Before Manassas & After Appomattox.* Alpharetta, GA: Booklogix, 2005.

Sears, Stephen W. *Gettysburg.* Boston: Houghton Mifflin, 2003.

Schulte, Terrianne. "A 'Visionary' Plan? The Proposed March 1865 Peace Conference, Part 2." *Emerging Civil War* (blog), https://emergingcivilwardotcom.wordpress.com/2017/08/11/a-visionary-plan-the- proposed-march-1865-peace-conference-part-2/.

———. "A 'Visionary' Plan?, Part 3," *Emerging Civil War* (blog), https://emergingcivilwardotcom.wordpress.com/2017/08/12/a-visionary-plan-the-proposed-march-1865-peace-conference-part-3/.

———. "A 'Visionary' Plan?, Part 4," *Emerging Civil War* (blog), https://emergingcivilwar.com/2017/08/13/a-visionary-plan-the-proposed-march-1865-peace-conference-part-4/.

Sexton, Jay. "The Civil War and US World Power." In *American Civil Wars: The United States, Latin America, Europe, and the Crisis of the 1860s,* edited by Don H. Doyle. Chapel Hill: University of North Carolina Press, 2017.

Schafer, K. Judith. "The Battle of Liberty Place: A Matter of Historical Perception." *64 Parishes* online, https://64parishes.org/the-battle-of-liberty-place.

Shadgett, Olive Hall. *The Republican Party in Georgia from Reconstruction Through 1900.* Athens: University of Georgia Press, 1964.

Sheehan-Dean, Aaron. *Why Confederates Fought: Family & Nation in Civil War Virginia.* Chapel Hill: University of North Carolina Press, 2007.

Shinn, James M., Jr. "The 'Free Cuba' Campaign, Republican Politics, and Post–Civil War Black Internationalism." In *Revolutions and Reconstructions: Black Politics in the Long Nineteenth Century,* edited by Van Gosse and David Waldstreicher. Philadelphia: University of Pennsylvania Press, 2020.

Silber, Nina. *This War Ain't Over: Fighting the Civil War in New Deal America.* Chapel Hill: University of North Carolina Press, 2018.

Singal, Daniel Joseph. *The War Within: From Victorian to Modernist Thought in the South, 1919–1945.* Chapel Hill: University of North Carolina Press, 1982.

Smith, David G. *On the Edge of Freedom: The Fugitive Slave Issue in South Central Pennsylvania, 1820–1870.* New York: Fordham University Press, 2012.

———. "Race and Retaliation: The Capture of African Americans During the Gettysburg Campaign." In *Virginia's Civil War,* edited by Peter Wallenstein and Bertram Wyatt-Brown. Charlottesville: University of Virginia Press, 2005.

Smith, Karlton. "The Best Staff Officers in the Army—James Longstreet and His Staff of the First Corps." In *Papers of the Sixteenth Semiannual Gettysburg National Military Park Seminar, May 12–14, 2017.* Washington, DC: National Park Service, 2018. Available at http://npshistory.com/series/symposia/gettysburg_seminars/16/essay3.pdf.

Steckler, Robert M., and Jon D. Blachley. "The Cervical Wound of General James Longstreet." *Archives of Otolaryngology—Head and Neck Surgery* 126 (March 2000).

Sternhell, Yael A. "The Afterlives of a Confederate Archive: Civil War Documents and the Making of Sectional Reconciliation." *Journal of American History* 102 (March 2016).

Taylor, Amy Murrell. *Embattled Freedom: Journeys Through the Civil War's Slave Refugee Camps.* Chapel Hill: University of North Carolina Press, 2018.

BIBLIOGRAPHY

Thomas, Emory. *The Confederate State of Richmond: A Biography of the Capital.* Austin: University of Texas, 1971.

Thomas, Wilbur D. *General James "Pete" Longstreet, Lee's "Old War Horse": Scapegoat for Gettysburg.* Parsons, WV: McClain Print, 1979.

Thompson, Shirley Elizabeth. *Exiles at Home: The Struggle to Become American in Creole New Orleans.* Cambridge, MA: Harvard University Press, 2009.

Tunnell, Ted. *Crucible of Reconstruction: War, Radicalism, and Race in Louisiana, 1862–1877.* Baton Rouge: Louisiana State University Press, 1984.

United States Military Academy, West Point. "Notable Graduates." US Military Academy at West Point online, https://www.westpoint.edu/about/history-of-west-point/notable-graduates.

Varon, Elizabeth R. "Andrew Johnson: Domestic Affairs." Miller Center online, https://millercenter.org/president/johnson/domestic-affairs.

———. *Appomattox: Victory, Defeat, and Freedom at the End of the Civil War.* New York: Oxford University Press, 2014.

———. *Armies of Deliverance: A New History of the Civil War.* New York: Oxford University Press, 2019.

———. *Disunion! The Coming of the American Civil War, 1789–1859.* Chapel Hill: University of North Carolina Press, 2008.

———. "The Fall of Petersburg and Appomattox." In *The Oxford Handbook of the American Civil War,* edited by Lorien Foote and Earl J. Hess. New York: Oxford University Press, 2021.

———. "*From Manassas to Appomattox*: James Longstreet's Memoir and the Limits of Confederate Reconciliation." In *Civil War Witnesses and Their Books: New Perspectives on Iconic Works,* edited by Gary W. Gallagher and Stephen Cushman. Baton Rouge: Louisiana State University Press, 2021.

Vincent, Charles. *Black Legislators in Louisiana During Reconstruction.* Carbondale: Southern Illinois University Press, 1976.

———. "Oscar Dunn." *64 Parishes* online, https://64parishes.org/entry/oscar-dunn-2.

Walther, Karine V. *Sacred Interests: The United States and the Islamic World, 1821–1921.* Chapel Hill: University of North Carolina Press, 2015.

Waugh, Joan. *U. S. Grant: American Hero, American Myth*. Chapel Hill: University of North Carolina Press, 2009.

Wegman, Jessica. "'Playing in the Dark' with Longstreet's 'Georgia Scenes': Critical Reception and Reader Response to Treatments of Race and Gender." *Southern Literary Journal* 30 (Fall 1997).

Weigley, Russell F. *A Great Civil War: A Military and Political History, 1861–1865*. Bloomington: Indiana University Press, 2000.

Wert, Jeffry D. *General James Longstreet: The Confederacy's Most Controversial Soldier* New York: Simon & Schuster, 1993.

Wetta, Frank J. *The Louisiana Scalawags: Politics, Race, and Terrorism During the Civil War and Reconstruction*. Baton Rouge: Louisiana State University Press, 2012.

Winders, Richard Bruce. *Crisis in the Southwest: The United States, Mexico, and the Struggle over Texas*. Wilmington, DE: Scholarly Resources, 2002.

Woodward, Colin Edward. *Marching Masters: Slavery, Race, and the Confederate Army During the Civil War*. Charlottesville: University of Virginia Press, 2014.

Wooster, Robert. *The American Military Frontiers: The United States Army in the West, 1783–1900*. Albuquerque: University of New Mexico Press, 2009.

Wynes, Charles E., ed. "Lewis Harvie Blair: Texas Travels, 1851–1855." *Southwestern Historical Quarterly* 66 (October 1962).

Yellin, Eric S. "'It Was Still No South to Us': African American Civil Servants at the Fin de Siecle." *Washington History* 21 (2009).

Yiğit, Tarik Tansu. "Reconstructing the American Under the Most Unimaginable Conditions: Civil War Veterans in the 'Arabian Nights.'" *Journal of the Civil War Era* 11 (December 2021).

Contemporary Newspaper Opinion Pieces

Bouie, Jamelle. "Running Out the Clock on Trump Is Cowardly and Dangerous." *New York Times* online, Jan. 8, 2021: https://www.nytimes.com/2021/01/08/opinion/trump-capitol-riot-impeachment.html.

Foner, Eric. "Confederate Statues and 'Our' History." *New York Times* online, Aug. 20,

2017: https://www.nytimes.com/2017/08/20/opinion/confederate-statues-american
-history.html.

Holmes, Steven A. "Where Are the Monuments to Confederate Gen. James Longstreet?" CNN online, Aug. 23, 2017: https://www.cnn.com/2017/08/23/opinions
/where-are-monuments-to-confederate-general-longstreet-opinion-holmes/index
.html.

Landrieu, Mitch. "New Orleans Mayor: Why I'm Taking Down My City's Confederate
Monuments." *Washington Post* online, May 11, 2017: https://www.washingtonpost
.com/posteverything/wp/2017/05/11/new-orleans-mayor-why-im-taking-down-my
-citys-confederate-monuments/.

———. "Only Accountability Will Allow the U.S. to Move Forward." *Atlantic* online,
Jan. 30, 2021: https://www.theatlantic.com/ideas/archive/2021/01/only-account
ability-will-allow-us-move forward/617876/.

Lane, Charles. "The Forgotten Confederate General Who Deserves a Monument."
Washington Post online, Jan. 27, 2016: https://www.washingtonpost.com/opinions
/the-forgotten-confederate-general-who-would-make-a-better-subject-for
-monuments/2016/01/27/f09bad42-c536-11e5-8965-0607e0e265ce_story.html.

Richards, Doug. "Ex-Governor: Replace Capitol Confederate Statue." WXIA-TV
online, Atlanta, GA, May 4, 2021: https://www.11alive.com/article/news/politics
/ex-governor-replace-capitol-confederate-statue/85-572e670b-8319-4fe3-b07c-f
08b405cbd0e.

Serwer, Adam. "The Myth of the Kindly General Lee." *Atlantic* online, June 4, 2017:
https://www.theatlantic.com/politics/archive/2017/06/the-myth-of-the-kindly
-general-lee/529038/.

Sinha, Manisha. "What Those Monuments Stand For." *New York Daily News* online,
Aug. 18, 2017: https://www.nydailynews.com/opinion/monuments-stand-article
-1.3423887.

Waite, Kevin. "The Missing Statues That Expose the Truth About Confederate Monuments." *Washington Post* online, Aug. 29, 2018: https://www.washingtonpost.com
/opinions/2018/08/29/missing-statues-that-expose-truth-about-confederate-monu
ments/.

INDEX

439

INDEX

Atlanta Constitution, 272, 273, 281–82, 283, 284–85, 291, 294, 297–98, 317–18, 323, 325–27, 330, 337–38, 344
Atlanta Custom House, 275
Atlanta Daily World, 356
Augusta Constitutionalist, 144
Avoyelles Parish, 193

Bacon, Augustus, 326
Badger, Algernon Sydney, 166, 183, 193, 196, 202, 203, 209, 214
  arrest and capture of, 182, 206–7, 209
  in Canal Street Coup, 203–9
  Longstreet blamed by, 216–17
Ballin, Ralph, 275
Baltimore American, 197
Baltimore Sun, 249, 314
Banks, Nathaniel, 140–41
"Banks County Ku-Klux" case, 268–76
Banner-Watchmen (Athens), 273
Baptists, 346
Barber, Alexander E., 174, 176, 183, 187, 193, 196, 198, 199–202, 205, 210–11
Barnes, Roy, 362
"Battle of Liberty Place" memorial, 361–62
Battles and Leaders of the Civil War, 281
Beall, Curtis, 331
Beauregard, P. G. T., 29–31, 33, 89, 102, 133, 286, 321
  on acceptance of Reconstruction, 143
  Longstreet letters to, 100–101
"Beefsteak Raid," 108
Behind the Scenes. Or, Thirty Years a Slave, and Four Years in the White House (Keckley), 153–54
Beisner, Robert L., 257
Bell, Caryn Cossé, 156
Bell Aircraft Corporation, 355
Bentford, John, 58
Berlin, Treaty of, 245, 252
Bible House (Istanbul), 250, 255–57
biracial politics, Longstreet's support for, xvi, 158
  see also Louisiana State Militia and patronage positions
Birmingham Ledger, 344
Blackburn's Ford, 29–32
Black citizenship, 126, 140, 150
"Black Codes," 137, 141
Black enfranchisement, adoption of and celebration for, 168–70
Black enlistment, 149
  See also Union army, Black soldiers in
Blackford, Charles Minor, 106
Blackford, Susan Leigh, 106
"Black Leagues," 213
  rumors about, 200–201
Black Methodists, 344

Black militiamen, xiv–xv, 171–77, 199, 205, 212, 211–17
  See also Louisiana State Militia
Black policemen, in Canal Street Coup, 211–13
Black press, 279, 291, 336
  Helen Longstreet praised in, 355, 356
  Longstreet assessed in, 278–80
  Longstreet's memoir reviewed in, 315
  in muted response to Longstreet's death, 347–48
  see also specific newspapers
"Black rule," as term, 158–59, 189
Blacks:
  citizenship of, 126
  Confederate debate over enlistment of, 111–13
  economic progress as essential for, 300–301
  education reform for, 178–79
  in Georgia political scene, 266–67
  in Louisiana State Militia, xiv–xv, 171–77, 199–206, 212, 217
  job discrimination against, 352
  Longstreet's support for, xiv–xv
  Longstreet's support from, 182, 279, 324–25
  in Metropolitan Police Force, 165–66
  in muted response to Longstreet's death, 347
  old-age home for, 327
  patronage positions for, 167, 330–32
  in postwar Congress, 218
  in Spanish-American War, 334–35
  in Union army, 63, 112–13, 140–42, 156–57, 218
  violence against, 133, 137, 141–142, 160, 188, 191–96, 204–6, 218–22, 242–44, 268, 330–31, 335–38, 354
  in World War II, 355
Black Sea, 250
Black Southern Unionists, 125–26
  Confederate punishment of, 57–58
  see also enslaved people, resistance by
Black suffrage, 124, 150, 151, 155, 221, 260, 271, 292, 311, 320
  in Georgia, 266
  in Grant's election, 159
  Longstreet's characterization of, 278
  Longstreet's support for, 145, 171–72, 244
  in Louisiana, 140–42, 156–57, 185–86
  suppression of, xiv–xv, 188, 221, 242–44, 268, 282, 330, 337, 355
  US marshals' role in, 268
Black tenant farmers, 322
Black veterans, 236
Black women (New Orleans), 169–70
Blaine, James G., 253, 274, 276, 280
Blair, Lewis Harvie, 16
Blight, David, 235–36, 281, 324, 335
blue-gray reunions, 298, 301
Board of Levees (La.), 190

INDEX

INDEX

impressment, 101
    of Black laborers, 57
    of gold, supplies, and resources, 110–11
Independent, 335, 337
Independents, 271, 280
    in Georgia politics, 266
Indianapolis Journal, 216
    Longstreet's Canal Street Coup interview in,
      214–16
Indiana University Press, 357
Ingraham, James H., 140–41, 156, 168, 169, 173,
    183, 198
"In the Land of the Sultan," 252
Institute on Race Relations, 355
insubordination, debate over Longstreet's, 70–71
integration:
    in federal patronage positions, 167
    in postwar Louisiana, 156–57
    school, 178–79
intelligence operations, enslaved escapees in, 53,
    55, 57–58, 112–13
internal revenue assessors, 163
International Statistical Congress, 26
Inter Ocean, 203, 216, 230, 243, 260, 300
Ireland, John, 339, 343–44
Irish immigrants, 165
Isabelle, Robert H., 166, 169, 178
"Isabelle's bill," 166
Istanbul, 250, 251, 254, 255–58
    Longstreet's move to, 245
"It's About Time" slogan, 359–60

Jackson, Andrew, 174
Jackson, Thomas Jonathan "Stonewall," 37, 40–47,
    53, 54, 58, 285, 304, 344, 359, 438
    death of, 58–59, 61
    military failings of, 306
    removal of statues of, 362
    wounding of, 106
Jackson Square, 205
James Longstreet (Sanger and Hay), 357
James Longstreet, SS, 438
James River, 107–9
Janney, Caroline E., 122, 129, 300
Japan, 329, 331
J. B. Lippincott Company, 296, 303, 317, 342
Jefferson Barracks, Mo., 8
Jenkins, Albert Gallatin, 63
Jenkins, Micah, 107
Jim (enslaved man), 130, 131
Jim Crow South, 133, 328, 347
"jingos," 333
Johnson, Andrew, 130–31, 158, 166, 311, 361
    amnesty and Reconstruction policy of, 134–35,
      136, 141
    Longstreet's critical assessment of, 155–56
    pardons granted by, 137

    political shift of, 136–37
    presidency assumed by, 124, 141
    white supremacists supported by, 142
Johnson, Eli, 57–58
Johnson, Robert Underwood, 281
Johnson, Walter, 325
Johnston, Joseph E., 62, 87, 96, 101, 118, 124,
    237, 262, 283
    in defense of Richmond, 35–36
    Longstreet's letter to, 49–50
    Longstreet's praise of, 33, 306
    Longstreet's relationship with, 36, 89–90, 93
    surrender of, 124
    wounding of, 36
Johnston, Samuel R., 76
Jomini, Antoine Henri, 7, 306
Jones, John William, 224, 226–27, 237, 315–16
Jordan, Thomas, 31, 102
Joseph, Peter, 210
Joubert, Blanc F., 163, 165, 169, 178, 198
Justice Department, US, 267–68, 272
    Longstreet investigated by, 274–76

Keckley, Elizabeth, 153–54
Keiley, Benjamin J., 343, 345
Keller, Christian, 359
Kellogg, William Pitt, 160, 162, 168, 187, 194,
    196–97, 200, 202, 207, 216, 217, 222
    in battle of the Cabildo, 191–92
    in Canal Street Coup, 203–5, 212–14
    gubernatorial run and win of, 185–87, 190
    Longstreet's rift with, 214, 215, 222
    removed and reinstated as governor, 207
Kelly, Thomas S., 335
Kennedy, John D., 317
Key, David, 244, 279
Killer Angels, The (Shaara), 358
Klonares, George, 255–56, 258
Knights of the White Camellia, 160
Knoxville campaign, 94–100, 104, 309
Knudsen, Harold M., 50
Krick, Robert K., 73–74, 359
"kukluxing," use of term, 268
Ku Klux Klan, 133, 183, 188, 273, 356, 362
    congressional legislation on, 268–69
    in Supreme Court case, 268–76

Landrieu, Mitch, 361–62
Latin America, 244
Latrobe, Osmun, 32, 48, 52, 109, 126
Law, Evander M., 71–72, 74, 75
Lawley, Francis Charles, 228, 234
Lawton, Alexander R., 102
Le Carillon, xvii
Lee, Fitzhugh, 120, 224, 286, 304, 310, 315,
    334
    Longstreet critiqued by, 234–35

INDEX

INDEX

INDEX

INDEX

PHOTO CREDITS

1. Library of Congress
2. Library of Congress
3. Library of Congress
4. Tennessee Virtual Archive
5. Library of Congress
6. Library of Congress
7. Georgia Archives
8. Library of Congress
9. Library of Congress
10. Wikimedia
11. Library of Congress
12. Library of Congress
13. Georgia Archives
14. Library of Congress
15. Library of Congress
16. Georgia Archives
17. Wikimedia